D1742480

ACROSS THE ABYSS

OTHER BOOKS BY PAUL ROUBICZEK

'Warrior of God': the life and death of John Hus (*in collaboration with Joseph Kalmer, Nicholas and Watson, London, 1947*)

The misinterpretation of man: a study of European thought in the nineteenth century (*Kennikat Press, New York, 1947*)

Thinking in opposites (*Routledge and Kegan Paul, 1952*)

Thinking towards religion (*Darwin Finlayson, London, 1957*)

Existentialism, for and against (*Cambridge University Press, 1964*)

Ethical values in the age of science (*Cambridge University Press, 1969*)

PAUL ROUBICZEK

ACROSS THE ABYSS

Diary entries for the year 1939–1940

Translated by GEORGE BIRD
with an introduction by ERICH HELLER

CAMBRIDGE UNIVERSITY PRESS

Cambridge
London   New York   New Rochelle
Melbourne   Sydney

Published by the Press Syndicate of the University of Cambridge
The Pitt Building, Trumpington Street, Cambridge CB2 1RP
32 East 57th Street, New York, NY 10022, USA
296 Beaconsfield Parade, Middle Park, Melbourne 3206, Australia

Originally published in German as *Über den Abgrund Aufzeichnungen
1939/40* by Fritz Molden, 1978 and © Fritz Molden, 1978.

English translation, introduction and notes © Cambridge University Press
1982

First published in English by the Cambridge University Press, 1982 as
Across the Abyss. Diary entries for the year 1939–1940

Printed in United States of America

Library of Congress catalogue card number: 81-17993

British Library Cataloguing in Publication Data
Roubiczek, Paul
Across the abyss.
1. World War, 1939–1945 – Personal
narratives, German
I. Title   II. Über den Abgrund. *English*.
940.54'82'43   D811
ISBN 0 521 24288 6

CONTENTS

INTRODUCTION

by Erich Heller

Paul Roubiczek, born in Prague on 28 September 1898, died, two months before his seventy-fourth birthday, on 26 July 1972 in Gmund, Upper Bavaria, in the beautiful house where he and his wife spent many of their summers and, after his retirement from Cambridge University, most of their time. In Cambridge he was a popular teacher of German literature and philosophy. Prague, Cambridge, and finally the house in Gmund, designed by an architect friend as the annexe to a farmhouse above the lake, the Tegernsee, were the three main stages in Robi's life. Robi was the name by which all his friends called him. Of course, there were other places in his life, and activities less academic and literary than those he pursued in Cambridge and Gmund. But from the point of view of the present writer, whose friendship with him began in Cambridge in 1939, those other places and activities appear more like prologues: the two years, after Hitler came to power in Germany, that he spent in Paris, starting, together with Peter de Mendelssohn, one of the first anti-Nazi publishing ventures; the years which he spent as a publisher in Vienna, fleeing once more from Hitler in 1938; and the short time in Prague which it took the Führer to add Czechoslovakia to his conquests in the spring of 1939. But probably the most important among those prologues was the 'prologue in hell' that plays such a decisive part in this diary: the years during the First World War when he was a soldier and officer in the Austro-Hungarian Army.

After two years in the family business in Prague, he spent thirteen years, an unlucky number, in Berlin. It was the time when that extraordinary city, once the proud capital of the German Empire, had become the symbol of a precariously divided continent, passing through turbulent years of political and economic disorder, intellectual agitation and the kind of cultural liveliness and nervous creative energy which some people took to be the promise of a new civilization. It ended in the terror of the Third Reich.

Paul Roubiczek devoted his years in Berlin to the study of literature and philosophy. Although he was much less affected than many of his intellectual contemporaries by the uneasy Republican freedom that Germany acquired with her military defeat, and certainly very much less impressed than they by the illusory expectation of limitless cultural progress, there is no doubt that Berlin contributed much to his development as a German scholar and thinker. It is characteristic of a mind affected by the climate of Berlin in the 1920s, that an unforgettable moment in his life as a young soldier on the Italian front should be recalled years later by the situation of Mephistopheles in the Prologue to Goethe's *Faust*. The young soldier, after a seemingly endless nocturnal march, had found himself in a pale, timid, icy sunrise, shivering with cold and facing death. Leopold Jessner, a famous director of the Berlin Theatre, places Mephistopheles in a similar state when, after the disappearance of the Lord and his heavenly hosts, he stands alone on the empty stage.

Yet it was those deadly battles fought by the River Isonzo that, more than anything else, made this son of a Jewish manufacturer in Prague into the Christian, the philosopher and the teacher that he became, and remained, to the end. His experience of the First World War has evoked some of the best-written pages of a diary that was never intended to display virtuoso writing. On the contrary, it is the paradox of this publication that what above all has made it worth publishing is the absence from it of any implied claim to publicity. It is the *journal intime* of a man of integrity who refrains from recording 'interesting' intimacies. Therefore, it is a unique diary in an age which, ever since Rousseau's autobiographical loquacity, has been inclined to take indiscretion for veracity, shamelessness for courage, and exhibitionism for honesty. By contrast, Roubiczek's journal seems almost anonymous. I always feel it was significant that my last conversation with him – in Gmund on the very day of his death – was about anonymity; he talked about the unknown builders and masons of the medieval cathedrals, the anonymity even of some ancient poets we do know by name, 'Homer, for instance'. He compared this with the desire for individual fame which, since the Renaissance, has led to the growing fascination of artists and their audiences with the peculiarities of the creative self.

Three themes dominate this diary. There is, first of all, the inner conflict of a man who detested war and every form of violence and yet was unable to be a pacifist in the war that Hitler was waging against the world, an onslaught that the world, hesitatingly and in the beginning ineffectually, made ready to answer by force.

That sentence written on 3 September 1939 appears simply to record the fact that war has been declared – *'s ist leider Krieg* (Alas, it's war!).

viii

But these words come from a deeply moving poem by one of the German poets he loved, and any German reader will instantly recognize the allusion to Matthias Claudius. Terrible, the diarist adds, but continues with the question whether it is permissible to say, like Claudius, *leider*, that is, simply to deplore the event. For although war at all times is indeed terrible, the two days during which England seemed to be hesitating to fulfil the promise she had given to Poland were perhaps even more so. They signalled not merely the possibility of betrayal, but of utter helplessness in the face of a monstrous threat to the whole world. The true measure of the inner conflict shown by the initial sentences of the diary will be realized by anyone who reads Roubiczek's memories of the First World War. They begin with the entry of 5 January 1940.

All this leads straight to the second dominant theme of the diary: the philosopher's determination not to shirk the intellectual task imposed upon him by this conflict, indeed by the collision of all manifestly irreconcilable opposites. *Thinking in Opposites,* his most important philosophical work, appeared in 1952, and many pages of this diary are rehearsals for that book.* Of course, the struggles of a conscience, caught between the abhorrence of war *per se,* and the affirmation of *this* war, between wishing to be obedient to Christ's admonition not to resist evil, and yet convinced that in *this* case it must be resisted, cannot possibly be resolved by 'thinking in opposites'. The acknowledgement of the perpetual clash between the 'external' and the 'internal' reality, the primary opposites of Roubiczek's philosophy, cannot alone solve that problem; yet it is true to say that his wartime experience of incompatible responses helped to shape his philosophical thought and to promote his final dialectic.

The opposition between those two 'realities' is again and again hinted at, explained, insisted upon in this diary. It is a theme that has directly and often tyrannized over the speculations of philosophers ever since Kant separated Pure Reason, our intellectual organ for coming to know the

---

* Paul Roubiczek's other books are intimately related to this work without being simply preludes to it or afterthoughts: *The Misinterpretation of Man,* a collection of essays on some of the great literary and philosophical minds that helped to form his own philosophy (it first appeared in 1934 under the German title *Der missbrauchte Mensch;* its English translation was published in 1947); *'Warrior of God': the Life and Death of John Hus* (1947, in collaboration with Joseph Kalmer); *Thinking towards Religion* (1957); *Existentialism, For and Against* (1964); and *Ethical Values in the Age of Science* (1969). His last book was to have been *The Necessity of Contradictions.* He nearly finished it during the last year of his life. It is to be hoped that it will be published before long, edited and completed by his friend Gregory Needham.

world as it appears in space, time and in the web of causal connections, from Practical Reason, our access to the domain of aesthetic, ethical and religious values; or ever since Hegel's enormous elaboration of our mind's dialectical mechanics, first discovered by thinkers of Ancient Greece and brought to their theological climax by Nicolas Cusanus. But the consequences of those thoughts are not only philosophical. Certainly, Marx was a thinker. Yet he was also the founder of a powerful political movement, Utopian in its nature despite his anti-Utopian protestations, a movement that was meant to revolutionize the 'external' reality of a world deeply at odds with the 'internal' reality of the human being – 'alienation' is the modishly Hegelian word that instantly comes to mind – and change it so radically that Within and Without would at last be at one. If Marx proposed a solution to this opposition within the realm of 'political science', Rilke's extreme recommendation for a poetical resolution of the very same conflict called for a profound metamorphosis to be brought about by the power of the inner human being. The offence given to our inner sense by the incurable corruption of the external world, endlessly fostered by the poisonous atmosphere of the epoch, must be answered by transforming everything into the invisibility of pure inwardness:

> . . . Earth! invisible!
> What, if not transformation, is your urgent commission?

Rilke asked in the ninth of his *Duino Elegies*, after having said in the seventh that before long there will be no other truly human world than the world within. In Roubiczek's philosophy there is no thought of thus claiming for human inwardness the Rilkean status of the only valid reality, and there is no Hegelian–Marxian expectation of an ultimately happy synthesis of those opposing domains. There is only something that is incomparably more modest, and therefore more Kantian and more 'real' than those grandiose abstractions, be they historico-philosophical, political or poetical. Roubiczek himself, in the entry of 13 October 1939, denounced all the manipulations of abstract thinking because this so often purchases its consistency by buying up, as it were, and removing from its path, all the impediments of irrefutable facts. He himself was content to define the point at which the intellect, having made its thoughtful way through the outward world, meets the inner reality, acknowledges its otherness and, contemplating those opposites, derives from them the strength for the right thinking and the right feeling and, perhaps, the right living.

The right life can be discovered in the example of Christ. Nobody who reads Roubiczek's reflections on Christ and Christianity can doubt his will to live in this manner even in the midst of an unchristian age, just as nobody who has known the man can question the honesty of his living. I have even heard it said that he was one of the few just men for whose sake God refrained from destroying the world. The way to Christ that first opened before the young man in the battles by the River Isonzo was certainly not without obstacles. These were not of his own making; they were due, once again, to conflicting opposites: on the one hand, the uncompromising spirit of fellowship demanded by Christ and, on the other hand, the 'externalities' of the churches. He was unable to reconcile himself to the frequent conflicts between the faith professed and the life lived, between the teaching of Christ and the practice of Christian institutions.

Roubiczek's struggle for the life in Christ, a life that would be firmly supported by his manner of thinking, is the third theme of this diary. For his own living existence it may well have been the most important one, the more so as it was inextricably bound up with the searches of the philosopher.

In his entry of 23 June 1940 Roubiczek gives his interpretation of the Marriage at Cana in Galilee (John 2: 1) and of the part which Jesus played in it. When Jesus' mother told him that there was no more wine, Jesus behaved as if he did not know her; yet he changed the water into wine, and a wine of such quality as to cause the governor of the wedding feast to marvel. Roubiczek's intense and intelligent contemplation of the person of Christ is by no means the only such revelation in this book, but it is I believe the most penetrating and the most beautiful. It is inspired by Dostoyevsky (who appears as an almost omnipresent guide to the author, much as Virgil does to Dante in his *Divina Commedia*). Roubiczek sees the Biblical passage as revealing two opposing tendencies in Jesus – his pitiless denial of *this* life, of the unbaptised life his mother gave him ('Woman, what have I to do with thee?') and yet his miraculous and joyous affirmation of it. These disturbing and harsh words that Jesus addressed to his mother could imply a rejection of her. Is not this an extreme assertion that he was not of this world? Yet, what does his first miracle mean, if it is not his wish to heighten the pleasure of this marriage feast? Truly a conflict of opposites! Like most of the later miracles Jesus performed, this shows the importance he attached to living a full life on this earth, be it only as the journey through the 'vale of soul-making' as Keats called it.

Time: in this diary there are meditations on the subject of time that read as if they had been suggested by Bergson or Proust or even by Thomas Mann's *The Magic Mountain*. I am as sure as one can be in such cases that they were not, even though he cannot possibly have been ignorant of those works. These observations emerge too immediately from Roubiczek's own experiences to be looked upon as mere literary reminiscences. Besides, he was too honest a man not to acknowledge his sources, had he been conscious of any, even in his own diary. Once again he remembers the moment in 1917 by the River Isonzo when he was convinced he was about to die. It was a moment of truth, and, therefore, of eternity, and therefore beyond time. Then there were three days, according to the calendar, when he and his comrades lived in a hut, hiding from death. Yet in the memory of the survivor these three days were not merely three days. Their minutes and hours and days and nights expanded immeasurably and could not be measured by any mechanical means. The same memory, however, hardly registers, all but violently contracts, what must have been long stretches of routine living. What an unreliable, capricious thing is time recalled, dependent on the mood of the moment. It is 'lost time', *temps perdu,* as Proust knew; and that mountain of Thomas Mann also shows its magic power by what it does to time. But the philosopher Roubiczek, at this point, reminds himself of the Kantian concept of time as the invariable mood of perception that man's consciousness cannot escape. How invariable is it? We need not think of Einstein to answer the question. We need only think of the birth, by that Italian river, of Roubiczek's philosophy, of the indeed invariable *opposites:* time measured by clocks and calendars compared to time lived with intense awareness or shrunk by boredom, time fully used and realised as opposed to time unresponsively, irresponsibly, wasted. It is here that for Roubiczek the problem of time touches upon ethics and becomes important in a way quite distinct from the explorations, carried out with superb artistry, of Proust and Thomas Mann. *Thinking in Opposites* was to deal more systematically with the question, urgently raised by the diary: the ethics of time.

Yet it would be wrong to assume that the diary contains nothing but the record of Roubiczek's preparation for his main philosophical work, nothing but his thoughts during the first year of the Second World War, the 'phoney' war, that was after all not as uneventful as it may have seemed. Roubiczek, in his diary, is also a faithful chronicler of everything that ominously either occurred or, not less ominously, failed to occur in the course of that year. But there is still more in this chronicle of a thoughtful, rich, wise, pained and yet serene mind. Take, for instance, the long entry of 12 October 1939. There the questions are asked that were inevitable at that time and especially important to a man who, intellectually formed by the German tradition, now entirely shared the hostility that Hitler's Germany had stirred up in the rest of Europe: 'Is not this tradition, about to be destroyed by Hitler, at the same time the tradition that brought him forth? Is the glorification of power at all costs, the power gained through murderous betrayals and deceptions, the power that finally consumed itself, not also the essence of the greatest national epic of the Germans, the *Song of the Nibelungs*?' What follows in the diary is a penetrating and most illuminating analysis of the saga that used to attract so much German scholarship and literary pedagogy, not to mention the dramatic use made of it by Hebbel and indeed Wagner. As in the *Song of the Nibelungs* there is an uncritical acceptance of the heroic ideal or of the heroic fallacy, so too nations at war unfailingly evoke an uncritical acceptance of the figure of the hero. In protest the mind turns to Shakespeare, who even in his most patriotic dramas, views the hero with scepticism; and who in his later works, notably in *Troilus and Cressida* and in *Coriolanus*, treats him with sublime derision. After a sleepless night, when sitting on a bench in an Elizabethan courtyard Roubiczek, in a kind of waking dream, 'saw' Shakespeare. The comments that he is moved to make about Shakespeare show Roubiczek as the profoundest critic of 'the hero' as well as the provider of an interpretation of Shakespeare more fascinating than many to be found in literary studies. The passage in which these comments occur appears in the entry for 8 November 1939.

It is not only such passages that more than justify the much-delayed decision of the powers-that-were at Cambridge to make him a teacher of literature, a Fellow of Clare College, and an honorary Master of Arts. But there is also a discussion in the diary (14 October 1939) that contains a most happily succinct essay on the poetry of German Romanticism. The poem discussed is Eichendorff's *Mondnacht*, exquisitely beautiful at its beginning:

> Es war, als hätt' der Himmel
> Die Erde still geküßt

but strangely disappointing in its last verse. It is, like all poetry of its kind, untranslatable. Why is it, Roubiczek asks, that not one of the later Romantic poets of Germany has written an entirely perfect poem, as perfect as are many of Goethe's poems or many by Matthias Claudius, those, for instance, that are quoted in this context? And his answer is: because of those poets' uninhibited cult of sentiment; their fear of letting reason impede the flow of feeling; their suspicion that the clarity of the intellect may destroy the misty charms that the light of the moon gives to a landscape which for them had become the single objective symbol of the soul;

their determination to sustain emotion even when it becomes powerless to infuse their words convincingly; their desire to smuggle, as it were, the passions like valuable contraband over the frontiers of territory foreign to them. But, says the diary, the true way of feeling and therefore the truly perfect poem leads to the transparency of thoughtful contemplation, just as the profoundest thoughts awaken the mind's true feeling. It is in this quite unforced manner that the discussion of poetry, indeed of one particular poem, issues in the affirmation of the interplay of opposites, the opposites of thinking and feeling, Roubiczek's persistent philosophical concern. Here is proof enough of his intellectual integration, of the integrity of mind of the man who wrote this diary.

TRANSLATOR'S NOTE

The text of the translation is a little fuller than that of the original German publication. In a few places this results from restoring editorial deletions which have inadvertently given rise to some obscurity, the paragraph beginning 'For what is a scientific law?' in the entry for 19 November 1939 being a notable example. But in the main this results from the restoration in full, for their own sake, of the entry for 26 November 1939 (headed *Night*) and of the entries for 28 May and 11, 13 and 27 July 1940. Quotations from Dostoyevsky I have translated directly from the Russian where I have been able to trace it; and I have made a few comments, mostly of a bibliographical nature, in footnotes.

My work has been greatly and most generously assisted by Hjördis Roubiczek, whom I thank wholeheartedly.

G.B.

ACROSS THE ABYSS

Diary entries for the year 1939–1940

3 September 1939

So it's war. Terrible. But can I say, with Claudius, *Alas?*[1] More terrible perhaps have been these last two days of apparent hesitancy over whether

> 1. The reference is to Matthias Claudius' poem *Kriegslied* written in 1779 during the wars between Prussia and Austria:
>
> *Kriegslied*
>
> 's ist Krieg! 's ist Krieg! O Gottes Engel, wehre
>   Und rede du darein!
> 's ist leider Krieg – und ich begehre
>   Nicht schuld daran zu sein!
>
> Was sollt ich machen, wenn im Schlaf mit Grämen
>   Und blutig, bleich und blaß
> Die Geister der Erschlagnen zu mir kämen
>   Und vor mir weinten, was?
>
> Wenn wackre Männer, die sich Ehre suchten,
>   Verstümmelt und halb tot
> Im Staub sich vor mir wälzten und mir fluchten
>   In ihrer Todesnot?
>
> Wenn tausend, tausend Väter, Mütter, Bräute,
>   So glücklich vor dem Krieg,
> Nun alle elend, alle arme Leute,
>   Wehklagten über mich?
>
> Wenn Hunger, böse Seuch und ihre Nöten
>   Freund, Freund und Feind ins Grab
> Versammleten und mir zu Ehren krähten
>   Von einer Leich herab?
>
> Was hülf mir Kron und Land und Gold und Ehre?
>   Die könnten mich nicht freun!
> 's ist leider Krieg – und ich begehre
>   Nicht schuld daran zu sein!
>
> *War-song*
>
> It's war! It's war! O Angel of God, restrain
> and intervene!
> Alas, it's war – and my desire
> is not to be to blame!
>
> What should I do if in my sleep, afflicted
> and bloody, pale and wan,
> the spirits of those killed should visit me
> and weep before me – what?
>
> If courageous men who sought for honour,
> should roll, maimed, half dead

to give Poland the promised aid. Because I thought that a vigorous attitude on Britain's part would be sufficient to bring about a German retreat,
my wish was for peace. Such a peace might, I was aware, prove very
dangerous, possibly gaining time for Germany to consolidate her relations
with Russia. Nevertheless, that was the peace I was hoping for, having
lost faith in war as a means of creating a new world, and this is as a result
of experience since the last war. What, first and foremost, is to be achieved
by a war which, for all that it is a war against National Socialism, is manifestly lacking in any positive idea? All the same, a new Munich, a new
bloodless victory for the Nazis is a fearful thing to contemplate. So, with
the choice between war and yielding, are we now obliged to assent wholeheartedly to war?

But what then of my conviction, also fruit of the last war, that we must
say no to *any* war absolutely, to war *per se*? Can I still maintain it? What
sort of a war is it that is now being fought?

What more than anything is so terrible about it is that it is completely
unnecessary. Up to 1937 there has, every year almost, been at least one
opportunity to tackle the bogy of National Socialism without war; it might
still have been possible even during the Czech crisis in 1938. At the very
beginning a rigorous boycott would have sufficed, a complete severing of
all relations – no railway, no ambassadors – and in six weeks the nightmare would have been over. Then came the occupation of the Rhineland
– the French ought simply to have mobilized; Abyssinia – the Suez Canal
should have been shut, and the fall of Mussolini would soon have brought
down Hitler after him; Spain – an all-out blockade of the Fascist countries
and they would have collapsed. Czechoslovakia could then easily have
been defended in Austria. And even in 1938 definite and vigorous action

> in the dust before me and curse me
> in their dying agony?
>
> If fathers, mothers, brides-to-be in thousands,
> before the war so happy,
> now all wretched, now poor people all,
> should be lamenting over me?
>
> If hunger, evil plague and their distress
> friend, friend and foe should gather
> to their graves, and in my honour crow
> down from a corpse.
>
> Of what avail to me crown, land, gold, honour?
> They could not give me any delight!
> Alas, it's war – and my desire
> is not to be to blame!

4

would still probably have saved Czechoslovakia and all else with her. It is only because all the opportunities have been missed, and because Hitler, in building on the weakness and half-heartedness of his opponents, has been proved right again and again, that war has had to come.

Opportunities have been missed because there has been no feeling of human outrage amongst the Democracies. It has always been present of course in individuals, and may have been too weak with the mass of the people because no one could really believe that the atrocity reports were true, or that such things were possible in the heart of Europe, or that reports were not terribly exaggerated. But this disbelief could easily have been removed if the ruling classes had wished; to have directed the stream of political refugees to Britain two years earlier would have been enough! But the ruling classes have not been outraged, their humanity has not been stirred – they, being primarily interested in capital – have still found the Nazis more congenial than the communists. If the powers of government had been stirred as human beings, their politics would have been the better!

What applied yesterday applies in high measure also today. Had the Nazis moderated their foreign policy and managed to create the belief that they would now at last let there be peace, they could have executed the remaining Marxists, roasted the Jews on spits, even annexed the Czechs, and people would gladly have come to terms with them, perhaps even have thrown in a few colonies. The war has come not because justice is being trampled or Western civilization destroyed at the heart of Europe, or because the self-determination of nations is being infringed. It is simply a battle against an attempt to achieve hegemony over Europe and grab world power – or a considerable share of it – for oneself. If Poland has not been sacrificed it is because it has at last been realized that the decisive trial of strength has come. The sufferings of the Poles would, in other circumstances, have been no more decisive than those of any non-Nazis in the Third Reich.

Now that it's war all these considerations have, of course, lost their force. The fight for the small nations and for justice and freedom has as a result become more than mere pretence. Certainly, the war has been brought upon us only by errors on the part of the Democracies, by the human and ideological weakness of the capitalist world, and by the unhappy amalgamation of democracy and capitalism which is destroying the Democracies. The terrible thing is that it is not the Nazis who have brought it upon us! For in a world that was genuinely civilized they would never have been able to provoke war. But as war is what we've now got, relative freedom and relative justice in this relative world are on the side of the Democracies. It would be dreadful if the Nazis won. We must wish wholeheartedly for their destruction and do all in our power to bring it about. Nothing would be more fatal than that pseudo-pacificism which so favoured the rise of the Nazis, that blind pacifism on the part of the British and French workers that was unaware of how it was playing into the hands of capitalist desires!

And yet for all that, am I not rejecting this war? What would happen if all thought as I do? World domination by the Nazis would be certain, and the final downfall of this civilization of ours upon which I depend with every fibre of my being. And as this civilization is for me first and foremost the German, how would it ever again be possible?

Still, all these thoughts concerning the fault of democracy again become of great moment immediately we consider the kind of peace that is to follow this war. Is again nothing to survive save national hatred, that hatred which today, when Germans are enslaving Czechs and shooting Poles is bound to be infinitely intensified? How is there ever to be peace when from every war national hatred emerges strengthened? True, the British have been admirable to date, drawing a distinction between the German government and the German people, and treating us in a way that cannot be set highly enough to their credit. But will this attitude survive the first British deaths? And even if it does, it is not one that will survive in France or in Central Europe. The fearful dearth of vigorous ideas which has brought war upon us will again destroy the peace. Also this war, like the last, is an imperialist war. If the ideas which today are being strengthened primarily by the war, again remain, and continue to remain, too weak, this war will have the same results as the last. This century will be condemned to become the century of great wars, as foreseen and, regrettably, praised by Nietzsche. After this war, Germany and France may be too weak to risk another. But the material for conflict between the Anglo-Saxon world and the Russian is, from an imperialist point of view, no less great, and this struggle too is again bound to be the destruction of Europe.

And above all, if ideas are not brought to bear this war is bound to go on for a terribly long time, to the point of exhaustion like the last. Or else, in some unforeseeable way, it will stop prematurely, changing nothing fundamental in Germany, and from the very moment of the peace agreement, our feet will have been set upon the road to the next war. From a theoretical point of view, it is astonishing that the British should drop leaflets over Germany to begin with, but their effect is crucially weakened

6

by their being unsupported by any reorganization of the world that might be attractive to the Germans also. A mainstay of the Nazis has been the inability of anyone to conceive what is to come after, except perhaps communism, which the majority fear. The antiquated modes of life of the Western countries, modes which in recent years have merely been salvaged by the Nazis and the armaments boom they have provoked, and behind which, if there is no rearmament, lurks the threat of millions of unemployed, no longer have any attraction for Germany, for it is inconceivable how they should be restored there! Certainly the great mass of the people would even welcome a harsh military dictatorship, if only they could get rid of the Nazis – though it is no coincidence that the military should obviously lack the power to establish such a dictatorship – and an equally great mass of the people would contend violently against it!

On the other hand, how enormous the effect of leaflets would be if it were known in Germany that here, in the West, something entirely new was developing, apart from Marxism, a solution of social problems that would guarantee freedom and justice. It needs no more than tolerably concrete rumours to this effect. But these there cannot be.

On the one hand, therefore, it is certain that the Nazis must be defeated. On the other, it is equally certain that ideas of freedom must take on new shape if this victory is to have any meaning.

A great misfortune of the last war was that those who died were the very ones who would have had things to say in the peace. This much was apparent to everyone shortly after the war, and everyone would have thought that such men were doing right to keep themselves safe.

But in the last war this problem was quite universally simpler. Barbarism was not plainly on the one side, and the war was more manifestly still an imperialist one. Conscientious objection was, quite universally, an outstanding Christian act. It seemed desirable to end the war as such, for civilization and imperialism were almost equally strong on both sides. Also the consequences of a suddenly enforced peace seemed quite plain: the war-weary nations would have overthrown the old empires and put peaceable republics in their place. Against which, conscientious objection now would be a positive act only in Germany. In Germany's opponents it would be disastrous.

But at the same time it was shown that the forming of republics is not enough. They must also know what purpose they are there for, and they must also be viable. Ideas are thus enormously important. So do those who are fighting for ideas have a right to keep out of this war too?

4 September 1939

I have remembered a Gospel passage that brings much light into this darkness. Jesus finds a man working on the sabbath. He tells him that if he does not know what he is doing, he is damned, but that if he does know, he is blessed. Does that apply to conscientious objection also? To be damned if we do not know what we are doing and are doing it only out of fear or selfishness, or to save ourselves from the common fate? To be approved if we know what we have to do, and are therefore doing it not for negative but for positive reasons?

One of the essential points here is 'Resist not evil.' This commandment I understand not as a negative one, not as a call to submit and simply accept any evil – that would be absurd. To me the true sense of this commandment seems to be this. Our task is not to combat evil but only to strive for what is positive. Our lives must not be directed against something, must not continue in ever negative opposition which, without positive backing, is bound to remain absurd. We are to pay no heed to evil. We are to walk past. We are to persist in our work at that which is good. If this work is right, if we are really able to do good, the good will also overcome evil. The result does not lie with us, and it is not what we are to worry about, because to achieve any result, we need conflict with something else. We are to do that for which we are here, undismayed and with all our strength. Whether what we do prevails or does not prevail, whether we perish with it or not, does not concern us, for that is outside our power and in the hand of God or fate, call it what we will. If we believe in that which is good, we must also believe that it is effective and that it prevails, and we must also have the strength not to resist evil but to work unperturbed at that which is good.

I always have something of an odd feeling at not really managing to hate the Nazis, and in a way I find it painful that the refugee intellect should exhaust itself reviling Hitler and all those criminals. That is what they are, certainly, dreadful criminals. But that they should have managed to come to power is not their fault but ours! The terrible thing is not that the Nazis have come, for a desperate people – and the German people *were* desperate – clutches even at the straw the devil holds out if it believes it can save itself or merely deaden its senses by so doing. What is terrible is that even the Nazis should have failed to stir any counter forces into life, and that nothing positive should have arisen or anything of the old positive have been reinforced as a result of the Nazis, for it is under enemy pressure and in the upheaval of terrible experience that the

8

creating of something positive is easiest. But nothing new is to be felt, either amongst the political refugees or in the West. Whether anything is to be felt in Germany probably no one yet knows. And this is precisely why the war is our fault, and the fault of everyone outside the Third Reich who has had the possibility of working for and creating this new thing, and not the fault of the Nazis alone.

Do we then all have to atone for this fault by marching to war?

We must know what we are doing! If we do not know what to do with our lives except revile the Nazis, and if resist evil is all we can do, then we very likely *do* have to march to war. If, however, we know what we are doing, and what work we have to do, and why we are keeping out of the war, then we must keep out of it! So that never again shall the disaster be repeated that, when the war is over, those who are missing, dead, or simply weary, exhausted to the point of death and thereby condemned to silence, are precisely the ones who would have had something to say!

For we who are fighting for an idea are at fault for having been too weak in the struggle for this idea, and for not being strong enough to create it and give it living form so that it might prevail. This is not a fault we can atone for by marching to war, and so wholly abandoning the struggle for the idea. For still, and as ever, the idea is what matters. We can only atone by remaining true to this struggle for the idea even today when it is an attitude that is likely to be held in contempt and proscribed, and when it would be so much easier and so much more liberating simply to go and volunteer for the front, and when it is only by so volunteering that we can stand high in other people's estimation.

5 September 1939

A vast number of objections present themselves to my thinking of yesterday. Although, in an absolute sense, it is certainly right not to ask what the result will be, it is probably more than anyone can do not to ask whether today, when the issue is Nazi victory or Nazi defeat, this attitude is not tantamount to that pacifism which has already been such a help to the Nazis.

But this objection does not to me seem valid. The very fact that it has had to come to war shows that far too few are striving for the idea, and that they have no power and carry practically no weight. For them to keep out of the war will not affect it either way. If, on the other hand, they are the majority, victory will not be the Nazis' salvation.

For all through history, almost every defeat has resulted in the spiritual

9

victory of the defeated. The Christians, after burning, persecution and extermination at the hands of the Romans, prevailed, without recourse to arms, against the whole Roman Empire. The Teutons conquered the Roman Empire only to be overpowered by Christianity and Graeco-Roman culture. The French Revolution was defeated from without and from within, yet its spirit triumphed over the victors. The unfortunate thing is of course that Germany should have failed to realize what enormous chances she has had in the world as a result of her defeat; if she had managed to create something new, the spirit of defeated Germany would have conquered the world – never has it looked so expectantly towards Germany as it did after the war!

How little can be achieved by external victory is now again being shown by the suppression of the Czechs. Their national resistance will remain unbroken as it has since the defeat of three hundred years ago. And if the Czechs had had more to offer than this national resistance, if they had had a faith and created a form of social community independent of things national, then, there can be no doubt, the entire Third Reich might have been shaken as a result of occupying the Czechoslovak Republic. The Germans would soon have realized that no garrison could be sent there without that garrison's becoming lost to them spiritually, just as after the war the *Entente* was forced to stop short of occupying Germany for fear of the army's being stirred to revolt. The task of the Czechs today is to teach how to resist oppression, and this lesson too can have a great effect, especially if Nazi rule is shaken by the war, but it is one that must remain without significance for the peace. Against which, a nation having something to offer for the peace need not fear defeat or conquest. Defeat and conquest may bring personal suffering, but at the same time they bring the victory of the idea!

But quantitative proofs are no proofs and the lessons of history are very unclear. Very contradictory things can easily be gathered from a reading of history, and conclusions of this sort can be deceptive. This objection cannot therefore be invalidated by such considerations alone.

What is more important perhaps is that peace has got to be prepared for even during the war. It would be a great misfortune if again those were to die who are able to prepare the peace. But who can claim with certainty to have this ability? This objection cannot be invalidated by external considerations alone.

I am also reluctant simply to reject war only for a definite sort of people. It must be possible to arrive at a generally valid judgement. That is the only kind that can have any meaning! Christ on the cross asking for-

giveness for his persecutors is perhaps the most powerful proof of his
purity and greatness, a wonderful example, but not one that excuses those
who do not know what they are doing. For that is the most terrible thing
ever, they have crucified Christ. We cannot therefore simply let them
have their way and wage war. Universally we must find our way to a world
in which Christ will be crucified no longer.

6 September 1939

I must, I think, go back further. Another shocking contradiction that
goes to the heart of this problem is the commandment 'Thou shalt not
kill.' This commandment, whether construed from a Christian, Jewish or
purely ethical point of view, seems to me valid unconditionally. It is, and
remains, inhuman to kill humans. But how is this commandment to be
reconciled with the necessity of waging war against the Nazis, a necessity
I still allow to exist for all who are not striving for the idea?

The churches manage it by quoting Jesus: 'I come not to send peace
but a sword.' Yet Jesus stopped Peter using the sword, and for the first
hundred and fifty years the early Christians refused to perform military
service. There may have been Christians who fought, but only because
men who fought became converted to Christianity, and not because the
original Christians waged war. So this saying of Christ's was either not
yet in the Bible at that time at all, or it was differently understood. To me
another explanation seems quite easy and obvious – these words are a
prophecy! Christ knows that blood will be shed for the sake of his teaching
– a fearful amount of blood, but this prophecy still does not mean any
setting aside of the commandment 'Thou shalt not kill.' Prophecy is not
teaching. So that way round which enables churches to bless colours and
pray in every country for that same country's victory, can be totally disregarded.

Christianity must not simply *manage* this unconditionally human commandment but must adhere to it absolutely. It is by means of this very
commandment that must be shown whether Christianity can be reconciled with life in this world. It is this very commandment that again poses
the crucial question 'Is Christianity today still (or again) possible?' The
problem of the war – *my* problem – is one of the most important in this
respect also. If Christianity merely beats about the bush again with evasions and improbable interpretations, and if it cannot help man in this his
greatest distress of conscience, it will not manage to come alive in peace
either.

11

The promise of a beyond which the churches fob us off with is today no longer valid. All the phrases, dogmas and this-is-exactly-what-you-must-believe-edicts are dead. If these forms of Christianity are all that there is, National Socialism will win as a religion too. Against that, the human example of the life of Jesus, the most glorious human life ever lived, is more than ever alive. Where are we to find help in our distress of conscience if not here? Because of this great life, my problems seem to me to be of equal importance as both human and Christian problems. For if Christianity stands the test with them, we gain simultaneously a most comprehensive and imposing model of human life that can and must help us with all its questions.

But it cannot be denied that, doctored by the churches, this model is hardly of any use to us any longer, or that it is alive still only for a limited circle and that even they are incapable of shaping it to take the deep hold that apparently only nationalism is now capable of. New ways must be found to this example.

And yet Christianity is infinitely rich in human ways of conduct and in answers to the most burning human questions. The British like to confront people constantly with Biblical texts, even renting advertising space in buses to do so as extensively as possible, a custom both unappealing and senseless, serving merely as a naive advertisement for Christianity. As a result the texts themselves may well have hardly any effect. Just the opposite. They may even become worn out by this frequent use, as no one thinks any more about what he is reading. They assist towards that enfeeblement of Christianity which is powerfully enough catered for by schools and churches anyway. And yet if trouble is really taken to read these texts and ponder their content, what infinite riches they contain, and how effective even in this form the riches of Christianity become! Yesterday I read posted to a church wall 'You cannot convert unless you are sure of your conviction.' In this too there is an answer to the doubts that torment me. That, of course, is just what I want to do – continue my work to become sure of my conviction and give it clear and simple shape. Is here too perhaps an answer to my objections?

'Thou shalt not kill.' And 'You must know what you are doing.' In this juxtaposition a great deal becomes clearer. If we simply parrot the commandment in a superficial way, obey it without knowing what we are putting at stake, and follow it without inner compulsion and perfunctorily, simply because that is what it says and that is how we have learnt it, we do not know what we are doing, and in that case it does not apply. It can apply only if we do know what we are doing, and know with every

12

fibre of our being that that is how we must act, and why we are acting like that.

If there is nothing we are able to do except fight the Nazis, and if that is the only thing we feel we must do, we must not keep out of the war for the sake of a commandment we have not experienced. In that case, other of Christ's words may apply to us. 'Forgive them for they know not what they do.' And what they are doing without knowing it in this fight for humanity as they understand it, is violating their own deeper humanity.

I write that so apodictically, and yet really it still does not clarify anything, or dispose of any objection. The ideas have really merely been shaken up together. I must start again.

I want to keep myself, and those like me, out of the war to fight for the idea. This idea is closely bound up with 'Thou shalt not kill.' But am I not qualifying this commandment and saying that the others who cannot work for the idea, *are* to kill? Is it possible to fight for the idea in so qualified a fashion? In that case, has this idea not received its death blow, and am I not doing the same as I reproach the churches for doing?

This contradiction is, I believe, only caused by our wrong thinking. We are accustomed, and it has penetrated deep into our minds, always to think first of result and achievement. If we say the commandment applies generally we are then already thinking that it must in fact be obeyed by all and be universally effective. The early Christians too were a little band against a whole world. And even if it were not possible for the good to be pursued in a single case, that, says Kant, alters nothing concerning its validity. The validity of a commandment is one thing, the number of people it is obeyed by is another. 'Resist not evil.' It is not for us to urge that others should fight. Our task is to urge the idea and that it should be obeyed, to urge simply, 'Thou shalt not kill.' The more this idea is obeyed the more alive will the idea become, and the more alive it becomes the more irrelevant will become victory and defeat. If we believe in good it cannot be our concern to seek its victory. It can only be our concern to translate this good into reality so that it shall become alive. The farmer buries the seed in the ground. It has to grow on its own.

But we must know what we are doing. We must therefore work at the idea and strive for its realization. Only from the full life of the idea can we experience the commandment 'Thou shalt not kill' in such a way that it becomes completely alive, and the obeying of it no longer springs from any dogmatism or remains purely negative but becomes a positive experience. We – I, therefore, have a right to keep out of the war even if only working at this idea which is to revivify this commandment. To wish to

13

be perfect would be arrogance. No one is. I can, to begin with, only demand of myself that striving for the idea that leads to this end. 'You cannot convert unless you are sure of your conviction.'

7 September 1939

Again, when I read over what I have written, the objections are many. First, a not very important one. It does not seem right to me to emphasize the struggle for the idea as harder than the decision to volunteer for the front. Certainly it is; in many respects to volunteer would seem a release. But again, it also is not. The front is appalling, perhaps, after experience of the last war, no longer to be endured. Be that as it may, that is a point of view that is of no importance. Again it is merely to be put down to our habitual reasoning which is for playing the hero, for it is the hero alone that modern man considers to be worthy of esteem. Whether the struggle for the idea is an act of sacrifice or of cowardice is of no consequence at all. If the idea is all that matters, and it *is*, it can only be good for it to be achieved under the best possible conditions.

If I know, say, an author whose work I should like to think protected and preserved, then, even if I myself am that author, my wish must be for him to work under assured external conditions and in a country which allows this to be possible. Provided of course that this personal security does not lead to a blunting of terrible experience. But if the idea is really alive, there is no cause for fearing that feelings of guilt and horror will be paralysed by a little personal security.

But above all the fundamental objection, 'Thou shalt not kill', remains. Is that to be an absolute commandment, yet not apply to all? That cannot be right!

Let us be honest – would we dare today to stand up and proclaim that no one should kill? Or would we too only approve if someone else did? No, a thousand times no! We would rush forward crying, 'You madmen, what are you doing? Don't you see that you are only helping the Nazis?'

And yet something in us is opposed to that also. If in this war too people do not live by the Christian commandments, we can carry Christianity off and bury it, and that must not be! Who in the last war were deserving of admiration? The Quakers, who did not fight but helped. But ah, in that war everything was still much clearer and simpler! Or does it merely seem so?

I keep rereading what I have written to find a way out of this circular

14

thinking. These contradictions must after all be resolvable! I cannot keep starting completely from scratch!

Suddenly it seems to me that the answer to these objections has already been given. 'You cannot convert unless you yourself are convinced.' How can we stand up in the market-place and demand, 'Thou shalt not kill', while our conviction is not clear and while the idea has not acquired life within us so mightily that it is a whole, a life form, so that we have power to say what we have to say, truly and completely? 'Thou shalt not kill' – that is the negative delimitation of the human. But this human must first be delimited positively, be clear what must not be destroyed, be Christ's example again become alive and accessible. Only then can we make any demands. What, to begin with, applies to us and those like us is that it is our fault that the idea is too weak, and that we have not been able to live and proclaim this idea convincingly enough. And we can only atone for this fault by remaining, in all the torment of this war, loyal to the idea, and by striving with redoubled commitment to make it a reality. We can proclaim commandments only when we are aware. First, we ourselves must be aware. The commandment must be valid absolutely. But we cannot proclaim this validity until it is an isolated commandment no longer and has become an essential part of a whole life. And until we are able to exemplify this life, a full Christian life, with all our power.

Is that an answer?

8 September 1939

Not a final answer. For the war is still so peculiar, and not really getting going in the West, almost as if people are waiting for the peace offer that Hitler will have to make, having conquered Poland, and this again is a dreadful notion. And during sleepless nights the anxiety of this raises the same old burning problem. 'Is it permissible for us to keep out of it?' But the answer is still probably right in a sense. However difficult, we must, to begin with, have the strength to break away from this problem. We must not become obsessed with the most difficult problem. We must really strive for the idea, probe it from all sides, and achieve it gradually. Then even this the most difficult problem will be capable of solution.

Certainly I manage each day to advance my philosophical work just a little – work that is to make possible a new form of thinking. For to me that seems important above all. So long as we think in the old, out-lived, deadlocked way prevalent today, these thoughts will also again and again lead to an unchristian, heroic, bellicose existence, for that form of life is in accordance with that way of thinking. Only a turn away from that way of thinking and a new thinking built up from rock bottom can lead us also to new aims.

But this work is still in its infancy. There is still a long way to go before it can answer any questions. It is of course for that reason that I have begun this diary, because without an answer to the burning questions life is unbearable. But now I have also to do here what I am doing there – with all my strength and supreme self-conquest, create distance so as not to get hopelessly lost in the topical!

How important a new way of thinking is bound to be is shown whenever we repeat a text from the Bible.

Knowledge, for instance, is a word that has lost its original sense almost completely. Today any special knowledge or ability such as to do with natural science, business or languages, is accounted knowledge. Real knowledge, knowledge of man, of the totality of one's own style of living, knowledge of the world that goes beyond politics – this has been lost to such an extent that hardly anyone hearing the word knowledge thinks of anything of that sort, even in the remotest way. And yet this is the only knowledge that matters!

But how is the solution of any problem to be achieved simply by using the old hackneyed words without clarifying their meaning. I really must proceed more slowly!

A caricature of the Nazis in a British paper today was backed up by the indictment 'For they know what they do!' A terrible indictment indeed, for them to know what they are doing, torturing, crucifying and destroying Christ quite consciously. The battle is clearly for the extermination of anything remotely Christian, even at its humanistic vaguest.

But do we know what we are doing? In a superficial sense, we do, certainly – fighting the Nazis, making room for relative freedom and a peaceful private life. But what about in that deeper sense that we attach to the word knowledge? If Christ were to reappear amongst us today, would we recognize him? Would we not, unknowingly, cricify him again? For he would not, of course, come to the church as a parson; he might indeed stand up in the market-place and preach 'Thou shalt not kill, for thou shalt love thy enemies, and if anyone strike thee on the right cheek, turn to him the other.' But then would not we too shout 'Stop his mouth. Off to prison with him! Down with the Nazis!' But what, in that case, do we really know of Christ?

16

9 September 1939

Beset by my problems, I have forgotten to report something of importance. Last Sunday, the day of the outbreak of war, there was a joint
Anglo-German religious service. The British pastor thanked the German
refugees he had invited, for giving him, on the first day of war, the opportunity of translating Christianity into action. There was really none of the
atmosphere of showing charity to poor foreigners. It was honest and very
moving accord.

Once again it has been shown what enormous possibilities Christianity
has in this world! What other organization today is capable of upholding
true internationalism? What other organization can unite men of good will
across all battle fronts? It would be wonderful if this small start were
really to outlive the war. Maybe there will be other such starts. On the
very day of the outbreak of war it was a powerful and invigorating impression.

The service as such was also very impressive. Both pastors preached on
the parable of the Good Samaritan. The British pastor a little superficially
– too much about prayer and divine service – but the basic idea was very
fine: 'We may, even in the most terrible times, be glad, for to us, with
Christ, has joy been given.' And the pastor himself made a cheerful and
down-to-earth impression, as a result of which the sermon itself became
very human and convincing. Pastor H.'s sermon, on the other hand, was
really perfect and gave the answer to real and burning questions. 'Go
forth and do the same. Be merciful to your neighbour where you are
placed and where you find the sufferer. Do not trouble yourself about the
robbers, trouble only about the sufferer. Do not resist evil, but help.'

Which, I must admit, touches on only one aspect of my problem. The
question as to whether one does not in fact *have* to fight the robbers
remains unanswered.

My objections to the church are legion. I have been drawn to these
services only because the Confessional Church, being, for the first time
in a long while, obliged to fight for Christianity again, seems also to have
the possibility of again becoming Christian. The services even of this
church have not so far been able to remove my fundamental objections
either, although much that Pastor H. is well aware of and does, springs
from a critical attitude towards the church similar to my own. At the same
time, however, he is not prepared to take that step which, in my view, is
indispensable if it is not the church one wants to save but Christianity.

Still, so strong is the impression made on me by the last service, that I am going to defer my objections and await tomorrow's service unprejudiced. For it would be so much simpler, so much easier, so much more of a relief if one could indeed entrust oneself, together with the battle for Christ, to the church, which is an established and powerful organization. This is a hope I have long since abandoned. Overhastily perhaps?

Sunday 10 September 1939, morning

During the night I have been overwhelmed by a fresh serious objection. A qualification of the commandment 'Thou shalt not kill' does in fact seem possible, and that is *except in self-defence and as a last resort.* In law books this qualification is probably correct. Tyrannicide, on a large scale and on a small, that delivers men from monsters, may remain a sin at the personal level but for others it is a deliverance, a sacrifice that one makes for others. And is this war which is destroying the tyrant's army not *self-defence as a last resort*? Impossible as it may be to decide in other wars who has been the aggressor, in this one it is Hitler – the others would never have started it. There would have been no war if Hitler had not opened the attack.

But there is another objection which seems to support my views. If we do not understand how to fight for the idea we must take the suffering upon ourselves. It will not do to take up arms in the name of civilization which is civilization no longer. If, within that civilization, the idea can no longer be helped to come into its own, then that civilization deserves to be destroyed. In that case there will have to be a new beginning, a new barbarism. So that from it a new form of freedom and justice can develop, a new Christianity that will prove more vital than the old dead Christianity we are attempting to revitalize.

We must therefore either be capable of creating a new idea, or we must take the suffering upon ourselves. Both ways are opposed to the sword. And perhaps also to applying to this war the concept of self-defence. A purely human law can be qualified only for the sake of purely human values. But are they really on our side? Or do we not have to create them before we are entitled to qualify the commandment?

However great the suffering we take upon ourselves in that, we must not be discouraged by it. But are we entitled to affirm suffering in this fashion?

18

Sunday, evening

No, the church won't do. It is just when Christianity is taken seriously that the church won't do. Not even this very comprehensible form of Confessional Church. Maybe I would judge differently if, in coming to church, I was not coming from battling constantly with all these problems. But is not this battling the very point at which to start criticizing it? For there is a war on. Every minute men are dying – being killed by men in a most barbarous way. All the horrors of the old war are again alive. Added to which, cities are being shelled, vast areas are trembling in fear and terror, women and children are dying, a whole population is fleeing – is not this just what the church should be stirred to the core about? Have not we who are today in safety, the duty and the obligation to make an all-out effort, using every minute of this undeserved safety bestowed upon us by mysterious fate? And can the church shut its eyes to the extent to which this war must, in spite of everything, be affirmed, and to the battles of conscience which must arise for him who truly believes?

The last service seemed a starting point, both outwardly through the bringing together in Christianity of enemies, and also inwardly. The example of the Good Samaritan raises all the questions which occupy me here and which ought to occupy everyone. Further answers should now follow, or at least be sought. Yet the sermon did not betray so much as a sense of this need, and neither the service as such, nor the hymns nor the sermon were capable of helping a questioner today even in the slightest.

I do not believe the fault in this to lie with Pastor H. He himself feels the distress that I feel. But as he does not wish to step beyond the church's sphere of influence he has tried to reinforce what the church today has to offer, consolation and faith. But consolation and faith are not, I believe, the things that matter to begin with, for, offered in their usual form, they are bound to remain external, and they involve a bypassing of the fundamental problems upon which Christianity has got to prove itself anew. The important thing is not at all that we should take comfort by indulging ourselves with, apart from this life, the luxury of an old non-living faith. It is not solace we need, it is a *living* faith!

Whenever others are reciting the Creed I get a deep, painful stitch. I simply cannot recite it with them. And who of them does recite it with conscious honesty?

Who today can still believe, honestly and literally, 'I believe in God,

Maker of heaven and earth, in Jesus Christ his only-begotten Son, conceived by the Holy Ghost, born of the Virgin Mary'? Who, mechanically repeating, '. . . descended into hell, sitteth on the right hand of God . . .' etc., etc., does any thinking for himself? And is that what really matters?

It is, in quite a different sense – we have got to break through these antiquated forms in order to reveal the example of Christ! As long as words are recited without anyone thinking for himself no one will have any vital thoughts of his own at all, and life will remain unaffected? What is of absolute importance is to present the figure of Christ freed completely from dead tradition and literal school-faith, in so new a way that people must, and can, at every word think for themselves, and therefore begin to ponder his life and each of his parables completely anew! That alone is what matters! And if the church cannot do it, then it will have to be done outside the church.

I know of course what the answer is to that. We must preserve communion. Where else is there a possibility of establishing communion? Does not Christianity then lead to a pallid humanism devoid of communion-building power? Certainly this is a serious objection, real communion is infinitely important, is what is important today also! And yet this objection is invalid. For this communion is ever dwindling; not only that, but the bonds that bind it are growing looser and looser and more and more tenuous. It has hardly any influence on the real life of the congregation any more. Communion can be saved only as a result of a new life of Christianity.

Yes, and if result can be taken as any yardstick, does not this argument already show that the church can only still be preserved externally if it does not decide for anything new? For the sake of external communion one would have first and foremost to endorse Catholicism, with all its saints, and, as befits a faithful Catholic, stop reading the Bible.

I know that there is also a deeper objection. Many hymns and probably today's sermon too are to be explained by it. I must sometime clarify for myself the full extent of this objection in order to judge of its importance. Too late to do that today.

But let me also record that the British parson was present at this service too. He is placing the church at the further disposal of the Germans, and the Anglo-German service is to be repeated when there is an opportunity. He is even trying to make social contact between the two congregations possible.

This and other experiences here in Britain make me realize that *outside the church* does not necessarily have to mean *against the church*, as has always seemed to me. Here too the Christian community has scarcely any influence on real life and people's practical decisions, but it does to a high degree determine people's attitudes. Here one can in fact see the Christian convention exerting a civilizing influence over a wide radius. The general readiness on the part of the British to help refugees, their guilelessness in always assuming the other person to have the best intentions – which cuts out so many conflicts, especially the almighty row which finds such favour in Germany and France – can certainly be attributed to it. But this is to say that the church is likewise human material, and perhaps even specially good human material, which is worth winning. Here too it is not a question of opposition. Do not contend against the church but strive to win it, and it perhaps above all.

In Germany this civilizing influence is much weaker, but against that, the Confessional Church, despite its inadequacy, offers a special chance. Today it is living primarily on the martyrdom of Niemöller. That is a big danger, for that seems to take the place of any reshaping; it does not allow the need for it to become sufficiently clear – the apparent effect of martyrdom is to reinforce many old elements in the church. Within the Confessional Church too nothing new is to be felt, apart from the struggle against the Nazis which really had of course to come, and which it began too late and too hesitantly! Niemöller does indeed provide an admirable and deeply stirring example nevertheless, and one that will require to be given effect to and interpreted in definite fashion as soon as the martyrdom is ended – that is, as soon as reshaping actually becomes possible. And will the state of being stirred not then have to transform itself into readiness for the new?

11 September 1939

Not long ago, talking to Pastor H., I mentioned the book *Das Heilige* (*The Sacred*) by Rudolf Otto. He replied, 'I'll accept that you admire this book if you'll admit that it is not a Christian one.' I thought I would have to, but was that not being overhasty?

This is one of the most fundamental books I know of, and it best clarifies the deeper objection I have mentioned. But to me its title does not seem sufficiently clear, as if at this point even this outstanding theologian had been forced to be cautious. Clearer would have been *Das Göttliche* (*The Divine*).

Otto attempts to clarify the feeling that is bound up with real faith in God. On the basis of a comprehensive body of examples drawn from all religions, he arrives at roughly the following.

21

When we try to talk of the divine 'not only do statements seem to result which are contrary to reason, its standards and its laws, but which themselves become disunited and state contradictions concerning their subject which appear to be irreconcilable opposites'. The divine is always enthralling and monstrous, full of horror and of wonder. It contains rapture and terror, the wondrous and the fearful.

One of the plainest examples of this is the fate of Job. But not only does Job suffer the most fearful things that man can suffer, he also, and this in order to make clear the greatness of God, speaks of hippopotamus and crocodile as completely meaningless and incomprehensible creations. They are examples not of divine wisdom but of 'that in the power of the creator which is mysterious in its crassness, manifestly stupendous, near-daemonic and enigmatic, and of that which is incalculable and wholly different, defying all comprehension, yet stirring and fascinating mind and heart in all their depths, imbuing them at the same time with a most profound sense of recognition'. In the completely meaningless is revealed the mystery which quietens the soul.

Jesus, child of a time that still, almost exclusively, knew God only as a God of wrath and as a nightmare, has above all to present the gentle, fatherly God. Yet he too knows the wrathful, fearful God, and crying on the cross 'My God, my God, why hast thou forsaken me?' he experiences him. Luther shows a very good understanding of Christ when he says, 'For God is a fire that consumes, devours and is envious – that is, he destroys us as fire consumes a house turning it to ashes and dust . . . Indeed, he is more terrible and appalling than the Devil for he treats and deals with us violently, plaguing and martyring us and heeding us not.' A God who cannot be wrathful, cannot love either.

Set down baldly and without Otto's detailed arguments, that probably sounds very blatant, but to me it seems as important as it is correct. A living faith in God must reach out far beyond all that is humanly tangible, surpass the human so far as is ever possible, and evoke most powerful, most extreme feeling – all of which can be achieved only by means of extreme opposites visualized simultaneously. Only when thinking is forced to extreme opposites, i.e., not only to that which is best, greatest, most imposing and glorious, but at the same time to that which is most atrocious, absurd and meaningless, only then does a feeling arise that elevates us beyond the limits of the human and conveys to us that awe which is the premonition of the unattainable and unimaginable, and of the divine.

This idea can also be explained in a way that is simpler and perhaps more humanly comprehensible than Otto's.

God cannot and must not be the Good. For good and evil are human ideas. Indeed, what sort of a god would it be who conformed to *our* petty standards? How can *we* dispute with God that there should be good and evil in the world – *we* who so often experience apparently good turning into evil and evil into good – *we* who have only fluctuating standards and are aware of no final purpose! How can *we* demand of God that he should organize the world in accordance with *our* petty wishes, and *our* relative conception which does not have the overall view? What sort of a world would it be that *we* thought good? A small, limited one, full of faults, based upon error and shortsightedness – not a divine world but a human one, or, to extend the idea, an ant heap, a bee colony.

God is not the Good, God is the Whole. Anyone who believes in God must feel this world to be divine. And he will be able instinctively to feel God only where, through all joy and pain, he manages to experience the whole, and only where, despite all pain, he is able to assent so fully as to say yes to this world as it is, with all the good and all the bad. Only where our feeling elevates us out of and above our torn, divided lives, out of and above the world divided into good and evil, which we alone are capable of perceiving – only where our feeling allows us to experience, beyond all discord, the unity, the whole – only there do we draw near to the divine.

The feeling is a remarkable one that the words *sublime, divine, over-powering* convey only allusively. Its hallmark is reconciliation to the point of unity of that which is contradictory. Our being overwhelmed by the sublime permits us simultaneously to experience that awe which is engendered by the terrible. That which is infinite about this feeling is the redeeming release created by the removal of limits and at the same time the fear and the terror produced by the infinite. It is the satisfaction of total interpretation and the turmoil of at the same time recognizing that this interpretation is not to be apprehended. It is security in God and the feeling of being lost in the infinite vastness of the divine sphere.

This feeling is to be experienced only in the opposite, and in extreme opposites. There is no need for these opposites to resort immediately to that which is cruellest, most terrible and most senseless – these are provided in human terms far more directly. With Otto these extreme opposites are justified because what he is trying to describe is the feeling of the divine. The Whole involved here, the fusing of good and evil, the perfect affirmation – these we experience every instant.

For when suffering the terrible, we are already experiencing the good, and the very suffering which arises from the good makes the good a reality. When we reject evil, we apprehend and are aware of good. In the pain occasioned by the bad, the cruel, the senseless, already lies its removal, for if it were appropriate to us, and if we were not aware of the other, we would be unable to feel pain.

Indeed, more than that: whether thrust into the abyss by a terrible fate or blinded by a glorious light, our first impression is of pain; whether great grief is our experience or excessive joy, both release our tears; whether we are overwhelmed by torment or by bliss, we suppose both to be unbearable. And it is in this marriage of the opposites which carry us forcibly outside our limits, and only in this marriage, that we experience the divine.

I do not believe that lively humans can, in our day, literally and naively believe in a God who has created the world and is directing it all-wisely. Nor do I believe this feeling I have described to be normal and common. We have learnt to direct our efforts away from the bad, from pain. We are concerned to shape life, even if our shaping is unable to make the good a reality. We move within the relative. Yet if there is a way in which we can still speak of the divine at all, and describe and apprehend it, then certainly it is only in this. And yesterday that might still have appeared to be intellectual dallying – Otto's book when I read it ten years ago, interested me as a historically abstract experiment. But today, when brutal and atrocious primitive forces, long since thought to have been overcome and cultivated or civilized, are suddenly again smashing through to the surface, does not this feeling acquire new weight? Do we not at least need to take it into account?

To me this feeling seems almost an end towards which we must strive. I do not believe that it can easily be made a reality. But I do believe that revivifying the example of Christ and making a reality of that human quality that we must aspire to, ties in with this feeling and will give it a more concrete content and a clear meaning. I do not believe that we can today just believe in God, or that this belief is today still really alive even in its pious church form – alive in the sense of being equal to this life. But I do believe that this feeling can today again shine at the ultimate limits of our experiencing and perceiving, and that it is by virtue of this feeling that what was feeble and non-living about humanism, liberalism and the nineteenth century is being corrected. This feeling, which all of us may have experienced clearly at least once, must be retained in our consciousness if we are not to be too quickly satisfied with the purely human. The example of Christ can be fully revivified only whenever we too re-experience this feeling. And a new Christianity will be possible only if it again gives clear content to this feeling. What is important in this is not

24

God [*Gott* – Tr.] as a name, but probably this feeling which, in the meantime, is still most clearly conveyed by the word divine [*göttlich* – Tr.].

But why is this feeling supposed to be unchristian?

12 September 1939

I understand why Pastor H. asserts that and why I have conceded it to him so readily. Yet to me it seems wrong.

The sermon which so greatly disappointed me, and also an earlier sermon, said roughly the following:

We know that God is with us. It was Christ's mission to bring this certainty. However our hearts may contend against it and all appearances deny it, however far we may depart from it, we cannot fall any more from the state of being children of God. Thanks to Christ, God is with us always and in all circumstances, for Christ has taken our guilt upon himself and extinguished it in the sight of God. Christ is not floating in the clouds, remote and unattainable. He has performed this act for all and forever, now and here. Therefore, pure or guilt-laden, good or evil, we can always approach God as the Father, and as a kind Father, entrusting ourselves to him with our cares and sorrows, praying to him for ourselves and our nearest, for our family and for Pastor Niemöller, knowing that God – in his, perhaps to us, incomprehensible way – will give ear, and we have the comfort of having a Father who has sent us his Son so that we should become and forever remain his children. Those abysmal depths of despair which man is not able to endure have been removed from the world by Christ. We know, even in our worst despair, that God is with us.

The removal, through Christ, of unendurable despair seems to me fundamental and correct, but even here there is probably no need for us to resort to a mystical faith. He has made despair endurable because he, in his life, has been able to give meaning to even the most fearful suffering. And it is by that means that he makes accessible to us experience of the whole. In the despair which we are unable to bear, we are also unable to experience the whole. Only when despair is bound up with knowledge of the meaning and of the good does it produce that opposite which brings us closer to the divine.

But anything that goes beyond this seems to me a blind process of humanization by Christianity. It is precisely because I first accepted this kind of Christianity that I have realized that it cannot be true Christianity.

I do not want to make myself out to be better than I am. When I get into a situation against which I am completely powerless and which can be resolved favourably for me only by an external turn of events, then the words 'Dear God, help' force themselves to my lips. But I have never yet spoken them without a deep sense of shame.

For what sort of a God would it be who allowed himself to be moved by our petitions, who, to help us, had first to be asked, and who, by our petitions, could be moved to alter in our favour the course of the world that he had determined?

No, we cannot approach God as children do their fathers! Even for Christ, God was Father but he was also the God who abandoned him on the cross. It is no good simply reducing Christianity to the certainty that God is with us, that it is sufficient to pray to him to be heard, or that it suffices merely to do good deeds in order to be rewarded, even if not until the world after this. It is no good conceiving Christianity simply as consolation. We do not get any nearer to God by relying upon the redemption of all sin through Christ.

Look at the old prayers and hymns. They quite clearly help engender the feeling I have described, praising God as glorious and terrible, and depicting the inconceivable in good and evil. Only the more modern hymns, from Paul Gerhard on, are primarily consolation.

As long as belief in God was alive, so too was the devil – the adversary and yet also part of God. Christ speaks of him. So does Luther. It was simply a different world. With God we have lost the devil also. And it will not do to maintain the old God now without the antagonist that made belief in God a living belief. Because we no longer shun the devil, the *evil* in *The Lord's Prayer* having acquired a purely human sense, we can no longer turn to God as Father, or else, automatically, he becomes for us *the good God,* that is to say a naive conception no longer having anything to do with the divine. We must, by revivifying the example of Christ, arrive at a wholly new realization of the divine.

Perhaps the redemption of all sin will then acquire a wholly new meaning too.

In the meantime however we cannot rely on this redemption. Otherwise God becomes simply the Good – a superfluous, empty word for a human idea. And the existence of evil in the world remains a constant, inevitable and inexplicable blow to a belief in God of that sort.

13 September 1939

The church services have led me to circle too much around belief in God. So far are we from that belief today that this is something that we

26

must not do, or else we easily get into mystical explanations at the point where it is still a question of human example. Thus Christ's enigmatic 'My God, my God, why hast thou forsaken me?' may, considered from the outside, serve to clarify the divine feeling. On the other hand, considered from within, they do not seem to me at all enigmatic. On the contrary. Indeed, if any proof were required of God's intention to give a human example, these words supply it.

Jesus is not eager for death. Three times he prays, 'Lord, let this cup pass from me.' Only when he discovers that his disciples are sleeping, does he make up his mind to take this death upon himself.

For how is his example to be effective if, at the most crucial hour, not even the disciples know what is taking place inside him; if not even the eyewitnesses and most intimate friends who are appointed to spread his teaching; if even those upon whom his example must first work for it to be passed on at all; if not even *they* understand him?

He has said to them what had to be said. His example, his teaching are complete. And yet they are sleeping. Nothing remains now but to perfect that example so strikingly and so disturbingly that it can never more be lost. Nothing remains but to take upon himself this terrible death, creating the symbol that preserves for all times the essence of his human life.

He has not wished for death. He has taught his disciples that, if threatened while proclaiming his teaching, they should flee. He has often eluded informers, and would be ready to do so now too, and let the cup pass if only there were one person he could trust – if only one of the disciples was not sleeping. Yet as they *are* sleeping he realizes that he is still terribly alone and that he must therefore follow his way to the end alone. Only the most terrible of shocks can resurrect his image in the hearts of his disciples, and complete what his words have not been able to complete, and will not be able to complete, alone. As long as he lives he will be betrayed, even by Peter.

He takes death upon himself not as deliverance, not as the culmination of his life, but as a terrible necessity. His life having been a human life, this death is as terrible for him as for any human. He suffers it entirely as a human being. So great is his torment that even he cannot suppress the words 'My God, my God, why hast thou forsaken me?' These words are evidence of a human life being terminated in human fashion. Dostoyevsky refers somewhere[2] to the supreme genius of Holbein's painting of *The Entombment of Christ* for depicting Christ's body as wholly human with

2. *The Idiot*, part 3, chapter 6.

all the fearful signs of decay. The death of Christ is deprived of its sense if it is not recognized in all its awfulness as a human death. Not without reason do those who pass by blaspheme 'If thou be the Son of God, come down from the cross.' The man Christ dies as man.

The (to me as yet not clear) symbol of the redemption of sin is not affected by that. A man can also take all sin upon himself. But this death may still show something else. The example lies not in the death. How can Christ set up so fearful a death as an example. His death becomes necessary only to save the example that he has given in life. It refers back to the life of Jesus, and sets us another aim – that of making the uncrucified Christ a reality.

How far we are from this! In the thick of a war that will call for any number of victims. And how far from it am I who do not even know whether it is permissible for me to keep out of this war. . .

14 September 1939

When I start writing in this diary again and think, as I do so, of the sort of conversations I am mostly forced to have, I hardly know what to make of anything. How many people *do* know what they are experiencing? How many have grasped that it is war? How many know what is at issue today? And when *are* they ever to understand, if not today when they are bound to be stirred up by the war?

Again and again I am shaken at the impossibility of talking about all these things with congenial, pleasant, apparently sensible and certainly nice, middle-class people. They react correctly as long as they are moving within their own circle. But now they have been dragged out of it, and it's war – a most terrible war – when *are* they to be liberated from their encapsulation if not now! It is here that the contrast between education and half-education is very marked. How very much more productive it is talking to really simple people, and how much freer and more natural the reaction of those who have not been miseducated! But how rare they have become too.

Can you seriously wonder at it? It is easier to explain colour to a blind man than to a colour-blind man. The blind man is obliged to develop a wholly new conception out of a completely different kind of conceptual world, and as a result is able to take it in. The colour-blind man first of all considers his partial and false conception to be correct, for that is how he sees, and it is difficult to argue him out of it. And even if we manage to show him that his conception is false, his false conceptions obtrude con-

28

stantly into the new ones, and he builds the new with the aid of the false.

But you must not be misled by that! Innocence does not admit of being restored artificially. Half education can be overcome only by real education. And even innocence needs real education, for its peculiarity is that it can be led astray, or, as Kant says, cannot alone prevent itself from falling. It needs the protection of genuine knowledge.

15 September 1939

Disillusioned by men, today I have once again been for a walk through this enchanting city of Cambridge, forcing myself, in spite of the war and the horror, to see and feel and experience the town. And it has perhaps been a better form of *recueillement* than church!

What impresses me most, time and time again, is the old Norman Round Church, a perfect example of that style. It is as man ought to be, outwardly earthly and inwardly divine! As man is basically intended to be and ought to become again.

And time and time again also it is powerfully borne in on me what a total absence there is here of baroque excess, and how unequivocally Britain is the land of no baroque.

On the continent I see Gothic as the baroque of Norman. Here Gothic, however ornate sometimes, lacks any inner baroque strain. And if baroque elements are later employed rarely and with care, baroque is never the result. Preserved throughout all styles there is a uniform English style related first and foremost to Renaissance. The Norman Round Church alone forms an exception. That was obviously the one time of a unitary European style; the time of a uniform Christianity.

There is the gigantic hall of King's College Chapel – enormous, overwhelming in its dimensions, and therefore not Renaissance style but Gothic. However, the space is strictly quadrangular, not striving upwards but exactly balanced in all directions, the windows – so that one shall not forget the war even here, are in process of being removed to safe-keeping – the windows being set regularly in the walls, filling them out exactly. In English churches there are scarcely any Gothic roses, never a solid wall pushing into the sky, the front always homogeneously proportioned so that it can be taken in at a glance, always treated from top to bottom as a whole. A distinct relationship can be sensed with the eighteenth-century town houses whose architecture consists only of clear arrangement.

The Gothic style of which this baroque upward surge is characteristic is here protected against any baroque extravagance, the buttresses are completely suppressed and the ceiling overemphasized instead, it bears down on the space, often it is made artificially lower than it really is by means of self-supporting Gothic shapes, the form of the basilica is constantly preserved. This Perpendicular style is a special Gothic of its own.

This exclusion of baroque ought really to signify a great liberation. How peaceful these many college courts are, extensive but clearly limited, the space opened up, yet at the same time restrained, always with complete lucidity of arrangement. Even the rigidity of the architecture is still humanly softened by lawns, trees and flowers, and so simultaneously reintegrated into nature. It is no accident that the architecture should so often lead on towards beautiful old gardens.

And yet this architecture lacks something. It provides neither final uplift nor final satisfaction. Why?

Remember Italy. What full, redeeming resonance is provided there in early Renaissance by the breakthrough of unambiguously clear, lucidly arranged human proportions! And yet there too Renaissance is completely arresting only in its early form, and only for as long as the enormous felicity of the first experience and immediate liberation can be felt. Later it becomes colder, more pompous, emptier. Man is not all, the superhuman refuses to be excluded completely, and the turn to baroque becomes essential.

That probably is the essential thing, in so far as baroque is an empty gesture, a side-scene of the world beyond, it becomes intolerable. But man is not satisfied by the earthly alone. Outwardly earthly and inwardly divine – that is the point. The style without baroque liberates to begin with because of the exclusion of the externally divine which is unable to say anything more to us today, but the liberation is not a lasting one because the inwardly divine is missing which is today precisely what we ought to be creating.

That only is what matters. The God who reigns above the clouds can today say nothing to us any more. We must rediscover him in ourselves or we shall not rediscover him. The moral commandments proclaimed by a superhuman power have ceased to sound and have lost their force. We must rediscover them as the core of our being.

16 September 1939

A constant source of delight is the clarity and vitality with which human knowledge can be gathered from the art form.

30

In itself the art form is inexplicable and enigmatic. To describe it only to some extent we have, rather as with the feeling of the divine, to resort to contradictions. In every consummate work of art the time-conditioned is united with the timelessly valid, the individually and nationally peculiar – with the universally human, a particular subject – with a general meaning. But where, with the feeling of the divine, the contradictions have something that is disquieting about them, in the art form they produce a liberation.

How powerfully a simple verse, a simple rhyme is able to heighten and clarify a statement. How much more is said by Goethe's lines:

> Willst du ins Unendliche schreiten,
> Geh nur im Endlichen nach allen Seiten.

> [If you would stride into the infinite,
> just walk in all directions in the finite.]

than by the same sentence in prose:

> Wenn du ins Unendliche schreiten willst, mußt
> du nur im Unendlichen nach allen Seiten gehen.[3]

In the verse the infinite does in fact encompass the finite and we can picture the strides measuring the infinite. The prose leaves us with a logical construction which we have first to think out exactly in order to grasp. Indeed, more than that: in the verse, the pervasion of infinity and finiteness is felt by us, and becomes clearer to us, than could be expressed by words. The art form produces a strong feeling that really does direct our strides out of finiteness and into infinity. It marries, interconnects, finity with infinity.

Far be it from me, even remotely, to elevate art into a religion. I know the arguments against – not only the possibility of great discrepancy between artistic gift and character which is bound to work out disastrously for the human, if giftedness is elevated to a heavenly level; but also, first and foremost, the fact that every work of art is ambiguous. We can gather the human quality from it very clearly if we experience the work powerfully and entirely without prejudice. But if we half experience it, or experience it falsely, or try to put something definite into it, we may gather something quite different. It is in ambiguity that its appeal and its riches lie. At different times we shall experience it differently – it will

3. The difference, which is one of construction, cannot be conveyed with sufficient contrast without inappropriate poeticizing of Goethe's lines after the style of 'Would'st thou stride into the infinite . . .'

always have something fresh to tell us, and we shall be able to return to it again and again. But it also has its danger – it remains nonbinding. It remains, even if in the highest sense of the word, enjoyment. It first awakens inspiration, and a strong spirit is required to know for *what*. And even the strong spirit will, by virtue of this inspiration, be strengthened above all in its own striving.

So is there a contradiction here also? Not wholly. The art form is an unprecedented means for communicating powerful human experience. Whoever has eyes to see and ears to hear will, by virtue of this experience, also arrive at human clarity. It therefore suggests the question whether it ought not to be possible to carry the form over into other spheres of human thought: perception and aspiration in order to clarify and intensify their results.

Is there a way of making this productive means of the human spirit productive *for* that human spirit?

Does not here too lie an explanation for why I so insist on the example of Christ, and why his teaching is for me not enough?

17 September 1939

Every day in this diary I make an effort to suppress mention of the events of politics and war in order not to get lost in the unproductive. But I do not find it easy. For the necessity of example there is a simple explanation. Dogmatic orders are inadequate because external fulfilment is never the point at issue. What is right for one situation can be wrong for another. That is why example is so important because at the same time as the commandment, it gives the situation with all its contradictions, and can therefore be transferred to other situations and interpreted and adapted for them; and because, in the greatest essential, the human attitude, it is not non-binding but wholly clear-cut.

The association with form is correct – it lies in the comprehensive elaboration of a situation with all its contradictions. In carrying the example over to a different situation an artistic element is no doubt even involved too. And the binding force which the art form lacks is produced by the human attitude.

But I still have it in mind to develop form more generally for the purposes of thought. It is about this that I am concerned in my philosophical work which is still progressing just a little each day. Maybe I should try sometime to explain here what I am trying to do. A simple review of this sort could not fail to be helpful to me in every way.

But I cannot do that now. We have been blessed with all too cruel a problem by this already sufficiently cruel war. So Poland has been crushed. And what is important now is that the most terrible thing of all should not happen – a new Munich. There is much in favour of it – the war in the West has still not clearly begun. There is much against it – it hardly seems likely that Britain will pull back this time, having stated so unambiguously that it is Hitler she is fighting.

And yet, and yet . . . The battle for Poland has been a definite war aim. But also, in itself, a dubious one. Why did we have to fight for this of all countries? It was the first to introduce dictatorship. Its frontiers in fact are artificial. It has persecuted its minorities, Ukrainians, Jews and So-cialists more cruelly than any other, and it did, let it not be forgotten, invent the concentration camp. Is not the dubious nature of this ally bound to be of more decisive moment now that it is no longer a question of saving but of re-establishing him? Can a peace be imagined that gives the Corridor and the Ukrainians back to the Poles, and the Sudeten Germans to the Czechs? Would a peace of this sort make any sense? For ending the last war there was always the disastrous idea of the self-determination of peoples. What sort of an idea is there today?

Of course, I know – it's not a question of Poland but of fighting Hitler, a question of freedom. For the British the elimination of Poland may come as a relief, because as a result it becomes perfectly clear that they are fighting for a cause of their own. But after six years of letting freedom be trampled, is it now possible suddenly really to fight a war for it? It may be of some consolation that the real point at issue is world domination. But is that any reason for war if peace is being offered in the West, and if world domination is something that really mustn't be talked about? If we are obliged to talk of freedom, having claimed for years that another coun-try's form of government is of no concern to us? And have recently declared as much, as a bait for the Russians, and are still not quite deny-ing it yet either, perhaps as a bait for Mussolini and Franco?

Again and again the vigorous idea is lacking! If that were there, all would be simple. But how are we going to serve it if we are not able to concentrate on it?

This compulsion to put the idea right in the forefront, in defiance of all the oppressing and pressing immediate perils is the same difficulty that used to beset me over the problems of socialism. There was a lot of truth in the socialists' reproach. 'You and your abstract problems! First we've got to feed the people, better their living conditions, then we can start worrying about the idea. When *you*'ve got nothing to eat that's when

33

you'll just have to start worrying *your* brains about it too. It's belly first and morality second!'

And yet they were wrong. For the difficulty of course lies precisely in the fact that a new social order and the fair distribution of goods cannot come about at all without a new idea and a new human attitude. However agonizing the need, we must find the strength and the rigour to strive first for the idea, because we do not, on the seemingly direct road, achieve even the betterment of living conditions. We must, despite all the need, take the long laborious detour because the direct road leads to nothing.

None of which is in the slightest altered by the fact that I myself cannot work at the idea if starving to death. Work on the idea has nevertheless to be done. Besides, *starving to death* is a very broad term. There are always enough who are not. To starve to death is rare, even when the majority are badly off. Care must be taken with absolute terms in this relative world: to starve to death is still the exception, even when understood figuratively.

Meanwhile the Nazis have supplied additional proof for what is an old view of mine. They are not to be fought with material arguments. Even were they to succeed in creating good living conditions that would still alter nothing concerning the absolute necessity of fighting them in any case. Indeed, they *have* bettered the living conditions of the lower classes, and this from having even themselves started from the idea. But the idea is what matters, and that it should be the right one. For the only, the sole thing to be endorsed, is humane socialism. What is the use of filling our bellies if at the same time all morality goes to the devil! Strength and rigour must be found to refrain from compassion, and, even if in distress, to fight for humanity!

And so then, in this war too, the important thing is not to let oneself be overwhelmed, and in spite of all, to strive for the idea.

18 September 1939

But just distancing ourselves obviously won't do. I have to write in this diary again too, and probably shall have to constantly throughout this war. For something quite crucial has happened today – the Russians have marched into Poland. With this it becomes plain that the Russo-German pact is, as has been feared from the beginning, an alliance. True, voices are now also heard to the effect that this Russian invasion may prove more unpleasant for the Germans than for the Western Powers, and that wholly ingenious plans are involved aimed now, as ever, at wearing down the capitalist states and plunging Germany into revolution. The communist paper is jubilant – '*Russian blow to Nazis.*' And it is not even completely impossible that something of the sort is correct.

But whatever the practical consequences, they will make no difference to the abomination of this total cynicism on the part of Germans and Russians, or to the significance of this double, and later perhaps, triple betrayal. And this betrayal, this complete independence of ideologies loudly asserted by both power systems – this possibility of concluding an alliance with the arch enemy just when it suits one's purpose, is the point. And so let that alone be the subject here before perhaps this clarity is obscured again by further twists.

The one point of interest would seem to be whether Britain is to blame for this about-face by Russia, not having pursued the alliance seriously enough, or whether Russia has been determined on alliance with Germany from the beginning. But even that would seem only of importance if the wish is to assess Britain's policy. In assessing Russia's it plays no part, the fact that an alliance with Germany has been possible being decisive in itself. Apart from which, of course, there is also the underhand, treacherous manner of the breaking off of negotiations with Britain.

What I see as important above all about this alliance is the rending of the veil of Marxism. Hitherto it has been difficult to lump the two power systems together. One has had to speak cautiously of *similar methods*, for communism is at core a good thing, and Marxism too strives after justice and, in the long run, even freedom. This confusion is now removed. The rule of force, of lies, of terror, of inhumanity, is plainly on the one side – the German and the Russian. The opposing fronts are at least clear – tyranny and lie versus freedom and justice.

Although that is not to say that freedom and justice are in fact already on the one side, otherwise this whole diary would be superfluous. It has merely become clear that effective help can be found only where there *is* freedom and justice, that tyrannies are only to be resisted with their aid, and that the essential thing is force, not the programme of left or right. It is becoming clear that Marxism must be eliminated from consideration completely, having become guilty of fearful errors and a fatal intermarriage. And if communists are today still praising Moscow they are again proving that they have no idea what is at issue. One cannot, praising Moscow, fight the Fascists.

Marxism was in line to reshape the world, and seemed after the last war to have every possibility for doing so. The fact that we are now having to pay so very dearly is first and foremost the fault of Marxism, and of its failure. We must not shrink from openly disowning Marxism, and here Russia's about-turn may indeed be of great advantage. The fact that the Nazis have been against Marxism is definitely no longer any argument for it. For it is entirely possible that tomorrow or the next day the Nazis will effect a Bolshevik revolution that will take account of most Marxist demands, and yet there will, as a result, be no chance that might influence our attitude towards the Nazis. As regards this nothing will be altered in the slightest.

Marx somewhere calls freedom, equality and fraternity, 'lip-service to modern gods'. And by that he does not merely intend a criticism of bourgeois society that would indeed seem justified, for these words are all too often posters hiding quite different motives. No, he means these ideas themselves, the ideas pure and simple. To him all ideas are only the *superstructure* of the economic order, an inessential trimming. To him the economic order is what matters, not the idea. And in this is a very precise indication of Marxism's most momentous and disastrous failing.

Marxism itself is based upon very powerful ideas. It traces every value back to labour, giving the old formula of justice a very vital modern content. It claims to help the proletariat – those who are deprived of rights – and that would seem a realization of justice and fraternity. And the new social order it claims to create is to guarantee for all the freedom which today only few enjoy.

But it denies these ideas – it does not profess them – it attacks ideas. In their place it puts a rational, thought-out economic system in which necessarily inadequate prophecy plays a disastrous part, and takes itself so seriously as to regard economics – eating – as the primary and solely decisive interest of men. The eternally true '*Man shall not live by bread alone*' it forgets.

At every point it throws the baby out with the bath-water. It claims to be fighting against capitalism and is in fact fighting against bourgeois society where it ought to have found powerful and helpful ideas, for the ideals of bourgeois society do not necessarily have to remain lip-service. It claims to be fighting the churches and is in fact fighting Christianity which might have become the new movement's strongest support. It claims to be fighting false ideologies, and is in fact fighting any ideology, not grasping that it is itself merely creating a new ideology, and one which is becoming disastrous because, in contradictory fashion, it is disavowing its own ideas.

Whatever way you look at it, Marxism proves time and time again that without ideas things won't work. Man does not act only in his own interests. On the contrary, for the sake of an idea he is ready to make the greatest sacrifices. Marxism, appealing as it does to interests, is unable to affect man deeply enough and gets overrun by nationalism. Believing in rigid material facts, it gets forced towards the concept of the class war, membership of the working class alone legitimizes. But in this it is obliged to disclaim the convictions of its opponents and dispose again and again of those best forces from other classes that have been ready to come to its aid, thus robbing itself of the possibility of renewal and adaptation to changed situations. Indeed, more than that, it is being destroyed by a class that it has disregarded and denied – the employees and *petit bourgeois* who have not let themselves be persuaded that they are proletarians.

Marxism calls for revolution, but, not believing in the effect of ideas, develops at the same time a history of philosophy proving that things are bound to happen as it claims anyway. As a result of this contradiction it splits the movement – the Social Democrats rely on essential evolution, the communists preach violent revolution. They both, in so doing, miss any possibility of carrying their ideas through. The Social Democrats are ruining the 1918 Revolution, for now, really assured that evolution is working for them, they are letting slip every opportunity of standing up vigorously for their ideas, whereas so keen are the communists on force that they are missing any opportunity of influencing that evolution peacefully. Finally, for the sake of power, they are even agreeing with the Nazis, thereby digging their own graves.

That, of course, applies only to Germany. But in France too the Marxists have achieved nothing, while in Britain the Labour Party has, at best, been of assistance to the Nazis, and the communists are today still idolizing Moscow. Only in Russia has Marxism had any explosive force because there the machine has still been something in the nature of an idea – a good god – and because there Marxism has been elastic enough to act counter to its programme, and firstly in giving the peasants private property. Against that, its failure has become apparent subsequently. That it should have been possible for Stalin quietly to take over power, speaks not against Stalin or the defeated Trotsky, but against the system.

Marxism overlooks the ideas in its own teaching, thereby depriving its adherents of any possibility of passing a correct judgement. They are unable to grasp what is of importance. For the materialistic concept of history is simply false. Slaves may well rebel if treated too badly, but Rome was overthrown not by rebelling slaves but by the Christians. Reliance on rebellion alone and on the fight for bread ushers in the new barbarism – destruction, not progress. Only ideas have a history- and civilization-building effect.

20 September 1939

I do not want to be misunderstood. I believe in ideas in the sense of being convinced that it is ideas that make history. I believe it to be beyond doubt that ideas are capable of making men ready and willing for extreme efforts and the greatest sacrifices. Christianity has reshaped the world. The battle for freedom, equality, fraternity kindled the French Revolution. And even Fascism and National Socialism, as I keep stressing, came into power initially by the aid of the idea.

But that does not mean my simply endorsing any idea merely because it is an idea. There are right and wrong ideas, beneficial and disastrous ideas. The important thing is to stand up for the right one. But this is just the important distinction that Marxism is unable to make because the idea is something that it denies.

It is probable that our time will have to make socialism in some form or other a reality. But that alone is not what is crucial. For the lesson of recent evolution has been primarily that there is a fearful, enslaving, army-barracks type of socialism, and there is a socialism that is liberating in the human sense. So what is important is not socialism as such, but the form – the idea underlying it.

Unfortunately the German–Russian alliance makes imminent the danger that most Marxist demands will be satisfied, and that for this very reason the most dreadful form of socialism will become reality. It is already hardly possible to imagine any other outcome to the war than that of Germany's being plunged into Bolshevik revolution either by Hitler or against Hitler.

But will that not be an enormous success for Marxism? Can we in that case speak of its failure? Is that not a premature assessment? Will not the success or failure of Marxism be decided only by the war?

No. For Marxism has wanted progress, and that clearly in the sense of an earthly paradise for men. It has wanted to free and not enslave them. Only a Marxist blind to ideas and adhering solely to external signs, can consider the victory of army-barracks-type socialism to be the victory of Marxism. That the terrible form of socialism has become a reality is seen by any right-thinking person as proof of the failure of Marxism. And the fatal thing is that this crucial distinction should, as a result of materialistic teaching, lie totally beyond Marxism.

38

21 September 1939

I do not want to be misunderstood in another sense also. I have the greatest respect for Marx for being able to wrest such work from the torment of exile. With him the materialistic attitude is understandable for he is opposing Hegel, that is, the immoderate overrating of mind. But this personal insight does not alter the fact that his work is to be condemned – his *work,* and not primarily the mediocre Marxists, they are merely extending the master's errors.

For the heroic struggle of the Marxists in Germany, and for the communists who have now been in concentration camps for six years and are unbroken, I have the greatest admiration. But that does not alter the fact that they are suffering for the sake of an error.

The Communist Freedom Station broadcasting from Germany is today saying 'Don't go to war – all you are fighting for is Krupp and Thyssen's dividends.' What a terrible thing! This transmitter is kept on the air by very great courage and an admirable contempt for danger – men are risking their lives for it, and it is bound to cost many more – and that heroism is in the service of absurdity of this sort. Does that not at bottom confirm what I was saying here yesterday? For what difference will it make to National Socialism if, as is not so unlikely, it dispossesses Krupp and Thyssen? Next to none! The Marxists have simply lost any chance of distinguishing what is at issue. And as a result they are depriving themselves of their effect; the broad mass of the German people is longing for decency, justice and personal security, and for that reason is as afraid of the communists as of the Nazis.

But again and again no less terrible is the weakness of the other side. If we imagine Bolshevik revolution in Germany, it seems probable too that the Western Powers will then lose interest in the war. And that again will be terrible. It will be the beginning of a world revolution. The final collapse of the West.

The Western Powers ought to be inclined to leave a Bolshevik revolution to itself, because it is with regard to socialism that the weakness of their own ideas is most manifest. They float free in the air, having so little penetrated into real life as to be able to tolerate a social reality of a totally different kind, without the contradiction being seriously felt and their bad consciences forced to rouse themselves. But that is not to say that what matters first and foremost is the socialist economic system. On the contrary! If the war is a long one it will in any case impose a more-or-less socialist economy on the warring states. But state socialism of this sort is far more of an evil than a blessing, and the very likelihood of it is why we must fight today for the ideas capable of reforming it in a human fashion.

Tolstoy uses a very good image. Anyone wishing to cross a rapid stream will not swim toward his goal on the opposite bank or he will get carried well downstream. He must swim against the current. The same applies here. If a socialist economy is what we are aiming at, we land deep in barbarism. We must, in the dreadful current of this war, also swim against the stream!

22 September 1939

Tonight is the beginning of the Jewish Day of Atonement, and it confirms from quite another quarter the necessity of swimming against the stream. For days now, young Jews have been insisting that they, who have never hitherto fasted, are going to this year.

There can be no objection to practising Jews fasting. But these are not practising Jews. They are doing it for quite different motives.

Of course, there is a good human motive involved also. If you are persecuted as a Jew it would be lacking in character to say that you are not one. In the very anguish of persecution it is right that one should own to being a Jew.

But how does one do that? By considering what it means to be a Jew, by immersing ourselves in the Bible and the Jewish scriptures, and by clarifying for ourselves what we really profess. How good that would be! The Jewish religion is rich in humanity and wisdom.

And a very remarkable thing might even happen which could prove most beneficial at the present time – we might become good Christians. That can very easily be the result of a serious study of Judaism, for Christianity preserves in purer form what in Judaism has first to be sifted out. And it would be good for Christianity also. The Jewish religion is the very one able to correct a great deal that the Christian church distorts in the pure teaching of Christ.

And who, setting about this task seriously, will not, after the Old Testament, be tempted to read the New as well!? And it is the New Testament that might be absorbed more vitally and directly by Jews than by Christians. Jews come to it possessing a very great advantage – for them the figure of Jesus has not been spoilt by school and church, nor has it been put beyond their reach and made lifeless by a tradition of mechanical parroting and by false dogmas. At a mature age, they can experience Christ fresh and pure.

40

This happened to me and to many of my friends some twenty years ago. Why should it not be possible more generally? In those days we were dreaming of a new task for Judaism – these last Christians might be the first real Christians. Ahasver returning home at last after two thousand years.

But no, they do not think that far. They do not think at all. They simply take over the antiquated forms without a thought. They protect themselves against the Nazis' nationalism by becoming nationalists themselves, copying in the most superficial way what they most condemn. They are like the Nazis. They believe only in external, tangible facts.

Judaism teaches that we should not make unto ourselves any image of God, or take his name in vain. It conveys the word God by *Jehovah,* that is, *the Eternal* or *Unchangeable,* in order not to emphasize the external too heavily. Similarly, Christ did not turn the stones into bread, spring from the pinnacles of the temple, accept dominion over the kingdoms of this world, or come down from the cross, because the external is not what matters, ever, anywhere.

If only men could be led away from faith in external facts! How much would then be gained.

For what is a fact? The thing of an act – that which you make out of reality.[4] Only when you devitalize it does reality become lifeless. And you *do* devitalize it by keeping only to the external.

23 September 1939

Facts apprehended only externally are probably the solely genuine values-to-be-believed-in of our time, and that is their chief evil. All of them – nation and state, heroic ideal and socialism are to be recognized in the elevating into an end of something obvious; of an assumption that as yet states nothing at all concerning the content of an aspiration. And it is as a result of this that they cripple man – for nothing can be added to an assumption, and if such facts are elevated into an end, man's activity is deflected into the false or the negative.

But how are they to be got at? Deeply and firmly they are rooted in the people of our time. Did I not myself, to be honest, feel bold to be condemning the German communists although their conduct is heroic?

The heroic ideal more than any other has again eroded its way into language and falsified it. We call any main character of a novel a hero,

4. 'Act' (*Tat*) and 'thing' (*Sache*) are components of the word for 'fact' (*Tat-sache*).

even if he is the reverse of one. We are even inclined, and a short time ago it was even generally usual, to call any man of genius – even Christ – a hero. But clarity is never to be achieved in that way, and the clarification of concepts is again the first prerequisite, for again it is only by means of clear language that we can think at all. An artist, a martyr, Christ, are not heroes. A hero is one who displays courage and daring in battle by martial deeds.

If this concept is clarified thus far, then already plain also is that heroism is not a content of human action but a form of it. In all civilized times heroes have been held in high esteem only when the content of their deeds could be endorsed, be it service to fatherland or to an idea or, as with the medieval knights, incongruously, to Christianity. It fell to the nineteenth century to idolize heroism as a value in itself, as an ideal, quite independently of its content, and today it is becoming plain that in this there has been a return to primitive times.

But as with any late and inopportune revival of the primitive, so too with heroism, the original sense is being perverted into its opposite. As long as the constant battle of man against man was a matter of course, heroism had a civilizing influence. Then, when the battle was not judged only by result, but by daring and magnanimity, regard for the code of combat, and a refusal to resort to cunning and needless cruelty which might have made the mere result easier, it was an enhancement. But at a time when battle no longer is a matter of course this civilizing significance is lost, and as what is now endorsed is a form which is in itself an empty one, emphasis on heroism just becomes emphasis on result.

For heroism, as a human ideal, suffers from a contradiction. Its original service is to purity, but it is bound up with the killing of the opponent – with murder. Overcoming dragons or showing clemency to the adversary is always the exception. The rule is the vanquishing, the murdering of a man. Thus as soon as murderous battle is no longer a matter of course, man must decide whether he wishes to remain pure and forgo heroism, or whether he wishes to become a hero and renounce human purity. If he decides for heroism he moves greatness of deed to central position in his striving, in place of purity; an empty form as an end is bound always to enforce a raising to monumental proportions; only empty greatness can serve to express its own emptiness.

But that means that the point at issue is again result, for as content is of no consequence the hero can be satisfied only by the maximum result. Out of single combat grows the battle of the masses. The more men the hero is able to engage, the greater the results he can achieve. And with that, magnanimity and daring disappear. In the face of the battles of the growing armies the concepts of cunning and cruelty simply become invalid. It is no accident that it should be the greatest hero of our time, Napoleon, who enforced the change towards mass armies and universal conscription. Heroism, as an end, leads perforce to modern mechanical warfare which almost completely devalues personal courage. Never perhaps has such an enormous number of heroic deeds been performed as in the last war, and yet they did not influence the war, and will be forgotten when the Greek heroes are still remembered. The visible deed of heroism is performed by the general or by the ruler who need display neither courage nor daring. All they have to do is sacrifice a vast number of human lives, and be successful.

Emphasis on the external leads to the false and negative; to destruction. And not only the outward but also the inner destruction of man. Heroism can no longer ennoble him or develop him inwardly. The modern hero is of no use in real, normal life. It is no accident that after the last war the reversion from soldier to mercenary set in.

In former times this inner unproductiveness of the heroic ideal was even corrected by means of a further contradiction. The hero was supposed to be victorious, but his image was perfected only by a hero's death, which brought another human element – the sacrifice – into this endeavour, masking its humanly sterile effect. For if the deed led to death its inner sterility could no longer be betrayed. The great deed appeared to be the culmination of life. But Napoleon was right in saying 'A Napoleon is beaten but he does not die.' Modern heroism is detached even from death. All it wants is victory. The glorious shadow of heroic death is only still employed to make the masses more willing to go to war. But Napoleon was unmasked by his survival. The six years on St Helena were merely the tragicomical epilogue to a great life, and the memoirs he proceeded to write, revealed more than anything the extent to which he was burnt out and empty. They preserved of his career only what his idolators strove to conceal. And the modern hero risking, but striving to avoid, death, is still only a destroyer and self-destroyer.

24 September 1939

Reading reports of the Russian occupation of the Polish Ukraine one becomes very conscious of the weakness of Western ideals. Land is being immediately expropriated and handed over to a peasant collective, the property of the rich is being distributed amongst the poor, and schools are being opened. Equality and justice seem to be moving in.

Of course, this prelude is only in the service of an all-the-more thorough enslavement and incapacitation of man. But can any who are suffering bitterly under the existing social inequality and injustice, consider consequences such as those? What can the West set against this process? How can real ideas of freedom and justice be effective when even today still no signs can be discovered of even just modest social conclusions being drawn from them?

The Western worker and the Western workless still, I know, fare better than the liberated Ukrainian peasant is now going to. But this popular argument is no argument. A dividing up appears attractive in a rich country too, because there is that much more to divide up.

This circumstance has been of little importance hitherto only because socialist administration has obviously worked badly, and seemed more manifestly to mean general impoverishment than general enrichment. Its importance has increased with unemployment and decreased with the new armaments boom. Will it not be bound to gain in importance again, and this time decisively, if the horrors and sufferings of war go on for years? Will it not have to be overwhelmingly effective if, in addition, there is a longing for an end to the war?

Is perhaps what I have been thinking all wrong? Is perhaps the terrible form of socialism appropriate to modern man's mental capacity, and is it thus perhaps pointing to the necessary detour that leads to the realization of socialism?

All ideas become falsified when they come into power. Christianity has led to terrible wars. The ideals of the French Revolution have, above all, liberated capitalism. Why should we fare any differently with socialism?

That is something that has long haunted me. It was after all what happened with early Christianity. The Arians who held Christ to be a man were undoubtedly the more genuine Christians. They must with good reason have seen the apotheosis of Jesus as a reversion to heathenism. But it was they who were exterminated, and obviously as a result Christianity was preserved. For it was thanks to the falsification that the people of that time were first able to assimilate it all. Could National Socialism be the needful adaptation to our time that prevents the idea of socialism from foundering?

But such considerations show only how dangerous external conclusions are! *We* are concerned with human ideals – so how can we sit idle? How

44

is a human socialism ever to be possible if the struggle for it is given up? The constantly renewed striving for pure Christianity which began centuries before the Reformation and has gone on unceasingly since, has wrung closer approaches to Christ even out of triumphant Catholicism. And it is only by such efforts that the meaning of Christianity has been preserved.

Nor must we let ourselves be influenced by the philosophy of history. The philosophy of history is not philosophy! The course of history is ambiguous – anything can be read into it or proved by it. The scientific accuracy of such interpretations can only become manifest if predictions are fulfilled over long periods, for history does of course also interpret long periods of time in the past, but that means never being able to prove the accuracy of historical interpretation in the present. The philosophy of history proves whatever anyone wants, and for that reason proves nothing.

Nor must we allow ourselves to be influenced here by consideration of the external result. If we think ideas right and good we must stand up for them. Our thinking them right can only be expressed in our placing trust in them, and so we must then, trustingly, leave their fate to history.

25 September 1939

It sounds banal to keep stressing that result is not what matters, and it sounds obvious to declare ineffective noble striving to be more worthy of affirmation than effective brutality. And yet it cannot be stressed often enough. For the sense of this has been lost by our times completely. The word *result* is itself somewhat disreputable. Everyone knows it to be unprincipled and contemptible to hazard good for the sake of result. But can anyone today afford not to consider what the effect of his activity will be? Who, judging an idea, does not immediately think whether it can, and how it will, work? But consideration of this, which is undertaken quite freely, is equally directed at result.

Our times give forced prominence to a magic word that heavily veils this connection in order to repress any scruples, and like to talk of *achievement*. This is a word that had a very important meaning in regard to the Romantic tendency to wallow in feeling. Then it seemed contemptible for people to devote themselves to any definite but limited activity by which something might be achieved; instead they lost themselves in some amateurishly head-in-the-clouds endeavour leading absolutely nowhere and serving merely to satisfy personal vanity. This word was a curb on personal vanity, pointing instead to the tasks of real life, and the limitation needful and appropriate to man's gifts when he considers them without vanity. And this very limitation of vanity which was originally bound up with this demand, is what today makes it so suitable to take over from the word *result*.

But since the war – the last war, that is, and I am constantly shocked at having to say this *last* – this productive sense of *achievement* has been lost. Our age is so credulous of reality that intellectual striving still seems at best contemptible, and certainly vanity is more easily satisfied by a turning towards this world. What today is declared to be achievement is sheer result.

For when today the call is for achievement, what is meant is that something has got to happen – there has got to be a visible result – something has got to be done, quite regardless of whether it is a good or bad, human or inhuman something. There must be order – it must work – something visible has got to arise, if only the inactivity of an organization that seems splendid by reason of being enormous. Who can deny the Nazis the fact of having *achieved*, and this idolizing of achievement does, in spite of all, support Nazi propaganda! And though it may all enslave and destroy man instead of helping him – quantity, greatness, is the hallmark of achievement, however empty that greatness may be.

Of the old meaning of achievement perhaps only a little still remains – it is not so much a question of personal achievement as of collective. Personal vanity and mania for result are achieved not directly but by the roundabout way of the work of a group, a party, a nation. Result has here adapted itself to the technical conditions of our technical times. But that is only so much more to the bad, for as a result of that those restraints of conscience get dropped which have stemmed the individual's all too brutal mania for result.

But this rejection of distorted achievement is still not enough. Even if humanly valuable achievement is taken as a criterion, we are still subject to the disastrous worship of success.

How often I tell myself that it is probably permissible for me to keep out of the war, but that against that I must legitimize myself by achievement. What I have in mind of course is my philosophical work, that is to say an achievement which I hope will be of help to men. Is this a correct viewpoint?

No, it is not! Of course I must endeavour to achieve – that, after all, is natural with any activity. But the success of that achievement is not mea-

46

surable in human terms. Talent is a very mysterious quality which can probably be increased by diligence but not decisively influenced. So whether my gift is great enough to assure the success of my achievement does not depend on me. Consequently I cannot be legitimized by my achievement. I can be legitimized only by my intention and by the meaning of my endeavour. What matters is the human attitude. And that can be justified only by human reasons, and its rightness recognized only by the aid of human reasons.

And what applies to talent applies quite generally to any kind of result. Effect, achievement, success, external recognition, visible result, advantage to other people – they do not immediately have to do with the substance of the endeavour, but depend upon a thousand external circumstances more or less beyond man's influence. Man must therefore never be judged by whether these circumstances come to his assistance, but always by the content of his endeavour. And he himself must similarly never make this casual assistance by external circumstances his yardstick. He must pursue unconditionally what he has recognized as right.

There are, certainly, men who well understand how to put to account those external circumstances which force a result. But this calculation is the more possible the further the withdrawal from the human and from the intellectual, and it is easiest in the shape of egoistical and ambitious demands. This very calculation therefore is again an argument against result.

26 September 1939

But result, achievement, effect are still not all. Also important is the withholding of help and sympathy.

I hesitate somewhat. Is it right for me to be critical at such length? How does that accord with the principle 'Resist not evil'?

But how can one make oneself understood; how can we think clearly if the language we are speaking remains unclear? How can we get away from *heroism* if language is allowed to conceal the substance of that ideal by calling Christ a hero? How can we judge achievement unless we establish that it masks result? There's nothing for it – I must go on being critical of language too. The only thing is to keep at it at every opportunity.

And like any intellectual process, this being critical is not solely negative. By virtue of the fact that obvious assumptions can be picked out of false aims, the human attitude that matters gradually becomes clear also.

In place of result, trust moves into the forefront, and that that is a considerable gain will be made substantially clearer by a critical examination of help.

Thinking of help we cannot help thinking of the Gospels. And here we are struck by the remarkable fact that it receives hardly a mention. It is never 'Help your neighbour' but 'Love your neighbour, Love your enemies'. Even in the parable of the Good Samaritan, which does in fact deal with help, help is not mentioned as such. It is a question of 'Exercise mercy'. And when Christ does help in that real material sense which we today understand first and foremost by the word *help*, then it is through miracles. But what does that mean?

If it was Christ's intention to set help before us as an example, help ought to form part of his natural life, for that of course is the only way we would be able to follow it. And that help would, like so much else, be made plain to us through his parables. If help in the materially effective sense is the very thing reserved for the sphere of the miracle, there must be a pointer in this fact.

The nature of that pointer has already been made clear. Every result is the product of the coincidence of favourable external circumstances beyond our control; and calculable though it may be to some extent in humble spheres, in the human sphere it is a miracle!

But that, applied to help, means that the readiness and the desire to help ought also to be something that is obvious. If we love our neighbour then we shall obviously be eager to help him and happy if we succeed. This happiness in being able to help is even a very general, very natural human feeling that with warmhearted people requires no special prior emphasis.

But help is not an end. If it were, we ought to be able to accomplish something with it – it ought therefore to have a result. But how can we strive for a thing that does not lie within our power? Imposing help and forcing its effect is only the cause of human havoc. For as result cannot be forced, we are obliged, in order to produce a result for our help, to do violence to the person.

Christ knows what he is saying in emphasizing 'Let not thy left hand know what thy right hand doeth.' That is not only a rejection of vanity and of self-glorification through the help that we give. Man is also not to allow himself to be dominated by help as an end. It is to be a natural component of every one of his activities but it is not an activity in itself. For 'Inasmuch as ye have done it unto one of the least of these my brethren, ye have done it unto me.' The consequences of help do not therefore lie in its result but on quite a different plane – in coming closer to Christ, and in the realization of his human relationship.

Christ's help is given essentially in quite a different way – by means of example. That is, he translates wholly into reality what he has recognized to be right, and without regard to external result. The fact that this example has been lived is the crucial aid, but a wholly internal one that even excludes the possibility of applying the yardstick of result. This example leaves the other personal freedom. He must decide for himself whether to accept or reject it. He must ultimately help himself. And he helps himself first and foremost by translating into reality a love of humanity of which readiness to help is a necessary component.

As this attitude ought to be obvious, but is not, Christ is obliged to illustrate help by means of the miracle. But the miracle points plainly back not to the help but to Christ.

In other words, just as when standing up for a cause we must not be cowardly, and just as in any course of activity we must be concerned to do our best, so we shall have to be ready and willing to help wherever there is an opportunity, and ready to endorse only a course of action that is designed in general to help men. By exerting ourselves to help others, by devoting ourselves to men, we help ourselves. And this inner self-help is what matters, not the external result, for only by means of the former are we able to give an example that is able to help the other person essentially. Again, we must not ponder the effect but trust in the thing we have recognized to be right. With help – and for help – it is the inner, the human, that matters.

From which can also already be understood why in this context I have mentioned compassion, and why a short time ago I was having to call for rigour, which, at the time that I wrote it, seemed disturbing.

It is when we respect and love man that we make the highest demands of him. Genuine love of one's fellows will share powerfully and painfully in the suffering of others – and it will be a great relief to be able to help – to be able to lessen this suffering. But this shared suffering must not be reduced to the level of compassion. The aim is still to make the human, the example of Christ, a reality, and suffering can to a great extent be the means of attaining this end! We must find the strength and the rigour unfailingly to serve this end, even if compassion threatens to overwhelm us. It is precisely for man's sake that it is above all the idea that matters, and not compassion that so easily turns into disastrous, violence-doing

49

aid. With all who truly love man this rigour will be directed against themselves. Yet even if the man is himself broken in the shared suffering – it is the example that matters!

Christ knows that through his death on the cross he is bringing infinite suffering into the world, that it will kindle wars and inspire martyrs to die, which is why he prays 'Lord, let this cup pass.' But realizing that the disciples are sleeping and that his example cannot be completed or made clear in any other way, he takes upon himself that agonizing, horrible death, trusts his inner compulsion, and does not heed the consequences. He himself is broken – 'My God, why hast thou forsaken me?' But his image is able to rise again, pure, in the hearts of his disciples and outlive those times.

Does this perhaps also shed light on the expiation of sin? In fact, if love of humanity is made a reality, this life is of course unendurable. Can anyone thinking clearly today about the siege of Warsaw, still be happy, or think or live at all? But we must not break. As it is the human quality that matters solely and above all, we must nevertheless, and now for the first time, really fight to make it a reality. Christ had to accept death on the cross to complete his example. But now that this example has been given we must struggle to make it a reality: struggle for the life of the uncrucified Christ! And we can, as the British pastor rightly said, even be glad. So great is this example and so purely has the idea revealed itself in Christ that we can trust in it, and amidst all the suffering be nevertheless glad at being able to fight for it. For how can we fight for it unless we delight in its beauty?

27 September 1939

But is it not an overemphasis of the inner to devalue the external in this way? We want to make the example of Christ a human reality, that is to say in a human life in this reality – we reject God-above-the-clouds, we reject heaven and the beyond and seek the divine in man – can we then renounce the external so sweepingly? Is this reality not external reality? And are we not obliged to live our lives in it?

Of course we are, and what I have said up to now does not contradict that either! For all of it does, I think, dispose of the overvaluing of achievement, but does not upset the idea of the act, and restores its meaning which usage has effaced.

If we work at our idea, and at its inner development first, sooner or later we shall come up against reality and have to decide in what way we are reconciling the idea with our real life, and in what way we, who have to carry it through in real life, can serve it there. It is not achievement that is demanded of us but a decision, a resolve that operates for the inner idea in external reality. What is demanded of us is an act!

The model for such an act again seems to me to be the death on the cross – Jesus' decision to go to Jerusalem and there suffer death. Jesus, having inwardly completed his teaching, has to decide whether to go on eluding the informers and lead a life of his own, as a result of which his teaching and his example will be clear but just not sufficiently so, or whether to complete his example. And his crucial act is consciously to choose the death that completes and vindicates his example.

The chains of reasoning which we have rooted in us are terribly dangerous. We must be quite clear that this resolve does not spring from pondering the effect. Jesus' intention is only to complete his example. The fact that he vindicates its effect becomes clear to us alone, not to him. If the effect of his resolve was something he considered, everything ought to have argued against it. For he knows that by this death he involves in sin all who are crucifying, mocking and betraying him; knows that by so doing he is bringing infinite suffering into the world – the sword which he takes from Peter's hand. And the very suffering that he accepts for himself by this death does not accord with his teaching and his humanity. Remember the Marriage at Cana and his turning of water into wine for the purpose of enjoyment. He is no martyr, no ascetic. Emphasized again and again is the joy of sheer humanity – the more genuine happiness of the truly human life! He ought really therefore to shrink from this resolve. But he does not because his inner development, an inner compulsion, prescribes to him how he is to act, and because he finds the trust to follow the inner voice in spite of all external doubts, and this because he does not consider the effect but trusts that which is within, this trust giving him the strength to shrink neither from suffering nor from only externally recognized consequences.

That seems to me the hallmark of the genuine act: that it should arise from an inner compulsion, an inner necessity so strong that it has to be trusted in, regardless of the consequences for oneself. And with Christ this trust holds good, for the act does indeed vindicate his example, and it holds good for every genuine act. For the act differs from mere activity and mere achievement by virtue of the fact of bringing something new into the world, of being a beginning in which new activity, life and growth are kindled, and of altering the world. With achievement a terminal point, a result, is always reached. Activity can be continued and achievement

51

thereby heightened, but with achievement one also has some reassurance for all achievement alters the world only quantitatively, not qualitatively. The act, on the other hand, is always a beginning, whether, as with Christ, a new beginning for the world, or, as in most cases, a new beginning for man himself.

For this example which I employ to clarify the concept is not supposed to mask the act as something that is general and a possibility for every man.

I have twice made mention here of acts – the 'act–thing' and the heroic act.[5] In its original meaning the fact is the personal grasp of reality and of its shaping and adoption – a breaking of convention in favour of direct apprehension. There are, I believe, only a few people who do not experience this at some time or other, even if few may have the strength to confess to this experience and base a resolve upon it. And the heroic act is originally the decision for courage, for daring, for integrity as opposed to cheap success – the deeds of the Greek heroes who, in the face of a world paralysed by despotism, demonstrated what freedom can do, and of the knights who upheld a code of honour that today seems ridiculous and who, for that very reason, gradually enforced civilization. This renunciation of personal success for the sake of higher values is a challenge that confronts all, even if today no longer in the form of heroism. And to every man comes too perhaps the need to reconcile his youthful dreams with reality. He may do it without any kind of act – be it by conforming to external necessity or to convention, or by continuing to dream as well as live. But he may also resolve to reconcile the inner and the external. How often this kind of thing comes about quietly between father and son!

Here too it is again not a question of result. With great talents and great personalities, such an act will acquire significance for the world, with others it will be effective only within a very small circle. But that is not what is crucial. What is, is that such an act should always mean a beginning, a creation, and be it only for one's own life; that it should be produced by the collision of internal and external reality; and that it should of necessity create a new reality.

With this, however, it is the very emphasizing of inner challenges that does better justice than anything external to external reality also. For it is of course this very constant renewal and enrichment of reality which matters.

Yesterday, incidentally, I supplied the answer to an earlier question of

5. See footnote 4, p. 41 above.

52

mine, as to whether it was permissible to endorse suffering. Suffering will hardly be avoidable in any human endeavour; the act too will be bound almost always to be a sacrifice, yet those too are only external signs, concomitant phenomena which must not become an end. If a man is really by nature pure and humanly perfect, or if a human act without suffering is possible, it is then senseless still to call for suffering. In our times of course, when suffering is so much on the increase, the ability to stand aside from this suffering may well betray no more than an inability to share suffering, or a human coldness. But that also is still no reason for setting suffering up as an end, or for simply unduly emphasizing it either.

28 September 1939

I was born on 28 September 1898. Twenty years later, on 28 September 1918, Bulgaria collapsed and it was plain that the war was coming to an end. Twenty years after that, on 28 September 1938, came Munich and the averting of war. Those two birthdays were even more plainly crucial days for me personally: in 1918 I went on study leave, and that was in fact for me the end of the war: I did not go back to the army again. And a year ago it was at once clear that for me the war was not going to begin, and that I was again going to be demobilized, and without a war. A remarkable coincidence!

But when I think back, how different from each other these two decisive moments are!

In 1918 I was walking on air! I was going on leave, the war was coming to an end, and everything else was of small importance. I was still very young then, and very dependent on others. I lived according to the general convention, hoping at bottom for the Central Powers to win. I was horrified at first when friends in Prague made clear to me that victory for Wilhelm and what he stood for, would be terrible, and that we must hope for his defeat. I was horrified at the extent to which preparations for Czech revolution were advanced, although at the front I had always professed to belong to the Czech Party. I was guided simply by the general desire to get out of the war at any price. The important thing for everyone was that the war was ending; that, and nothing else. It is a feeling which will have to be taken account of again in this war also, and especially as so many seemingly unshakeable systems have been shaken since!

Against that, when I think of last year I still cannot suppress a feeling of deep bitterness. I went to war with a very bad grace – even then it was clear to me that it was not in accord with that service to the idea which I consider solely essential. I reproached myself for hanging on in Prague for so long and getting into the position of not being decently able to keep out of this war of self-defence. I did not keep out of it, but had I died, it would not have been with an easy conscience but in despair.

And yet, even if it had come to war then, and by September – and only for want of a vigorous stand in the summer – it was probably no longer avoidable – and even plainly accepting that I should very likely be dead, that war would still have been better than the Munich Agreement!

Evening

In honour of my birthday, I have once again been for a walk through the quiet autumn gardens and peaceful courts of the colleges. This quiet, this peace, is almost uncanny, with war raging outside. How often I was impressed by the same thing at the front in the last war – the most glorious weather and at the same time the most terrible fighting – unspoiled nature in the thick of man-created horror!

And as for me, and my having, for a second time, escaped very probably, almost certain death – is that a gift, a favour, or merely a second, and this time, briefer postponement?

One of the courts set me dreaming of a Shakespearean stage. There, in front of the old wall of a Gothic hall, visibly the product of dark and confused times – despite softening in English fashion by pre-Renaissance windows – is a little porch, a few pillars, a regularly delimited wall, a few steps, – an escape to the clear forms of the Renaissance. And the other sides of the court really are Renaissance, very simple, very restrained, liberatingly lucid.

Is that not the world of Shakespeare's comedies? Still a background of inhumanly hard times, grinding superstition and disastrous passions constantly confounding the merry foreground. The human and cheerful world appearing only as a small front projection to the stage. But it is this very world which finally keeps the upper hand; we escape into a humanly comprehensible, humanly shapeable life divested of horror. What, a short time before, was still overwhelming, crushing reality, vanishes like an unreal spectre. And what seemed merely stage, becomes reality. When will such an escape from our dark and confused world be found? When will the spectre disappear which, in spite of all the better awareness and all the manifest better opportunities, is grinding and destroying us? Has Britain – human, moderating Britain – that, if not soul-uplifting, still so happy land of no baroque, again perhaps been assigned a special task?

54

29 September 1939

Yesterday morning's entry suddenly shows again with terrifying clarity that I am getting nowhere with my main problem! Regretting that there was no war last year? Is that compatible with my conviction that 'Thou shalt not kill'?

But with yesterday's entry an answer has in fact been given, a further answer – if only I follow what I recognize to be right! I must not keep pondering the possible consequences, the result. What is important here too is to trust the idea. If that is strong and alive, then in the collision with reality which sooner or later is inevitable, the act will be bound to follow also. Whenever we aim at the external we are swimming with the stream, and the stream is then the more powerful by perhaps a drop or a tiny tributary. Yet it is only when we swim against the stream that a new reality can arise – only then can we reach the opposite bank higher up.

Trust – so easily written, but a great and difficult task that is bound to influence the whole of one's thinking, the whole of one's life. Can one really, when all is at stake, not ponder the effect? Maybe I cannot, but whoever can will really be able to give something to the world.

Here perhaps is an explanation for why it is so difficult to combine intellect and politics. Politics call for consideration of effect – immediate intervention for the purpose of result. The intellectual act has to mature slowly, and when it has matured it is a long time before it comes to the awareness of the general public, and before the general power of comprehension catches up with genius as it hastens on ahead.

Therefore the usual reproachful call for intellectuals to go into politics is wrong. It is no accident that in the German Republic our experience was that intellectuals who sacrificed themselves to politics achieved nothing but self-destruction. And here too in Britain accurate discernment on the part of intellectuals has, over recent years, been entirely without influence.

It is not that the two provinces seem independent of each other. The crucial political changes go back to intellectual achievements: the changing of the world by Christianity as also by the French and Russian Revolutions, and perhaps too by the Third Reich which is translating all the evil ideas Nietzsche had into reality. But this political effect is produced only when the idea is able to mature – i.e. when the intellectual serves it and does not, with an impatient hand, attempt to impose the immature idea upon the world. He must trust in the idea. He must not replace trust by political efficiency!

55

When an idea has come to maturity, then it is perhaps possible for intellectual people – and above all for those who are not themselves creative and who are serving no idea of their own – also to concern themselves with translating it into practical reality. But our idea has not yet matured. And so for us pioneers there is nothing for it but first to struggle for this idea. We must be rigorous enough to dispense with immediate aid and put up with the long wait for possible effect.

30 September 1939

Today in a British paper I came across an anecdote which sounds frivolous but contains a profound truth. A literary person was asked in the last war why he was not going to the front to defend civilization. 'Because,' ran the answer, 'I am part of the civilization they are trying to defend.'

That answer seems to me to be a fundamental one and to call attention to something I have not yet considered. How, amidst the monstrous machinery of war, is it to be possible to select talent that is genuine? How is a state able to select justly? Indeed, how can any clear judgement be made as to who really has anything to say? There is nothing for it but to select oneself, and one has that right. Who today would not be grateful to a Franc Marc, a Trakl or a Stramm for selecting themselves?

This self selection certainly also adds to the responsibility and obligation. But is not that all to the good?

1 October 1939

It is a month to the day since the Germans invaded Poland, and they have, it must be admitted, achieved a great deal. The *Blitzkrieg* in Poland has gone perfectly, according to plan, and faster perhaps than the Nazis themselves hoped. And in other respects too the Nazi programme is becoming reality; the war in the West has in fact not yet got going, and the Nazis can, as announced, now blare forth their peace offer to the world. Except that for two days, Russia has been behind the peace offer also. The alliance with Russia, about which there are still doubts, is obviously being extended consistently, step by step. Why not? So far, Russia has done well out of it! Already it has swallowed half Poland, and, cleverly, the half which it can digest without difficulty, at the same time increasing pressure on the Balkans, and it has brought Estonia into dependence, likewise a very important gain.

On the other side, a lamentable spectacle is presented by America. The neutrality law is now to be amended in favour of the Western Powers, but Roosevelt, in whose good intentions and clear view I believe, can only put this amendment through in disguised form. Deliveries are to be made only to those powers who pay cash and who are able to ship the goods off in their own vessels. Is it not a disgrace that in America they should not be allowed to say 'We are standing by the Democracies against the Fascist and Bolshevik aggressors'? In practical terms this amendment is probably to the advantage of Britain first and foremost. Nevertheless, its masked form is bound to take its revenge. It means that China is being dropped, and already some British papers are asking with concern 'May not Russian gold be brought into play in Germany's favour?'

All America seems interested in is getting rid of Roosevelt, the one man who has attempted to carry through social reforms on a path of sound development and who is attempting to remove the crucial weakness of democratic ideas. He has got to woo his capitalists with good business, otherwise it's no go. And so America will obviously make the same mistake as Britain, disguise her policy, and for that very reason drift into the war she wishes to avoid.

Or will this policy prove disastrous sooner? What if the peace appeal is directed at Roosevelt, carrying on from his own frequent peace appeals which have not been exactly appropriate anyway? It is to be hoped that the treading of this road will be prevented by Hitler's vanity. Britain's firmness certainly now seems beyond all doubt, and France's too if the British papers are to be believed. But France has had to ban her communists . . .

Many of Britain's arguments even seem to me correct. That the war has so far failed to get going in the West may not be wrong strategically, for this slow strategy is the very thing that is destroying Hitler's hope of a short war, and a long war may still be something he is afraid of, even if Russian material aid does not prove as insignificant as the British are always stressing.

But another British argument seems to be disastrously false. It is that the pact with Russia is in any case a defeat for Germany. Already Hitler has had to hand over half Poland and give up the Ukraine, and already he sees his superiority over the Baltic states and the Balkans disappearing and the real danger of a Bolshevization of Germany instead. All of that may be correct, although it needn't be – for why should the two criminals not share the booty further? But even if it is true, it proceeds from a false supposition. It presupposes the Nazis to have some concrete, established ends which they wish to attain. But the alliance with Russia ought to have

57

taught the world that they have no end other than that of themselves remaining in power. They may very well alter their plans for world conquest completely. Why the Balkans? Why not colonies? Division of the Empire? They may pervert their conviction into its complete opposite; nationalism is no longer all that far removed from Bolshevism in any case – they *may* do anything – all they want is to stay in power!

But for that purpose the alliance with Russia is not a bad device. To date the Nazis have lived by looting – it was the turn of big business to be looted anyway, and if, following the alliance with Russia, that now has the appearance of a communist measure, the threat Germany represents to the world is only increased. A Bolshevik Germany may pose more of a threat to the Democracies in peace and war than a National Socialist. And may it not be that engineering in Russia has already progressed to such a degree that production could be given a rapid boost by German organization and Russian coercion? We must hope not!

But does it really have to be a very long war for a powerful sense to be gained of the danger which Russia alone already represents as a national enemy?

The final hope for the war against the Nazis has always been for the Third Reich suddenly to collapse like a house of cards. That is still possible, but as a result of the alliance with Russia, the very thing that is no longer probable. And even if it does, is it still possible to imagine a peace that would be even half respectable? Is not the fearful world change, imminent for years, now at last under way?

Evening

I constantly get lost in speculations about this war which may be completely false. But to abandon them is difficult, not just for external reasons, but also for a very substantial inner one.

For the moral commandments which it is possible to establish are never supposed to be of dogmatic validity – they are supposed to be absolutely valid only internally, not externally. Our task is not to pass this life by or be broken by it. We are to serve these ideas in this life, reconcile them with the practical demands of this life, make the uncrucified Christ a reality! To propound an absolute commandment and follow it blindly would be easy. And how easy it would even be then to accept any danger! The difficulty and magnitude of the task consist in living this life in a real way and at the same time morally. In not shirking, in not bringing about that supreme sacrifice and producing tragedy, but in fulfilling life, not as regards effect, but morally.

A particularly fine and clear example of this battle for real life is provided by nineteenth-century Russia. A happier life than Tolstoy's can hardly be imagined. Following the success of his great novels he was the most celebrated writer in Russia. His fame was beginning to conquer Europe. He was wealthy and independent, friend of the people and of the Tsar. Life in the city was blissful intoxication, but whenever he tired of it he could withdraw to his estate, and there, with wife and children, he knew better than any man to the last fibre of his being how to enjoy – and shape – every happiness that nature was able to offer. Yet there, at the height of his fame and happiness, he was overcome by the power of Christianity, and unable any longer to stand aloof from its commandments, began following them to the letter.

With admirable resolution he put from him everything that constituted his life's happiness. Renouncing his gift, he wrote only social appeals and interpretations of the Gospel. Renouncing his riches, he led the life of a simple peasant: chopping wood, going to the fields with his barrow, refusing to allow anyone to serve him. Renouncing happiness at home, he attempted to convert his family. He renounced every pleasure. And yet his distressing life, his great and moving renunciation did not become an example. The fault lay not with his new literary activity – that he had already begun side by side with his creative work. The unfortunate thing was the very means by which he believed he was fulfilling the Gospel – his literal adherence to absolute and dogmatic commandments. This man was, as no other, endowed to create unique works. Had he the right to withdraw from that vocation and do peasant work that could be done by anyone? In so renouncing his gift is there not a contempt that devalues the outwardly Christian standard of living?

In fact, Tolstoy's attempt to adhere dogmatically to absolute commandments destroyed his life. One of the most important commandments is charity, but that prevented him from keeping the commandment of poverty which he interpreted equally dogmatically, for his wife and his children resisted his renouncing of wealth, and he did not dare to do them harm. Thus his peasant life became a farce. Amidst luxury which he declined to enjoy, he lived the life of a poor peasant on his rich estate. And it proved equally impossible to renounce his gifts. In secret he wrote some of his best *Novellen* and plays. But was there not, in that concealment, a doubly tragic error? His life, previously so happy, now drove him again and again to the brink of destruction. But this too has a sterile two-facedness about it – a note of boredom enters even into his fanatically sincere diaries. Death, when finally he feels its approach, is an inhuman absolute which he himself is unable to bear: a sick man, he flees secretly into the snowy wastes, revoking his false life by his final recovery and final act!

Dostoyevsky rightly says of him,

> Strictly speaking, there is no need to distribute one's property, for here, in the work of love, any absolute quality becomes like a uniform, a rubric or a dead letter. Being persuaded of having fulfilled the letter only leads man to pride, formalism and idleness. You must do what the heart commands you to do, and if that be to serve all, then serve all, but not as many dreamers, straightaway seizing a barrow and saying 'I am not master. I am going to work like a peasant.' Again the barrow is only a uniform. On the contrary, if you feel that you can be useful to the general public as a scholar, then go to the university and obtain the necessary means for doing so. It is not necessary for you to distribute your possessions or don a peasant smock. All that is necessary and important is your determination to do everything for the sake of active love, everything you possibly can and yourself sincerely recognize as possible!

What you yourself sincerely recognize as possible!

But Dostoyevsky, who plumbed the full depths of passion; who knew every bottomless pit of the chaos of our time; who, in his own life, discovered what temptation – be it that of gambling, injustice or chauvinism – can do; and who, by remaining true to his writer's gift, experienced suffering to a degree without equal in the nineteenth century – Dostoyevsky it was who was also able to grasp Christianity in a profoundly new way, and perhaps as no other has succeeded in doing. But he comprehended it undogmatically, and in any case in only the essence and not the details of its commandments, and only by so doing was he able to fulfil his life! He endured *The Dead House* in Siberia which drove robuster friends of his into madness. He endured poverty which threatened constantly to compel him to destroy his world and his own life. He endured his illness which again and again drove him to the brink of madness, suicide and breakdown. He endured terrible and, as a result of unimaginable poverty, degrading isolation in alien Western Europe. He thought only of his work which, in a profound, undogmatic sense, was serving the figure of Christ, and by this it was that he was able to perfect his life as an example. This work – Tolstoy repudiated his own work – took him beyond all suffering to that hour when he could cry to the whole of Russia 'Proud man, humble yourself. Idle man, work.' And the whole of Russia listened – an hour that Europe will re-experience in time to come – as he explained non-dogmatically and for the inner self – 'The truth is not outside you but within you. Master yourself and you will see the truth. Not in things is this truth, but in your own exertions upon yourself.' Shortly after this he died, a calm, peaceful death, plucked from his labours when they were at their height and yet confident in having done what was to be done. And it is in the redeeming completion of that harassed life that the image appears, perhaps for the first time in all clarity, of the uncrucified Christ, the image he was no longer able to complete in his work.

I cannot help thinking of this very example today, it being so inconceivable that in a few decades Russia should have sunk so low! Is it not perhaps just here and now, when Russia has so obviously betrayed all good ideas, that there is hope? Is not perhaps concealed there unrecognized greatness that may come unexpectedly to the aid of the idea?

Be that as it may, Christ also said, 'Be wise as serpents.' Christ also could not have taken upon himself the death of the cross if he had dogmatically followed the commandment of charity. Christ's example also compels us to do justice to this life.

So how can I exclude this life from this diary? How easy and how false that would be – simply to set up old or new dogmas and demand that they be blindly followed!

2 October 1939

Yesterday there was again a joint Anglo-German church service. It was simple and impressive without being particularly profound. Both preachers said what had to be said once on this occasion, that they put Christianity, unity in spirit, above nations. The church was packed, and the preachers' challenge was very effectively underlined by the presence, in the midst of war, of the two hostile nations. Maybe this example will have an effect beyond the small circle. But is that enough to make an impression on perhaps the most powerful of false gods, the nation?

The nation is also one of those obvious assumptions which are elevated in superficial fashion to the level of an end. It is perhaps the plainest example of the power and the fate of such inversions.

61

The power of the national bond cannot be disputed. It is expressed in the language, that incessantly active, perhaps supremely important medium of human life that forms our intellect and dominates our daily existence. How few people are able, just within the circle of Western and Central European civilization, to learn a second language really perfectly. How our thinking is blunted and our lives reduced to one level by having to make do with a language whose finer points and ultimate ramifications we have not mastered! No one, surely, will speak contemptuously of language, that original creation of man's which first made the world human, and which must always be the way and the means to the highest humanity? And can anyone with emotional experience of the power of language, ever renounce his mother tongue?

Mother-tongue, Fatherland – can anyone, saying those words here, in a kind, indulgent foreign land, and without prejudice, escape a feeling of profound emotion? And *without prejudice* means not thinking of those who are today abusing and distorting that language, and besmirching and destroying that land – means not thinking of the calamity it has brought upon the world! And how much these words evoke! The land we know – that has embraced us as our home – that holds the memory of our childhood, our youth, our growth. The people we know quite naturally and do not first have the difficulty of getting to understand, including many whom we love with that attachment which is possible only in early youth. There are the common traditions which make life easy because its external forms are naturally provided, because people understand each other, and not having to agree about what is natural, are able to make progress. There is the civilization to which we owe what we are, and which we have to cultivate ourselves further by, it alone being what we know to its fullest extent and are able to understand. And in that land reside the dreams we dreamt as children and cannot dispense with even today, and the plans and wishes which can give firm shape to an unclear future and enable us to seize it firmly, clearly and purposefully.

All of which, if one has experienced Europe, need not mean narrowness or inhibiting ties! I was born and grew up in Prague, and spent the most important and crucial years of youth in Berlin. The most crucial impression of those years was Italy. I love Paris like a second homeland. I have a longing for the Alps and the North Sea. And now England is growing into a new, powerful and beautiful experience. Yet to all that there is still a nucleus – German language and culture, friends in Prague and Germany, the forests of the Bohemian and South German *Mittelgebirge* – a nucleus giving a very definite sense to the word *homeland*.

Those are the obvious assumptions which are bound to provide strength for continuing one's human development, out of narrowness into full life, towards other, higher objectives! But how these assumptions become perverted into their opposites and a fatal thing when the nation is elevated into an end!

For we are German or we are British, and we cannot add anything to the fact or aspire to become one or the other, it being, through no fault or merit of ours, what we are born. We cannot become more German or more British. The *better German* on whom Germany lays such stress has always been simply the false pretension of some party concealing its own ends under a national cloak. But human endeavour, whenever directed towards an end to whose realization it can contribute nothing, and severed from the positive, is bound to take refuge in the negative. Nationalism is of necessity discharged in hatred and contempt, violence and destruction.

Every form of nationalism is aware of that and therefore invents pretensions to conceal it. 'To be German is to be loyal.' Maxims of that sort are simply nonsense. If loyalty were really the point at issue, the loyal Frenchman would be German and the disloyal German not! Maxims of that sort serve only to ascribe all good qualities to any one nation indiscriminately while denying them to any other. There is hardly a good quality to be found which any one nation would not claim to have the monopoly of.

Even national character, on which there is such overemphasis today – a nation's characteristics specified with great precision – is only a disastrous generalization. Certainly, the common tradition and particular history of a country, the language, and the scenic and climatic conditions create certain common characteristics that distinguish one nation from another. Whether a nation knows the sea or lives inland, on the plain or in high mountains, in the north or by the Mediterranean, is used to a difficult climate or an easy one, whether it has two hundred years of democracy and world power behind it or absolute rule and suppression – all these are distinctions. But these are characteristics which strike us particularly when we first encounter a nation and get to know many of its people slightly. On closer contact with individuals they become steadily more imprecise and blurred. Superficially they are correct. There *are* certain general guiding principles which should still be taken into account even as regards the individual. To generalize them dogmatically only does the individual injustice. Precise knowledge soon brings the realization that the good and the bad qualities which arise as a result of these national

63

limitations balance each other out, that the individual can alter them or develop them to his advantage or disadvantage, and that material and spiritual interests, and the level of humanity and of education create more powerful common interests than do the national. To emphasize characteristics and dogmatically generalize them serves only to elevate the nation into an end. To determine these characteristics is only meaningful and justified when they are seen as means serving a higher end, and when they are supposed to clear the way along which each nation can best and most effectively serve a higher end, and smooth that way and show the contribution which that nation can most productively make to humanity!

This becomes particularly clear if we seek to root these national qualities where they mostly do get rooted today, and regard them as innate characteristics. If we move away in that direction, i.e. away from tradition and history and external living conditions, they become completely intangible! It may be that these acquired characteristics are also further strengthened by heredity – a view supported by there being a certain predominant type in most nations – yet it is no coincidence that the transmission of inherited characteristics is still the most obscure and least clarified area in the field of natural science. If these characteristics are innate, and thus wholly inevitable and invariable, how does that agree with the fact that nations obviously do alter their characteristics completely, indeed to the extent of reversing them. Thinking of the Germans and Russians as they were roughly a hundred years ago, it seems scarcely possible to find any fundamental connections with the Germans and Russians of today! And even the British of today may have little in common with the British who conquered India. To regard these superficial characteristics as unalterable is to deprive any nation of any possibility of development. These characteristics are indeterminate because they are variable and apprehended in process of development, and so it is they that must be made into a means – a process of development towards other ends.

National Socialism has clearly perceived this weak feature of nationalism, and has therefore invented its bolstering racial theory. But that very theory is more revealing still. Its real purpose is to make the Jewish race contemptible. But, as any honest National Socialist will admit, none of the efforts to date have succeeded in discovering as much as one clear-cut characteristic distinguishing the Jewish race from the Nordic. The only clear purpose served by this racial theory is to ascribe all good characteristics to one race while at the same time making the other as contemptible and hateful as conceivably possible, and, while claiming to be

64

a science, not being able to adduce any kind of scientifically tenable proof.

How much clearer such distinctions are in language! As even superficial examination shows, German is particularly rich in philosophical and metaphysical distinctions, emotional values and mystical elements; English is outstanding for conciseness and precision, brevity and pithiness, and positive and practical distinctions of the utmost complexity; French – for logical richness and formal and intellectual clarity; and Russian, before being choked by lifeless words produced by combining initial letters – an automatic abbreviation process which today threatens to deface all languages – was distinguished by an abundance of expressions concerning man, God and the devil.

But can anyone disclaim these human riches? Is not here a clear indication of the way that nations should, by virtue of their characteristics, contribute to the enrichment of humanity and to translating the human into reality?

The nation is deeply rooted in man – every man – however free of it he may think himself. Which is why such power over men is gained by all misleaders who elevate the nation into an end, making those convenient characteristics which need no contributing to or working at, its sole content, thereby liberating those orgiastically satisfying bestial forces never wholly extinct in man. The negative, destruction, self-extinction are a deep craving of man's, for they alone enable that profoundest of intoxications, that intensest of lusts from which he is estranged by reason and civilization. But that intoxication also releases horror and that dreadful fear which man has been unable to bear since primitive times and which compels him ever more powerfully towards reason, culture and civilization. In civilization, in a superficially comfortable life, however, man's deep feelings threaten to atrophy, and he again begins to crave destruction and intoxication. National Socialism is no more than this destructive urge in modern guise!

Which is why also it cannot be overcome by a superficial internationalism that denies reality and replaces it by unreal logic. Nationalism is today again beginning to produce that sense of horror that drives people into civilization, but civilization will only be able to develop – develop anew – when it is really able to banish fear. That is, when it creates a clarity and security that neglects none of the humanly provided assumptions and does not have to shy away from the idea of man thinking to conclusions, – a civilization that takes account of, and overcomes, tradition – that does not dismiss anguish or negativeness but opposes both with a positive, and that does not explain the divine in terms of a denial

65

of evil but shows God in good and evil. Only when God is the whole is he able to banish fear and with it, the craving for analgesic and destructive intoxication!

Which is also to say why assumptions can become ends and how they can be turned into assumptions again. In the absence of an end really capable of extending all of man's powers and taking profound possession of him, he makes an idol of what is provided, and this idol is super-powerful because, simultaneously with man's deep-down forces, it liberates intoxication. We cannot, however, eradicate these disastrous ends by fighting them, but we can by opposing them with real ends for which man is able to engage himself wholly with all his strength, feelings and thoughts. But when such an end does take possession of man, the obvious assumptions will quite obviously become mere assumptions again.

What a long way this has brought me from yesterday's church service! Certainly I do not underrate the fact that these joint services are a great step forward which in the last war would still not have been possible. And it is a great advance that what is being prayed for is no longer British victory but a lasting peace in which nations can live together in friendship and concord. That that should be possible makes life more bearable, and I owe these Sundays a deep debt of gratitude.

Yet it is precisely gratitude and respect that make one's demands the greater! Is what was said and done yesterday really enough? Last Sunday was a day of prayer in English churches, and the sermons too were in line with the prayers. Is not that one of the church's very weak points?

Jesus says, 'When ye pray, use not vain repetitions, as the Gentiles do: for they think that they shall be heard for their much speaking. Be ye therefore not like unto them: for your Father knoweth what things ye have need of before ye ask him.' And Jesus teaches the *Our Father* as the only prayer.

Is it permitted to ask for special wishes to be fulfilled? Are we allowed to pray for men and peoples, for peace and the achieving of a world that is good in our sense? To me it seems plain that that cannot lie within the meaning of Christianity, and that by so doing we do make ourselves like the Gentiles. For what becomes of faith if it rests upon prayers of that sort? Prayers of that sort are obviously and necessarily for the greater part unheard. If, however, faith does rest upon prayers of that sort it must count on their being fulfilled and be shaken when that fulfilment is not forthcoming. That is Christianity destroying itself as the result of adopting an unchristian element.

66

I know that prayers also serve another purpose. Real and fervent absorption in prayer creates a sense of unity with God, and produces that sense of the divine which I have sought to describe. Yet this purpose too is only ill served by prayer. Prayers, since they embody wishes, point to a wholly concrete end, and even if we do lay stress at the same time on God's will and God's glory, but a sense of the divine can originate only in the aimless tension existing between extreme opposites. Psalms, hymns and songs serve this purpose purely and well, but these prayers do not.

Christianity has saved the world from intoxication once already – not that of nationalism but the orgiastic sensuality of the Graeco-Roman world on a scale no longer conceivable. Will it again find that strength? This time it has not only to create a new world in order to do so, but also to free itself from its own dead forms. And that is perhaps just as difficult as unmasking ends consisting of obvious assumptions.

Evening

But this second meaning of prayer does not satisfy me either, nor do the psalms and hymns. They may, if it is present, serve the feeling for the divine. But as I have already said: as it is no longer alive, at least in its real force, another way to it has to be taken, the human way via the example of Christ.

For in times when intoxication threatens, we cannot be saved by ecstasy, its near neighbour. What can help us is clarity, purity, certainty. We have to be able to think to a conclusion, move on sure ground with our thoughts so that they are not constantly upset by feeling but upheld and imbued with life. We have to create a new world of thought, in which the whole man together with his thinking, feeling and willing has a place so that every human impulse is not forever tumbling him from his world of thought and compelling him to take refuge in insensibility. If man has no worthwhile end, all he will be able to do is deny his impulses, and mere denial remains impotent here also, doing no more than release the impulses' destructive power. Only when an end has been established towards which man can strive with all his powers, will impulses be forced into this powerful stream also.

The feeling of the divine must not be confused with ecstasy either. At all times of faith, God has been a certainty, which, however, is to say that what is involved is a serene, level, well-balanced feeling, but that is to say that the feeling involved is a serene, level well-balanced one. This feeling may well be realizable only by means of extreme opposites, but these balance each other, not driving man beyond himself but producing a tension that keeps him too in equilibrium.

My mention of Dostoyevsky as an example must not be misunderstood. I have deliberately chosen quotations which prove how far he advances in the end beyond the ecstasies of his early period and into the realm of reason.

Reason is what matters, that is to say, unity of consciousness, the balanced accord of man's loftiest powers of intellect and his fully developed powers of feeling and will.

Today when a dark feeling akin to intoxication is threatening to break through all bounds, it matters more than ever. And the way to reason is always completely clear thinking – thinking so clear that it does not lose itself in empty logic but does justice to the totality of human nature. That human nature is provided for us in its highest perfection in the example of Christ. Are we then not entitled to demand of the church that it should exert itself to interpret it?

3 October 1939

I try all the time to make the optimistic British standpoint my own. For it is supported by the calm, cool, respect-compelling attitude of the British, an admirable renunciation of any hatred, and by a smooth functioning of Parliament, even in the present difficult state of affairs, which may redress many political blunders of the past.

They argue that Germany has already lost the war in the East, for Russia has cut her off not only from her dreams of the Ukraine but also from domination of the Balkans and the Baltic. Poland is not a gain. Her industrial regions do not even compensate for the Saar, which is already useless, and she on the other hand is adding to the insecurity in the hinterland which in any case is already tying up troops in Czechoslovakia and maybe also in Austria. In the West, however, Germany is bound to lose. Germany's population is less than that of France and Britain together, and the Germans have been leached out for years, were exhausted even before the war, and are without essential reserves of raw materials, whereas Britain has the wealth of the Empire behind her which is simply inexhaustible and can make good any loss, and sooner or later she will have the material and perhaps also the manpower wealth of America. Germany cannot fight a long war. Britain, however, supported by half the world, and the richer half at that, will fight a long war, however terrible, and that long war she is bound to win.

I am inclined to believe these arguments, although they do presuppose that Russian aid to Germany is not going to figure essentially, even as regards raw materials, which is very questionable. Still, even that may be correct. But does not that view neglect other very essential factors?

If Russia *has* won the war in the East does that not also mean that Britain has lost it? And if Russia manages to go on benefiting from other peoples' quarrels is there not the threat of further and more momentous Russian victories? Already the Baltic states have been crushed, Russian domination of the Balkans is probable, and what is to happen in Asia, Turkey and China? And even if Germany is beaten, is there not then the threat of its becoming Bolshevized, which will be a further plus to Russia and a further threat to the Western Powers? In this country at the moment a great many defenders of Russian policy are clinging to the fact that Germany is being done out of the fruits of its victories by Russia. But by what right do they regard these Russian victories as to Britain's advantage?

The more I try to make British optimism my own, the greater my misgivings. I see Russia as the main danger, even if it stays neutral, and this danger has either not so far been recognized by the British in its full significance, or it is being consciously denied. What point is there in defeating Germany if by so doing it is hardly possible to deal a blow at Russia?

Approval of Russia's policy is probably only possible if one approves the world revolution. For Russia's plan seems in fact to be to let the Fascist and capitalist powers destroy each other in a long war, thus preparing the ground for world revolution, and this plan seems to be materializing in fearful fashion. How so devilish a plan which has deliberately precipitated so terrible a war can be approved of, is hard to understand. For it is of course becoming ever plainer that Russia has wanted this war in this way. But of course there are also some who think the terror in Germany atrocious and think the same, even bloodier, terror in Russia desirable, and who will not realize how dreadful that socialism is until they experience it for themselves. Which is something that must be taken into account.

But that is further to the Russians' advantage. To me it seems much more likely that Stalin's thinking is imperialistic, but even if that is correct he need never betray as much but can pursue his imperialistic ends behind the screen of the world revolution which is bound to be of service

69

to him. For Russia, world revolution and imperialism are identical, and so world revolution can mislead even those who are affected by the imperialism.

But if Stalin is an imperialist, what, in a long war, are our prospects in Asia? Has not Napoleon's dubious dream of an attack on India become for the first time a realizable possibility? But such far-ranging and, I hope, fantastic thoughts even apart, is not Germany the right confederate for Russia after all? Russia can win imperialist-fashion only at the expense of Britain. Germany, on the other hand, as these first weeks of war have taught, can be deflected towards aims of no interest to Russia. And from the standpoint of imperialist world revolution it is even a matter of indifference whether Germany achieves these aims or founders upon them. Russia at all events will win and Britain lose. A defeated Germany that may in all probability become Bolshevized will have a further explosive effect on the capitalist world.

The inestimable value to Russia of being able to conceal her objectives behind world revolution is apparent in every small detail.

So this war, whether we like it or not, is also about the liberation of the Poles and the Czechs. Notice has already been given of a demand for the re-establishment of the old Czechoslovakia, and difficult as it may be to reconquer the Ukrainian territories for Poland or promise them to her, she will, in the event of Germany's being crushed, demand all the more German territory in return. And with that we shall again find ourselves up to our eyes in the insoluble problems of the post-war period: national self-determination and nationalism which can only destroy but not build.

Certainly part of the freedom of the individual is also the freedom of his people. So the Czechs have a right to their own state. If this state is to be viable it must retain the territories of the old Bohemia. But on this territory live Germans who have no wish to come under Czech dominion, and they too must be conceded the right of self-determination. But how is this right of self-determination to be reconciled with that of the Czechs?

It cannot be as long as there is a failure to find new, constructive ideas for the coexistence of nations – ideas that overcome nationalism! Has Britain such ideas? Has she also anything approaching a clear idea of what kind of peace it is to be that she is trying to win?

These are problems that Russia is not beset by. To her autonomous Soviet republics she can attach further autonomous Soviet republics, regardless of the extra peoples she assimilates! She can without difficulty split economically homogeneous regions nationally. She can create cultural autonomies nationally satisfying to multilingual territories. Her

70

problems already lie beyond nationalism, and those problems seem also to be proving so momentous that nationalism is no longer capable of doing any damage. Whatever one's thoughts about terror, it must be admitted that world revolution in favour of that system and Bolshevization is a clear aim capable of being made intelligible to anyone.

Up to now Britain has merely been preaching the overthrow of Hitler. That means assuring the rights of the small nations *vis-à-vis* the superior strength of the big, and freeing Europe from the constant danger of military attack. But has not this negative and therefore inadequate end already been corrupted by the fact of conceding Russia's neutrality although she too has attacked Poland? Where are the justice and freedom we claim to be fighting for, if the Estonian Protectorate is accepted without a word, – is it so very different from the German Czech Protectorate?

Well yes, we have got to try to keep Russia out of the war and exploit her neutrality. Freedom and justice are not so alive as to drive people into a state of absolute indignation – people are again being realistic, in default of any compelling idea in favour of consistency. But will this realism not again prove shortsightedness? A Russian defeat on the Western Front, indeed, even the fact of Russian troops being forced to fight might have unforeseeable revolutionary consequences. There might here be a possibility of presenting the other side with a threat of revolution also! And that revolution, as distinct from the first, might still be the saving of all.

But for that a powerful, intelligible, clear-cut, living idea would be needed!

No, I can take no comfort in British optimism. Again and again I am filled with very great horror at the lack of ideas.

There is still perhaps comfort in the fact that one knows so little of the real policy and these combinations may, for lack of real foundation, so easily be wrong. World history seems to prefer half solutions: perhaps even this war will end suddenly and in a way quite different from that foreseen. But this can be a comfort only if we are working at the idea, and if, from this respite in the process of fate – for a half solution can mean no more – we are hoping to gain time for work on the idea. We must find the confidence to serve it without any pondering of the exigencies and effects of the moment.

4 October 1939

I am dreadfully depressed by my thoughts of yesterday. Whatever way we look at it, how humiliatingly clear the Russian ideology is, against which the inevitable emptiness and vagueness of all that can be said about democracy's ideas, and the high degree of falsification to which they are still being subjected, drives one to despair. The battle being fought by the West makes sense only if it is regarded as a battle against National Socialism, and as such it merits approval. But exclude National Socialism – and it is only when we do, I believe, that we arrive at the essential problems, next to nothing remains of the war aims of the West. Russia serves as a direct illustration of the profound sense of the commandment 'Resist not evil,' and of the fact that it is not enough to know what is being fought *against*. We must also know what we are fighting *for!*

For what is the use of defending freedom and justice, having no idea what to think at those fine-sounding words, and then a glance at Central Europe shows the impossibility of any longer realizing there what, thanks to little-shaken tradition, still holds out in Britain, although scarce able to make itself felt socially. It is still holding out today, but will it be able to withstand the rocking of the Empire by a world in revolution? Will not Britain also soon be in dire need of a new and living idea?

But then is there still any sense in struggling for this idea in the abstract? Do not we, just as much as the Russians, need first to know what a supra-national constitution and a new social order ought to look like, so as to be able to fight for them? Is there not even a need for a fully detailed plan for a new Central Europe – for a renewed Europe?

Alas, the sequence does not, I am afraid, admit of being reversed. First the idea must be clear, for only then can be seen what kind of concrete consequences to derive from it. The Soviet Union has also only become possible by virtue of decades of theoretical preparatory work. This apparent detour cannot be avoided, and there is no getting around the need for confidence in the idea, however difficult that may prove.

But am I not here getting lost in a contradiction? This demand for trust in the idea is a very absolute one, but at the same time I am rejecting absolute demands and requiring that we fulfil life. But for that surely is not some consideration of effect, even, indeed, of result, essential? Are we not otherwise bound to be broken by life?

I do not think that there is a contradiction here. When I attempt to grasp and formulate an idea, that means of course that I attempt to formulate it as clearly and intelligibly and well as possible. My concern to achieve the clearest possible grasp of it must be just as great as my concern to achieve the best possible presentation of it. My task is not to select a form that will encapsulate the idea from the world or even make it impossible for people to use, but to select that form which people can do something with.

There is one valid formulation of an absurd striving for the idea – *Don Quixote*. But what we are to think of that kind of striving has been stated with unsurpassable clarity again by Dostoyevsky in bidding farewell to this favourite figure of his youth. In Don Quixote he once again honours the power of the idea, but now also recognizing how terrible it is

> that the supreme fineness of man, his greatest purity, inno-
> cence, good nature, gentleness, bravery and finally even his
> great intelligence, far too often serve no purpose, fade without
> benefit to humanity and even become a mockery to men be-
> cause man, possessing all these most noble and abundant gifts,
> lacks only one final one, namely the genius to control this
> abundance of gifts and direct all this power onto a real, and
> not fantastic and insane, road towards the good of humanity.

What is said here of Don Quixote is valid for all. I have already had occasion to say that what is important is not just the idea, but the right idea. I must now add that what is important is not just the right idea but making it productive for men.

To achieve this effect we need not think first of effect. In keeping with the struggle for the idea itself is that we should strive for its supreme clarity. The better it can be apprehended, the more clearly can it be formulated. The simplicity of a formulation is never its beginning – never an abandoning of the improving and developing process – simplicity here is the ultimate, and most difficult, perfection! But this ultimate simplicity is also a guarantee of the most powerful effect.

Certainly there is also an artificial simplification which in most cases will even have an external result. But that simplification is an impoverish-ment that rapidly ends in a vacuum. It cannot in the end be mistaken either for the simplicity of nature or for ultimate perfection. The real act creates a new reality. The completed idea becomes simple again, becomes nature again and, with that, as powerful as a natural event.

It is the old battle between end and means. The end does not justify the means, ever, under any circumstances. For as long as the means does in fact correspond to the end it does not need first to be justified at all, not being in that case under discussion. It needs to be justified only when it does not in reality correspond to the end, when the lie is supposed to serve the truth or force is supposed to serve justice. But that justification cannot succeed. Any means serves only the end appropriate to it. Lie and force always serve only untruth and injustice, and destroy the end that is supposed to justify them. The means, consideration of effect must not be a matter for discussion at all. It must result from the laws of the idea – if *they* are elevated into an end they will always serve only the result that destroys the idea.

We cannot get around the need for trust. Any idea needs time for perfection and then again time to be apprehended more generally. Its effect cannot be expressed immediately, cannot help externally and visibly. But if any help is to be given at all, and in the real sense, then it can only be through the idea.

Evening

But I still cannot say that I am satisfied with this. I think it probably correct but not complete.

On the way towards perfecting the idea problems of form will arise, problems of the means of formulation and expression which will have also to be examined for effect. This endeavour is very plainly subject to restraints. It is correct as long as it subordinates itself to the inner laws of the idea and does not falsify it. It immediately becomes false inasmuch as it impairs the idea. Emphasis on effect is always dangerous, for it can all too easily mislead into transgressing these limits. But it is for that reason that this conditioned endeavour towards it remains important.

We are set in an external and an internal reality. External reality is today predominant, and the important thing above all is to develop the internal. But this can be developed only within external reality and upon it. We must prevent overemphasis of external reality, we must refer effect to its limits. And we must not at any price falsify the idea. But within these limits we must become clear concerning external effect.

It may, for example, be only beneficial to the development of the idea if, at an early stage in clarifying it, we make ourselves clear as to its effect, if, say, we consider what the concepts of freedom and justice state in concrete terms concerning the coexistence of nations. Certainly that too cannot be translated into reality until those ideas have become powerful, and they do not become powerful until taken deeper and revivified. But clarification of their content today can take us a big step forward towards this revivification.

Basically, of course, that is what I am doing. The personal and political thoughts, the examination of concepts, analysis of assumptions and ends are a confrontation with the idea, that is, of inner reality with the external. This diary too does not move in a void but in the domain of external reality.

But for the fulfilment of life that is the very thing that matters. We must examine the idea and the possibility of its effect against the test of external reality, in order to reject what is bound to remain non-living in the shape of mere empty speculation, and what, under false assumptions and as an artificial thought creation, does not do justice to real life; and this so as not to ride past reality and into a meaninglessly confused dream, like Don Quixote, but to find the way to make the idea really productive for humanity.

Night

I cannot get away from this diary today. I have always seen Christ's death on the cross as the ultimate example of an abandoning of effect. How dreadful the effects of that death were bound to be, and how utterly the reverse of success! Yet that very death on the cross which was brought about only by the internal compulsion of the idea, which served only the perfection of the example, really has perfected that example alone preserving and vindicating it for all time. If today we are still able to trust at all in the possibility of a fulfilment of life, then it is to this act of Christ's that we owe it.

But very plainly and very emphatically this death also had regard to external circumstances. Because of his teaching Christ prays 'Let this cup pass from me.' But when he sees the disciples sleeping, and when three times it is impressed on him how alone he is, he knows that he must perfect his example in this the most plainly visible way.

But it is by virtue of that very fact that this death acquires another sense and become firstly the profoundest fulfilment of life. For what distinguishes this death is that it is not a failure, not a martyr's death, not tragic destruction, but the profoundest fulfilment of this life. This death makes us see that life can and must be fulfilled in death also. Death comes to all of us: what matters is to transform death from a negative, casually meaningless conclusion of life into a meaningful perfection of it. The task of making the uncrucified Christ a reality refers us to natural death, but this natural death must also not remain an external conclusion. It must meaningfully perfect an inwardly rounded life. The fulfilment of life demands death, and demonstrates itself only in its fulfilment.

75

7 October 1939

It's hard to catch breath in this war. Now again Hitler's peace offer. Although admittedly it is not to be assumed that it will cause much confusion, being too little like a peace offer and too much like a threat and a demand for submission for that. Still, it has made an impression not only on the British and French communists – which is probably of no significance – but also on Lloyd George who may only have said as much to prevent its having any effect on those more pliable. The confusion caused amongst the German people and elsewhere in the world by this offer is something that we probably shall not discover.

But that alone is not what matters. Is it not terrible that we should again be having to approve of war and disapprove of peace in this fashion?

8 October 1939

We must, I suppose, also distinguish between one peace and another, and between peace and pacifism.

Peace too is an assumption and not an objective. Bound up with peace will probably be all positive ideals, for they will need it for their development, and if able to develop, will also bring it about. But that is still not to say that peace as such is a productive end, and that it can be worked towards unconditionally. When civilization is strong enough, and when all peoples are equally swayed by this civilization, then probably we shall be able to demand peace, but not in face of the barbarians, not in face of force, for both of them, force and barbarians, are only encouraged and supported by a readiness for peace. Pacifism *vis-à-vis* the Third Reich leads perforce to war, as experience has proved. We cannot fight for peace but must fight for the idea that creates it. The idea, if it prevails, will bring peace as a necessary consequence. Mere pacifism makes victory for violence easier.

But that is a long way from saying that war is something to be worked for, and if only to prevent attack – far from it. For years the Third Reich could have been conquered with greater certainty without rearmament than now, after complete rearmament, if only a living idea had been at work instead of pacifism. And the same goes for other situations also. Rearmament before the last war did not prevent war but simply brought it about. But pacifism alone is not enough, it must be the concomitant phenomenon of a peace-making idea, that is the extent of its significance. Everlasting peace may be an age-old and glorious dream of humanity's, but it is one that cannot be realized by dreaming but only by striving for an unconditional, real end – namely the realization of positive ideals.

I am constantly shaken at there being so many people who can do nothing but talk about their adventures in the last war. For what sort of a peace is it that fails to become an experience for men, and one that seizes and absorbs them! I have experienced a very great deal since the last war, and what a full and rich life it has been although its course has not taken me to special heights or away from the general, and I have experienced only what any can. How rare it is for me to be moved to speak of my adventures in the last war, although I had some! Is it really impossible to create a peace containing exciting, stirring, meaningful things?

I cannot believe that war is a necessity. But I do, I suppose, believe that lasting peace will remain a pious dream until it is forcibly brought about by a living idea capable of giving it living content.

But what is the sense of these thoughts in the middle of war, and when one is unable to approve or disapprove of either war or peace unequivocally?

9 October 1939

I have an answer to that too, but must first express it figuratively because it is not yet fully clear to me.

If we are climbing a mountain and come under a rock avalanche there is no sense in standing and facing the plunging boulders. We have to save ourselves and let the avalanche go its way. To try to stop it would be madness. Our only choice is between saving ourselves and being crushed. Only the first makes sense. Only then shall we perhaps be able to help any of the victims, and when the avalanche is over, again set about climbing our important mountain.

If we find ourselves not in the line of the avalanche – out of danger, it is not of immediate concern to us. We must not leap to certain death to stop the plunging boulders even if there are people below. We must try to rescue them of course, but for their sake too we must choose a sensible way of doing it. They will not be served by our killing ourselves, but only by our helping them. Of course, we may, in so doing, ourselves meet death, but braving the avalanche as such does not justify us in that, but only our attempting a feasible way of helping people. We may, employing all our strength, be able to deflect a single rock fragment, or hold someone until help arrives. It may be that all we are able to do is fetch help, and in some cases it may be crucial for there to be one survivor to fetch

77

help. But whatever we attempt, our action must not be directed against the avalanche itself, *that* we must let hurtle to the valley.

To interpret and apply this illustration I am obliged to speak of free will, and that is one of the most difficult problems. I am endeavouring, in my philosophical work, to discover a new approach to free will, and believe I have to some extent succeeded. But that, here, would take us too far. However, basing myself on this, I may perhaps succeed in indicating here the practical results of these considerations, which, I believe, will speak for themselves, even without exhaustive substantiation. This shall be appended one day when I clarify for myself in these pages the essence of my philosophical work, which is of course something that still has to be done.

Concerning the act, I have stressed that it creates a new reality, which is to say more precisely that the consequences of the act are again subject to the laws of a general necessity, and that the act itself on the other hand is an expression of free will. These genuine acts, the moments of free will, are extraordinarily rare. They occur only when, into collision with reality, comes a man inwardly so firm as to be able to withstand it, whose inner reality is of such clear definition as not to be effaced but to prevail. These moments apart, free will is unable to prevail, and except for them, we move in a stream of external necessity, be it provided externally or created by our own act. This external necessity is something we are unable to alter. We can strengthen free will only in its inner working so that it shall become effective if there is a crucial collision with external reality and the act becomes possible. Nothing remains but for us to let external reality hurtle its course and strive for inner reality until such time as a new moment of free will, a new turning point, can be introduced by virtue of a new act.

It is of this external necessity that we must take cognizance and account. We can submit to it – for it does not always resemble the rock avalanche, it can also be a stream heading for the sea, but always it is implacable; we can exploit it for our inner development, we can divert it somewhat, we can distance ourselves from it, we can save ourselves from it, but at all events there is no sense in going against the essential issue. We are not to resist evil. We must let the avalanche hurtle and the stream flow. We are to do what we ourselves honestly recognize as possible for us, and that applies not only internally but also externally, and consists also in acknowledging necessity. All that is permitted to be at issue is our striving, and this cannot consist in resisting necessity but must consist in preparing a new reality which can be founded only upon the fact that it is our internal reality that brings about the act.

In this perhaps lies the meaning of the word necessity. The exact meaning of need[6] – and one which has not been entirely effaced by the generalization of modern usage – is not simply the misery and misfortune that befall one – not something terrible to be borne or avoided, but a *position compelling action*, an internal tension demanding remedy, indeed itself impelling towards help. As soon as a necessity has arisen and been recognized, need will be averted, the further issue being then indicated and defined. This necessity may well be a misfortune for us but it can and must not any longer mean need for us. Need lies only at the point where help is possible, where we are impelled towards help, and where we ourselves are able to contribute towards this help. What is needful and shall alone create need is therefore that for which we can strive – the inner reality and the free act which are alone able to bring about a new turning point of need, a new necessity.

Again this stressing of internal reality does not mean any neglect of external reality. On the contrary, it is in this that it first becomes really clear why the act is what does most profound and perfect justice to external reality.

If we attempt to intervene absolutely in the events of external necessity we are either destroyed by life, or, if we are not clear concerning the necessity of this failure and are nevertheless saved, we become so very disillusioned by life that we are forced completely into a remote, non-living world; either way we are not doing justice to external reality. Only the knowledge of the possibility of the act, that knowledge which helps inner reality into its own, compels us to keep our eyes fixed incessantly on the avalanche, be it to achieve something in small particulars, or spot the moment at which to continue the ascent or begin it anew. Our external activity will only be able to become meaningful at all by virtue of internal reality, it is by its aid alone that activity will be able to begin always at the point where it can be effective.

Indeed, more than that. The necessity in which we are placed will not of course always resemble the avalanche. There are also times of construction, and we can also be in a reality that has been created by an act of

6. 'Need' (*Not*) is in German more plainly a root of 'necessity' (*Notwendigkeit*) than can be conveyed in English, and later there is play on the *-wend-* of *Notwendigkeit* with the meaning of 'turn' in the sense of 'avert', so that 'necessity' is understood as 'need-averting'.

which we are able to approve. We must let external necessity roll on, but our submission to it and our external activity will have to be differently evalued at different times. At a time of hurtling avalanche when we can expect only incidental helpful achievements, it will be of small significance, but its importance will be great at a time that serves the building of the idea, when it is able to work in the sense of a positive idea, and when therefore the internal reality can develop upon the external. We must try to recognize which time we are in – whether we have to save ourselves from the hurtling avalanche, or whether we can trust ourselves to external necessity. This distinction will only be possible if we know the meaning of the internal reality – knowledge of the internal reality and of the act appropriate to it saves us from senseless activity at any price, and turns it into a means for the fulfilment of our lives.

The emphasis on internal reality is thus necessary also and above all for the sake of external reality. For we must not of course think of all that in terms of waiting until knowledge impels us to action. In external necessity is where we stand – life will almost always demand action from us – our task is mostly to strive only for the correct control and assessment, and for the proper engagement of our person so that our sense of life shall not be destroyed or blocked by the action. It is precisely this meaningful fulfilment of the given external *demand of the day* which is only possible by shifting the emphasis onto the internal reality, and when in spite of the given external activity, or in it, we help make the internal reality valid – and that especially in our time when external reality is in any case overrated.

How important this distinguishing of different times by the aid of inner reality is, will become especially clear if we once again consider the striving for result. At this point I must somewhat correct my description of this striving. What I have said applied absolutely to personal result, and, in negative times to general result, to effect, too. Concessions to negative times will allow result to become possible only at the expense of the idea. On the other hand, in positive times a different striving for result is possible. Striving for result can sometimes also mean renunciation. It can, under some circumstances, be easier to live absolutely for one's ideal ends than to try to assert them, and in positive times such a concession to the times can have a positive sense. If the idea is in the process of realization anyway, such a sacrifice may serve the idea better than positive striving.

For Rathenau, say, it would certainly have been easier to live for his work than to sacrifice himself – and very consciously – for the result that

80

was to be for the benefit of the German Republic. And perhaps for Masaryk it would have been easier also to remain true to his opposition to war than to bring himself to send rescued prisoners of war to war again and death, as legionaries.

Yet both examples show too that we must not allow ourselves to be overwhelmed by external ends, that we must not yield overhastily to the desire to help, but that it is necessary to identify our time accurately. Rathenau's sacrifice was a vain one. He would perhaps have served German civilization better by keeping himself in reserve and completing his work. How very greatly we miss his intellectual power today! And had Masaryk remained loyal to his conviction and the Old Austria in consequence not been destroyed, would he not have been able to serve democracy in quite different fashion?

Such considerations do not affect the admiration due to these two men, even if they were in error – for who would presume to judge! But they show the rightness of condemning the pondering of effect, and they show too that our distinguishing of the times must follow from internal reality. We must compare the times with our own internal reality: if we have more to give than they have, our own internal reality is then what matters. If the times have more to give, we must subordinate ourselves to them. Thus it is not the effect that matters but the internal reality. The development of the internal reality is the crucial contribution that we are able to make to this world, and it is that we have to serve, whether with the world or against it. The crucial thing is not whether or not the result is a sacrifice, but whether or not that result is justified. We must not sacrifice ourselves to the result if enticed to do so by a possible effect, however useful it may appear, but only if urged to do so by the idea – i.e. when the external activity in the sense of the times corresponds better to the idea than what we would be able to achieve by completing our own work.

The demand of the day was a phrase of Goethe's and his own example most clearly shows how accurately this distinction can be made and that it must be made from within. It is to this demand of the day that he submits in returning to Weimar from Italy. In Italy, relying on his talents, he could have led a carefree and happy life. Yet it is by his very renouncing of that special position that his talents might have created for him that he manages to set the first example in modern times of a meaningful human life. He sees the positive possibilities of this time, and only by subordinating himself to them is he able to develop his internal reality to its full extent. It is not effect that concerns him – the Weimar Duchy, the

Weimar narrowness which he fears and has happily just escaped, is not all that important – no, he sees only that he needs external reality for the sake of the idea, and so this crucial act of his life serves the idea also. But he at once turns his back on the times and distances himself from them as far as possible when they turn into the hurtling avalanche. He might have sacrificed himself in the battles against Napoleon, and his involvement then would probably have brought great success, much depended on him at that time, and, thanks to him, on the little duchy also – but by very reason of the fact that he did not so sacrifice himself – that even during the Wars of Liberation he fought solely for the essential, he was able to perfect an example that did not get buried beneath the internal collapse following the Wars of Liberation. It is only by this turning away from reality that he vindicates the significance of his turning towards internal reality – of his return to Weimar – it is by virtue of this that he has become not only a poetic figure whose loss we should regret, but a human example retaining a validity beyond its times.

Deciding between these two forms of striving may be difficult in times which give the impression of serving construction – as towards the end of the last war when it seemed possible to press that which was productive into the service of the idea, or during the German Republic which seemed to be serving the idea. Today however that decision cannot be difficult. This war which came about because all the positive opportunities were missed, leaves us with no opportunity for opposing fate. The avalanche which has started here, has got to roll. The only possibility for us is of being crushed or of working internally for a different future, for a turning point after the avalanche is done. This war, however much we may be affected by it, does not essentially concern us at all, our task is, so far as possible, neither to let ourselves get dragged into it, nor to waste strength opposing it for the sake of an impossible or false peace. Our task is, so far as possible, and apart from any personal assistance rendered, not to concern ourselves about this necessary course of events but hold ourselves in readiness for the new ascent. For the sake of lending assistance and in order to recognize the right moment for a new act, we must, I suppose, keep our eyes on the avalanche. Apart from that, we have every right to save ourselves because only then can we hope to serve the idea.

10 October 1939

Expressing it more plainly – the call to recognize the times is, in itself, already a call for external activity. For in times of peace it will not be so simple to recognize whether it is a rockfall we are dealing with, or obstacles, the overcoming of which lies in the realm of necessity and is possible by virtue of it. We shall probably only be able to distinguish reliably by first of all attempting to overcome obstacles.

As a result of this call, the given external activity in any case receives internal meaning – it has to sound the limits of necessity, for it will be disastrous to consider necessary what is not yet necessary at all – disastrous to submit to a positive necessity, because we are then not able at all to exhaust the possibilities it offers – and also disastrous where the necessity is one that we have to escape from, if we flee it prematurely, if we do not recognize it completely, we shall also fail to recognize the right point at which to bring in the act. Either way, the internal reality will atrophy – if the external activity does not make all its possibilities known, internal reality cannot develop upon it, nor can a collision of the two realities result leading to a breakthrough of the internal reality – in this collision the act will be impeded by the neglected parts of the necessity.

The activity must also teach us how we have to assess the external obstacles. But we must also allow ourselves to be instructed by these attempts and apply our personalities only where they can be applied, be it in support of external necessity or in turning away from it. This unflagging and constant process of attempting, however, this application of the personality which must not lead to disappointment even if the attempt has a negative result and has to be repeated in quite a different way, this constant beginning again and timely breaking off, will only be possible without paralysing disappointment if we are aware of the internal meaning of the activity and of the internal reality of the act. Only then can we have trust – otherwise we are bound to despair.

However, in the two commandments of which I have made frequent mention we have been given distinguishing marks for this recognition, aids which free us from the uncertain historico-philosophical approach upon which my considerations of yesterday were forced in part to support themselves.

'Resist not evil.' We have got to be able to do something positive. Possibly necessary resistance also has got to be in the service of a positive activity, the stress must always be on the positive. As long as we are aware only of the negative content of our action, our action is false. We are then setting ourselves against the necessary sequence of events, against the plunging avalanche: then it is high time for us to save ourselves. Our internal reality is a positive thing – it can only develop and unfold in the positive – so long as we merely resist, however important that may seem, we are bound to destroy it, and with it, the essential contribution that we are able to make to this world. And not only that – by resisting we achieve nothing at all – we have to let the avalanche plunge to the valley – all we can do is prepare a new reality, and *that* requires a positive aim.

'Thou shalt not kill.' We are allowed to clear obstacles out of the way, we are allowed to destroy what we are able to rebuild differently or better, we are allowed to inflict a final sentence of that sort where we really are able to know exactly down to the last detail, and therefore able to recreate. But how can we then arrogate to ourselves a sentence of that sort upon a human life? How can we be permitted to destroy a human being? Here something unknowable, something other is at work, before which we must bow! It is terrible to fall into the hands of the living God – overstepping this limit we deliver ourselves up irretrievably to this power of the other and are finally buried beneath inescapable necessity. We may perhaps be saved by Grace, but can that be counted on from the outset? As long as external necessity is threatening to drive us to the point of being forced to kill, we have to escape or be crushed by the hurtling avalanche!

Here are the two limits set absolutely upon any activity if it is to remain meaningful and internally and externally productive – the negative that refers us to the positive, and the killing to which the positive must not lead. We must not renounce our power and we must not do what goes beyond human power. It is within these limits also that my thoughts must move.

So be wise as serpents and innocent as doves. The disciples are permitted to flee and use any cunning to safeguard the teaching from external necessity, but they must remain innocent. For otherwise the teaching, the internal reality, will be endangered. And we cease to be innocent in that which is negative, when we serve no teaching: render unto Caesar what is God's and sacrifice the innermost to necessity. From the turning point of need which it ought to be, necessity will in both cases become the productive, living God by whom we are consumed.

11 October 1939

I keep rereading what I have written over the last two days. For the problems involved here are, of course, the most essential and fundamental. This is where we must be as clear in our minds as we possibly can.

Yet the more I reflect, the better I think the illustrations and distinctions chosen. Necessity is the avalanche or stream which cannot be halted. But thanks to internal reality, we have the good fortune always also to be standing to one side of the avalanche; and that good fortune is something we must exploit and make something real of! It is here that we must apply our powers and use everything at our disposal – external and internal reality – in order to help become operative in our human lives which occur in external reality, that human quality which is more than the external alone, and still something fundamentally different.

Maybe the following illustration will also help. The necessary course of events, however far it may still extend into the future, we are simply to regard as unalterable past. We are to transform future into past constantly and every instant. The present can be only our endeavours and with them, inner reality which does not lead to the future predelineated by necessity, but which can produce a new act, and with it, a new future. We must, every instant, complement external necessity by employing humanity.

External necessity is our fate. Our fate is something we cannot escape – but that is not what matters – what *does*, is what we make of it. We may be broken by misfortune, we may consume ourselves in impotent resistance to it – but we may also make it internally productive. The same blows of fate will have devastating effects on one and productive effects on another. To be able to re-mint our fate we have constantly to assail it in order to recognize the full extent of the necessity, but at the same time we must not pursue these attempts into the absurd for their own sake, but must learn from them; being broken, however great a proof it may be of our powers, is not what matters, but the internal re-minting of our fate. It is in and through our fate that we must make our freedom a reality.

But that means – but no, I must not go on any further here yet. I keep letting my thoughts race ahead. To translate the human quality into reality we have got first of all to know it. I cannot solve the ultimate problems if I do not lay a foundation for them, if I skip the connecting links. In the stream of my thoughts there is no preventing my touching on them constantly, but I must, in touching on them, also be able to turn away from them constantly. It is for the very sake of these thoughts that I have constantly to make a fresh start where details, where the simple things of this life, where individual problems are concerned. I have to fill out the framework ever more powerfully and clearly, for the important thing is that the feeling which has forced me to keep this diary should not be lost in fantasies which do not stand firm against life, but that it should receive a clear content capable of being lived. The moment I touch upon an ultimate problem, I am absolutely obliged to go back to the beginning, and for as long as I no longer need to explain everything in detail and ultimate simplicity is the result. Again and again I need to catch breath!

12 October 1939

The avalanche is rolling, and above all, the Russian one. Already the Baltic States have been forced into dependence, after Estonia and Latvia – Lithuania, which has got Vilna back, it is true, but has had still more plainly to surrender her independence in exchange. Now Finland is under threat. Troops are concentrating in the Caucasus. Against Turkey? Persia? India? Can anyone calculate in advance where an avalanche will roll to, or how far?

But Britain has today concluded a trade agreement with Russia. Well, yes, I know – Russia must not now be made an enemy of as well. It's good tactics to force Russia into plain neutrality. Maybe it will still be possible to play her off against Germany who up to now has already had to pay considerably above the odds where this alliance is concerned.

Yet I cannot help feeling that this realistic policy is again merely short-sightedness. Let us for once leave the idea out of it completely. One of these days Russia will negotiate with Finland, and these negotiations will be dangerous for Britain. For if Sweden stands by Finland, as she says, Britain will probably have to trouble herself about Finland too. It is already remarkable enough that the Baltic States should have been dropped like this without a word. Negotiations with Russia have apparently foundered first and foremost on Britain's not wishing to sacrifice the sovereignty of these states. But will not Russia be strengthened in these negotiations when she sees Britain weak and giving way? Would not Finland's position, and with it Britain's, be better if Britain were more reticent, if she were to veil her intentions towards Russia? Yesterday the Commons even turned down a proposal to publish a Blue Book concerning Anglo-Russian negotiations – must not that too be an encouragement to Russia?

And even if things end well with Finland, what then about Turkey? The Turkish Foreign Minister is still apparently in Moscow and not being received – obviously he is to be subjected to pressure. It is in Britain's own very special interest to counter this pressure also!

Almost equally uncanny is that Germany should be recalling German minorities everywhere back to Germany. Southern Tyrol has been given up. Germans from the Baltic countries, whether they like it or not, have got to go to Germany, and it is already being said that even Germans from the Balkan countries are to be forced to return, and that Volga Germans are to be exchanged for Czechs.

Why is it? Man's rootedness in the soil, in the countryside he has belonged to for centuries, is of crucial importance – the tie that mustn't be broken but strengthened. But that is of no account. The Nazis' dogmas are always no more than a means of effect and never a belief. They can be interchanged as the situation demands. But what is the intention that lies behind them?

To pronounce on that we must not let ourselves be moved by the misery of the people who have been expelled and robbed, nor must we grieve after German culture. In the old Austria these scattered German minorities were still upholders of culture. They had their good theatres, their concerts, lectures, schools, universities. They seemed a wonderful means of imparting to the Slav world what German culture had to give. How great my own gratitude – and I am not alone – to German institutions in Prague, and what a fruitful reciprocal effect these energetic splinters had upon German culture! But in Austria, minorities were already being abused as a means of domination, and to the Nazis they were merely another means of destruction. By their aid the way was paved for the demoralizing of the states to be subdued. And having let themselves be misused for this purpose, and having themselves brought the greatest misfortune upon people, upon all Germans who were not Nazis and upon the Jews who felt themselves part of German culture, these minorities have forfeited the right to be pitied or regarded as upholders of culture. The wonderful legacy of the German past, German culture, is being destroyed: can anyone mourn that other legacy of the past, the German minorities! They might still have been the special means of peacefully propagating a peace-bringing culture, but as they have simply been a means of domination it is good for them to disappear.

But what is the significance of abandoning this means of domination?

Rauschning, in his book,[7] stresses repeatedly that the real Nazi plan is for world domination, and that everything being done and demanded in East and South-east Europe is merely secondary to this, and being used as a front only for as long as it is needed. The Nazis, he says, seem aware that German youth is not likely to be moved to start a hard and dreary peasant existence in Eastern Europe, whereas an adventurous and lordly life in the colonies would be highly appropriate and, by virtue of National Socialist education, become still more so. That is also why the coloniza-

7. Hermann Rauschning, *Die Revolution des Nihilismus*, 1938 (English translation, *Germany's Revolution of Destruction*, 1939).

tion of East Prussia has not been continued, and not just because of the Junkers. These plans alone, Hitler is supposed to have said, would justify a war involving the sacrifice of a whole German generation.

For these plans, says Rauschning, two lines of action have always been considered. Either with Britain against Russia, in which case Eastern Europe would have played a big part. Or with Russia against Britain, although Rauschning does not argue this possibility further, considering it improbable. In this respect he has been wrong. But the abandoning of further European plans, which is confirmed by the destruction of German minorities, shows him to have had a good knowledge of the Nazis nevertheless.

Is Germany gathering together all Germans in order to stake all on one card – in order to deal a final blow? Is it already a question of the insane alternatives – world domination or destruction?

With any other nation such insanity would have to be considered unlikely. Especially when what seems so much more likely is destruction, and when, through the pact with Russia, it has in any case become so ominously imminent. But with a people whose national epic is the *Song of the Nibelungs* can this idea be dismissed?

I have always felt uneasy about this epic, for it is one of treachery. Siegfried wins horny skin and the cloak of invisibility to ward off treachery, and himself betrays Brünhilde, at first unknowingly in forgetting her for Kriemhild's sake, but then knowingly too in falsely winning her for Gunther, and betrays Gunther when he betrays his treachery to Kriemhild also. Gunther betrays Brünhilde in letting her be won by Siegfried, and Siegfried in giving Hagen, at least tacitly, permission to kill Siegfried. Hagen betrays Kriemhild having promised her to protect Siegfried, and betrays Siegfried, his brother-in-arms, in treacherously stabbing and murdering him. All the Nibelungs betray Siegfried by continuing their loyalty to Hagen, and Kriemhild betrays Etzel in marrying him only in order to be able to take revenge. And finally Hagen betrays the Nibelungs by keeping silent about the danger of which he alone is aware, and knowingly leads them to their deaths. In this epic all acts – and most, it must also be added, are false – arise from, and lead to, treachery.

Certainly this treachery brings doom. But this doom appears not as something terrible, not as a just punishment, but as the desired thing, the approved and glorious end. For the sake of that end approval is given to all the falseness and double-dealing, putting all that has gone before so very much into the shade that it is possible to talk of Nibelung *loyalty!* And the true hero of this epic is not Siegfried either but Hagen. Hagen is the most significant figure, and after murdering Siegfried he comes wholly to the fore. It is Hagen alone who brings the course of the epic to its crucial and overwhelming conclusion.

Very clearly to be recognized in this displacement is that transformation of the heroic quality which I have sought to outline. Siegfried is by nature a hero, dauntless and strong, courageous and daring. His every act becomes of itself a heroic one. How can he strive consciously to become a hero! He is concerned with quite different things. He wants to win the treasure, win Kriemhild, live a rich, glorious life. The enriching and cultivating of life is what matters. Gunther, whom he could vanquish with ease, he subordinates himself to, willingly – Hagen's envy is alien to him – his mind is not yet confused by the ambition of every conscious hero to be greatest. He wants to live – live better in the material and spiritual sense, not rule.

Hagen, on the other hand, the ambiguously sombre, whom no one dare actually to attack but even less actually to admire, is no longer a shining hero, and so becomes the conscious hero, the heroic quality becoming his ideal. 'Dares he still to fight who cannot fall?' he flings at Siegfried. His treacherous murder of Siegfried seems to him justified by his inability to vanquish Siegfried, protected by his horny skin, in any other way. And in fact, if it is only the heroic act that matters, and nothing else, the murder is justified. But Hagen also mocks Siegfried, and scorns his striving after purity and honour – he who wishes to be hero must also will the means, be it the infamous stab in the back. He taunts Siegfried with his cloak of invisibility and horny skin, but how can Siegfried renounce them as what he wants is not heroic single combat at any price, but, in every sense, battle with the dragon, the liberating act, life! Certainly Hagen would not renounce them either, not, however, for the sake of life, but because his desire is for heroism and he knows that it is only the greatest act that matters, and that all means must be employed for its sake that are conceivably effective. The stab in the back does not weigh upon his conscience, it is his triumph. He has found the way to be victor nevertheless!

Hagen is the true father of the heroic ideal. Apparently the curse of his act is still a burden upon him – the epic does not yet quite dare to declare itself for him – but this burden serves only to bring about what the heroic ideal cannot dispense with, heroic death. Awareness of the ignominy that the heroic quality can no longer dispense with, serves only to make heroic death desirable to conceal how little justice to life can be done by this ideal.

Hagen alone knows what awaits them all at the hands of Kriemhild. He knows they are lost, yet is silent. A word from him can save the lives of them all, and one would think that the lives of his brothers-in-arms would be worth more to him than the gold of the Nibelungs which he will not surrender – more than all the gold on earth – yet he is silent. Consciously and deliberately he brings about the disaster. For he knows that all the treachery and ignominy that they have been obliged to heap upon themselves can be effaced only by death, and that only heroic death will stamp them beyond all doubt finally as heroes, and as the greatest. This ideal that desires victory is obliged nevertheless to complete itself in death. And behold, having countless times proved too weak and incapable of preventing treachery in life, here at last it really stands the test. Loyalty and honour, sullied again and again, stand firm in the face of death, and for the first time no traitor is found. Only now, when all are aware that what awaits them is not the victory they proclaim and pretend to desire, and when they at last know the destruction they glorify to be certain annihilation, does the sham ideal hold good that ought to have shaped life and yet was too weak. Only now do they become really worthy to be heroes of an epic. Only now, having chosen the way of madness and annihilation.

Today, when Christianity is being assailed, the *Song of the Nibelungs* – an old Teutonic tradition, revised in Middle High German, and readopted by the Third Reich's idol, Wagner, by Hebbel (the justification of Hagen is his) and others – is more than ever the Germans' national epic. May not Hitler have had Hagen in mind when, with apparently a clear conscience, he caused the murder of his loyalest comrades-in-arms? The signs fill one with horror, will this nation, pursuing an ideal whose value is proved only in death, seek that death? How large is the *other Germany* that wants to live, and has she just such an ideal? The German's fondness for destruction is strong. For that he finds no price too high, and it is more attractive to him than the *rotten peace* he does not know what to do with, or the victory he pretends not to desire, or the life he does not know how to deal with.

Is this sinister epic, which from any human viewpoint remains totally incomprehensible, simply a prophecy? Is it now going to be fulfilled?

Perhaps. I hope not. But the flames that destroyed Etzel's palace are still smouldering in German hearts and in the heart of Europe, ready to destroy even that glorious edifice, and be it only for the sake of their own destruction. They ought to be smothered, these flames, but how? Is annihilation all that is left?

90

Even the craving for annihilation is not a *national characteristic* of the Germans, but it is a powerful tradition. Also alive has been, and still is, the other, spiritual Germany of the glorious achievements. But her tradition has often proved too weak. Can it be hoped that the very threat of annihilation will give her strength for a decisive act? Domination grows weaker the greater the areas dominated and the more overwhelming further plans become. Can we hope for a humane counter-revolution when the Bolshevizing of Germany begins?

When a powerful ideal is at work making demands of the powers of the individual to their full extent and in worthy fashion, many things sink back into the deep dark places of the human heart and cease to be dangerous. But where is the ideal that can save the *other Germany?* Much would be easier to bear if that were at last to become clear at least here, outside the frontiers of tyranny and the urge for destruction and self-destruction!

13 October 1939

Thinking is easy when we are thinking abstractly. We have no need to fear the obstacles of reality, the objections presented by the facts – we can be uncannily consistent.

This danger is also present when we proceed from a reality that we know. How much greater it is bound to be when it is a question of political conclusions, where we are bound to lack a vast amount of crucial knowledge!

Am I not also in danger of succumbing to this false consistency? We must hold to the reality that we know – that the idea is what matters needs no further proof!

14 October 1939

To draw breath and get away from the thoughts that keep gnawing away at me – is it now imminent, that dreadful stepping-up of the war that is bound to come? I have been immersing myself in an anthology of German verse.

Reading verse, rejecting poems I once liked, and discovering new ones which previously I paid no attention to, I keep wondering if there is not some objective feature by which to make a reliable judgement of poems. The answer would be of importance to me, attempting as I am to penetrate the mystery of form.

There are probably no single features, the form possibilities of the lyric being too rich and varied for that. Yet the longer I compare those poems that have held their own over the years, with those of which opinion differs, the more I believe it possible to distinguish perfect poems from imperfect. Differences of taste turn first and foremost on poems which are not wholly perfect. Where they are concerned it depends upon one's own state of preparation whether the faults or the merits seem the more decisive. But that apart, it will probably be possible to choose a number of perfect poems that no one able to disregard personal preference or aversion – i.e. no one capable of judgement – will object to.

Certainly, here too there will be deviations. Form cannot be fathomed rationally, it has to be experienced, which is why personal considerations cannot be completely excluded. But experience is guided by form into definite channels which extend beyond the personal – upon a personal path is formed that which is of general validity – the means of forming remains personal and requires the kindred personality to receive it, but the result extends far beyond it and can therefore be judged all the more objectively the more the means is overcome. Comparison of various anthologies confirms even this most personal of forms to be so determined that a whole number of poems are to be found in every such selection, confirms too that it is in fact a question only of inessential deviations and not of fundamental uncertainty.

It might, say, be laid down that all poems which, for the sake of the form, do violence to the language, should be excluded. That may, to begin with, when the feeling, the thought, the image seize us, be something to put up with, but it will not endure in the long run. Poems that let themselves be overwhelmed by one thought or feeling without completely clarifying it or creating the form appropriate to it, will be identifiable as imperfect when thought or feeling has been completely grasped, for then the inadequacy of the form will become evident. Feeling and form, thought and image are the basic elements of the lyric. However beautiful or essential the shaping of any one of these elements, the important thing is that they should all be made perfectly congruent.

Imperfection will be more difficult to recognize in poems whose form is too easily achieved – which simply take over and exploit for effect possibilities of language made pliant by generations of poets before them – those poems which fall lightly on the ear, which merely beautifully rearrange the familiar in language, imagery and thought, without extending it by means of new experience. Or in poems which create one of these elements anew and, for the rest, settle for that which has been created by others or for a modification of it; poems, possibly, that reproduce an image or natural mood without awakening a deeper feeling, clarifying a new thought, or clothing an experience, new in itself, in external images. We have only to think of Heine to know that this is a difficult distinction. Undoubtedly fine poems too can be imperfect and shaped for effect instead of developed from experience.

But here too there is considerable scope for objectivity. In German there are, for example, such glorious songs addressed to the moon that the feelings and thoughts awakened by a moonlight night, as also the image of the moonlit night itself, are very generally accessible. And with the aid of the already pliant language it is easy to find new variations for these things which externally can be very fine. And yet they are imperfect, and this imperfection is identifiable.

Mondnacht ('Moonlit night') is one of Eichendorff's finest poems. It immediately draws us into a gleaming moonlit night that awakens memories of love and dreams:

> Es war, als hätt' der Himmel
> Die Erde still geküßt,
> Daß sie im Blütenschimmer
> Von ihm nun träumen müßt'.

> [It was as if heaven
> gave earth a quiet kiss,
> so she, in gleam of blossom,
> had now to dream of him.]

And from this mood, the description of the stillness of the night proceeds powerfully and clearly to prepare the transition to the feeling, which has been made intelligible, and to the thought.

> Die Luft ging durch die Felder,
> Die Ähren wogten sacht,
> Es rauschten leis die Wälder,
> So sternklar war die Nacht.

> [Over the fields the breeze went,
> the corn ears gently swayed,
> the forest rustled softly,
> so starry was the night.]

But then suddenly a stock image appears which does not fulfil the expectations raised.

93

Und meine Seele spannte
Weit ihre Flügel aus,
Flog durch die stillen Lande,
Als flöge sie nach Haus.

[And my soul extended
wide its wings for flight,
flew over the silent country
as if flying home.]

The soul extending its wings is a fine image which in the old hymns has a strong content of feeling. It is fine too in the many moon songs where the light clouds become wings of the soul. But here, in the moon-clear night of this poem not only is that image missing, but the note struck in the first stanzas is not carried through to the end, and nothing is to be found in the poem capable of investing the soul's wings with meaning, or of giving this adopted image any substance. The image is supposed to lead over into religious feeling, but the contribution to this ought to be made by the poem itself. Switching the transition to a conventional image deprives the religious feeling of any power, or more correctly, betrays that it has no power. It is simply filling space that ought to be filled differently. The poem rolls smoothly on instead of being completed.

Reading the poem and under the spell of its beauty, we are at first only slightly irritated. But rereading it and comparing it with perfect poems, we find it less and less able to captivate as a whole. Against that, let us consider just two verses of Claudius' simple poem:

Der Mond ist aufgegangen,
Die goldnen Sternlein prangen,
Am Himmel hell und klar;
Der Wald steht schwarz und schweiget,
Und aus den Wiesen steiget
Der weiße Nebel wunderbar.

Wie ist die Welt so stille
Und in der Dämmrung Hülle
So traulich und so hold
Als eine stille Kammer,
Wo ihr des Tages Jammer
Verschlafen und vergessen sollt.

94

[The moon has risen,
the tiny gold stars shine
in heaven bright and clear;
the wood stands black and silent,
and from the meadows rises
the white mist wondrously.

How silent the world is
and, wrapped in veil of twilight,
as homely and sweet
as a quiet room
where the day's affliction
you shall forget in sleep.]

Eichendorff's world is closer to us than the simple pious world of Claudius. And yet how the eternal validity of Claudius' poem contrasts with the mere atmosphere of Eichendorff's while being in no way deficient in atmosphere itself. But there is much more to it than that. Strongly and surely in the verses that follow there is a transition to prayer, and so clear and firm a transition that even the most irreligious of readers will be unable to escape its effect. But can this difference also be explained?

It can be, more precisely than I have done so far. In Eichendorff's poem the point of break can be identified. It is plainly in the line *So sternklar war die Nacht* ('so starry was the night'). The image has been completed, we have been made part of the stillness and moon gleam, one in which the stars can be visible only very indistinctly. The picture lacks nothing, the stars merely round it off externally and in contradictory fashion. We can be reminded of the stars, certainly, but *reminded* is the operative word. This line is simply a conventional supplement. The religious motif receives some slight preparation in the first lines, but heaven's kiss initially awakens other ideas. If this religious feeling had been there from the outset, how easy to produce a decisive turn in this line, whether through the stars – which would have had to break through, however surprisingly – or through the breeze's agitating the forest and leading to the wings of the soul. The slipping in of that false *so* is no accident. The meaning, I suppose, is merely that the night is completely starry, but not being essential internally, this line has to be strongly connected to the preceding one, thus producing a false logical construction. Forests can rustle softly even on dark nights, they do not do so because the night is starry. And as this line refers back falsely and does not extend the image, the image of the soul remains hollow too. There is no compelling transition to the thought, which itself remains weak because it is not rooted in the poem and imbued with feeling, and merely completes the poem and rounds it off.

How different in Claudius' poem. Here too the stars, but *shining* because the moon is *rising*. So clear is this image that even the long outworn *wondrously* still sounds new and original even today. How firmly this forest stands upon the earth, and how softly and easily the veil of twilight envelops it, and the white mist wondrously. In the third verse there is also express mention of there being a half moon, so that the stars are not outshone, and the thought then attaches itself to this. But how preparation of the thought which will elucidate the feeling in the moonlight grows from the image itself as early as the second verse. How graphically and intuitively clear God's solace becomes here, even before it is mentioned. Do I really have to quote Goethe as well? Claudius holds his own beside him, Eichendorff does not.

But that is perhaps the most remarkable result of this examination. Only an infinitesimally small number of Romantic poems would manage to find acceptance in the anthology of perfect poems. That is surprising because it is the Romantics who revel in feeling and school themselves in the folksong, perfection of which was seen as an end even by Goethe. And yet Eichendorff's is undoubtedly one of the most powerful Romantic poems ever!

I am not in this connection thinking of the bad habits which ruin so many Romantic poems – the diminutive suffix – *lein* which, with Claudius and Goethe, still sounds genuine but later gets worked to death; and the elves and sprites, magic and miracles which are part of the creaking apparatus of Romanticism. What I am thinking of are the fine, the best Romantic poems which, like Eichendorff's, are free of any external faults. They are fine but hardly any are perfect.

Can that also be explained? It can, and the explanation even directs us to a flaw in generally accepted notions of ours.

We always believe that thought should be restrained in order not to destroy feeling. And as to us feeling seems more natural and original, we are inclined to curb thought for the sake of feeling and repress it to a primitive level. We fear *destruction of the earth by mind*. This mind-hostility, even on the part of the intellectual, is one of the main causes of the incursion of the new barbarism, for this fear is simply false.

Every strong feeling urges towards clarity. Feeling that is not artifi-

96

cially preserved but real is not to be satisfied with half-truths. Certainly, purely intellectual thinking that does not do justice to man as such, will not do justice to feeling either. But mind does not of course mean intellect but reason – that is, comprehensive thinking that does entirely do justice to man – and it is this comprehensive thinking, *thinking to a conclusion*, which does justice to feeling, indeed, does so solely and exclusively. It is for the sake of feeling that we must think to a conclusion!

How clearly that is demonstrated by the Romantics. They above all are the ones who curb thinking in order to revel in feeling: revive the fairytale, throw themselves into the arms of the church, cling to the folksong, make diminutives of words to take them straight into the realm of feeling; simply accept any readymade result of thought merely to save thought and arrive quickly and directly at feeling and to heighten that feeling. And those are the very means by which they ruin feeling. As the bad habits of Romanticism make it impossible for us to think for ourselves, we are not able to feel either – the finest poems are thus simply distorted. And what is true of the bad habits is also true of where they are absent. Eichendorff's moonlit-night poem also adheres to a scheme that saves us thinking any further but, against that, promises a wealth of feeling. And as we see, that wealth of feeling does not emerge because it cannot lie in things but must lie in man. But human feeling can only become rich and full when man thinks, does not evade experience but introduces it, looks reality in the face and clarifies it for himself so happily or so painfully and to such an extent that it cuts into his flesh and rouses feeling to the full. We do not see when we are screwing our eyes shut and holding fast to the images of someone else's memory – can that essential aid of the blind be recommended to anyone who is sighted! And equally, we do not feel when we are forcing our thoughts into worn ways – when we are artificially levelling reality. If we force ourselves down into dark underlying depths and keep ourselves from obeying the urge towards clearness which is inherent in all dim feelings, we shall be pulled down into the confusion that destroys us. And if, broken of the habit of the dark underlying depths, we hold to images which promise to rouse this more powerful feeling, be they of enchanted forest or pre-formed belief, we shall always be able to have only a pale after-sensation of these images. Feeling comes only from experience – dim feeling from unclear experience, and clear feeling from considered, identified experience. And the way of feeling leads from dimness to clarity. If we restrain ourselves from considering deeply, we shall hinder the development of feeling and deaden it.

To conclude these thoughts I cannot, by way of example, resist setting

down a perfect poem – one alien to my thoughts, so that preference shall
play no part in the choice – in a free form that does not too clearly reveal
my own thoughts concerning form – an unconventional poem from a world
of simple faith, again by Claudius. It is the poem of a believer and
strongly felt, yet how clear – and how fully thought out every one of his
thoughts is! The Christian tradition in which Claudius lived, and which is
what matters to him, could easily have provided images which would
have rendered any painful reflection superfluous, but he rejects them –
he does not take the easy way, and it is for this reason that he is able to
awaken our feelings also, through all the strange veiling externals. But let
the poem speak for itself.

> Der Säemann säet den Samen,
> Die Erd' empfängt ihn, und über ein kleines
> Keimet die Blume herauf.

> Du liebtest sie. Was auch dies Leben
> Sonst für Gewinn hat, war klein dir geachtet,
> Und sie entschlummerte dir.

> Was weinest du neben dem Grabe
> Und hebst die Hände zur Wolke des Todes
> Und der Verwesung empor?

> Wie Gras auf dem Felde sind Menschen
> Dahin, wie Blätter; nur wenige Tage
> Gehn wir verkleidet einher.

> Der Adler besuchet die Erde,
> Doch säumt nicht, schüttelt vom Flügel den Staub und
> Kehret zur Sonne zurück.

> [The sower sows the seed,
> earth receives it, and in a while
> the flower appears.

> You loved her. Whatever else this life
> has of profit, you esteemed it small,
> and she was taken from you.

> Why weep at the graveside
> and lift your hands to the cloud of death
> and decay?

Like grass upon the field are men
gone, as leaves; but a few days
do we walk disguised.

The eagle visits earth,
yet tarries not, shakes from its wings the dust and
returns to the sun.]

How firm and perfect the form becomes by virtue of this clarity in which thinking and feeling, image and sense are united. Form is probably not to be explained by means of the thought – this poem shows that much with final clarity. But form can also only be achieved when the thought is not curbed but carried through to a conclusion.

15 October 1939

Thinking of *the other Germany* one is forced to acknowledge with wonder and amazement the power that *the other Britain* has over people here. She may not have experienced the ups and downs which have cast the German mind this way and that, but she has withstood the test incomparably better as regards tradition-building.

Every day a tribunal sits in London before which all those objecting to military service on grounds of conscience have to appear. Where the conflict of conscience is a real one, approval is given for unarmed auxiliary service. But where it is merely a question of evasion, objection to military service is regarded as punishable.

At a recent hearing there was uproar. The objector was objecting even to serving in the Medical Corps. He was willing to help civilians but not soldiers because that would be performing military service. This stung the otherwise calm President of the Tribunal into exclaiming, 'If Christ were to appear today he would approve of this war – of that I am as sure as I am of sitting here.' The public, who were clearly present in strength, protested, the President cleared the court and adjourned the hearing, threatening in future to exclude the public completely.

But at the resumed hearing yesterday the President opened with an apology. He had, he said, at the end of a long and tiring day, permitted himself to be drawn into expressing his own opinion. The remark he had been led to make, had, under the circumstances, been ill advised.

In what other country could a scene like that have been enacted in the middle of a war?

16 October 1939

Good British tradition is also revealed in the fact that Chamberlain's speech is not simply being accepted. Generally people are pleased at his speaking out plainly and vigorously against Hitler and rejecting the shabby peace offer outright. But the absence of any clear statement as to war aims or of a *constructive peace-offensive* is regretted, and apparently widely.

Chamberlain's defenders counter that it is impossible now, at the beginning of unforeseeable events, to tie ourselves down to detailed objectives. Obviously at the word *peace* they are thinking in conventional fashion first and foremost of changes to the map, and from this point of view are no doubt right. They carry their point too, I am afraid, when they examine the deliberations of the Socialist Opposition speakers. Is it not shocking and grotesque how little they too are able to extricate themselves from old thought habits. They call for a world in which all nations can live peacefully together, and for disarmament – and above all, disarmament of the mind. The experiences of recent years seem to have passed them by completely and utterly. They still have not grasped that the existing ways to that goal have failed, and that the one and only thing that matters is to find new ways. Their utter helplessness is betrayed in their express mention in speeches of Schleicher and Fritsch as chief witnesses against present-day Germany – Schleicher, the inefficient grave-digger of the final republican governments, and Fritsch, the imperialist, who probably drew up the war-plan against Poland.

So is nothing left but the use of force? What would happen if through some upheaval in Germany there were today suddenly peace? The Socialists would have to admit that they had been wrong, and that the use of force had saved the world from war. And would not I also have to bow acknowledgement to that?

Of the Socialist speakers, only one, and he, characteristically, an outsider only recently received back into the Party after a lengthy period of expulsion, seems to know what is important. He is calling for an attempt at planning a new world order. That is at least a move in the right direction. Supposing, for instance, Britain were really now for the first time to draw up a programme for a new, viable League of Nations imposing far greater obligations on the nations than the present League, and above all, economic ones – but also offering great economic advantages? Will there then not be a real possibility of nipping any imminent attack in the bud by means of an effective economic and moral boycott? Against Nazi Germany there would have been, but today, following the turn of Russian politics, the certainty is less. But a League of Nations of this sort will still not be enough. It will have to be supported by a living idea, and its power will thereby be decisively increased also against Russia. For it will deprive American isolationists of all their means of propaganda – today they can still claim with a certain amount of justice that the war is not being fought for democracy at all. And above all, a clear expression of the idea, however imperfect to begin with, will be a weapon in the hands of the weaponless German people, and then perhaps something may come of the definite hope of their timely participation in the fight against Hitler.

No, I do not need to bow to force! If there were suddenly peace today the successors of Schleicher and Fritsch would have very likely to intervene, and what sort of a peace would that be? Quite apart from the improbability of that intervention as being bound up with a renunciation of conquests, would not the important thing in that case – and in that case specially – still be what was made of the peace? A sudden peace on that basis would be first and foremost a victory for Russia!

But if a feeling for the need for constructive peace proposals is already so general, if therefore the lack of the idea is already being painfully felt, how good its chances will then be if development and revitalization of the idea succeed!

17 October 1939

No, I cannot accept the use of force. Whatever its power, force, viewed from the idea, is simply weakness.

The seductive power of force is something I can understand only too well. It is difficult, while battling to clarify the idea, to hold out and not be diverted from the struggle by immediate exigencies and the very urgent demands of the day – difficult not to intervene prematurely and to the danger of the idea. But then how much more difficult it is bound to be still to go on waiting, imagining ourselves in possession of the idea, believing that we know how to help people and change and redeem everything, and being obliged to watch how mortally slow the idea is in asserting itself, how hard it is to propagate it by persuasion, and how much time goes uselessly and fatefully by, when the mature idea would be capable of helping at once and directly. It is here, waiting for the natural development and general effect of the idea, that faith is put to the crucial test.

Anyone who fights for the idea using force will have to demand suffering and sacrifice not only from himself but also from others, will have to sanction and require the killing of men, but to be able to bear this he will, in order to endure it at all, have to set an external end beyond man, but in so doing he becomes incapable of serving the idea, which can take root only in the human. He is forced to destroy in himself and in others the inner reality from which the idea can alone grow and through which it can alone become a reality. As a result the finished idea itself is deprived of its fostering soil and forced to transform itself into an external end, an external institution, leaving behind nothing any longer of its content. The noblest motives are unable to prevent this development having once resorted to the use of force. Material power over man is bound to destroy man and with him the idea. It is not the murderer who can become an example, but only he who is murdered. The murderer falls into the terrible hands of the living God, and in so doing renounces the possibility of the free act which is alone able to make the idea a reality.

Certainly, for service to the idea I have called also for rigour towards ourselves in order not to succumb to compassion. But this rigour means fellow suffering: it does not direct itself violently against the other man in order to make him subservient to an external end, but it does direct itself against itself for the sake of an internal end. It directs itself towards perfecting the idea – it is to make the idea capable of convincing men. And it is, above all, the act that calls only for the engagement of our own person – it is not until the act succeeds – not until a new reality is being created, that this reality can force men into its own essential path. He who resorts to the use of force for the sake of the idea may first of all demand of himself only that rigour which the idea as such demands, and this step will mean for him the greatest personal sacrifice, for who, when he is struggling for the idea, will be able with an easy heart to hazard human lives? Yet in reversing the priority appropriate to the idea, he succumbs to the use of force, and however admirable his motives or great his sacrifice, the rigour is directed no longer against himself but also against others – he will have to show them definite external ends, and as men are sacrificed for these ends, they are bound also to seem more important than the human sacrifices. The compulsion of an external reality becomes operative even before the act has created a reality in the sense of the idea. And as this external reality consists in the conditions of the struggle and the general and unalterable laws of any use of force, so laws and force are bound to overwhelm man also. And the more so as, through murder, he is at bottom renouncing his freedom.

102

But with that there sets in the enjoyable sense of power that is inevitably bound up with any use of force. Power over other men is one of the most potent pleasurable sensations of which man is capable. The intoxication of destruction is mingled with the elevating of one's own person. All disquiet concerning our own inadequacy can be silenced, all inferiority, all fear. What torments, harasses and pursues man is unloaded upon another, what man cannot deal with is deflected outwards, and if he destroys his opponent as well, the intoxication deadens the last nagging and gnawing doubts, at least for moments. But in a power apparatus everyone partakes of this enjoyment. He who gives the orders does so doubly, in power over subordinates and in the struggle against the enemy, but so does the subordinate also, for he is permitted not only to hate the enemy but also to scorn him as a representative of the idea. But this pleasure relentlessly completes what the use of force has begun. It is a sweet poison which permeates man and transforms him and gradually brings out the final destruction of all that is human in him, and as a result of it he becomes, deeply corrupted within, estranged from the idea he pretends to serve.

That is the vicious circle in which mankind seems inescapably caught. Again and again it seems necessary to carry the idea through by force in the face of superior strength, no other way any longer seeming possible. It is apparently for the very sake of the idea that we are obliged again and again to resort to force. But it is force which also again and again destroys the idea, making the use of fresh force and the destruction of fresh ideas a never-ending necessity. No sooner is a way out of this vicious circle discovered and a fresh idea found than the passionate obsession with it leads to the use of force, and at once the vicious circle is again complete.

Is there no escape from this seemingly eternal cycle? Christ alone has indicated it in preaching that we should love our enemies, and requiring that 'whosoever shall smite thee on thy right cheek, turn to him the other also'. He has made a reality of loving humility which is in fact the greatest power, the greatest force, which no man is ultimately able to resist. But who can still make it a reality?

Evening

Today's thoughts have brought me back to Tolstoy and Dostoyevsky. It is from Tolstoy that we have a clear understanding of the apparatus of power, and so his conclusion 'Do not resist evil by using force' suggests itself also. But this conclusion is a narrowing down. We are not to resist evil at all, either with or without the use of force. And force is also to be rejected in active service of the idea.

Dostoyevsky depicts the poisoning effect of power, and in this context makes a very important discovery. Arriving in prison he expects to find criminals and murderers shattered by remorse, and is deeply shaken to find them not, and even proudly boasting of their dreadful deeds. But is there, in that case, anything internally evil at all, and is there a human standard at all if the conscience can accept even murder? Agonizing doubts threaten to destroy any possible faith, but gradually he is forced to recognize that he has merely been constrained within too narrow a Christian tradition. Again and again he is filled with new happiness at discovering redeeming human features in even the most terrible criminals. In not one has the human quality withered completely. But the keener his eye becomes for humanity in even its strangest disfigurement, the more plainly does he recognize too that the inhuman deed manifests itself not in self-reproach or remorse but in the disfigurement of man. We may commit a murder, may sleep well afterwards, may even boast of what we have done without a qualm, but the influence of it is sure to transform us – we shall become different persons and the image of man in us will be besmirched and destroyed. The concept of conscience is too narrow. What is involved is the whole man, and there are many places for the destruction to begin. And gradually Dostoyevsky discovers also that the disfigurement of the warders is similar to that of the criminals. What all of them are poisoned by is the enjoyment of power, the intoxication of destroying a human life as much as the constant opportunity for exercising power over other men.

But in this he also finds a way for himself and for us, the way which makes the life of Christ – the perfection of which would otherwise be bound to oppress us – into an example. If we relied on conscience, the use of force could be justified – either by our being given a clear conscience by the idea, or by our accepting the struggle with conscience.

But it is not that which is important but the translating of the human quality into reality – we have to recognize the ideal image of man and accept it wholly into our feeling, in order to be able to strive towards it with all our strength. Knowledge and feeling will not perhaps be strong enough to bring us close to perfection, but that is not what matters. They are the only way that makes any sense at all, and we are given no choice. The supreme master of psychology demonstrates most comprehensively in his immense work that it is not the result that matters, or how far we get along this way. Any tiny step upon the way to the fulfilment of our own being will strengthen us in incalculable fashion, and for the very

104

reason that it is our most innate being that is involved. And it is all the less possible to direct ourselves externally according to effect. 'Everything is contiguous, – you touch the world at one spot and the echo comes from another.' The ramifications of effect are far too complicated to be taken in at a glance. We have no alternative but to orientate ourselves by the laws of our being. They are the one certain thing that can give us support.

This superseding of the concept of conscience is a very essential correction. Conscience seems to be a vague something that functions automatically. We may well be able to force ourselves to heed it, and we can by this constant heeding make it more acute, but we are obliged largely to rely on it, being able neither to create nor alter it. Man's nature also is something that is provided independently of us, yet by virtue of our recognizing it, our thinking is also assigned that place in the realm of ethics which is its due – it corresponds to the urge for clarity which is inherent in feeling, it does not refer back to the vague something. And it corresponds also to that strengthening which all innocence is bound to experience through knowledge – even the naive conscience is corruptible – even this innocence can only resist corruption with the aid of clear knowledge.

But this knowledge teaches Dostoyevsky and us that 'loving humility is a force, the strongest of all, and there is nothing to equal it in strength'. It has been proved by the example of Christ and by all who have followed his example. How can we then let ourselves be turned from this path by dubious reflections concerning effect, or by fear of our own imperfection? It is the only way of breaking the vicious circle – are we, contrary to our better knowledge, to remain in it? Also, to attempt to break out using our limited means will still always be better than to choose force, i.e. the means that is absolutely bound to destroy the end. It is not foreseeable how far even the smallest steps will be effective, but against that it is certain that force banishes us inevitably to the vicious circle.

18 October 1939

Now I can also add to an entry which I made at the beginning of this diary only with great hesitation. I described tyrannicide as the exception admitted by the commandment 'Thou shalt not kill', and so, exceptionally, as a justification of the use of force. That may in essence be correct, but we must make the meaning of that exception very clear to ourselves for it not to have a destructive effect.

Such a deed burdens him who performs it with the full gravity of murder, while at the same time seeming justified by implying an equally great sacrifice. For no tyrannicide will be able to count on saving his own life. But that sacrifice must not mislead us into regarding such an act as an example to be followed. It is still a dreadful thing in itself, an expression of despair justified only in extreme need and in very desperate situations. In such special situations it may mean deliverance and liberation, and so that sacrifice will have a very high value set upon it. Nevertheless it is not an example for our lives, it does not directly contribute to them, it merely removes one insurmountable barrier. Its elevation into an example would be bound to mislead into seeking the opportunity for such an act in any case, even where the compelling situation is not present. It would be bound also to reduce the gravity of the murder. Only too easily does the use of force creep into the realm of the idea.

Indeed, more. Such a deed is also only meaningful if genuinely ideal forces are pressing for development – if something positive is there that can in fact be liberated by the removal of the tyrant. That too determines the rarity of this situation. Premature tyrannicide remains murder, and may do incalculable harm, perhaps frightening off still-shaky adherents of the idea or putting the idea morally in the wrong. The sacrifice only becomes meaningful if it is made not out of hate but out of the superior strength of the positive.

This final qualification certainly seems almost superfluous. It seems that hate alone is really not sufficient for such a deed, and that what is needed is fanatical possession by the idea. For how else to explain the apparent absence of any serious assassination attempts against the present-day dictators? Here also is revealed the weakness of the idea. And so it again becomes apparent that tyrannicide cannot be demanded. By what, if not the idea, could it be justified?

So as not to be misunderstood, Schiller, in *Wilhelm Tell*, contrasts the true tyrannicide Tell with the parricide Parricida who has killed only out of hatred and personal interest. And in so doing he draws the necessary line very precisely – any egoism, however greatly it may coincide with the general desire, is bound to devalue so terrible a deed.

19 October 1939

Man is a tiny speck of dust lost in the infinity of space. As a result of which he is made constantly and most powerfully aware of his minuteness and helplessness. Even the earth is enormous compared to man, so big

106

that he is unable to perceive its curvature, and above it is the firmament of suns, moons and stars whose distance and size are wholly inconceivable. Astronomers have calculated both, but what do these imagination-surpassing figures say to us? They merely confirm our first naive impression, – that we are specks of dust overwhelmed by an infinity of worlds. Every glance at horizon or sky reminds us of this hourly.

Like any source of anxiety, this one also is transformed into a stimulus, and being ubiquitously and inescapably plain, acquires a crucial, generally effective power. Man must know and master this space before which he forever stands as an inferior, and must do so in order not to break. Here is one of the deepest roots of the heroic ideal – of its power which has been scarcely affected by the whole of human experience – heroism always is also a passion for conquest. Here is one of the roots of the desire for external effect – one of the usually unconscious sources of ambition and of the thirst for fame – even the effect upon people, even the fame that spreads through countries, is capable of conquering space.

But the size of the earth condemns this striving to failure. Even if Alexander or Napoleon had succeeded in conquering India, they would still not have been lords of the earth. The more they conquer, the more plainly does merely a new, larger part of the earth move into their field of vision, and their gain – though it be the whole of Europe – is small. They are driven inevitably on from deed to deed until the one which is bound to break them. And even *their* fame is not able to conquer space. Magnitude is the measure of space. Only the greatest fame is able finally to dominate the earth. It is also the desire for fame that drives them on so long until they break. Tragedy seems inevitable for all who join battle with space. The predominance, since the Renaissance, of external reality, the urge for knowledge, the power of invention and the passion for conquest have enabled a mastery of the space on earth hitherto quite inconceivable. The whole earth is, for the first time, known, almost everywhere habitable and dominated by the same civilization, and all of it has also been brought ever closer together by technology – distance having been almost totally devalued by plane and radio. The stimulus of space has here brought about a gigantic and undoubtedly non-tragic achievement. And yet this has altered nothing of the fundamental state of affairs either. This collective, more-or-less abstract mastery of space is not enough. The overwhelming magnitude of space acts as a further impulse to the greatest deed and the greatest possible conquest. The conquerors' successors are proof against this temptation, for direct experience of the superiority of space is effective upon those who have been obliged to endure it. But the effect is obviously not that of an example but merely that of a spur to spur others to the battle for world domination. And technology is, equally, no comfort. The possibility of conquering distances makes new plans for world conquest only still more *gigantic*.

Resolutely another section of humanity attempts a completely opposite path, that of forcing heaven down to earth by mysticism and ecstasy. Intensification of feeling to its highest degree has apparently the ability simply to eliminate space – simply to draw all things in heaven and upon earth directly into feeling – to permeate feeling and embody it. The ecstatic heightening of feeling produces the tangible and thereby per-ceptible mystical connection of all things with the infinite. All mystics, although also tied to finiteness, experience infinity in a wholly concrete fashion, whether by fancying to know the Beyond – God and his angels, hell and paradise – or by knowing about transmigration of souls, or merely believing to be in possession of the magic key which, given a supreme effort, will unlock the way to the unveiling of the secret. But even this conquering of space by excluding it does not stand firm against reality. It leads man away from life and makes him long for death. He wishes to look with his own eyes upon this glory he believes himself to be aware of. And also this manner of dealing with space means destruction of life. If there is nevertheless a collision with reality, even ecstasy will not be able to do justice to it. Ecstasy will either be broken upon the hard reality of things, leaving man behind, helpless, in real space, or will now all the more seek a violent solution in death.

This destruction of life admittedly has not a tragic but a mystic signifi-cance. This striving produces not heroes but martyrs, and the martyr does not perish, he is redeemed. His example appears the greater because he is willing to sacrifice his life, and because he does not first think of victory and domination and the use of force, but lays down his life for a belief and the absolute consistency of his life, and with them for a common ideal – not for the supreme act which is supposed to elevate the hero himself. And yet the martyr is not a valid example. It is no accident that we speak of the Christian martyrs without in so doing thinking of Christ himself. The death on the cross was not a martyr's death.

The death on the cross perfects an example. It becomes the fulfilment of death because it is the needful consequence of the fulfilment of life. The emphasis is upon life, and simply because this life has been so rich, this emphasis has been able to liberate even death from external necessity and transform it into an internal fulfilment. With the martyr, on the other hand, the emphasis is upon death. The paths of life are indicated by Christ or by another idea – what is validated is not the strength of the idea – but the disciple of the idea in paying even the highest price for it – that of his own life. With this, however, the martyr's death acquires a significance similar to that of tyrannicide – deliberate self-destruction is terrible too – *that* is not the meaning of this life; under certain circumstances when no other way of keeping faith with the idea any longer remains, it may be justified, but it must not be demanded. The martyr is of course worthy of admiration, and who can grudge him the very highest? Nevertheless it is wrong to elevate him into an example, for as a result, the terrible deed of self-destruction will seem desirable at any price – the weight of the special circumstances which can alone justify it, will again be lost. If the idea is strong, the sacrifice, if essential, will also be made. Ecstasy and mysticism which lead to martyrdom awaken a longing for death which is the absolute destruction of life.

Is there then no way of holding our own against space? Is the overwhelming superiority of it bound to drive us to our doom? There is a way, and I will give it first as described by Kant with unsurpassable clarity in one of his finest passages:

> Two things fill the mind with ever fresh admiration and awe the longer and more persistently they are pondered: the starry heaven above me and the moral law within me. The first commences from the place I occupy in the external world of the senses and extends the connection in which I stand, into the immeasurably vast with worlds upon worlds and systems of systems, and moreover into the infinite times of their periodic movement, their beginning and continuance. The second commences from my invisible self, my personality, and represents me in a world that has true infinitude. The first view, i.e. of an infinite host of worlds, destroys, as it were, my importance as an animal creature that must give back again to the planet (a mere dot in the universe), the material of which it was made, after being (one knows not how) provided for a time with living power. On the other hand, the second elevates my worth as an intelligence infinitely, by virtue of my personality in which the moral law reveals to me a life independent of animality and even of the whole world of the senses.

The significance of this quotation can perhaps best be made clear by visualizing the development of modern astronomy. When, at the end of

109

the Middle Ages, the infinite universe was discovered, and the earth transformed from the static centre of all things into an orbiting star, this new, inconceivable and impenetrable infinitude to which earth was delivered up, seemed to cut the ground from under man's feet. The propagation of this knowledge was resisted by the church with fire and sword, for it must, it seemed, render any faith or belief impossible. Yet the greater the familiarity with the laws of the stars' orbits and the more accurate the knowledge of the laws of the worlds in the universe, the less the dismay. Today's astronomer approaches his exploration of the universe unafraid and the rest of us are no longer aghast at his work. Thanks to our knowledge of the laws, we are aware that we are bound constantly to rediscover in any detail the laws of the whole, and that new discoveries must penetrate the inherent laws of the whole. We may still be unable to apprehend complete infinity, but we recognize its nature by the laws which can be apprehended by the aid of the details we are provided with.

But that is the very thing that matters. It is not possible to gain external mastery over space, and it remains impossible so to intensify our feeling that space becomes of no account. But on the other hand, we have been provided within with a reality to which also belong feeling and will to power, but which is not exhausted by them. Internal reality is infinite too, and we must recognize this infinity in order to be able to withstand external infinity. Yet here too mere recognition is not enough – as long as in thinking, willing and feeling we live, without any law, on the brink of this infinity, we remain helplessly at the mercy of it and of space, and shall constantly be letting ourselves be driven out of this internal, alarming infinity into either tragedy or ecstasy. But internal reality, every bit as inconceivable in origin and compass as the external cosmos, also reveals laws, the laws of morality and humanity, the sure and knowable moral laws upon which human nature rests. Knowing, heeding and following the moral laws enables us to become just as secure in this internal infinity, as knowledge of the mechanical laws does in the universe: through law we may live in harmony with the whole, even though not able to exhaust infinity. Through law we take possession of internal infinity, and it, as a result, is able to counterbalance external infinity.

Here too necessity turns the need.[8] The stars are kept in equilibrium and enabled to follow their orbits in accordance with law by gravity and centrifugal force. We must include ourselves in the equilibrium of external and internal infinity in the same way. Only when we live in lawful

8. See footnote 6, p. 79 above.

110

accord with internal infinity does the infinity of space no longer acquire that overwhelming weight which drives us out of ourselves and into the destruction of our lives. Only then are we able to concentrate on the infinite task of knowing and realizing our own laws, and thus on the possible and real task of our lives. Then, and only then, shall we surely and unswervingly run the course of our lives. In sight of the orbiting stars and unperturbed by them, the human speck of dust will also fulfil its – in the sense of the infinite – little life.

21 October 1939

The papers are slowly filling with casualty lists. Related to the armies engaged in battle, they are still very small, but can quantity be brought into it? Each individual death destroys one whole irretrievable life, destroys for him who is killed a whole universe – *the* whole universe, bringing what sorrow to family and friends! Imagine women, parents, children and friends poring over the casualty lists breathless with horror to see if *he* is there! Can we, at that, go on being glad about and for those who survive?

Evening

I have already described how a sense of the divine arises as a result of tension between extreme opposites. If clear consideration is given to what I have just written, tension is also produced of the kind that brings us close to this feeling.

Man is included in a process of development for which human life obviously possesses no value. Every step, however small, in this development process consumes and destroys an immense number of human lives. Nevertheless, for the individual this life is his most valuable possession. For him the whole of reality vanishes with its loss and the whole process of development collapses into nothing. It can therefore, although human lives are valueless to it, still not make up for the value of even one single human life.

If we attempt to dispose of this contradiction in logical fashion by means of a plausible explanation, the development process has to be shown to be necessary. The value of the individual life is suppressed. But nothing is gained by that – feeling is not able to follow even the most convincing proof – it is forced into tragic conflict. We can then, to satisfy man, also still represent the development process as the way to a higher order by

111

making it appear as either a means of redemption or of progress. Plausible proof will here scarcely be possible, but neither will it be missed because feeling is, to a higher degree, satisfied. But as realization of these comforting aims cannot be looked for until the next life, feeling will have simultaneously to be forcibly intensified to the point of ecstasy, in order to hold its own with death. The mystical content of that solution will be bound to emerge, and mysticism, even in that form, cannot do justice to life. Any solution of this contradiction leads to a destruction of life and is therefore unable to offset the dreadful experience of this destruction. It can only confirm it and often this confirmation may be a great relief, but equally often too it will fail as a sedative. In any case it does not do justice to the humanly positive idea which the fulfilment of life demands.

For I cannot believe that tragedy even in its mystically ecstatic inversion is the necessary form of human life. I believe tragedy to arise solely from a false conception of life, and to emphasize the tragic as something natural seems to me a gross misunderstanding and an evasion of the most pressing questions of life. Any life, properly lived, can find its meaning. And an idea is only humanly positive and only holds its own against internal reality when it leads to the fulfilment of life. That is shown even by tragedy itself. The tragic thing is that the hero – the one who is being broken by life – does not recognize the correct path he should have taken until his downfall and it is too late. If his downfall were absolutely necessary, and if the idea had only the task of facilitating and confirming it, this end would of course not be tragic but simply be only terrible or only meaningful. It is tragic because it points away from itself to another missed possibility. Here too we must not let ourselves be misled by the general levelling of language – this alone is the original sense of the concept of *tragic*. It can be tested against every one of Shakespeare's tragedies, and alone explains Goethe's dictum that he could not write a real tragedy because he would be bound to be destroyed by it himself.

There is in fact another possibility. If we do not attempt to dispose of the contradiction at all, if we think of our lives as simultaneously infinitely worthless and infinitely valuable, if we hold fast with all our might to both thoughts simultaneously, if we allow ourselves simultaneously to be depressed into meaningless nothingness and elevated into infinity by the moral world within us, then there arises that feeling which I have described as experience of the divine. Here too we must force ourselves squarely to face reality without any glossing over; to clarify for ourselves the extreme unbridgeable opposites – we must make no attempt at all to bridge them. Then it is, and then only, that we shall not be broken by reality, and shall experience its inexplicable divine core.

To attain to this feeling in face of the senseless horrors of war is especially difficult. Yet are not senseless, fearful horrors ever present? Is it not simply our deficient vision, our lack of imagination that make it easier for us? That war makes the horrors plainer must merely be the way of experiencing the positive opposite all the more plainly in suffering those horrors! That is what we must achieve – that is what matters!

We must not rush into intoxication, not even in its noblest forms, the pathos of tragedy or the ecstasy of mysticism. Intoxication, if it does not lead to destruction, is unfailingly followed by disenchantment. Experience of the sense of the divine is not an intoxication, does not speak louder than the horror which must be clearly faced – the horror is kept in balance only by the simultaneous and equally clear recognition of the positive. Extreme opposites produce extreme tension, and this tension is resolved because in an inexplicable way it reveals the whole. This whole is not to be brought to life by words of comfort – we cannot know it, we can only experience it.

We must not conceal the horrors from ourselves, or become dulled to them, but assail them unceasingly with all the power of the joyous feeling which morality and humanity, Christ and the idea are capable of granting – then we shall not break – quite the reverse – then we shall perfect ourselves and serve humanity. Only then will it be possible for death to be fulfilled just as much as life.

Certainly, that too is easy in theory and difficult in real life. But it is the only attempt that is worthwhile: can we let the difficulty of it deter us?

Night

Just another brief postscript to the problem of tragedy. Every tragedy comes to a resolving and releasing conclusion. But it is precisely that which shows that the tragic as such must not be affirmed for this conclusion is brought about by the error being recognized and by the indicating of a nontragic way. Hamlet, Richard III, Macbeth and King Lear either themselves know how they should have acted, or the spectator knows for them; and Romeo and Juliet, who are destroyed not by their own mistakes but by those of the world around them, by their own destruction make it directly possible for this false life to be overcome. The tragic, while being formed, is also being neutralized; form, which always penetrates deepest into the nature of life, shows affirmation of the tragic to be an absurdity. That is not a contradiction that is irremovable and that must therefore be thought out in its opposites, but simply a contradiction in itself that remains senseless. The tragic can only serve to make us attentive to the right path – flight into its pathos is as destructive an intoxication as any other. Pathetic feeling arises from the overcoming of an insurmountable distance, from the forcible suppression of an irresolvable contradiction – we must not suppress the contradiction or opposite, we must make ourselves aware of it. Satisfaction in pathos, the inevitable concomitant phenomenon of the heroic ideal, is again an absurdity – pathos is almost a sign that no satisfaction is possible – entering the realm of the pathetic we should in any case be careful not to rest content!

Affirmation of the tragic was possible only to a time that had surrendered completely to external reality. The predominance of the natural sciences led to an overrating of logic – the contradiction, the insoluble opposite being intolerable – anyone recognizing the tragic to be undoubtedly present, had also to affirm it. But that time is past. How can we do justice to our time, using logic alone? No less dangerous however is the reverse way, that of submerging ourselves in feeling intensified to the point of ecstasy, which is the profoundest National Socialist means of effect. We have only to compare the factually mystical racial theory with the mysticism of the Middle Ages to know where we get to on this road! The only way that remains to us is to face, undismayed, the irresolvable opposites which are what teach us to recognize clear thinking. Only then can real and productive feeling in the sense of the idea develop.

22 October 1939

For days the newspapers have been celebrating the signing of the Anglo-Turkish Agreement. It is a great success when one considers that Romania now really could be defended against Germany, and that this bolts an effective door against German Balkan, and Berlin–Baghdad plans. But at the same time the reports also reveal that Russia did not wish to promise to remain neutral in this war. Really this treaty ought to serve towards building a new bridge to Russia. Of course, we can now attack Russia also from the Black Sea and from the Turkish frontiers, and that is essentially better than that Turkey should throw herself into Russia's arms.

But this part of the success is not yet so certain – Turkey is not committed against Germany. *Successes,* time and time again, are measures aimed at Germany – and is that fighting against the main danger?

If we at least knew what the picture was in Germany! I can imagine that the constant and certainly prominently advertised U-boat successes, linked with the reassuring lull in the West, are working to the Nazis' liking psychologically. But I can also imagine that the surrender of the Baltic States and the imminent surrender of the Balkans is creating bad blood amongst the Nazis especially. For the time being all conjecture is mere fumbling.

I must, after all, also add a little to my thoughts of yesterday. The impression may be gained that it is just the difficult tasks that I am affirming, as if difficulty were a standard of judgement. But that is not the case! The most difficult of tasks can be wrong, the greatest of sacrifices can be senseless, while easy, joyous accomplishment can be right. Not everything need be difficult that has to be affirmed, and not everything need be rejected that is easy. It is always only the task itself that matters – *its* intention and *its* meaning.

Chance sends an appeal pamphlet fluttering into the house, 'In Christ's name, peace!' It calls for the laying down of arms, using all the Christian arguments. British Imperialism, the pamphlet claims, bears a share of the blame for National Socialism. We therefore have no right to fight. We must set the world an example and renounce sovereignty, even though a temporary loss of freedom and great suffering be involved.

I take it that this appeal is being distributed by Fascists, for it is anonymous. To call for peace in the name of Christ and then not vouch for it personally would seem all too blatant a contradiction. No church community would be likely to be behind that.

Yet even if it did emanate from a church and was signed, would it not show the correctness and importance of my statement that it is not at all our task to bother about war and peace but only to strive for the idea?! Can anyone today, without unchristian arrogance, make demands in the name of Christ? To make them of oneself is one thing, but to make them of the general public is quite another. Is it not arrogance today for any church to abrogate to itself the right to make such a call? For who has power to make such a peace even merely the starting point of a Christian peace?

Just one small thing – the appeal is printed very sumptuously on expensive paper. But all churches say the *Our Father* with its 'Give us this day our daily bread.' This request in so striking and prominent a position is a powerful underlining of the minimum social requirements the Bible so often stresses. But how then can they, with this ostentation, also be obviously appealing to the wealthy? Another argument against this appeal coming from any church body.

But it is of course sad and shaming that today, just when it wants to act in Christian fashion, the church should no longer be in the position to raise its voice for peace. It too must bear the consequences of the falsification of the idea to which it has so greatly contributed. There is no alternative but to strive for the idea with seeing eye and in spite of all immediate distress – to strive for its renewal and pure realization, and to leave it to the power of the idea and of our service to it how far it is able to be effective in war and peace.

More encouraging than the church point of view is the political. It is astonishing and a testimony to the strength of this Democracy that such an appeal can be printed and sent out. But here too we must not let ourselves be lulled by a sense of security which makes the task seem simpler than it really is.

The boards which refugees have to appear before to be interned, or freed from all restrictions, were very lenient to begin with. Recently they have ordered a few internments which are very difficult to understand. No one would have felt it to be an undue hardship if all refugees had been interned. Now when individual judgements are sometimes hard to understand, one cannot suppress a feeling of disappointment. It is, and remains, difficult within the framework of a gigantic state apparatus to make a correct selection. We can and must not rely on externals. We must know what we have to do and bear the consequences.

24 October 1939

Yes, but how about it? If what this appeal says is true, and to a large degree it is, must we then not stand by it absolutely? Is it not above all and under all circumstances the truth that matters?

I wanted to state this challenge when speaking of modern astronomy because it is there that the absolute rightness of standing by the truth has become plainest. The church tried to suppress the new knowledge in order to preserve man's faith. Yet it was the very change in the image of the world that also created the possibility of a renewal and deepening of the Christian faith. Scholasticism had traversed the realm of its productive possibilities, and after centuries of very great cultural achievements finally lost itself in highly abstract speculations no longer having any con-

116

nection with life. And in this way too it had abandoned this life – and even that of the church – to profound demoralization. Christianity would ultimately have been buried under the rubbish heap that remained. Christianity was then saved not by the church politicians allowing themselves to be guided by considerations concerning the benefit of every piece of knowledge, but by the reformers ruthlessly proclaiming the truth.

The absolute profession of truth seems to me to be the concrete form of that trust in the idea which I have always called for. We must entrust ourselves wholly and unconditionally to the truth even if it nails us to the cross, and seems to bring man nothing but disaster. Its effect is deeper and more far-reaching than we are able to grasp. We cannot know whither it is leading us and leading man. Here too what alone befits us is trust that does not inquire after effect.

That statement sounds so obvious, almost like a platitude. And am I now actually making qualifications? Am I not again proceeding towards that dangerous and seductive region where effect becomes the means of judging the action.

No! For this banal statement is in reality a very difficult demand which requires to be very accurately understood if it is not to mislead. The possession of truth tempts us to fanaticism – but standing by the truth non-fanatically is what is important. For fanaticism also causes us to persist in error, and for the sake of the truth we must remain non-fanatical so as to be able to separate it from error.

Certainly – and yet, and yet . . . Is love of humanity not more important than truth is? Are we entitled to go so far with proclaiming the truth as to injure or destroy whoever we are proclaiming it to? May not a merciful lie be more humane and moral than a merciless truth? Does not the demand for mercy limit the demand for truth?

This contradiction is perhaps not necessarily a contradiction. A truth can be dressed in different forms. We can proclaim it with superficial clumsiness, we can be self-important over it, and we can put ourselves in the background and emphasize that in it which is comforting. Naturally it is for us to choose that form which injures the other least and is the most merciful. But we have no right to withhold the truth from another! That would be merely a violation of respect for man, a lack of trust in him, a confusion of compassion and love of humanity. We have no right to prevent that painful collision with reality which may become profoundly determinative for the inner development of man. There are truths which it is impossible to put in a merciful form – the death of a loved one, for instance. We have no right to keep such a truth from another because by

117

so doing we lead him away from real life, so intervening in his life in a way we cannot be responsible for because it goes far beyond the possibilities of our own power of judgement. Certainly the truth can destroy man also, but it can conceal unsuspected sources of a deeper healing and a new development too. The compassionate lie, on the other hand, can only result in the truth's coming to light in a far crueller way. It also lacks that inner healing power that the truth can have. Love of humanity means above all respecting no man less than ourselves. But that means that we must not lie to him, and that in human relations also it is the truth that matters.

This simple answer is however inadequate. It does not do justice to reality. For usually it is not such a clear-cut case as with a death. Usually it is a question of abstract truths, and here everything can be very dangerously falsified if the desire for truth is understood with superficial absoluteness. Nowhere does vanity creep in more easily than in proclaiming the truth, and it is just here that that urge for self assertion is most easily activated which is nourished by our own weaknesses and inferiority complexes. Proclaiming the truth so easily makes us superior to others! We must demand that the truth be proclaimed in a form that removes from it everything hurtful that vanity might add, but with that even the lie comes into its own! For as long as we are not yet capable of giving the truth the form appropriate to it, a temporary lie can also be the way of keeping us from proclaiming it falsely. We have the right to withdraw from an encounter with reality when and for as long as we know that we are in no way equal to it, and we are entitled to flee if we know why, even if this form of flight is a white lie! It is not at all important that we should, with exaggerated frankness, find takers for all the half- and quarter-truths, or that we should submit to situations in which we cannot yet become certain of the truth, and which in fact we are not yet equal to – all that would merely be vanity, self-love and not love of truth. But all these qualifications are valid only for as long as we are not certain of the truth, whether through not yet properly knowing ourselves or being still too weak to comprehend it to its full extent. And they only remain justified if we employ them as means of striving after truth, and if, with the ardent desire and firm will also to stand wholly by the whole truth, we wrestle with the angel until he blesses us. The way to truth can be confused and unclear and full of unavoidable evasions, but always we must force the way in the direction of the truth afresh; and the truth itself, when we believe we possess it, can no longer be evaded, not even by the supreme means, that of compassion for people.

Perhaps therefore the demand for truth might be more accurately defined as of absolute validity for the will to truth and for the proclaiming of the whole truth, but not for the difficult way to truth. Here there is no absolute commandment and each must himself recognize as honestly as possible which way is capable of leading him to his goal, and it will be disastrous to demand the proclaiming of half- or uncertain truths under all circumstances. Before we can convert we must be certain of our own conviction. So long as we are forced to recognize that we are not certain of the truth, we have tasks quite other than that of dragging other men into our difficulties by proclaiming views bearing the stamp only of our overhaste or our vanity or our fanatical desire for truth.

But this answer too still seems to me inadequate. What has actually been the case with the natural sciences? Here again to begin with, everything seems very simple. It would be senseless to try to keep scientific discoveries secret for the sake of love of humanity – that seems quite certain to us today. Today, of course, when external reality has been so extensively explored, scientific discoveries hardly have far-reaching effects any more from the human point of view. Where inventions that can be directed against humans are concerned, it is more difficult. But even the aeroplane has been the realization of one of man's ancient dreams and has seemed destined to bind nations closer together. And even dynamite has helped to blast tunnels, remove obstacles and so make the earth an easier place to live in. Even in war most weapons are still as much a means of protection as of attack. It cannot therefore be demanded that discoveries should be kept secret, although there are perhaps special exceptions. But even these – the death-ray, for instance – have usually proved to be fairytales. The invention of poison gas even, was originally in the service of vermin control.

Here however another aspect of the problem arises, for here it is no longer a question of the truth at all. Galileo was a seeker after truth because to a super-powerful, one-sided knowledge of internal reality he opposed knowledge of external reality. Today science and technology are a rolling avalanche, a super-powerful half-truth. Anyone who subordinates himself to them cannot claim to be seeking truth – that would be nothing but presumption. No complicated historico-philosophical considerations are required to see that. The human ravages caused by the one-sided predominance of the natural sciences are all too plainly evident. Today it is no longer discoveries and inventions that are all important. The discoveries of natural science are getting more and more lost in the abstraction in which scholasticism lost itself. They no longer have any influence on our power

119

of imagination and therefore no longer any on our whole life either; nor are they searching for any truth, but simply applying artificially devised, self-contradictory arithmetical and geometrical theorems arbitrarily where most expedient and practical. Their influence on technology is all that still provides the connection with life. Where inventions are concerned, it is not the invention itself that is important but only the spirit in which it is used and developed. It is not the dead machine itself which is a curse or a blessing, but what man does with it and makes out of it.

This difficulty also emerges with the other example I have mentioned, the death, news of which has to be broken. We must not keep it secret, we can only, as a supreme aim, translate into reality that fellow suffering within us which may perhaps be able to help the other person. But deciding to do this is still not sufficient either. We are prompted to give aid, to sacrifice ourselves. We are obliged to make that distinction which I have already made here between help as a matter of course and help as an objective. In our fellow suffering we must not yield to compassion – we must remain alive to higher duties towards ourselves – we must not destroy our own internal reality.

That too therefore is a part of the truth: the truth must correspond to external and internal reality, for we humans have to recognize it, and we have been placed in both realities. Neither external knowledge that exempts us from self-examination, nor an internal truth like love of humanity, is sufficient without examination of their external and internal conditions. Our task is to concern ourselves not with effect but rather with assumptions in external and internal reality. We must determine where external knowledge neglects the human element that belongs inevitably to knowledge of truth. And in internal reality we must distinguish between self-seeking – i.e. chance, externally conditioned expressions of our nature – and its true common core in which truth can alone take root.

Today when external reality has been extensively explored, it will above all be a question of abstract truths, and for that very reason it is also quite especially important to know this true core of human nature. And for that reason part of the striving for truth is also an endeavour which, at the very first, seems especially hard – we have to know man to know what really accords with his nature. Ruthless psychology, deep and merciless soul analysis are an inevitable part of the struggle for truth. Revealing man's weaknesses can be cruel when bound up with contempt for man and exploited against him. On the other hand, with true striving after truth, this very endeavour arises from profoundest respect for man, and stands therefore in harmony with love of humanity. If we know about

120

internal reality, know that with it we are in possession of the true laws of humanity – we and every man – then we can and must also probe our imperfections and every man's, knowing of course that in so doing we are merely uncovering his more essential and more perfect core. The life of every human should be a battle waged by his perfect soul against his imperfect character. If we love man, we must help him take up this struggle and support him in it. But that is something we can only do if, without any false considerations, we seek to provide ourselves with an exact knowledge of the elements of this struggle. For truth is only whole if it corresponds wholly to the core of the internal reality. Any half-knowledge of this reality puts us in danger of opposing the external half-truths which dominate our world with equally inadequate and equally dangerous internal half-truths.

But that being so, if anyone dares today to demand peace in the name of Christ, I am entitled to recoil and ask *who* it is and whether he is inwardly authorized to demand it. It is not enough simply to quote a book however true – even the Holy Scriptures – for from any book we read only what we understand. But so long as we have not wholly experienced and profoundly understood Christ's example, we cannot speak in his name. The external repetition of Christian commandments is only half-truth. Here we run always the danger of understanding one section of his commandments and forgetting another because we do not understand it. We can, and may, only proclaim the truth if we have externally wholly comprehended and internally wholly experienced it. Not even the finest collection of Biblical passages can get around that!

The appeal is obviously merely a collection of Biblical passages – but *its* inadequacies quite apart, who can honestly say of himself today that he is entitled to speak in the name of Christ? My attempt at a superficial probing of truth has already revealed such a number of contradictions – the limited justification of the lie, the need for ruthless psychology, and the call for brotherly love nevertheless – but how very much more difficult are the contradictions that arise in the search for Christian truth. Do we – does any priest urging children to love their parents, and burying the dead – know what is the meaning of having to love your enemies but forsake father and mother, and leave the dead to bury their own dead? Profound psychology permeated with humanity may help us upon this road, but it is certain that we must break through the Christian convention that veils these contradictions. And can anyone say today in what manner Christ would make his demands today? Perhaps not by going into the market-place as I originally thought, but perhaps by walking unrec-

121

ognized through the land in order that men might learn what it is that matters, and in order that the sacrifice that must be demanded of them should be a meaningful sacrifice. But certainly to begin with, he would have chosen different words from those in the Bible, and employed Biblical passages rarely and only when, as a result of a new clarification, they would have become immediately intelligible.

The Christian preparedness which obviously exists in this country must not be abused, but first and foremost must be transformed into a living, unconventional Christian attitude. That alone is what we can in truth demand today.

Evening

The most difficult thing is really not the absolute challenge but the day-to-day demands of this life. There they are, those people with whom we have all the time to deal – nice, ready to help and fairly reasonable for as long as they can move within that domestic compass which is appropriate to them, and at once intolerable when, as so often in exile, they are obliged to step outside it. They have become so set in their accustomed life forms that they are open exclusively to external arguments and either have no notion of the real problems or furiously reject them, the most ridiculous externals still being to them of greater importance than simple human considerations. Now, for instance, they are so overwhelmed by British friendliness and the necessity of making their way here that they unfailingly think everything English good and everything German bad. They are simply reversing Nazi methods and basically doing precisely the same. There is no possibility here for those conversations which make the conflict of contradictory opinions between people of the same level so fruitful. The moment human problems are touched on there is nothing but misunderstanding, bickering and spitefulness. If we want to strive after truth with them, there is nothing for it but to quarrel with them.

I believe that there is only one possibility here – that of not taking the relative absolutely. Our task is to go our way towards truth as unswervingly as possible, and upon this way we have every right to escape, every right to withhold from others the truth we have discovered to date if we believe that by so doing we do justice to human demands which will lead us further upon this way. Only the truth, only the example matters. When it has been found and completed, then we have a right to say, 'He that hath ears to hear, let him hear.' Until then however our sole task is to toil and engage ourselves for the sake of truth and example, we must not offload the problem on to inessential details, must not let our view of the essential be distorted by the minor difficulties. If, in face of the relative demands of this life, we do not wish to endanger our own way to the truth, we must endure in the manner possible to us at the moment, and as well or as badly as we only can.

25 October 1939

We speak so surely of the truth, but *is* there an absolute truth, and do we know of a means of reliably recognizing it?

But no, enough, no further now! I must not let myself drift, otherwise I am bound to come to hasty conclusions. Let me instead go out and enjoy these last beautiful autumn days. Already the showers are becoming more frequent and removing the leaves from the trees! When I began this diary it was glorious summer weather. Soon autumn too will be over . . .

Outside I am enveloped in the full glory. Only a small garden but how luminous the trees in their yellow, brown and red, and how the now rarer and darker green stands out against them! And flaming and darting on the walls of the house the red leaves of the vine. And in all this bright colour there is nevertheless rest and peace.

Walk through the extensive gardens of the colleges. Here you realize even better than in the all too artful gardens of France why horticulture was once numbered amongst the arts. How they nestle against the old buildings, these gardens, enhancing their impression, and how liberating then the way out from the court onto the Backs – into free and yet restrained space! Perhaps too it is only in autumn that this beauty shows completely to advantage. In spring and summer when nature's urge is towards exuberance, its taming has a cramping effect. But in autumn when nature is growing weary, it is in the very melancholy of the Backs that nature's beauty first shows completely to advantage. In open country this beauty is easily dispersed, and in the woods we apprehend it only in prospect, from a distance. When we are in the woods it is hidden from us. On the Backs it receives its proper setting, every detail showing to advantage, and it is the spacious English gardens that bind these details into peaceful harmony. Here, on the threshold of death, the beauty of life becomes once again manifest, and for the first time wholly so.

But in the evening just walk back through the meadows. Slowly the mists are rising and the air is turning blue, a peculiar, dull, translucent blue, more corporeal than that of summer, known perhaps only to the few days of the transition of October into November. Day is slowly transformed into night, and in that brief span where light and dark are in uncertain balance, the world is veiled and yet transparent. Beauty is detached from objects, we hardly still see it, yet feel it all the more strongly.

At this hour we believe we have an immediate grasp of the mystery. But who can say what the solution is – who can say what beauty is?

27 October 1939

As I have not been able to get away from the ultimates, I have again interposed a break, thereby adapting myself to the peculiar course of this war. Since the overthrow of Poland war has been going on only in the secondary theatres, and above all at sea. The actual front is quiet.

In this lull British optimism is assuming a more convincing form. The conviction is almost general that Germany is already in a hopeless position and that time must work in Britain's favour. Germany's only possibility today would seem to be to attack the Maginot Line, either direct or through a neutral country, and either way would demand enormous sacrifices and be doomed to failure. Germany's embarrassment is shown too in her concentration on the sea war. But that cannot bring decisive success, for the counter-measures will, it seems, grow ever more effective, and to date the sea war has neither seriously damaged Britain nor eased the blockade of Germany. The best thing for Germany, relatively, would be to sit out at least the winter in order to improve the prospects for the offensive, but waiting would seem, for internal political reasons, to be what Germany can least afford. Because of which we must not under any circumstances acquiesce in any peace overtures. Peace seems to be the Nazis' only chance.

At the International Club recently we had a socialist lecture setting forth the basic features of a desirable peace. It was a fine Utopian picture – a federative Pan-Europe in which would reign peace and unity. Still, the speaker did not rest content with Utopia alone. Examining the forces available for the realization of this ideal, he found them to be four: the democratic forces in Britain, France and Germany, and the socialist state of Russia, thereby betraying how Utopian his thinking and that of his party was. His reason for building on Russia who, in the Baltic states, is already destroying the basis for such a Europe – to say nothing of her internal constitution which is fundamentally opposed to the realization of freedom – he did not substantiate. Nor did he reveal what prompted his hope that the democratic forces in Germany, which would be of primary importance in this, could be powerful enough to serve such a plan effectively. He failed to notice that no idealistic force is, for the time being, available by whose aid we can hope to move even moderately effectively against National Socialism, unless it be dictatorial Bolshevism! He may be right in saying that for the sake of such a glorious ideal it would be worth renouncing the power of the British Empire. But in view of such a complete inability to evaluate the real position, it can safely be assumed that the Socialists would renounce Britain's power to the detriment of mankind, even though there were still no certainty of serving the realization of Utopia thereby. Just as the Socialists' pacificism, laudable in itself, has helped the Nazis over their most difficult first years, so might this inability on the part of all Marxists to see what really matters, save the Nazis from destruction!

This Utopia is not at the moment dangerous, because the Socialists still recognize that Hitler has got to go, and are backing the government. But this pacifism may in time become dangerous, for while the Communists are only a tiny band, the Labour Party is large and capable of government.

The fearful mistakes made by the Conservative Party notwithstanding, it must be said that their supporters are the clearest thinkers. The left wing which has always condemned these mistakes, today of course has a greater influence also. Here ever more clearly awareness of the importance of establishing constructive peace aims even today seems to be making itself felt – discussion of them is becoming ever more urgent. But even more hesitancy is being shown than by the Socialists, for people remain aware that National Socialism can be driven back only by an equally powerful idea, and that this idea is lacking. Unfortunately though there is also a hesitancy to draw at least the simplest conclusions from democracy's ideas – in social respects and in India – any step in the right direction could make an incalculable contribution to greater clarity!

28 October 1939

In the old Czechoslovakia today, the twenty-first birthday of the Republic, would have been a red-letter day. It is not a red-letter day anywhere anymore. It is probably not even an important date, but merely a sad one.

For the British are hesitant to promise the restoration of the old Czechoslovakia. This is probably not in order to keep open a possibility of retreat for themselves – they honestly do want to rid the Czechs of Hitler – but they do not want to be in a hurry to encumber the new Europe that will have to be created, with national states. Maybe we can, after all, build a Pan-Europe – maybe other moves will follow. There is at all events time to consider these subsidiary questions.

The Czechs have as yet found no way to do justice to this mood. Beneš speaks of Pan-Europe, and who can doubt that this most active of League of Nations Presidents is honest in his intentions. But he speaks too of restoring the old Czechoslovakia unchanged, and apparently he is trying too for a union with Poland and attempting to work towards a grand Czech–Polish State. It is possible that these plans offer better prospects than Pan-Europe. But for the time being, the notion of the sacrifices of the war being made only to facilitate a superficial re-ordering of Europe that harbours the germs of new wars, is not a pleasant one for the British and probably others as well.

The Czechs are an amiable and unhappy people. Interspersed amongst, and saturated by, Germans, they occupy no area that would admit of the formation of a natural state. As a result of centuries of suppression over-large sections of the people have been forced to emigrate. As a result of their being constantly suppressed by reactionary powers their struggle for national freedom, in Hus's time just as in Masaryk's, has been bound up with the struggle for a progressive idea, and this has created a very good tradition, allowing the spirit of democracy to become deeply rooted. (The ruling and wealthy classes having always been German is a reason also.) Nevertheless, it has never been possible to divorce the idea from nationalism. The nation has lived, and lives, hemmed in by an alien people. Reaction has therefore been overstrong and has won before the idea has been able to assert itself. It has taken the form of national suppression, and so again and again nationalism has been strengthened. And so the Czechs, more than any other people, are dependent on Pan-Europe and are in theory honestly ready for it also. But the new suppression must create a national high-tension that will almost block the road to this goal. From this experience they will be bound to make demands that will only with difficulty be reconcilable with the idea of a federative Europe.

Characteristic too is the attitude towards Poland. Poland has always been a feudal, reactionary state, but out of kindred feeling, and always only in the face of pressing danger, the Czechs have brought themselves to accept that and seek support. The Poles, in their slightly more protected situation, have then been not yet so directly threatened by the danger, and negotiations have failed, last year just as much at the time of the Hussites. Today, when both states are exposed to the same danger, is there any prospect of this age-old plan being realized? Of is it past the time for plans of that sort?

Evening

I cannot stop thinking about the Czechs. Memories come back making many things appear differently from the way they have appeared to me over the past years.

I was brought up a German but at the front became a supporter of the Czech Party. Contact with the healthy world of democratic thought came as a deliverance in view of the ultimately German and reactionary Austria being concocted by German Nationalism. With the Czechs I was dreaming of other objectives – real democracy, separation of church and state, land reform, social reform – those were the things we had in mind.

On 28 October 1918 I was in Prague, happily taking off the old Austrian uniform never to don it again. And my admiration for the Czech Revolution was total. Of our leaders, the First Guard – Masaryk and Beneš – was in Paris. The Second was just attending a sitting of the Reichstag in Vienna. It was only the Third Guard we had in Prague, and yet everything went off perfectly. Not a shot was fired, not a drop of blood was shed, and the very evening of the day of the overthrow which had begun at about noon, the new Czech police were patrolling the streets to keep order.

But by the third day I felt sad and lonely as I wandered through the crowds still filling the streets. For that was when the revolution began to change. Feeling was no longer against the Double Eagle but against anything written up in German, and it was dangerous to speak German in the street. The revolution had suddenly become nationalistic.

That was not the revolution we had been looking forward to! We were not going to repeat the old Austrian mistakes. In this state, the peoples now jumbled up together were all to live freely and in harmony – it was a question of different, human aims! A little later I was furious that the Sudeten Germans should make their proclamation of independence from Vienna, instead of accepting battle in Czechoslovakia and forcing that country not to stand by what had been promised – for as yet nothing had been – but to do justice to the hopes pinned on it.

Then, as the years went by, many things changed. Masaryk and Beneš came back and worked in the sense of the original intentions, even though no longer able to carry them through completely. Many reforms, such as

127

the land reform, did get carried out although, it is true, with practical shortcomings, but could anyone hold that against a country? And then when the German Republic did so badly, and Czechoslovakia withstood the onslaught of Fascism almost without compromise, the only country in Central Europe to do so, when, as the only genuine popular Democracy east of France, she stood the test in the teeth of immense difficulties, then, I think, everyone was ready to retract all previous reproaches and again give way to that admiration which I had felt on the first day of the Republic.

But was that right? The wounds inflicted by nationalism festered on and proved mortal! This was no Switzerland with an inner, supernational power of resistance to oppose to this onslaught. Certainly in the brief span of twenty years that was not something that could be justly demanded of them either. The blame for the collapse falls first and foremost on those Germans who were so nationalistic as to prefer even this terrible Third Reich to the free and healthy Czechoslovak Republic. And yet, all realistic scruples notwithstanding, the original impression immediately after the last war was the more correct one! Probably the attempt to create a Swiss constitution would not have brought many practical alterations to the course of events, but the position of the Czechs here and now would be different. There may be great understanding for that position – but the grievances of the Sudeten Germans are having their after-effect nevertheless. Generally, people are probably pro Czech, but not for some time so generally for the old Czechoslovakia. And as, minus the German borderlands, a Czech State is not viable, great difficulties may still result.

What can be the picture today in Prague? The Czechs are sure to be as firm as ever, sustained by great hope. But what will be the effect if this hope is disappointed, at least partially, for a second time?

29 October 1939

Perhaps, in spite of my aversion, I ought to think more often of my war experiences. Many last-war situations will be repeated – it can only be good to face them with last-war experience.

War forces man to think of what is essential by confronting him more immediately with death than life does at other times, it being more difficult in the face of death to be satisfied with superficial thoughts. At the front I found in the simplest men a readiness for good that was wholly new to them. It was as a result of this of course that in the last war the

128

hope grew that the war would usher in better times. Has it been justified – is it possible to affirm war at least in this fashion?

That hope has proved false because the ravages of the war, in the world and in man, strike much too deep, and because man too readily abandons himself to fatal violence. The revolver is ready to hand – murder is an all too easy, all too simple, argument.

But that still says nothing against the thoughts which have come or which can come in war. The encounter with death causes man to gaze into depths which at other times he is not able to look into – and those thoughts remain right, even if at the same time war seduces us into selecting the wrong means. Subsequent years and the relative claims of life have effaced many of these thoughts. But it is by the very aid of this experience that it must be possible to separate the right substance of these thoughts from the wrong means. And it would seem good to make this separation to prevent the right from becoming again hopelessly mixed with the wrong.

But in case anyone should ever read this diary let a warning be at once attached. Expect nothing of *the spirit of the front* – of the community of the front-line troops which Hitler and Daladier are so fond of talking about, and which seems to have its devotees here in Britain. I said *we* just now, but not in the sense of any subsequent association of front-line veterans. Those with clear ideas of the state they wanted to create, later – and usually much later – adapted themselves to political parties and practical life. It is those very people who are unable to deal with life who far more often are to be found in veteran associations.

Of those who have been genuinely involved in war, most return infinitely weary. The one thing they long for is a bit of quiet life, and it is not until years later that they find their way back into public employment. The ones who are quick about it are the superficial who are incapable of experiencing anything, even at the front. Indeed, of those who shout loudest hardly any have actual experience of the front. This modern, mechanized war, it must be remembered, calls for a very large rear – also, in static warfare, one need not be engaged for weeks on end. Many who moved up to the front with me were slightly wounded on our very first march, when we were still well back. They did not rejoin us until there was a lull, and before the next fighting, had, through some coincidence, disappeared, having been detailed off somewhere else, where again they experienced nothing. They spent almost as long at the front as I, but without knowing what the front is. On the other hand, of those who really were on the battlefield, a dreadfully high percentage were killed. Once, out of 236 of us, only twenty-five got back, and of those missing, almost all were killed. Of those who really were in hell, the war machine lets very few return.

The weariness may of course also express itself in great fear of hostile life, and of being again responsible for oneself – and these men seek to prolong the war by becoming mercenaries and joining the Spartacus or the Free Corps groups where the war is still going on. But these disturbed men are completely incapable of embodying any fruitful spirit of the front. And a similar disappointment with peace drives men, the weary ones included, into the front-line veterans' associations – they are unable to experience anything in peace, and the lives they shape on their own responsibility are not able to offer them enough. They are obliged to cling to their war experiences, and therefore they escape back into the comradeship of the front.

There is however one remarkable thing about this much-vaunted front-line comradeship. My own experience and that of all my friends is that the apparent friendships of the front have not endured the peace, and I have been forced to conclude that it is exceptional for them to do so. The unnatural living conditions weld men together in an unnatural fashion. The external threat of death forces the minds and feelings of all into the same path thereby making them comrades without their true personalities being expressed. This is shown when those conditions are removed – one no longer has anything to say, one laboriously reconstructs the old situation, often even hostile feelings appear which have merely been suppressed, and mostly towards those one seemed on closer terms with. It is here perhaps that those strange words 'Nibelung loyalty' are really appropriate, for one's behaviour is Nibelung-like. All of them hate Hagen and their relations with each other are dubious too, but in the face of death they maintain their loyalty. And this last gleam of human quality is in this extreme situation a great comfort also.

But friendship, genuine community, can come about only through community of mind or of feeling. Anyone who really returns to life and knows how to make something of his life is sure to prefer to avoid his comrades of the front – with certain exceptions, although here too the friendship will have to be built up again from scratch; and this because they remind him of that comradeship in which he was not himself, and in which mind and feelings were subject to extreme constraint. From a human point of view the comradeship of the front is a fundamentally unworthy one because there has been no original relationship to occasion

130

it, danger having been required to bring men closer together and they having acquiesced in that, either because war has suppressed human feeling or because men have set it aside solely in order to partake of this last comfort.

It is therefore probably to be expected that the thoughts produced by war will be fruitful, and also that people from the war will, in a long and painful process of development, find their way in a fruitful fashion back to life and then be able to give these thoughts expression.

But what cannot be expected is that they should found a veterans' association that represents these thoughts! True human community is founded upon positive human qualities and positive objectives, not upon the negative experience of danger jointly suffered. It is for that reason that it cannot be attached to front-line veterans who, from a human point of view, have become closer in hardly any way, and who have had no common aim other than war. When this negative external feature is made the bond of a community, it may be taken with certainty that the true meaning of community has not been understood, and for that reason no positive contribution to the reorganization of life can be expected from such an association either, but at most a reinforcing of those obvious assumptions, nationalism and heroism, which, as aims, become so dangerous.

30 October 1939

Do I in this diary have again and again to start afresh? But maybe that is precisely to the good. Variations make all the possibilities of a theme, its substance and its meaning especially clear.

Yesterday I was also at a meeting of the Society of Friends, the Quakers. I was particularly receptive yesterday to the stressing of friendship, and the subject of the lecture, 'Constructive Peace, an Alternative to War', raised my expectations very considerably.

The speaker began by establishing in detail the absolute incompatibility of war with the Gospel. The Society of Friends had become necessary because of the church's falling away from this truth. He then found a very convincing transition to the work of the Quakers. There could be no hope of creating concord between nations as long as social injustice reigned, and as long as the closest neighbours did not know how to live in peace. It was for this very reason that the Quakers were trying to make this human quality a reality by stepping in with aid wherever people were in distress. He went on to describe this relief work in the last war, and after

131

it, in Germany, Austria and Russia, and later in Spain and China, and now again – for the refugees. He quoted figures which are really overwhelming when you consider how small the Quaker membership is. And anyone who has seen the Quakers' work in Germany and in Vienna and Prague will remember it with deepest gratitude.

Frequently in the course of this lecture ideas occurred which have already been expressed here. Conscientious objection was not so simple in Britain in the last war as it today appears, and although objectors in many cases met with sympathy, of some 1,540, over 800 were imprisoned, and not in easy conditions – seventy-one died there. Some who declared themselves only when *en route* for France, were shot. And no one should be deceived, the speaker said, by the lenient treatment of conscientious objectors today – the longer this war lasted the severer would that treatment become this time also. This act was therefore meaningless if it sprang only from fear, and justified only if one was courageously prepared to bear all the consequences. In the last war, of the 1,400 to 1,500 British Quakers, only 540 had refused military service – no reproach was levelled at the others. Each should do only what he sincerely recognized as possible for him – if he were pro the war, then it was more courageous and sincere to fight than to seek personal safety behind a pacifism that he would in that case discredit. If however he was convinced that he was not permitted to fight then he must declare as much and not think of the possible or impossible effects. What was certain was that war must, and would, be overcome just as slavery had been. The supreme task was still to be a proclaimer and pioneer of this future.

Nevertheless it was a lecture that left me very dissatisfied. It is terribly difficult to stand there alone, with similar thoughts, and not be able to attach oneself to the existing pacifism in any way.

For what was the title of the lecture? 'Constructive Peace'! But are aid and conscientious objection enough to contribute towards such a peace? Are not vastly more positive ideas a part of it? Certainly Christianity contains these ideas but are the Quakers striving to make them accessible to our time and translate them for modern man? No, that is the very thing they are not doing, believing already with their conscientious objection and rendering of aid to have seen the whole truth.

The speaker himself stressed that the roots of war lay in social injustice. But is it enough to counter these injustices with charity, albeit in the best sense? No! For charity is always able only to alleviate injustice, not to counter it. Justice can be created only by the idea. But this idea is not made manifest by the example of the Quakers – their work, however they

132

may apply their money, confirms the distinction between rich and poor.

Fundamentally they are doing what even Tolstoy did, and what everyone who relies upon one particular of the Gospel is bound to do – they are resisting evil. Possession of one such single truth which, if stressed exclusively, becomes a half-truth, is not sufficient to supply a comprehensive example that can express itself completely in positive activity – and so we are compelled to become positively and negatively active. One particular does not do justice to reality – and so there can be no reliance on its natural growth, or on its creating a reality, room has got to be made for it by battling against other parts of reality. Every inadequate realization of Christianity is recognizable by its very failure strictly to obey the commandment 'Resist not evil.'

This very commandment it is which cannot be construed absolutely enough. Otherwise a crucial passage in the Gospel will remain completely incomprehensible. When Christ stands before Pilate the crucial charge is 'Are you the King of the Jews?' It *seems* so easy to refute. Christ will apparently not have to resist evil at all in doing so, but merely say what the fact is. But no. He answers 'You say it.' And with that he grants the main weight of this charge which is specially emphasized in the inscription above the cross: 'This is Jesus the King of the Jews.' Does that not show with overwhelming clarity that we are here at the very heart of Christianity – that it is this very charge that must not in any way be qualified? It is this very answer that clears the way upon which Christ completes his example!

31 October 1939

Opening the paper today I was shocked. The Government is publishing a collection of authentic reports concerning the horrors in the concentration camps, which are supposed to prove that methods have not changed in the last two years. And this together with the detailed explanatory statement that they had not been published earlier because it would have been wrong to destroy any possibility of reaching an agreement with the Nazis.

Yes, but can't it see what it is doing – not merely confirming the falseness of this policy but its hypocrisy, indeed criminality?! It was the suppressing of human indignation that was to blame for the wretched policy which led to Munich and to war, on top of which is now being proclaimed that that faith in the honesty of the German Government which the British Government had always used as a pretext, was not even genuine. For with criminals of whose crimes it had precise knowledge, how could it honestly hope to come to anything short of a criminal agreement? The publication consists of Embassy and Consulate reports containing scrupulously verified facts, and has been available to the British Government for the past two years!

The final sentence of the explanatory statement sounds somewhat more conciliatory. The Government was reluctant to publish, even in war, in order not to arouse feelings of hatred, and was only doing so now because it had been forced to by German propaganda. But why then cannot it also say – and it might still excuse the Government a little if it did! – that it had acted wrongly in withholding these reports from the press for so long and thereby leaving the people to believe the *horror propaganda* to be exaggerated as the Germans had always asserted. The explanatory statement shows that the Government obviously still has no inkling even today of what it has brought about by its anti-idea, idea-less attitude, and that it does not, and cannot, grasp what really matters, and will matter for the future too.

Obviously we must not yield to any illusions.

1 November 1939

But reading Molotov's speech one has to take back all one's reproaches against Britain. The British are being accused of waging an imperialistic war. Germany, on the other hand, who has attacked and pocketed Poland and is demanding colonies and other dominions, is merely contributing to peace. After all, it would be wrong to fight a war for the sake of an ideology – the Russians obviously no longer have anything to take exception to in the Nazi system. But Russia is the innocent lamb of course. All she wants is to preserve peace – and if Finland won't give way, and apparently Turkey too, then *they* are to blame for any failure there may be to preserve peace.

No practical change is introduced by this speech. It is perhaps more Germanophile than expected – British Socialists will find it harder to build on Russia. All the same, it makes no promise of war aid to the Germans, and regarding the future, all possibilities are left open – those of unpleasant surprises remaining entirely with Russia, the time for unpleasant surprises having apparently not yet come.

All the more illuminating is how closely the capacity of the Russians for saying exactly the opposite of what yesterday they were declaring to be absolute truth, approaches that of the Nazis, right down to individual

134

turns of phrase. Can anyone – apart from the Communists – really still refuse to believe that there is a very precise correspondence between the German–Russian façade and that community of ideas which has to be fought?

On the same day, in the British Parliament, special provisions restricting the liberty of the individual and freedom of expression are being defeated. These provisions come nowhere near those long since in force in all European countries, but the Government gave way to the opposition even though it could have secured a majority. It is a great shame that people cannot all the same simply say yes here also – and to this Britain also!

2 November 1939

The association of Tolstoy and Quakers brings to my attention a feature that perhaps does not always apply, and above all not for every follower of Quaker teaching, but that surely applies to the teaching itself, and is very instructive. It is that both are, to a high degree, suspicious of art.

Certainly Tolstoy was one of the greatest artists, but after turning to Christianity, he abjured art and persecuted it with most intense hatred. A more anti-art, a more uncomprehending criticism of Shakespeare than Tolstoy's has assuredly never been penned – and Tolstoy's late works were written in secret, with a bad conscience and against their author's conviction. His representation of the Gospels eliminates the figure of Christ completely, replacing it with colourless, clear-cut dogmas. And similarly in the Quakers' teaching there is also to be found no artistic element – the figure of Christ receives recognition certainly, but emphasis is again on definite dogmas, on an intellectually unambiguous teaching and not on experience of the example.

But it can be no coincidence that the Gospel should itself be also an artistic experience – that it should bring a character to life in a thoroughly artistic fashion, and over and above that rely upon another very perfect art form – the parable.

Do I still need to explain why that is so? Any intellectually unambiguous line of thought fails to do justice to life, life being never ever unambiguous. Only when we experience opposites – become fearlessly conscious of the contradictions to which our limited capacity for knowledge unfailingly leads – only then do we approach this life at all closely in essentials. That is mostly so in everyday life – it holds good absolutely for everything directly affecting the human – it holds good absolutely for the sense of the divine.

But the difficulty is to combine these living opposites into intellectual form, that is, to render their homogeneity accessible to the intellect without that intellect, whose striving is towards unambiguity, simultaneously resolving the opposites. This difficulty is overcome solely by means of form. Form is not tied to art form alone, as will become clear when, as soon I really must, I explain form more precisely – the Gospel not being an art work either of course. It is only today, when so many sources of life seem exhausted, that the art form is the clearest embodiment of that intellectual form. And for that reason we are entitled to place very great emphasis upon artistic experiencing and shaping, because form always contains that element which we are accustomed to describe as artistic – that ambiguity which arises precisely by virtue of the simultaneous, interconnected visualizing of opposites – that appeal to experience which arises from the intergrowth of irresolvable contradictions. Form stands forever in opposition to any clear-cut thought, to any unilaterally determined feeling: it creates an intellectually inexplicable unity that does justice to our whole life, and thus in a comprehensive way to external and internal reality. I shall later show ways of striving for this form – but all of them are merely the auxiliary means of an act of creation, mysterious in itself, that cannot be translated into words. Form results from the complete engagement of our lives, and we have to re-experience it in order to grasp its content – yet it is by that very means that it does justice to life.

Is it not our constant experience that understanding is best achieved with artistically gifted people or those able to re-experience artistically? They more than anyone are prepared to let opposites persist, and possess as a result the necessary receptivity and sensitivity for the imponderables of this life which really constitute human life. They remain open to man himself, whose nature is to be comprehended from a position of no rigidity. Man is himself a creation – and form is the sole image of that creation.

A man is born – however much we may know of all the natural laws that seem to explain this birth, we are ultimately, with these laws, merely laboriously probing the surface of the event. Why man lives, how he came into being at all, what led to the marvellous forming of organs, mind, heart and soul, and how this *man* became what he is – however factual we may be about it, there is, beneath the thin outer skin of the laws, a miracle before which we must bow. And which we perhaps, if granted success, can repeat in creating form. This repetition is a tiny thing against

136

the miracle of birth – to which of course it is also solely due – and yet one which can, if successful, be greater than man himself, outlasting its author, generation and times.

A man *has* been born. Here the day before yesterday, amongst us, the child of friends of ours. Let us bow before the miracle that even in war attests the power of life, that ensures the triumph of life in defiance of all the death. Here alone is the true miracle. Let us not be confused by the miraculous deeds which usually are the only ones cited as miracles – they merely conceal the genuine ones which are more mysterious than any magic – they merely diminish the miracle ever present to us in each breath and heart beat, in each glance out of the window at trees and sky, in each look at the light and at ourselves – that miracle which becomes palpable in every birth. False miracles, by teaching us to wait for the exception make us forget the ever-present miracle of miracles – that of life.

The important thing is for us to be aware of the genuine miracle – for breaches in the laws of nature which we can never expect for ourselves, only depress us. Against which, the true miracle elevates us, for we are not excluded from it – it is alive within us, and this life we are able to record in enduring forms by means of our minds. In form we are provided with our second weapon for overcoming death, and it is one which is not restricted to artistic talent alone. The forming of our thoughts and feelings, the forming of our lives, can also create a complete and enduring example! If, in this world dominated by life-destroying thoughts and forces, we live a vital life devoted to its human meaning, forming our thoughts and feelings, everyday life, marriage, calling, in the sense of this vital life, then too we create a form capable of working on unforeseeably and ensuring the triumph of human life in defiance of all war and destruction. Children must not just *arrive* – we must also be preserving for them a life that shows how this life can be lived in a manner worth living and worthy of man!

The important thing is for every flood to be survived by one righteous man bearing witness to God. For this, those works of art which bear, and will continue to bear, witness to all the civilizations that have perished, are not sufficient – rather must this testimony be borne by that living spirit which is as comprehensive as that which today finds clearest expression in art.

3 November 1939

Still, American arms shipments to the Western Powers now seem certain to be made possible. There has, it is true, been a substantial minority against this, but the argument that the Democracies have got to be helped seems to be making most impression. Is there the hope that democracy will yet see its way to acquiring force and substance? The reports from America do not supply much food for it – yet this first approach may be important for both parties nevertheless, and thus for democracy itself, and not only in a practical way.

Talking to visitors from London, I have been strangely disquieted to hear that a Russian invasion of Finland is expected, indeed, with even a threat to Sweden, and yet there is still a readiness to explain Russia's attitude as a threat to Germany. Of course it was admitted that Britain was bound to take this attitude, being desirous of winning the war and having therefore to keep invincible Russia in a state of neutrality. My idealistic objection to this attitude and the encouragement it offers to Russia was brushed aside. But is it not a very grave thing nevertheless? Will Britain's claim to be fighting for democracy still retain its force if she sacrifices the Scandinavian Democracies simply because she has given them no guarantees? War with Russia is certainly not an attractive proposition. But it is highly likely that Stalin is afraid of war. And that very war, grievous as it might seem, would perhaps bring about the collapse of the dictators which so far has been hoped for in vain. For what is bound to be the effect of bringing great numbers of this nation which for twenty-five years has been cut off from the outside world, suddenly into contact with the outside world again? Stalin knows why he has made this isolation almost impenetrable!

The British are very generous – employing a great many Germans in important positions in Ministries. All the same, even in Britain, nationalism is still operative to such an extent that no positive advice can be given in crucial matters because it would simply be impertinent. Certainly one's own house is something that one can only put in order oneself – from the inside. But is advice interference? Do those in power not listen merely because they do not want to, and lack the strength and the idea voluntarily to take that crucial step? But because of all this, all those dangers arise which we would be so glad to see kept away from Britain. Some kind of social new order is bound to come – social injustices and distinctions being greater here than in other countries – and if the idea remains impotent the new order will be enforced by means of the most terrible violence.

Ah, if the British could bring it off where the others have failed! The atmosphere in this country is so beneficial. The most important of the German politicians amongst the refugees have now been gathered to- gether into a committee that is supposed to make plans for the reshaping of Germany. That is bound of course to serve Britain's war aims also, but only because they are for securing not new dominion but a free Europe – and beyond that, concern for the German people is really genuine – hos- tility is perhaps concentrating too much only on Hitler – there is honest concern for the German people. But how do things stand with the British people?

7 November 1939

The word *people* is another of those dangerous concepts which are any- thing but precise and therefore a source of confusion. Today it has obviously two different meanings. Firstly, the totality of those speaking one language – the English, German, French *people*. And then it stands for the seemingly still more homogeneous, *more popular* lower and mid- dle classes of every people in contrast to their upper class – the simple, the poor, the great anonymous mass.

The splitting of the concept simultaneously reveals the prevailing con- fusion. Earlier, under absolute, divine-right rulers, *state* and *people* had been clear opposites. The *state* might embrace many *peoples,* and a *peo- ple* might be broken up into many *states*. The *state* did not serve the *people*. The *people* were employed for the ruler's purposes with which they had nothing directly to do. The Habsburgs ruled Spain, the House of Anjou – Sicily. The eternal wars of succession were no business of the *people's*. The *people* was a homogeneous concept – the upper class being at the same time international – the people bound to the language being at the same time the great mass of the lower classes. It was not until state and national unity became identical aims that the concepts *people* and *state* coincided also. The *people* were no longer a subsoil of the *state* that no longer had to be taken into account – these *states* were supposed to be created for the very sake of the *peoples*. But the *state* new order coincided with an only inadequate social new order. It was not the *people* who came to power but bourgeois capitalism. The new *state* too, which was really supposed to serve the *people,* again served only an upper class and made use of the *people* again for purposes that remained alien to the broad masses of the lower class. Even in the progressive Democracies – and democracy *does* mean *rule of the people* – it was not the *people* who ruled, but once again a ruling class. The concept *people* was not absorbed into the concept *nation* which was now made the basis of the *state*. The *nation* merely replaced the earlier divine right, but at the same time *nation* does properly speaking mean *people*, and thus it was the splitting of the concept came about. *People* was the whole *nation*, yet within any *nation*, *people* nevertheless meant lower and middle classes at the same time.

The National Socialists, who have a good understanding of these things, clearly make some allowance for this. The more the concept *nation* becomes the servant of absolute rule by a sparse upper class, the more they speak of the *people*, also taking pains to render harmless the legitimate claim inherent in this concept which is upheld by its second meaning, that is to say the legitimate claim of the whole people that it should be served by the nation state. No fellow German must go cold or hungry – the misery of the lower classes is abolished – the middle classes are forced into the lower class, nationality and folklore and tasteless rubbish and *Blut und Boden* are emphasized merely to create the impression that the national state is a people's state. Democracy, which in the national state ought to become the demand and sense of the concept *people* they replace by the artificial reanimation of the old features of the *people* in earlier absolute states, which, in the spirit of absolutistism was logical and expedient. It can only be hoped that the *people* having become aware of their legitimate claims, will not let themselves be enslaved by the empty phantom of a *nation* of the *people* and yet alien to it, as they were earlier by the doctrine of divine right, which was after all wholly different in sense and content.

Still prevalent in Britain on the other hand, is the bad conscience which democracy has regarding its own name. Hence this concentration on aid – this really admirable readiness to be helpful. The little British congregation which holds German services, recently collected things for the interned refugees, i.e. for enemy aliens branded as more-or-less dangerous by British courts. And this collection for enemies in the midst of war has produced a whole host of the very best and most suitable articles!

But it is precisely here that the weakness and inadequacy of aid is most clearly demonstrated. Aid reinforces the unjust structure of the state – anyone who considers it must recognize that there is no sense even in renouncing a large fortune, for no new order will be created by so doing, and as aid it will make no sense – a drop in the ocean, simply creating more people in need of aid – the man who gives up the money, together with his family, those who make a living from the wealthy and the workers whom wealth employs. It seems more expedient to leave wealth switched into the mechanism of the existing social order and producing work and prosperity, and apart from that still to use it expediently for aid that is in turn dependent on surplus. But private aid cannot help the whole people – it is hard put to it to alleviate misery in the slums of London and the poverty areas of Britain in only a remotely effective way – it needs such special tasks to become effective in a way that can be felt. It cannot be for the benefit of the classes of the people who seem to need this aid but only for isolated groups who, by virtue of some special feature, allow themselves to be easily detached from the whole.

It is with the German refugees that the positive and negative sides of aid become especially clear. Here a great relief task has been achieved, an unusually large number of people having been saved solely by the aid provided. But this aid has been able to become effective only by reason of the fact of its being part of the Nazis' cowardly tactics to direct themselves initially against small sections in order gradually to become master of the whole, and with time it has grown ever more important. And when today again and again we read with heavy hearts how Germany is going to resettle the Poles and the Jews and the Czechs – how these people, stripped of everything, are to be packed into appalling reserves, our first thought is how terrible that they should now have to go without the saving relief aid of the British! How will your mother, your friends, your relatives – all of them fare without the aid that has been the saving of us! But at the same time it must be admitted that in face of this mass resettlement even the most sacrificial of aid would be powerless. The 250,000 Polish refugees sent flooding over frontiers by war, are already presenting the relief agencies of the whole Anglo-Saxon world with insoluble tasks. Those under threat can now only be aided by the war, provided it is successful soon enough, and the only thing capable of effectively saving all would have been the timely suppression of the Nazis. Only if the danger had been duly recognized and resisted, and the idea powerful enough to overthrow the Nazis would the misery really have been prevented. For in any case large sections of the German people, trampled underfoot by the Nazis in just the same way, have gone without aid, and now, in war, are being destroyed first, whilst the Nazis' crack troops sit safely in the rear keeping watch on the people.

Britain therefore has something to learn from the concept of *the people*. Positive ideas, the social new order, justice, are what matter! Aid is also no more than an emergency arrangement that makes injustice tolerable

141

to heart and mind. It cannot replace the positive ideas which are lacking – it may alleviate misery here and there, but basically it is even bound to reinforce injustice.

Evening

Re-reading what I have written today I am seized with great anger against this war. It requires us to grin and bear Russia – the Russia who was yesterday making Germany out as the innocent lamb attacked by the wicked British, and who today, on the occasion of the twenty-second anniversary of the Bolshevik Revolution, is remembering her principles and making Germany – whom she is after all effectively aiding – suddenly out to be a wicked imperialist power; the Russia who, the day before yesterday, was declaring Finland an ally in need of protection in order to swallow her, who then, when Finland refuses to be swallowed, blares forth to the world that big wicked Finland is going to attack good little Russia; who today on the occasion of a supposedly proletarian celebration is cautiously silent concerning Finland, and who tomorrow will assert whatever suits her – any nonsense, the exact reverse of whatever she has just said. As regards Germany this war requires that we lie inactively in wait, allowing her time for all the crimes she plans so that countless more people can be plunged into misfortune. And even if this war were to be conducted differently, it would again still plunge countless other people into misfortune. And none of this need have been. The weapons Germany is fighting with were built in full view of the world, which could easily have prevented it, and have in part been supplied by the world which is now being destroyed by them. And this is the war we are supposed to give assent to!

Probably it is the last way of still beating the Nazis. But how can any good come of it? Resistance has been begun too late for it to be carried through humanely – too late for the many who have already perished and will now of necessity still perish – and can that *too late* ever be made up for now? The time lost is irretrievable, what has been done cannot be undone. Will not that dreadful process of development which we have been watching, inactive and in good faith, be promoted even further by war? The most obvious historical parallel is appalling; the last war produced splendid ideas but the soil on which they might have been realized was eroded away by the effect of the war. How is it to be this time with a completely different world precariously haunted by the mere shadows of those ideas?

142

At that time we still believed we had to destroy in order to be able to build. Today we know that destruction leads always to fresh destruction. How can a new war possibly create a positive new world – and this war especially which began with nothing but mistakes which are being continued today. It was too late. Is it not also now definitely too late?

Today, in a more serious and profound sense than ever before the call is 'Peoples of Europe, defend your most sacred possessions!' But do they still have those sacred possessions which they want to defend and must? What has become of this sacred Europe? Is there really anything else for it but to retreat into solitude to gather, sift and preserve for another world what Europe has to bequeath?

8 November 1939

After a sleepless night I have again sought refuge from my thoughts in the Cambridge courts and gardens, but the magic of those great works of man has refused to make itself felt. I saw only the sandbags to protect them against bombs, the glassless windows of King's College Chapel and the closed museum. The trees are now almost stripped of leaves. Only rarely does the sun penetrate the grey, and only rarely does it still conjure forth gleaming patches of colour. Thoughts turn to the winter which will give the Nazis time to perpetrate further crimes, and very likely fail to bring about the hoped-for revolution.

I did not stop until I got to my Shakespeare court. Here, in contrast to the old Gothic wall, the calm, clear shapes were so sure in their effect as again to draw me completely under their spell. Being tired I sat down for a while in a seemingly warmish corner, and suddenly, as I struggled for a moment against sleep, the stage was peopled, only not now with one of the earlier comedies that had recently been in my thoughts, but with his last, *The Tempest*.

But here too the desired harmony would not make itself felt. The beginning fitted the frame, but then, in all too tragic a fashion, the comedy seemed to shatter it, the cheerful intention of the play was shot through with real sorrow, and I at once became aware that even the ending which, as with the early comedies, overcomes the tragic element, would not this time make up for the discordant note. In the presence of this clear, firm style it seemed to me that all the magic means working towards the end only emphasized the tragedy externally.

Suddenly it struck me that I was not alone. In the middle of the court a single spectator, a prematurely aged man was sitting. His dress resem-

143

bled that of the actors but that did not at all surprise me for I recognized him at once. He had come down from London to escape the bustle of the theatre, the exertions and demands of court life, and reconsider his difficult decision once again, in peace. Uneasily and without the full force of his attention, he was following the nevertheless enchanting progress of the play, his every thought plain to read upon his work-worn brow. At one point he seemed satisfied – plainly all that he was hearing out of the whole play was the rightness of his decision to turn his back on the theatre and return to Stratford.

What a struggle that decision had cost him, and how much he had had to abandon, returning to that dreary, bigoted provincial town! Everything that hitherto he had thought the substance of life. But there had been no choice – he had had to follow his path to the end, and that last step he had been able to take only in solitude, away from the theatre whose practical demands had again and again kept him from that final logical step.

Twice he had reached the limits of his world. An enormous world, a veritable cosmos. Now, as he surveyed it, his work seemed almost greater and mightier and more real than the life he had been trying only to depict, and now dreaded. But by very reason of its being greater, and more genuinely and powerfully concentrated on the essential, this world pressed for a meaning to be found. That meaning he once thought he had possessed. Blissfully, with every fibre of his being, he had experienced that new time which was due to the Renaissance in Italy, the liberation of man from the enslaving bond of faith degenerated into superstition – man had become self reliant – it was, finally, each individual who mattered. And the supreme and noblest expression of that time he had seen as the heroic ideal – in this it was that liberated man seemed to achieve his most glorious perfection. But what had survived of that ideal in the course of his creative work, and how very alone it left him now that he felt death approaching and the question of meaning had become burning and imperative! Certainly he was not going to renounce the great, true achievement of that time: self-reliant man. But where to achieve his perfection if not in pure, clear, powerful heroism?

In his mind he reviews the long line of his works. How clear and certain heroism had seemed for as long as it had been merely suggested in contrast to other worse and weaker figures! The weakling Richard II, the villain Richard III, indeed, later still, even the eternal waverer, Hamlet – against that background of evil, the hero stood out as a glorious and saving promise. But the hero himself eluded him, every deed of King John's, for instance, had been vigorous and powerful but not at all suited

144

to making the hero seem a model. For he had, to be truthful, to allow that those deeds were founded upon baseness and cunning, and that power had had to be won through brutality and a lust for killing. Again and again the hero's way leads him through bloodshed that is impossible to justify, via victories of undoubtedly small significance to a downfall that seems just.

Again and again he had attempted to capture the purity of the hero. Henry IV relieves his son of all those seemingly inevitable misdeeds essential to the winning of power, and Prince Hal, bubbling over with life and strength and in sure possession of power seems easily able to become the pure hero. But he too, be it noted, fails – his glory-haloed transformation into worthy successor to his father can be bought only at the price of shameful treachery towards Falstaff. His coldly calculated rejection of his friend for whose high spirits he also is to blame, puts him in the wrong at his very first step. He becomes worthy to succeed his father, but in a sense other than the intended – using an empty pretext to start a war with France and treading the already-rejected road to pure heroism. 'Honour is a mere scutcheon.' These words, coined originally against Falstaff, the coward, acquire general and decisive weight throughout the kingship of Henry V.

More and more Shakespeare sees himself deflected away from heroism and towards portraying conflicts of conscience. Against his will, he attempts to depict the greatest heroic figure of classical antiquity. Here, at a clearer distance, it really must be possible to capture true heroism, and yet now he is forced to admit that it is simply the title that is wrong, he calls the drama *Caesar*, but the drama is that of conscience-hounded Brutus. And what are *Hamlet* and *Macbeth*, where he touches most powerfully on the general, but struggles with that predominance of conscience which his times and he himself wished to discard as infirm?

Was heroism really not an ideal? Was it to be condemned? Once already, filled with scorn and anger, Shakespeare had given vent to this realization in that remarkable comedy *Troilus and Cressida* – at bottom his bitterest tragedy – which had tormented him into giving it one reworking after another. The new translation of the *Iliad* had just come to hand, and that was not something he could keep calm about and just accept! Could not people see what it was about? 'All the argument is a whore and a cuckold, a good quarrel to draw emulous factions and bleed to death upon?' That, in a nutshell, was the heart of the whole matter!

Or was it? The cause was not what mattered. Very splendid deeds were performed in this war notwithstanding! But what of those deeds? In his

145

comedy, Achilles performs all the great deeds that tradition ascribes to him. But that does not prevent his still being limited and vain, hollow and puffed up, just as sensitive to praise and censure as he is ready to let himself be seduced by a beautiful woman's every allurement, by every form of excess. Hector does not fall in battle. Achilles' warriors fall upon him and dispatch him like an animal brought down by the hounds. Of course, Shakespeare does not know if Achilles was really like this or if the deed was really enacted in this way, but that this battle might have gone thus, or this character have been thus, without either being necessarily at variance with Achilles' posthumous fame – that deprives heroism of absolutely any validity. There are always the eulogizers who can, by lying, make the coward into a hero, the murder into a heroic deed – the truth comes to light only when the attempt is made to depict the hero. And the heroic deed, be it noted, still says nothing whatsoever concerning the man himself, heroism obviously having no purifying influence, the much-celebrated Achilles can even be replaced by a pitiful figure such as this without inconsistency, the whole merely becoming more probable.

With an ill-humoured gesture of the hand Shakespeare dismisses this whole strange Fair of Human Vanity that he has created. The aged babbler Orestes, scheming, hyper-cunning Ulysses, stupid Ajax who is the best of the warriors nevertheless, and the idiot Menelaus. No, he is not satisfied – once again he comes to grips with heroism, in his last tragedy. But does that really say anything different?

Coriolanus is so pure and unshakable, so proud and bold that Shakespeare allows him, without a scruple, that remarkable right demanded by the heroic ideal of killing – provided it be in impeccable combat. But what has become of Coriolanus when confronted with the truth of form? He too has lost his spiritual purity, his honour. His fine inflexibility is the very thing that deprives him of the possibility of the great deed – if he wishes to remain a hero he must in the end seize power, become a traitor. Even acceptance of killing to which Shakespeare has been opposed in all his dramas of conscience, is not able to save the heroic ideal.

No, he can conceal it from himself no longer – in this play he has finally and unambiguously passed sentence on the heroic ideal. Volumnia overcomes the most powerful of feelings, the most powerful of natural forces, motherly love – and a more sublime, more dearly-bought prize song to heroism than hers has never been sung, 'had I a dozen sons, each in my love alike, and none less dear than thine and my good Marcius, I had rather had eleven die nobly for their country than one voluptuously surfeit out of action'. Indeed, she proclaims:

146

    the breasts of Hecuba,
When she did suckle Hector, looked not lovelier
Than Hector's forehead when it spit forth blood
At Grecian swords, contemning.

But she who is so ready to sacrifice what is dearest to her – what is it that she herself must sacrifice to the God of War, to heroism – what is it that she must finally admit to herself? She too is forced down into deepest abasement, and retrieves her inner greatness only by confessing

    our suit
Is, that you reconcile them: while the Volsces
May say, 'This mercy we have show'd;' the Romans,
'This we receiv'd;' and each in either side
Give the all-hail to thee, and cry, 'Be bless'd
For making up this peace!' Thou know'st, great son,
The end of war's uncertain.

That alone retrieves her greatness – the fact that she herself overcomes her blind faith in heroism, and finds the strength to go, as herald of the unheroic peace, to the son she had brought up as a hero.

Shakespeare listens, ever more weary and perplexed. Have these last comedies, wrested so joylessly from himself, another meaning? That medieval world of unclarity, dark passions, life-destroying confusion which he thought he had overcome, again suddenly breaks into the open air of his comedies, no longer in its old form, it is true – changed – but no less disastrous for that. Before, his comedies have been a great sigh of relief, confirming him to be on the right road and allowing what had oppressed him to be dismissed with a laugh, now the calamity is beyond the scope of his merriment, and the light, merry ending is no longer proof against its power. What has before been sure deliverance is now merely a false miracle, external magic. This inhuman, man-destroying world cannot be true. There must be a way out – he had already found one – were not his people cheerful, merry and natural? Did not they stand surely in this world? Did not their lives fill it? He is not going to let himself be destroyed by this senseless love of the hero, and must not. He must find the true sense of this living life that he has won, must clear the way, albeit at the most grievous cost – that of renouncing everything that he has loved!

His face is suddenly clear and set, he is firmly decided – he must go to Stratford. He listens for another moment to the ending of the play, bewildered. It still holds him – and sounds better than the ending of the uneven *Winter's Tale* written shortly before! But probably only because

147

he had then already made his decision, and that had given him back something of his old vigour and merriment. He rises wearily, but his walk is young, the springy step of the actor, comes towards me, and the phantom vanishes. With an effort I drag myself away.

Slowly I walk back through the autumn gardens. Evening is falling, tempting one to dreams. What I have just been thinking seems to me more real than reality.

Whether my suppositions are correct can never be decided. The lack of understanding which Shakespeare found at Stratford, has deprived us of his final manuscripts which might have explained his decision. There is supposed to have been a *Life of Jesus* amongst them, but even that is uncertain.

But is it not attested by all of his works that what he was seeking in Stratford was really an answer to the paramount ultimate questions? The enigma of this decision, looked at externally, is that Shakespeare has actually repudiated his existence for the sake of it. For what awaits him is a provincial town where he is ostracized as a Godless person and an actor, and his fame is reckoned a taint. There is not a soul who understands him and with whom he can have a rational conversation. What awaits him is fearful solitude amongst bigoted and gossipy provincials! The darling of the people, the Court favourite, the grand gentleman is going voluntarily into almost intolerable banishment. What can he have been seeking if not the solitude and isolation essential to final composure, to profound change?

Even the unconfirmed reports of a *Life of Jesus* sound probable if his works are read with care. Certainly his works are alive with all that is human, and with practically all of the ideals, although in his last works most of them are already too weary, stale and discarded to have become the aim of this new and profound transformation which his decision reveals. One of the great motive forces in the turn towards the earthly effected by the Renaissance, was, inevitably, love. But in the final comedies, love which in *Romeo and Juliet* shone so effortlessly upon a numbed world, no longer has any supportive capacity. In *Troilus and Cressida*, Andromache, who would seem to be someone worthy of kindling love, no longer plays a part, whereas Helena and Cressida, who move the world, are figures of a destructive passion. And *Coriolanus*, where Shakespeare attempts to take refuge in motherly love, shows just how badly even this love can go astray. But to the people, whose fickleness he has seen through too deeply, Shakespeare cannot turn – he knows that what matters is what one says to them. One cry remains, and in his final works more than anywhere, the call for justice, and it is this yearning desire that permeates

148

the abnormal happenings in *Othello, King Lear* and *The Tempest*. But as, in *Macbeth* and *Coriolanus,* this desire is bound up with the power of conscience, the escape to Christianity is still a probable one. And how else should Christianity have presented itself to that great portrayer of men than in the figure of Jesus?

There is no contradiction in the fact that this interpretation should stand in opposition to earlier interpretations, or that we should not really understand until today what prompted Shakespeare. Men of genius are the contemporaries of later generations! Only today, after a hundred years of brushing aside Shakespeare's contempt for the people, do we understand how strangely real the people are! The devotees of dictatorship proclaiming their joy to their very butchers, have taught us how fickle the people are. And how alive again Coriolanus becomes as a result. And is it not also only today, when man has been denied most elementary rights that we again know the meaning of justice, and our ears are again attentive to this as being amongst the sources of torment to Shakespeare, and one which a few decades before was still hidden under picturesque action? And *Troilus and Cressida* did not rise from the dead until after the last war, for it was not until then that we knew the real face of the much-vaunted hero, the real meaning of military glory, and the extent to which all soldiers were identical with these hitherto seemingly strange figures!

Men of genius are bound to be the contemporaries of later generations. For genuine, perfect form is true in the sense that it penetrates to the essence of things, and exposes what the slow unfolding process which makes one part clear after another, reveals to people in general only in the course of generations. Nevertheless, form remains bound up with time: Shakespeare would drop into a void if he dealt with any time other than his own – that of the maturing Renaissance – he must strive for the heroic ideal – must overcome the medieval world the sake of that human image which we today see as the final achievement of that epoch which began with the Renaissance and has just come to an end. But in recording this image in perfect form he also illuminates it, disclosing the world which lies, beyond the present, at the end of this unfolding process. He may have felt that true life begins beyond tragedy and heroic ideal, and that the renunciation of tragedy is essential, and yet, confined to his time, he was unable to overcome tragedy except in the drama. Today, when time faces us with the necessity of this renunciation, we are perhaps for the first time in a position to understand this very far-reaching element in Shakespeare's work and thus to understand his final decision. We are acting in the sense of form whenever we set aside all previous knowledge concerning a work and interpret it completely anew, for in all genuine form the opposites that have created it remain alive and ambiguous, and we shall be bound again and again to find fresh possibilities for fresh interpretations.

9 November 1939

An abortive attempt on Hitler's life. First thought – bad luck that it didn't succeed. Second – let us hope, for the vindication of the honour of the German people, that this news is at least true. Third – so here you are, assenting to murder. I think though that I have already said enough of what there is to be said about tyrannicide.

But today is not only the anniversary of the abortive Beer Cellar Putsch which, characteristically, the Third Reich takes as its starting point – it is also the anniversary of the German Republic that failed, and whose weakness is betrayed particularly clearly by its not having had the heart to make this a red-letter day.

German Republic! What glorious years, great hopes and dreadful disappointments those words revive! I went to Berlin in 1920. How good the air of that city then, the air of young freedom – everything worth striving after seemed possible – the boldest Utopia could now be made a reality! A new kind of art was beginning – Expressionism seemed to be sloughing off the extremes of the trend and becoming a sound basis for genuine renewal. The rightly despised Imperial Institutes of Art were turning into the best museums in the world, the old abominations disappearing into the cellars to make room for the celebration-attended new arrivals. Every new theatre performance took one step further into a new land that awakened the very highest expectations, and literature, concerts, exhibitions and lectures kept pace with that tempestuous development. Berlin in those days was an international city. From East and West a sizeable intellectual stream had come flowing in with the years – the Russians arrived with their theatre, the British came and envied us – 'You're lucky – you've been beaten and as a result you've got room for what's new. In our country everything is fixed and rigid.' Here, and here alone it seemed possible to find a *synthesis* of Europe. Nor did it all seem just an airy thing. The People's Universities in each of Berlin's many districts were excellent. The young workers were eagerly imbibing everything that could conceivably be studied. A high standard in choral speaking and amateur dramatics was being shown even by the political organizations of the Left. Was there not also bound to be success in gradually altering the policy

150

that alone gave cause for concern? A most liberal constitution had been drawn up, and in Weimar which, after due consideration, had been chosen as shield and watchword of the young Republic. So powerful was the intellectual life that there was bound to be success in filling this splendid framework with the life appropriate to it.

In view of all that has happened it is difficult today to recall that rapturous and yet not remote-from-earth mood of those first years. It is hard and bitter to recall that unique experience of young freedom – the good, keen, stimulating atmosphere that was so wholly different from the atmosphere of the good, yet sickly liberal tradition that holds sway here in the West. One little experience may serve to illustrate this slightly.

When I arrived I knew hardly anything about Berlin. It was summer. Most people were on holiday. I was very alone at first. The ugliness of the city disappointed me. Only a few theatres were open and presenting the usual summer repertoire which disappointed me too. For days on end I saw only the ugly façade. At the beginning of September, when the former Court Theatre was playing again, I went, quite by chance and with misgivings – for the Imperial Theatre had been notoriously bad – merely to get my bearings. But then up went the curtain and I knew from the very first words that I was seeing real theatre – the theatre of which I had always only vaguely dreamt – here it was, realized to perfection! The old, the false and unclear had all been washed clean away – here was a new experience with not a speck of dust on it, bright as the sun, alive to the last word and the least gesture, with no free-wheeling, no mechanical aids. It had been all completely restored to life inside and out – created anew. A broad new path opened out before me, and I knew that that was the way I must go.

Of course, my surprise had been due solely to my ignorance. This was the already famous production of Wedekind's *The Marquis of Keith* directed by Jessner, the best producer, with Kortner, the most consistent and dedicated of modern actors, in the lead.

But however well one knew Berlin, this would happen again and again. I had occasion to visit a working-class suburb so nasty and dreary as to leave one breathless, and discovered outside one of those hideous suburban houses of the nineties a board stating 'Exhibition of Art by the People's University'. I went in only because it was beginning to rain, and found an excellent survey of the graphic work of Käthe Kollwitz. The ceilings of the rooms still had the old hideous stucco but the walls were painted in bright colours. No museum could have arranged the exhibition better. A young worker, seeing how long I lingered in front of each of

151

those splendid prints, came up to me and without the least shyness put a great number of questions which this unusual experience had touched off for him. They were naive and innocent of any acquired artistic jargon, and yet gradually they elicited from me everything that I had to say about these prints – indeed about art in general, helping not only the young man but also myself to arrive at greater clarity. As I left I no longer saw anything of the ugliness of the suburb. Happy, stimulated, optimistic, I was breathing in that unusually good pure sea air of Berlin which was so exactly in keeping with its intellectual atmosphere.

I would go down into the Underground and see an excellent new poster hitherto unknown to me. I would go into a bookshop, find a small exhibition by some unknown artist and be captivated. Walking past a small lecture hall, I would want just to see what was going on – and there, attaching themselves to some technical theme, would be the boldest ideas – ideas I had not yet considered myself. Even the ordering and engineering of this city seemed alive – seemed simply to be paving the way for a new art, a better social life. I would move into a new boarding-house and there would be a young painter, a Russian mystic, a Baltic writer, a German actor, and a religious socialist to have all-night discussions with, or a couple of musicians to tell me about the new world of a new music. It was the time of endless, all-night conversations – I got drawn into efforts and experiments which, however different, all seemed to be working purposefully and productively at reconstruction – and the only meaningful and desirable sort – the careful building up of a world renewed in all its parts.

Yes, in those days we believed what yesterday I chanced upon again in a publication of Rathenau's and today sounds so false, so untrue and Utopian, and so heart-rendingly sad. It did not seem Utopian then at all, but down-to-earth, meaningful and possible. It seemed the sole and true meaning of a defeat which was not depressing us, but rousing our powers. We might not have been able to put it so clearly, but we would have given our assent to those words which we have hardly the strength to read today. Rathenau was saying precisely what mattered to us, when he said:

> We can, and are entitled to, live only if we become what we
> were destined to be, what we were about to be, and what we
> have not become – an intellectual people, a mind amongst
> peoples. For that reason we have been granted a weak dispo-
> sition of external will and a strong disposition of the internal,
> and for that reason we have been given depth and knowledge,

152

objectivity and justice, versatility and individuality, capacity for work and power of invention, imagination and desire to bring this about. For what do these qualities mean jointly? They do not mean the conqueror, the statesman, the man of the world, the businessman. It is one-sided, inadequate and an abuse to pretend to be one of these amongst nations. They indicate the worker of the mind. And if we are a long way from being a people of poets and thinkers, it is our right and our vocation to become a thinking people amongst peoples . . . [That alone is what] withstands and fulfils the social epoch.

Was Rathenau's knowledge of the Germans really so poor? But he said too, of course, 'Here is a people that has lost its right of existence because, in blind authoritarian belief, it staked its existence on prosperity and power.' He said, 'We can, and are entitled to, live only if –', and wrestled with the looming shadow of the lost revolution which he recognized earlier than others. The shadows very soon became plain. I find, while now putting my things in order, a couple of diary entries of the year 1923 in which I say that nothing more can be expected of this Republic and, full of sadness, say farewell to hope. That was after the murder of Rathenau, which the Republic did not know how to punish. It was at the height of inflation and the government was not only unable to master it but also unable to explain to the people that it was not the wicked French alone who were to blame but first and foremost German large-scale industry. But in spite of having written that, I still did not, at that time, believe it, and for a long while tried not to. Such lively hopes are difficult to part with.

The German Republic was too weak to follow the path indicated to it in the first years – it was not able to transform into reality the enormous possibilities which it had been granted by defeat. Rathenau was murdered, and it is not he who is commemorated today but his murderers. Again the German Republic has staked its existence on force and power. Is it not able, and allowed, to *live*? Will the other Germany that still does live even today in the hearts of so many Germans, never come to power and develop?

We have a Republic – nobody seriously wanted it. We got parliamentarianism at the eleventh hour – nobody wanted it. We have a kind of socialism – no one has put faith in it. It used to be 'The people lives and dies for its sovereigns – the Hohenzollerns – to our last drop of blood!' – nobody denied it. 'The

153

people wishes to be ruled by its hereditary lords – will go
through fire for its officers – better death than yield one inch
of German soil to the foe.'

Was that delusion? No, it was the truth.

Those too are words of Rathenau's written in 1919. But he goes on,

This military obedience, this enthusiasm for war has been not
a political will for power and aggression but the docility of a
childish people that desires for itself, and can imagine nothing
other than, that which at present exists.

It was to this 'childish lack of political imagination' that he pinned his
hope – it was here that he saw the tasks and possibilities for 'responsible
thinking people'. How greatly they have been abused!

Will the hellish experience of National Socialism make this people more
mature? Or is it now, and above all as a result of this hellish schooling,
finally too late for anything good and productive?

10 November 1939

Today is the blackest of German anniversaries. A year ago the syn-
agogues were burning – something was taking place one would never ever
have thought possible in Germany – a great, cruel, officially approved –
indeed, organized, pogrom. And this year apparently a new monster crime
is in preparation – a sudden attack upon Holland.

11 November 1939

And today is Armistice Day again – the reminder of a vain victory gam-
bled away through bad policy, through weakness of the idea. But life in
the university city is showing its most amiable side so that one is inclined
to forget everything else. The students have all turned out to collect for
the war disabled, and at every corner there's a different sort of music –
jazz-band, pipe-band, noise of the fair. They are dressed up as Negroes
and Berbers, cowboys and animals – there's a genuine, only rather too
demoniacal storm-trooper who, whenever he meets the nice little don-
key, gives a Hitler salute. No one can get by without giving them something, but so boyishly high-spirited is their importunity that it is impossible to be angry. It is almost as if Paris has suddenly erupted into
Cambridge. But at the same time there is, even on this patriotic occasion,
that pleasant freedom which Paris, I am afraid, can no longer afford. Some

154

produce a great Siegfried Line on which washing gets hung. Others organize a procession to the War Memorial – as hideous here as anywhere – and call for immediate peace negotiations, although without revealing how exactly we are to envisage them.

Nevertheless it is on this Remembrance Day that I am unable to free myself of war memories. Have I not, in my judgement of the soldier, let myself be carried away too far by *Troilus and Cressida?* I witnessed, in the war, a great many acts of heroism, and almost all were performed either from fear, or in ignorance of the danger, in a state of intoxication, or from a mixture of stupidity, cowardice and brutality that fighting so easily brought to the surface even in seemingly harmless men. But I have known two men whom I must respect as real heroes. Quantitatively, two is next to nothing, but is not one example sufficient to confirm an idea?

One, a lieutenant, captured Height 209 in the Tenth Battle of the Isonzo with eleven men, it being a most important strong point for which in this, and in the battle that followed, there was perhaps the heaviest bloodshed. Completely calm and unmoved he walked through the thickest drum fire, not because he did not know the danger, but because he had overcome it internally. He was exceptionally intelligent, and in long conversations had made me as aware as possible of everything to do with war. He kept the overall view, took care of his men, knew how to use them properly, and so far as it depended on him, how to protect them. As a result of the drum fire it was not possible to inform our own artillery of the capture. Nothing could be seen for the thick clouds of dust, the telephone lines had been shot to bits, and runners were not getting through. He was dislodged from the position by our own artillery, but still got back with nine men – an achievement no one else could boast of. But he made so little of it that he never received any more considerable distinction. He mourned the two men he had lost. In neither case was it through any fault of his. One was blown to pieces by a shell. The other, a very good friend of ours, had been hit by a bullet at the very moment he had been yelling to him to take better cover.

My other hero, a captain, had above all the courage of his own convictions, which is something rarer in war. A Hungarian regiment having lost a position, a furious general gave the order for it to be recaptured by parade assault, i.e. with a mass attack in broad daylight, as a punishment. This, as any private could see, would have meant the senseless annihilation of the regiment as the position was not to be taken in this fashion. The captain, arriving with the relief troops, was ordered to storm the position that night. His answer was that he would take the position,

155

but that he would have first to familiarize himself with it and carefully prepare his attack, and that only then would he be able to decide *when* to attack. The general stood by his order. With each night that passed without an attack his threats became worse. He summoned the captain to appear before a court martial and threatened to arrest him. The captain did not allow himself to be deflected from his course. Seven days later he took the position, and that achievement, for which a regiment would have bled to death, and to no purpose, cost him two wounded and none killed. He then surrendered himself to the court martial.

The characteristic thing about these two heroes is that, despite their deeds, they had no internal relationship with heroism, and that with them it was only a concomitant phenomenon. Outwardly they were extreme opposites. The lieutenant was a little Jew, and conspicuously feeble. No one would have thought him fit for front-line service at all, and yet he endured more than the others. The captain was a tall blond German, wiry and slim, and much decorated. But both hated and despised heroism and war. The lieutenant devoted every spare minute to studying his beloved philosophers whose works he always carted around with him. The captain, who later organized assault patrols such as he had invented, throughout the Austrian Army – and properly employed they saved a great number of men! – was obliged to lecture on military science, which he did, but complaining that it was a desecration of the sacred name of science to speak of military science at all. He was the only one from whom we learnt anything of practical frontline use. But first and foremost he tried to free us of the great fear that war aroused in us and teach us what could be of protection to us. Both asserted themselves in war because so great was their human steadfastness that it withstood even the drum fire. Their strength was drawn not from the heroic ideal but from the idea of humanity. These, the only two heroes I ever knew, do not therefore correspond to the heroic ideal. They it is who have refuted it.

The true hero, one who measured up to the conception, was someone I also came to know. After the Tenth Battle of the Isonzo, when hardly anything was left to our regiment, I was detached to Brigade H.Q. In command there at first was a major of no special reputation. He let other ranks live in his safe dug-out. He himself made no special demands. He was popular but not respected. To relieve him a lieutenant-colonel appeared, preceded by a reputation for special bravery and efficiency and with hardly any room on his chest for any more decorations. His first act was to banish all other ranks from the dug-out to the village which, as the Italians had the range of it, was very dangerous, and only at the actual start of a bombardment were they allowed to crowd into a small section of the dug-out. For the lieutenant-colonel, on the other hand, proper rooms had been built in, complete with W.C., simply so that he would not need to go out when there was danger. And then to his many decorations he decided to add the Maria Theresa Medal, awarded in Austria for successful acts carried out without express orders and on one's own initiative, and went to work as follows.

Height 209 had been finally lost. It had now been consolidated with machine-gun galleries – and the rawest private could have told him that it could not be stormed without most thorough artillery preparation. But the lieutenant-colonel believed in surprise, and this on one of the best-guarded and most exposed points of the front. For form's sake he consulted with the artillery commander, and he, being all for a quiet life, approved the plan. And so sixty men and an officer were sent to the rear, fed well for a couple of days, issued finally with rum and told to deploy as assault patrols – an effective means here perverted into its opposite! – and take the Height. As was to be foreseen, not one of them came back, and the lieutenant-colonel did not get his decoration. When his relief arrived, I heard him phoning the artillery commander. He thanked him for his help, which had not been required, adding – and I shall never forget this, as a funeral oration to sixty-one human lives thrown away in an utterly senseless fashion – 'I'm handing the Height 209 affair over to my successor.'

It was my indignation over that, I think, that summoned me back to life. I had been, as I have mentioned, one of twenty-five out of 236 to survive – all my friends were dead – I could not believe that I had escaped for this one time at least, and was expecting my end hourly. But that stupidity, that senselessness was worse than death. The hero's reputation was of course in no way harmed by this *little experiment*.

Even more characteristic of this heroism in modern war were the court martial proceedings against the captain already mentioned. He was exonerated and the general was retired. Still, it must be admitted that the court was unusually discerning. Not to punish a general was a matter of course, however many lives he might squander. But it was not at all a matter of course, on the other hand, that insubordination should be approved, however manifest the rights and the success might be. In this mechanical war ordinary soldier and front-line officer had no overall view, and could hardly influence it in any other way than by carrying out orders well, and thus the prestige of the general was protected at any cost. Little now depended on heroism, and everything on the functioning of the

157

machine. And this machine and all who willingly obeyed it and strove for the favour of the wire-pullers, resembled to a nicety their models in *Troilus and Cressida.*

No, I have no need to worry my head any more concerning heroism, and this knowledge has been gained from countless very bitter experiences – my report of encounters with highly praised and highly decorated heroes could be continued for pages. These experiences became even more instructive when, later, I found strength to resist senseless orders – for most still emerged as cowards over this. But against this, I can cite no instances of a genuine hero who also actually drew his strength from the ideal of heroism.

13 November 1939

This constant news of the deportation of Jews from Germany to the Polish reserve is terrible. Now apparently the Vienna Jews are being transported to Lublin. Human imagination, human strength does not suffice to picture all the suffering and all the destruction embodied in that brief statement! At one time the talk is of 22,000 – then, out of 2,000, approximately 600 have disappeared – then eighty-two have committed suicide – those figures, even if exaggerated for propaganda purposes, are unthinkably dreadful, and in Vienna alone there are still 100,000 Jews! To make the thought bearable at all, there is really nothing for it but to hide away behind these inanimate figures and not attempt to bring them to life.

This revenge by the idea upon people who have fallen away from it is terrible. Almost all are so very much alienated from life already of course that they do not know at all why they are suffering – they only feel the horrible injustice afflicting individual groups at random. It is impossible not to think of the old saying that humanity is bound to perish once it falls away from God. But we must not take the word God in vain. We undermine any new idea when we cling to old words without experiencing them anew, and the fact that all this fearful suffering may serve the rebirth of the idea, is really the only hope that remains to us! What sense then is this suffering to have if not that of leading people back to the idea, and thus to an experience to which we may then perhaps attach the exalted name of experience of God?

16 November 1939

Always, walking through the streets of Cambridge, I wonder how it is possible with such certainty to distinguish the neo-Gothic buildings from the old. Most, to be sure, are to be recognized here just as anywhere by their hideousness, but some have been built very carefully and with great understanding, and the question is more than usually pertinent because the old buildings are often renovated so thoroughly as to look as if only just finished. To begin with, and until such time as we know the peculiarity of English style, confusion does in fact arise, but even then we have only to look closely, study a little and compare, to know what is old and what is new, and be left in no doubt. That may be simplest with Gothic, but when we become familiar with English style, we will only rarely be mistaken, even with the entirely plain buildings of later epochs.

Of course, there are criteria for this distinction even with the best imitations. The details are plainer, lacking in expression, the whole more regular, the proportions more mathematical. But that is not what matters. Even when building has been done strictly in accordance with an old plan and the heads and ornaments carefully made after plaster-casts – even then the difference remains plain.

It is not possible to build *genuinely* in an old style. As long as a style is alive it remains a problem, a task, an art. The construction of the pointed arch breaks perhaps the given form of the building which has then to be closed again, each window contributing to the shaping of the space, which the architect has in mind in an ideal form and is striving to approach. However accurate the plan may be, the construction is at some point too bold. It has to be balanced by some irregularity, some fault which again is counterbalanced by other changes. Or the reverse – the plan is surpassed, as a result of which the same process comes about – the intended impression has constantly to be rescued anew. Out of the living style details have flowed into the building which have not let themelves be planned or calculated for. Here space is left for the veneration of a saint, here the light draws attention to a surprising effect, there room is left for an ornament that, owing to the special place, itself again becomes novel, there a new need creates a new task. And it is as a result of that that the building receives simultaneously a relaxed quality and firmness, that inexplicable contrast that today excites our admiration. The form has, to the fullest possible extent, to do justice to the content which, being wholly life, is just as manifold and surprising as life, and the content, in turn, demands a definite form which it is a question of locking into itself – out

159

of which mutually contending demands a tension arises in the creator which impels him forward and restrains him simultaneously. From which tension he is able to permit himself any deviation because, as a result, tension will also be recaptured. Imitation can permit no deviation because the original opposites are no longer operative and tension can therefore no longer be produced. The imitator is obliged to keep to the rule which can be deduced from the results before him – maybe this rule was what they were based on, but in the process of creation it has been varied, altered, extended. It has been only the basis, and not the binding law that the imitator is obliged to accept it as. As the imitator sees and feels differently, variation will render him false, and it is by virtue of his being bound by this external austerity that life eludes the form – what is left is only the shell allowing a partial idea to be gathered of what is inside, although what *is*, is certainly no longer life.

The human and the time restrictions, the thoughts and feelings, the knowledge and the intentions, the seeing and perceiving operative within form are incessantly changing – they dovetail into unity only when accurately interjoined in their instantaneous state. For this interconnection succeeds by virtue not of a calculation, not of a rule, but of tension. And this tension can arise only when the two opposite parts are equally alive and equally important, and when man is profoundly moved by their unbridgeable opposition. It is engendered only by the equally powerful, equally full vitality of the mutually contradictory opposite parts, and their contradiction must also be alive in the same way.

It is only out of this experience that the inexplicable harmony within form can arise. If we cling to a detail – and with an imitation we have no other opportunity – either form becomes formal, that is to say empty and non-living, or life breaks through form and becomes formless – and even that intractability which eludes apprehension by the human mind, again leads to a void.

17 November 1939

Yesterday I asked an Indian what his attitude was towards Christianity. 'What we are interested in is not the Christianity of the churches but the Christianity of Christ', he said – an answer that deserves to be recorded.

18 November 1939

The lull continues. The attack on Holland seems for the time being to have been called off. The air attacks on Britain, while gradually increasing

160

in number, are not as yet any more serious in character, their purpose seeming to be more to provide the German press with news. And the U-boat war is becoming less and less effective. Many items are almost amusing. For instance, German aircraft dropping Russian leaflets over Paris containing Molotov's speech. Or British aircraft dropping appeals over Bavaria for the return of the hereditary Royal House. In Paris Otto von Habsburg has declared himself an ally of the Allies. Is it really going to be a quiet winter?

The British papers are explaining the lull in terms of serious political conflicts in Germany. Hitler wants an offensive. The generals don't. And Hitler, whose power is as yet unquestioned, has not so far been able to reach a decision. The morale of the German people meanwhile is becoming steadily worse and paralysing initiative. Reading between the lines it amounts almost to a prophecy that Hitler is first of all going to have a grand purge, probably with Goering and many generals as victims – this being the only reason for heaping so many offices on Goering – and will later himself have to give in to the generals.

How one would like to believe such news! Yet it may also serve to explain the inactivity of the allies themselves. Similar news about Britain is apparently being spread in Germany. Maybe both sides are merely playing into each other's hands so as not to have to risk a particularly heavy and hopeless battle in winter. It is probably true that time is working more against Germany, but also not certain as Russia's attitude is further unclear – negotiations with Finland having been broken off, Russia too is obviously watching and waiting. As to unrest in Germany, there is only one concrete piece of news – from Prague, where nine students have been shot and the universities closed. But terrible as that news is, I do not believe that the Czechs will let themselves be provoked but will know how to wait for the right moment. I therefore believe we should not give ourselves up to any premature hopes but maintain a lively mistrust of war news, even here in Britain.

19 November 1939

Is it really not possible to communicate experience and convey its lessons to others? Does everyone have first to expereience and suffer for himself before he understands? This is obviously the case today, but does it have to be?

I think that that too is merely a fault of our science-trained thinking with its absolute demand for unambiguity. Our thinking hastens from cause to effect and from this effect to further effects to reach a clear result as quickly as possible to take comfort in and exploit, and in so doing excludes life to a considerable degree. The inability to accept other people's experience consists of course in a lack of vision and imagination – we are able to imagine only what we ourselves experience, unable to share experience, and therefore obliged to experience everything ourselves. But this deficiency is caused by by-passing life in our thinking, by our proceeding too quickly from life to the abstract – by our not lingering but hastening towards an end. If we thought out our own lives differently we would also be able to accept other people's experience differently.

That seems especially plain to me in the so-called realistic thinking which is tied wholly to reality. It is this thinking which consists in weighing out cause and effect as accurately as possible in order to take account as faultlessly as possible of our own and other people's actions. This thinking wishes to arrive at reliable conclusions and is therefore bound to make its assumptions as unambiguous as possible. But that means that the assumptions are bound to be made more unambiguous than they are in reality – we have to abstract from the given in order to arrive at this unambiguity – and it is for that very reason that the conclusions of other people's experience cannot be taken over if it deviates from our own, for its assumptions then appear fanciful. What has not yet been experienced for ourselves cannot be taken into account because always only that can be extracted from reality which we already know – even that which is strange leads us back to the familiar abstraction. It is precisely that seemingly down-to-earth thinking which we are accustomed to describe as realistic, that requires abstraction, and is therefore obliged to simplify life just as much as the laws of science do.

For what is a scientific law? How do we explain a falling body? To calculate its fall precisely all we need to know is its weight, dimensions, perhaps its shape and density and the density of the air it is falling through. It is immaterial whether it is an apple falling or a pear, whether the body is blue or green, a good apple or a bad, beautiful or ugly, whether it will withstand the fall or break, and much else besides. These are all things which will only be considered in other cause-and-effect chains which will again exclude a multitude of other distinctive features. And the explanation of the falling body is founded, as are all these explanations, upon a pure abstraction – gravity. For, call it what we will, we do not know what electricity is or magnetic attraction – the force remains an inexplicable auxiliary conception of abstract thinking. But it is just that sort of explanation which is the ideal model, the aim of realistic thinking.

162

The havoc bound to be caused by neglecting so many details in the sphere of human life is readily apparent. Certainly, leaving out so many details in this sphere, will never work, and the exactitude of the natural sciences, is for this reason also unattainable. But the absence of this exactitude is perceived as a fault, and anyone who thinks this way – and who today doesn't? – is therefore driven further and further along the road of abstraction in a most disastrous fashion. Morever, in the sphere of life it is not possible to try out new hypotheses in order to make the results more exact, for there is not the possibility of the artificial experiment whereby the hypotheses can be verified. Which is precisely why the painful roundabout way of our own experience by which inadequate assumptions can be corrected, is all that is left.

Is there really no other possibility for human thinking? As often as I have spoken of form, essential knowledge and approaching the feeling of the divine, I have been obliged to indicate that they come about only by virtue of the opposites which we encounter in our lives having to be left in their own right.

Do not these opposites play a fundamental role in our thinking hitherto unconsidered which may correct the faults in our habitual thinking today? Only if we are able to think in opposites can we hope to apprehend life to its full extent! And only then shall we also be able to re-experience other people's experiences in such a way as to be able to learn from them.

20 November 1939

I am endeavouring in my philosophical work to show that opposites are the basic law of our thinking, and that by acknowledging this hitherto-neglected basic law, our thinking can, in unexpected fashion, be renewed and made fruitful.

Such a renewal, such a fundamental change in human thought is by no means an impossible or even unusual thing – it has occurred often in history. It is only today that causality, the basic law of our thinking, strikes us as absolute, whereas it in fact only originates from the turn away from the medieval world which took place in the Renaissance. To appreciate the completeness of this change, we have only to read the writings of the Schoolmen whose lines of thought we can at best reconstruct as pale ideas, but mostly are not even able completely to clarify. It is impossible to follow with lively interest the Eucharist dispute, for instance – the question as to whether Christ is present in the host bodily, or merely symbolically, or in the sense of his words, 'I am your bread.' Even this comparatively simple scholastic problem is today so inaccessible to us – and to the Church! – that the distinctions drawn in its solution seem small and immaterial – and yet men once gave their lives for them! The celebrated scholastic problem about the number of angels able to stand on the point of a pin, is not a joke but merely an oversubtilized expression of an intellectual world turning upon the opposition of corporeal and incorporeal – the reconciling of this life and the hereafter – an intellectual world which for centuries guaranteed the supreme fruitfulness of human thought, and which we are supremely indebted to for our civilization! And so complete a change in thinking is by no means unique. There is an equally plain one between the Classical period and the Middle Ages – a man of the former would have faced such problems with even slighter understanding than we – and between Classical thinking and our own. How could *we* have found our way about a world that did not yet know the domination of the clock. And these are changes which have occurred within our own cultural circle. The differences between different cultural circles will be all the greater!

The development of causality has come the way that every idea, every mode of thought comes. As a new, young mode of thought, it brought, to begin with, a renewal of human life. When medieval thought lost itself in highly abstract speculations, abandoning reality to supersitition, reality still seemed merely devil's work which was bound to hold man in fear and terror. Every flash of lightning, every comet, proclaimed a judgement. Every act of healing, indeed, even beauty itself, betrayed the witch. And the devil ruled for all to see, for there was thus no defence against lightning or plague. In those days it came as a deliverance that clear natural connections should be recognized and established within nature! Man was suddenly able to breathe freely again, and live vigorously, and the divine sphere too, purged of the turbid impurities of a misinterpreted reality, was able in the Reformation to reproduce itself in pure form. But today this stage of development has been passed: today natural science is losing itself in abstract speculations beyond our powers of imagination, the rule of causality has been shaken even within the realm of natural science, and these problems not having any direct influence on life, life is again being abandoned without guidance to itself and transformed into a nightmare. Reality, this time social reality, is bound to hold man again in fear and terror. A new thinking has become necessary.

In my philosophical work I show how our every thought is the product of opposites. We may experience body, event, man, ourselves, as a unity. But the moment we attempt to translate this experience of unity into

164

thought, we are obliged to resort to opposites in order to render it comprehensible intellectually.

We are unable to think of light without thinking of dark, of the body without thinking of space, of motion without thinking of rest, of good without thinking of evil. We are obliged to conceive Man as body and mind, as man and woman, as a vessel of thinking and feeling, of will and urge, and draw a contrast between individual and community in order to be able to think at all. We are obliged to separate idea from reality, external reality from internal, the force from its effect, the stars from the universe, their movements from other movements, dead from living, the valuable from the valueless, the means from the end, the intention from the sense – we simply are not able to think any differently. Any apparent unity in our thinking is based upon opposites, and I trust that I have succeeded in showing this comprehensively.

Since we experience unity, our striving is directed towards producing it in our thinking also. But this unity is always achieved through onesidedness. For the sake of this unity we are constantly obliged, as with the explanation of the falling body, to neglect most important parts of life. Life is too rich to admit of being forced into any homogeneous thoughtchain of our inadequate understanding.

On the other hand, when we decide to renounce this homogeneity – which is at first a painful process – thinking experiences an undreamt-of enrichment. In fact of course, we are only able to think in opposites, so that resort to them is not really renunciation but the only means possible of exploiting our thinking apparatus fully, of overcoming the inadequacy of our understanding, of exploiting it in all directions simultaneously without need of imposing the restraint of feeling, for its unfolding coincides with that of the feeling – understanding is widened into reason. Only when we are prepared to recognize opposites as ultimate given facts, are we also ready to consider all the infinite contradictions of this contradictory life and do justice to its full wealth.

Any opposite widens our view. We see the conformity with natural law underlying our practical experience, and at the same time the limits of all the laws asserting the human element; we recognize the validity of causality in its appropriate domain and its simultaneous eradication by the indispensable means of our thinking apparatus – all knowledge being, since we cannot think without thinking apparatus, only relative and never valid absolutely – and as a result of this, internal reality comes into its own. We are prepared to separate external reality fundamentally from internal, and as a result do not need, in contemplating reality, to exclude

165

feeling – for which it is today avenging itself by means of its hypertrophy – we can allow it as an opposite of thinking, thereby widening the sphere of consciousness without having to exclude the acuteness of the thinking. We are not obliged to find that which is practical beautiful, or that which is beautiful good, so as to be able to force it into a uniform view of the world. We do not need to despair because science reveals nothing concerning human values, for opposites also teach us to apprehend values separately. But thus it is that they also do not founder on the rock that causality is so obviously coming to grief on today. Causality pretends to absolute validity and yet is unable to state anything concerning the shaping of human life and the forming of human society – opposites teach how to solve these most burning questions also.

And it is thinking in opposites that leads to the possibility of creating in all domains of thought that living form whose fruitfulness here will very likely already have become sufficiently clear – it is thinking in opposites which leads to that tension of feeling which I have sought to describe as a sense of the divine. Thinking in opposites liberates our thinking from all those restraints as a result of which, enslaved by an antiquated tradition, it is in danger of becoming unfruitful – it is making this supreme perfection and most wonderful instrument of the human organism again into what it today no longer is and ought definitely to be – a means of access to all those mysterious sources of life which we cannot explain, but which, by the aid of genuine thinking, we can experience. Relieved of the unrealizable demand that it should provide an absolute solution to every mystery, thinking in opposites lets these almost blocked sources stream forth again – and it is in that stream only that we can fulfil our lives.

21 November 1939

How decisive the significance attaching to a change of thinking actually is, is shown in the following. At the end of every epoch men have presentiments of the epoch to come. At the end of the Graeco-Roman period philosophers' thoughts were revolving around ideas related to the Christian. In the late Middle Ages mystics had a presentiment of the high significance of the individual which subsequently dominated the Renaissance. These presentiments were already staking out the whole area to be filled by the new; and looking back, we believe that we can see contained in them everything of importance to the new. But these presentiments were not themselves able to produce any change and had no immediate effect – and what was really new in them was not recognized by contemporaries – for preparation of the soil for what was to come was being done only under the surface. The new becomes alive and effective only when brought about in a completely new way, as a product of fundamentally changed thinking.

There is one very clear illustration of this process. A hundred years before the onset of the Renaissance, its plain forerunners are Giotto and Dante. Their conscious striving was, it is true, concerned with portraying the cosmos of medieval belief, but in this, and for the first time since the Classic Age, they succeeded in bringing natural people to life. Giotto's drawing was still not entirely accurate, but his people were no longer expressions of the mind but equally powerfully true to life, while the Classical figures in Dante's hell were depicted so vividly as to overshadow the whole epic. The significance of this new element went almost unnoticed by Dante's contemporaries. They were striving in the old fashion to animate Biblical themes. Dante's *Hell, Purgatory and Paradise* joined their number as being similar in kind. It was only beneath this surface, only as a concomitant phenomenon that the influence of new standards made itself felt, with painters now at the same time striving to paint man true to life, and also gradually succeeding more and more in doing so. Nevertheless this change was, to begin with, insignificant, for it was during that very two-hundred-year period that art was almost in danger of stagnating.

Then, all of a sudden and above all with Masaccio, the Renaissance started. What had happened? This change of direction could not have been due to his capacity for painting people true to life, for perfection in this had almost been attained before him, and the distinction between him and his contemporaries who were bound up in the old, was only a gradual one. But Masaccio employed this ability differently. He resolutely threw overboard the old composition – the crowds of heads and figures, the two-dimensional quality of the picture – and at the centre of the newly opened space stood man, free and dominant. For the first time the world was being apprehended by a fundamentally new thinking emanating from man. The same Biblical subjects were still being painted now too, but suddenly they showed earthly man in the same manner as the classical subjects which soon appeared. But whereas with Dante revival of the Graeco-Roman world had merely had the purpose of intensifying Christian faith, man had now become an end in himself and was what mattered above all. The crucial step lay in the shift of thought from the world beyond to the world of the present, from God to man, and it was only as a result of this that the image of man pre-formed under the domination of the world beyond, was all of a sudden able to attain a new

167

significance. It was only as a result of this that the revival of Classical art, which in the intervening hundred years had also been no longer uncommon, became its rebirth, the Renaissance. It was only with the new view of the world that the new epoch began.

And it was then only with that that the significance of the presentiments and previous work changed also. If the Renaissance had not begun, the great forerunners would have remained forerunners of the old and the minor masters of the intervening period would have been lost. How often previous work of that sort has been lost without trace, especially with dying civilizations, we do not know. It was only the fundamental change of direction in thought which introduced the new epoch that made the work of the hundred desolate years, in itself insignificant, into a significant preliminary. For by virtue of this subsequent change of direction it proved extraordinarily fruitful, giving painters the new freedom which they would not have possessed if they had had first to strive for the technique – and without their preliminary work they would not have been capable of clearly recognizing and expressing their new faith.

Today we are again surrounded by presentiments of this sort. Since the Romantics there have been a number of attempts to set the other side of life against the one-sided development of the nineteenth century. French Symbolism and German Expressionism were – despite their failure – splendid attempts at creating that kind of new view of life. Even at the low level represented by National Socialism, the revolt of suppressed feeling and disappointed faith and the longing for a new humane society are still to be felt, at least by young people. And who shall say whether Dostoyevsky will not be recognized in Russia – and not just in Russia – as the crucial precursor of a new world? Intellectually unambiguous collectivism is also obviously caught up in a profound change of direction. And should there be a new epoch, a future history will surely be able to sift the preliminary work out of all these attempts.

But for the time being, and for as long as we cling to the old thinking, all these attempts are doomed to failure and all presentiments are bound to remain vague and impotent. It is no coincidence that they should all be more-or-less Romantic – for Romanticism builds a dream world apart from reality, influences life only by neglecting it, thereby assisting the breakthrough of dark and brutal forces, and is unable to change life in the sense of Romantic ideals. For it works using the old thinking, and the old thinking is able to apprehend only the old reality with which it is indissolubly bound up. A new reality is not created until there is a new thinking.

168

22 November 1939

Yesterday's thoughts certainly show of what little assistance to us historical conclusions can be.

All ideals are age old. The Christian ethic is foreshadowed in the Jewish and the Eastern religions and in parts of Classical philosophy – the ideals of the French Revolution accord with any valid ethic. The important thing is never a new ideal but the fusing of its eternal content with the substance of present-day life, and so to provide it with a new form that makes it vital and effective. It is from this fusing of constantly like ideals with the living stream of life that the ideas that make history arise.

Consequently it is easy to compile what is also bound to form the content of the new idea – it is possible to give shape to premonitions. History allows us to read with some clarity what change of direction ought to occur – and if also in so doing we fall into error in consequence of the inadequacy of any philosophy of history as already described, some of the possible conjectures will probably be correct. But that is still not enough – the requisite living form can arise only from a new experience, from a new act of creation. And an act of creation of this sort does not admit of being calculated, logically inferred, or forced.

The example of the Renaissance does, I believe, clearly show this conclusion to be false. Looking back at the preliminary work reveals that new creation of the type that introduces a new epoch does not occur suddenly, although it seems sudden, but is prepared gradually over a long period of time. And if we examine this preparation period more closely, we discover the line of communication between precursor, preliminary work and new epoch – it is the change of technique, i.e. that part of the task at which the painter must work consciously and thinkingly. The slow change of technique corresponds to the gradual change of thinking – and it is precisely in the field of thought that consciously willed work is possible. That is to say that it is precisely in the field of thought, which then also produces the fundamental and decisive change of direction, that deliberate preparation for the requisite change of direction is possible. The change of direction itself, the result which makes our work into preliminary work does not depend on us, but can never come about if we merely wait and do not do the preliminary work. Even genius needs maturity of means to be able to give expression to the new times – and this maturity we can only bring about by conscious work with ideas.

It was necessary, in my example, to bring Dante into the history of painting – however illogical that may at first appear – his work with ideas

169

which sends painters to paint Classical figures who can no longer be rendered in a medieval style, is every bit as important as the model provided by Giotto's frescos. But the very effect of Dante shows too the very great importance of technique, that is to say of preliminary work in that field in which work must be done consciously and thinkingly. Dante's literary effect does not create an epoch because he adheres to the old technique of the epic. The fanciful revival of the Graeco-Roman world is alone not enough. It has an effect only because Dante sends painters to a subject that demands and promotes a new technique: that technique, for which the way is prepared in the Biblical pictures of Giotto and put to use in the Biblical pictures of the early Renaissance, alone becomes the tool of the geniuses who produce the change in direction. And it was only thanks to this novel application of a new technique that the Classical world later acquired a crucial importance for the Renaissance.

But that means that compiling historical parallels and making fanciful excursions into unrevealed worlds is not the important thing for us either. It may, some time later, have the appearance of interesting prophecy, but does not represent preliminary work such as might also bring this *later* about. It is in the field of thought that we have to prepare this change of direction – we have to provide a new thinking technique – only then maybe will this change in direction also really come about.

For this aspiration there is only one distinguishing mark – and that is the ruthless striving for truth. Only when we refuse to be deterred by any tradition or tempting possibility from thinking absolutely and completely to a conclusion – only when, by our thinking, we shake whatever can be shaken and stop only when we arrive at unshakeable certainty – only then can we hope to create a new thinking. Today's thinking obviously no longer does justice to truth, for which reason we must abandon the accustomed modes of thinking, for it is only by the aid of truth that we are able to arrive at new modes which *do* do it justice. We must not cling to the old merely so as not to fall into the void which seems to yawn before us. Barricades built upon the sand of the untrue or of the no-longer-true are of no avail against the new things that are on their way. The torrent of the fearful development process of which we are already witnesses, will mercilessly sweep them with it. Our only hope of reaching new land is to leave material for new bridge-building ready for the builder of genius who we hope will come. But this new bridge will stand firm against the new conditions the development process creates, only if the material is technically sound, i.e. measures up to the truth as far as the development process possibly allows it to be approached.

170

It is in this new approach to truth, and in this alone, that for me the importance of thinking in opposites seems to lie, and with it the importance of my philosophical work.

23 November 1939

Yes, but *is* there an absolute truth? How does that agree with our recent statement that, as we cannot think without our thinking apparatus, any knowledge is only relatively, not absolutely, valid?

That statement is unshakable. We are utterly dependent on our thinking apparatus for recognizing anything. This imposes on our thinking, feeling and will definite laws which we can in no way circumvent, as without thinking apparatus we cannot think at all. We are also unable in any way to check whether the results to which it assists us, are absolute – to do that we should need a third point outside our thinking from which to compare these results with reality, and that third point does not exist. This barrier is not one that any scientific experiment can help us surmount – for again we can only establish whether it is correct by subjecting reality to the laws of our thinking.

Calculating the velocity of a falling body does of course obviously coincide with the real event. But at the cost of dispensing with such a very great deal! We force ourselves in the direction of one-sidedness, reducing reality so as to squeeze it into the framework of the laws of our thinking and make it evaluable. How then can we talk of absolute knowledge! And the fact that the account tallies is no proof at all. For it will do that, whether we base it on the theory of gravitation or relativity or anything else, the meaning of that being that we are not building on absolute knowledge but adapting the given result to the laws of our thinking – assigning it a variable position in the building of our world of thought. The calculation is bound always to tally because the starting point is the result, and as the thinking is supposed to explain this result, it must be applied in such a way as to lead to it.

How little our thinking is capable of in respect of the absolute, becomes ever plainer the closer we approach the human field. This, which we know from our own experience and apprehend not only from without but also from within, resists one-sidedness and simplification – the given result remains ambiguous, and this ambiguity prevents the establishing of firm laws. It is only when we deal wholly in the external that the semblance of absolute knowledge can arise – but it is precisely this sole, seemingly absolute knowledge which is also most manifestly a semblance

171

and no more. For we can deal wholly and freely in the external only where we have no possibility whatever of penetrating into the internal, and where, therefore, in place of this internal we can apply our laws of thinking wholly at will, as indeed happens with the abstract and empty concept of energy. It is only by virtue of the fact that *inanimate* nature – i.e. nature wholly inaccessible to us internally – can be apprehended exclusively from without, that it adapts itself so fully to our laws of thinking as to enable seemingly absolute mathematical laws to be derived.

Quite apart from this impossibility of absolute knowledge, however, there is within us, independent of any experience, the voice of the absolute, that dictate of the inner reality, of which I have constantly had occasion to speak. Within ourselves we not only apprehend reality from outside, but also experience it directly, independently of external experience and plainly separated from it. However we may contest the fact with our reason – however strikingly at variance with it the external laws we believe in may be – we have nevertheless at the same time been given internal necessities, moral laws, which we cannot refute or supplant, and which, if we are honest, we are also obliged, against our knowledge and against our will, to recognize. It is here, and here alone, that the truth has been granted to us. We may deny it, supplant it, subdue it – but we shall, if honestly striving for truth, be bound to find it here.

Even this truth is not absolute knowledge – we cannot completely translate it into knowledge, and we can know neither its origin nor its purpose. But we can, on the other hand, apprehend it as clearly as possible, and in so doing are directly apprehending the absolute. The example of Christ conveys no absolute knowledge, for we are unable even with its aid to answer questions as to how and why, or say anything concerning the beginning and end of the world and of man. But that example does, on the other hand, convey the absolute truth because it accords with the purest apprehension of the moral laws provided within us.

The ways to truth differ with the times. At the beginning of the Renaissance, when the growth of internal reality had got out of hand, the natural sciences were the way – today the only way able to lead to it is the way to the internal. But all ideals are age old, and if fusing the temporal conditions with the given ideal works, we again find ourselves on the way to the one invariable absolute truth. The conditions of human thought and experience change, but the inner core is always the same, and thanks to the change, we can only hope to experience it more and more comprehensively.

But the special importance of thinking in opposites as a new way to the old truth seems to me in this context to be as follows –

The impossibility of absolute knowledge does not mean, as the misunderstanding so often is, that there is no external reality or that the forming of this reality comes about only through our thinking. Our thinking being in every particular tied to our bodies, i.e. to external reality, is bound to be stimulated by it, and that we are, in fact, applying the laws of our thinking correctly, becomes evident only where the result is experience that can be put to practical use. 'Ideas without concepts are blind, concepts without ideas are empty', says Kant. Just as we are obliged to penetrate reality with the aid of the laws of our thinking in order to assimilate it at all, so too we are obliged to break into reality with the aid of the laws of our thinking in order to be able to use our thinking apparatus productively. The moment we entrust ourselves to completely abstract concepts, we are dealing in empty space in which the most capricious speculations are possible – but again and again these speculations will be bound to collapse because they are constantly refuted by our experience. We have to do justice to reality and to the laws of our thinking – we have to recognize this double limitation, for only then can it become productive for our lives.

But the same goes too for the internal apprehension of the absolute. This apprehension remains uncertain and dangerous as long as we simply entrust ourselves to all the impulses of internal reality and all the vague feelings and blind desires. The absolute then remains mingled with the relative in an impenetrable and unproductive fashion. Here too the correct and fruitful application of our thinking apparatus is assured only when we get as far as laws. Earlier these laws were given from without, by God, but today we have to reveal them within, in moral laws. Only when we apprehend these laws as a legitimate component of human existence can they recover the force they once had as divine commandments.

My present thoughts are based extensively on Kant – and Kant also went so far as to reveal formal moral laws and showed what general conditions the content of moral laws must fulfil. But that content has itself remained closed to us. The step which I take beyond Kant, to the opposites, enables me to apprehend that content in its conformity to law also, for these opposites have two aspects: as regards external reality they are formal conditions; for man, on the other hand, they prove to have moral content.

This has become clear once already in this diary – space, set against external reality, is a pure and an empty perceptual form; for man, on the other hand, it is a crucial reality. I have considered space here as a human reality – and it has as a result enabled far-reaching conclusions for judging man's moral behaviour.

26 November 1939

A curious thing about the British is that almost every day, on opening the paper, one first of all discovers their own losses set out big, and only with difficulty a small report to the effect that at the same time a German vessel has been seized considerably larger than the British one that has been sunk, giving rise to the sensational announcement. Is this kind of propaganda necessary to rouse the Britisher's will to resist or does it simply accord with the *understatement* so popular in this country?

Certainly, as a result of the all-out mine war the situation seems more serious at the moment than it did. And for all that there is no impression as yet that the war has really begun, it is beginning to look more and more likely that it *will* begin in the spring and in its most terrible form. Rumours to the effect that the Germans will be coming with thousands of aircraft may be tendentious and exaggerated – but it is to be hoped that the British will, as a result, really realize that the Nazis are capable of anything!

I am afraid that the restraining influence of the German generals is being overestimated. They may in some things prevent much that seems madness, but the final decision does rest solely with Hitler. Recently a French paper had a cartoon of 'Hitler's War Council'. There are twenty Hitlers sitting around a table, walking agitatedly up and down, asking each other questions – the whole room is crowded and with no one but Hitler. This cartoon comes, I think, very near the truth! Others may sometimes succeed in making an impression on him – but at the decisive moment he will give way to himself. And the fear is that he is deciding in favour of committing very large numbers, for doing this has got him where he is – and even if he is unable to retrieve anything for Germany thereby and merely drags Europe to destruction with him.

I would be glad to see myself proved wrong by events – even by the German generals whom I consider incapable of standing their ground at the crucial moment. It is now being said that General Fritsch was not murdered, but that he went up to the front line with suicidal intent – and that, I believe, is also the summit of what those gentlemen are able to achieve. More typical is the behaviour of Thyssen who, having provided

174

the Nazis with crucial finance and helped them into the saddle, now, seeing what he has done, escapes to Switzerland. Something that none of them are able to do is accept responsibility for what they are doing and fight to the last for their own cause – they like to stay in the background in order of course not to have to bear responsibility. Once only has the *Reichswehr* been induced to bear responsibility itself – when Schleicher became Reich Chancellor, and then it was that it showed its incompetence most plainly too. There is justice in Hitler's being Lord of the *Reichswehr*, for he is at least on a level with Fritsch, having also proclaimed that were Germany to suffer defeat, he would not survive her. Is it not grotesque that anyone should dare to put such a thing to his people – should allow himself to embark irresponsibly on an undertaking costing the lives of millions and the welfare of generations and imagine himself justified by promising either to reap the fruits of victory or evade the consequences of defeat? But that, as has been said, is still at an exalted level – the others will swear any oath you like to their lords of the future also, and break it just as they broke their oaths to the Kaiser and to the Republic.

Future historiography will be able to prove without difficulty that the domination of Hitler became possible only in consequence of the general development, and that he was a blind tool serving the logical continuance of this development. But we are experiencing with horror the inadequacy of this interpretation. The weal and woe of millions depends in fact on his decisions and on the human failure of his opponents. This logical interpretation again proceeds from the result and adapts to it all that has gone before. We who are living and suffering at the time are not yet so fortunate as to be able to simplify and therefore recognize that man is to a very high degree one of the moving forces of this development. Later times will name these forces, and in so doing, exclude man. We, on the other hand, see how enigmatic these forces are, and that it is for that reason that it is, above all, the people who matter.

Night

At the moment, however, our danger brings with it an enchanting concomitant phenomenon – we can, thanks to the blackout, wander this glorious city by moonlight, undistracted by artificial light.

The days have grown short and the rain more frequent. Even when, occasionally, the sun shines, the bare trees stand alarmingly naked against a pale sky. The eye has not yet grown accustomed to them, and a scrap of

175

foliage here and there still bears witness to what has just vanished. Only when the branches are again familiar will new beauty be discovered in their intricate ornamentation. The moon awakens a premonition of this beauty, for in its unreal light, what just now was naked and desolate becomes soft and mellow.

But finer than walking through the meadows with the mists rising, is to walk through the town. I am captivated first by the old gabled houses – the moonlight reveals what makes them so dear and near – they are the homeland, the familiar scene of all the fairy stories and childhood dreams – man, confronted by the next world and the ecstasies of heaven and hell, has always found in those stories and dreams a secure place that he can love, and where he can feel safe.

The severe, plain façades of all periods, remain unaroused. They need the sun – their element is plain daylight – the moonlight passes over them, they remain silent. But the dreamy moonlight, streaming past, turns them into stage scenery standing strange and meaningless, because the performance it is used for is not taking place – the moonlight conveys us into a freer and easier realm, into glittering mystery before whose pale reflected splendour bright day fades.

Loud, over-loud, heralds of this mystery are the lively Gothic churches. The shadows of windows and niches are deeper, the rare plain surfaces gather all too bright a light. King's College Chapel, filled with an almost oriental splendour, soars more loftily than by day towards the veil of heaven, rebelling against the softness of the latter. And even the plainer spires of the old churches still break through the divine harmony which they were supposed to serve, remarkably starkly.

And again, praise be to the Roman Round Church! Even in this light its form remains clear. Even in this light it stands strongly and firmly upon this earth. But it alone responds to the light! Its regular roundness generates a gentle counterplay of light and shadow, and with this the mystery that by day resides only in its interior, moves outside. The dark shadow gathers all earthly ponderousness, yet is gradually dissolved, gradually the gaze passes to where light has been gathered, and it is in this suspense between darkness and light that the mystery roused and yet not revealed by the moon, gathers. If now we could step inside, the mystery would, we believe, be bound to be solved. And we realize that the door is bound to be locked – for otherwise how should we find our way back to day?

176

27 November 1939

European Federation, the United States of Europe is gradually becoming an article of faith with the British people. Everyone seems to be calling for it – the Labour Party, the churches, the Quakers. This programme is obviously very popular with the students and yesterday even Chamberlain suggested something similar. The important thing will be not the alteration of frontiers but a new organization of a community of European states. And this community will also have to have a unified economic life and a unified leadership.

This line of thought distinguishes this war very pleasantly from the last. Nevertheless it is one that involves special dangers. The League of Nations was a wonderful instrument too – the convention on which it was based contained well nigh everything for the coexistence of peoples. But it became ineffectual, indeed harmful, partly because it had been from the start merely an instrument of the victors, and partly because it allowed itself to be guided by Utopian aims. Lacking a genuine, living basis in a change of spirit and of nationalistic autocracy it was obliged to seek refuge in Utopia. It sacrificed its best principles to the unattainable aim of bringing all states under one umbrella. The first danger seems eliminated today, but against that, is not the second all the stronger?

The purely Utopian form duly expounded at the International Club by the Labour Party representative, seems however to have been pushed into the background, and the more so the more the non-Marxists concern themselves with this demand. Asserting itself ever more strongly is another plan that is substantially more concrete. It was put forward again, and in its most realistic form, not long ago in the International Club, and characteristically by a German refugee. The British, certainly, are not as yet so consistent, but it does seem that they too will get there. We can therefore, in judging this idea, proceed from the plan in this form.

As a condition for acceptance into this League, Professor Kantorowicz calls for a fully democratic form of state. The League is to be small to begin with, an aristocracy of democracies. The democratic states are to join forces for the defence of democracy. This means common heavy armament, common control of foreign policy, a common economy and a unified currency, and a guarantee of internal independence and national security. Kantorowicz probably sees that even for this League a change of heart will really be necessary – but he believes that the advantages the League will offer for the economy and security of its members will be bound to make every state strive to become a member. And the condition of membership being genuine democracy, democratic aspirations will be strengthened in all countries, Europe educated to democracy, and, gradually, the attitude of mind produced that guarantees peace. A military attack on this League would, however, be unlikely, even today – the modern democratic states alone possessing so great a material superiority that no one would dare to attack them if only they were suitably armed and united. It is for this very reason that there should be a clear partial renouncement of sovereignty in armaments – small bodies of troops from other states should be stationed in each of the member states, so that an attack on one will automatically and unavoidably become an attack on all.

This form of the plan has, I must admit, many impressive features. It takes extensive account of the weakness of the human spirit and the spiritual weakness of the state machine. Nevertheless, even with this form I cannot shed the uneasiness which assails me regarding all Utopias. Let me try to fathom this uneasiness.

In the League of Nations the flight to Utopia came about because the real conditions for building the League were not present. Briand's proposal for the creation of Pan-Europe suffered the same fate – having been accepted by twenty-seven states but without the slightest practical consequences. Will not the same happen to this proposal too, even if it is accepted – even if a start is made to carry it out – unless there is a change of spirit first?

If the war really does end, as is generally imagined, with Allied victory and the turning of Germany into a tolerably human state, it is to a high degree probable that this proposal will in some form or other be made a reality. The lesson of the last war has been that as a result of the general exhaustion, possibilities are created for effects upon the spirit hitherto inconceivable, and following this war the exhaustion may be greater still. But this very exhaustion, the post-war period has clearly shown, contains a great danger – as a result of it, mental effect seems very easy, everything appears simple, we underestimate the counter-forces which for the moment have merely been forced into the background, and as a result the change of spirit remains superficial and does not produce the fundamental change of heart and mind which ought to guarantee its success. It enables the counter-forces to recover in a most disastrous fashion. This process was actually encouraged by the League of Nations which masked this unfortunate state of affairs – will it not also be encouraged by a League that again begins re-organization from a basis that is not as yet assured.

I am aware of course that the League of Nations was above all a tool of the victors giving out that it was serving humanity, and that it was as a

178

result unable either to assure the fruits of victory or really to serve humanity. This time the Democracies have got to win, and the League will have to protect the very fruits of victory, the saving of the Democracies, in the most forceful way possible.

But this time a new power is in play – Bolshevism. What is not certain is how far it will have pushed by the end of the war – the Rhine? China? Sweden? But even if its sphere of influence *is* not much different from today's, it will still be that totalitarian power against which the Democracies will have to be defended, and will it be possible to set up a defence line of that sort in France and Britain unless these Democracies undergo a fundamental change internally? Almost all of us came back from the last war socialists, having all of us become disaccustomed to property, the close circle of home, and life as an individual, and though we might long for them it seemed to us right and fair – indeed, completely self evident – that everyone who had risked his life should now also have a share in the goods of this world. In Germany Socialism seemed inevitable – it was only its ignominious failure that made way for the opposing forces. Today's senior Nazis were all Social Democrats in 1918.

At that time this effect was potent only with the conquered, after this war is it not bound, under Russia's influence, to become general? Will it then still be possible to fit into a capitalist economic order soldiers expected to stop at nothing and accustomed to danger, death and killing. And form an army to protect this capitalist world against a communist one? And even if it is, will not the apparent realization of Utopia once again mask a state of affairs that is of necessity producing a totally different development? Will Utopia not again contribute to a failure to bring about what, in the immediate post-war – and spiritually favourable – period, might in fact have been brought about?

One remark of Kantorowicz's seemed to me especially instructive: 'There will then be no more neutrals. Neutrality will then be nothing less than a crime.' But is it not a crime today? Is it not disgraceful that Holland, Belgium, Switzerland and the Scandinavian countries whose weal and woe depends solely on whether the Allies are victorious, should be clinging anxiously to their neutrality – indeed, even be protesting in Britain against the blockade of Germany? Again, I am aware that the neutrals are justifiably afraid of German invasion which the Allies would not be able to protect them against directly, and that it is also in the Allies' interest that no pretext should be given for this invasion. But that invasion is really being prevented by this is highly uncertain – what, on the other hand, *is* certain is that invasion will come as soon as it suits the German

179

war plan. And it is equally certain that Germany's conduct of the war depends to a high degree on Swedish ore and on the products she receives from and via these neutral countries. And it is certain too that the Nazi propaganda potential would be much smaller and the psychological situation in Germany fundamentally changed if these neutrals were allies of Britain.

Today is when this League ought to come, then it might help! What part the Nazis see neutrality as playing was shown clearly when they were planning the attack on Holland. As long as they believed Belgium would pursue neutrality to the point of insanity, they were going to march in, but when Belgium so far infringed her neutrality to the extent of standing by Holland conditionally, they dropped their plan, at least for the time being. If it is left to the Germans to decide which countries are entitled to remain neutral, and if it is always only the state under attack that takes up arms, it will always be to the Nazis' advantage. On the other hand, if the Democracies even today – and today is perhaps the last possible moment – were to go over *en bloc* to the offensive, the Nazis would suffer a crucial blow strategically, economically and morally.

28 November 1939

The past is ambiguous – we can read into it almost whatever we like. It can, for example, be equally well proved that the fall of Napoleon was a misfortune because the emergent centralized state failed to materialize, as that it was fortunate because it hastened the birth of nations. The first conclusion will satisfy pioneers of Pan-Europe, the second – the nationalists, and both, from their conclusions, will derive laws which will lay down for the future what they have interpreted from the past. The correctness of such conclusions can only be verified if the laws derived from long periods of the past were also to remain valid over long periods of time in the future, but verification of that sort is not possible. We have no means of looking into the future and seeing whether the laws stated by philosophers of history are right or wrong. Still, we can today take in at a glance that most of the earlier philosophies of history have been refuted by developments – the laws propounded having always been completely wrong – although isolated prophecies have been fulfilled, by chance, albeit mostly in a manner different from the manner prophesied.

For that reason we also have no possibility of counteracting the wish-fulfilment element of such allegedly scientific predictions. Mostly this element is clearly evident – the name *Third Reich* is eloquent of the extent to which it has been based upon interpretation of history, but certainly no admirer of the Third Reich will demonstrate that European federation is bound to come, and no socialist will conclude that socialism is impossible, although that too might be demonstrated. We might perhaps in these cases still say that it is the realization of what is to come that brings about the struggle for it – but that that is in reality not so is shown particularly clearly by one of the most remarkable of historico-philosophical works, Spengler's *Decline of the West*. What Spengler prophesies is dreadful, he himself shrinks from what he sees coming. But as he describes the final epoch which is now supposed to be preceding the decline, it becomes clear that in spite of all his reservations and pessimism, it is to this epoch that his own heart belongs. It is the epoch of technology, the engineer, great wars, Prussian Socialism, and ruthlessly heroic man dominating by the aid of technology, whom it is ushering in, makes that dangerous life which Spengler alone considers worth living, a reality. Even in the gloomiest form of the philosophy of history, the wish forges decisively ahead.

This work is typical of the philosophy of history. Philosophically it is in part plainly untenable, and it is demonstrably based upon many violent distortions of history. All the same, it remains an important and remarkable book by reason of its exceptional power of vision, and it may be as a result of this that it is right in the end for all its false and inadequate assumptions. But we must nevertheless not let ourselves be seduced into believing it today, although developments at the moment appear to make this very prophecy probable. Only later times will be able to decide whether he is really right or whether he wrongly assesses a minor section of history. We should therefore merely be acting prematurely and letting ourselves be unnecessarily discouraged in our resolves if we accepted these conclusions as scientifically founded guidelines for our own lives! But the same is true of all good historico-philosophical works – the arresting thing about them is their power of vision, which is the very reason why no great validity attaches to them. We can just as well follow our own wishes with the same certainty or lack of it.

In the political plans of recent times the wish has now already made itself independent – people are renouncing the historico-political basis, and reinforcing and illustrating merely the intention of creating a more desirable world. But the philosophy of history is producing an after-effect, in that people are simply constructing the external form of what is coming, and are neglecting the human forces which are able to give the form content and make it a reality. But that is precisely the method of the history of philosophy – it derives from history external laws which lead of necessity to the end, but to which therefore man has no need to contribute. With Hegel reason automatically becomes reality, with Marx capitalism leads inescapably to socialism, with Spengler decline is unavoidable and the rule of the engineer inevitable – and in the same way, with federation the gaze is pinned on external development. What is forgotten is that the wish can only be fulfilled if people change accordingly.

Indeed, more than that – it is not external form that matters at all! Socialism, as I have already had occasion to stress, can either be humanly desirable or also fearful and terrible. Any external form contains these two possibilities – federation too can be desirable as a community of free democracies – and it can be terrible as a semi-Fascist community desirous merely of saving capitalism. So it is not at all the ends being fought for today which are important, but solely the furtherance of the human quality. But Utopia, in any form, misleads into viewing external form simply as an adequate fulfilment of the wish – in the same way as the Communists are even today still standing by terrorist–Fascist Russia, federation too can lead to Utopia's being furthered by the genuine democrats when its realization is already setting the seal on the decline of the Democracies.

Here again the example of Spengler is characteristic. His preference for the warlike Prussian Socialist age has been a great help to the Nazis, and his encouragement of them has been his real contribution to development. But when they came to power Spengler was obliged to dissociate himself from them – that was not how he had imagined the future he had wished for. He died lonely and embittered. But he it was who had demanded that we should submit to the development process and said that any evasion was wrong. But even if he had wanted to evade it he would not have been able to. The Nazis used his ideal but rejected his work. His pessimism was of no use to them. His work created only obscurity and confusion. Spengler's attitude towards humanity – and that of many Germans who believed him – might have worked out quite differently had it not foundered on its false assessment of external development.

The example of the natural sciences must, I believe, be followed unfailingly in one respect – we must be ruthless in arriving at the basic elements and we must build up from them! But we must liberate ourselves from causal thinking which cannot teach us to know the basic human elements – we have got to find a new way to the human.

182

29 November 1939

Yes, but am not I too continually citing historical examples? Am not I too straying into the field of the philosophy of history?

To include history in our deliberations seems to me of the greatest importance. Human life is short, the radius of our own experience small. History can and must supplement what our own lives are not able to offer. But we must regard history as *experience*, and not read into it what experience is never able to offer – the general and absolute law. Interpretation of that sort is merely a disastrous statement of the fact that history is easier to simplify than our own experience. We must attempt to obtain a thorough knowledge of the individual event; we can get to know the connections in a particular field; we can investigate definite changes of direction which teach us to understand the technical composition as it were of the change of direction we are co-experiencing; we can also read from an epoch what kind of path is being followed by thinking, the idea, faith and art. But we must never forget that we know nothing of the limitation of birth and death, little of the mental processes within human society, nothing of the apportionment and dependence of aptitude and genius, and that we lack all the basic elements that would enable us to see in human history a necessity that conforms to law. We must be especially careful over the interpretation of external processes, for the points of reference are so slight here that such interpretation leads quickly into the boundless and groundless. We must never forget that we cannot possibly answer the question that so often assails us and asks what would have happened if Caesar or Lenin had lived longer and if Napoleon or William I had died earlier. Where mental and artistic processes are concerned, we can go further, for they have already been transferred to that realm of thought in which interpretation also moves, and we are therefore able to penetrate them more directly, although here too we must not forget that our knowledge is confined by the impenetrable mystery of life and death, of aptitude and effect. Neither must we in this field of knowledge assail limits which are insurmountable, but endeavour to enter deeply into the internal, not the deceptively abstract internal of unidentifiable forces, but the human element which we are alone able to re-experience. Then, and then only, will the science of history remain clearly separated from the philosophy of history, and only then will it become productive.

We must understand the teaching that our time provides. Sixteen years ago the word *war* had no concrete content at all for most Europeans – and who, a short time ago, reading or speaking of the French Revolution,

183

Spanish persecution of the Jews, Russian pogroms, civil war, slave revolt or a mercenary leader's reign of terror, would have had any real thoughts as he did so? Our time is giving us a fearful object lesson in history – we are learning daily that we only understand what we are able to re-experience. But this re-experiencing can only be intensified by research if, with the aid of our minds, we enter deeply into the history of the mind, investigate facts so closely that they become humanly immediate, and if, where people are concerned, we do not call it a day at psychology, which is equally unreliable and ambiguous, but endeavour to apprehend their thoughts and feelings directly and without connections we have attributed to them subsequently. But even doing that we only get to know our own minds and never the mind of history! Even history remains mute if we strive beyond the limits of our knowledge, for in so doing we always plunge into the void – but our possibilities for knowledge are immense when we employ it within its limits and in conformity with its nature.

Evening

Spengler may perhaps once again serve to illustrate this distinction. A fine feature of his work is his portrayal of past civilizations. He shows how, like a plant, they grow, unfold and bloom, bear fruit and die. This approach is productive and helpful where isolated epochs of the past are considered, but becomes manifestly false as a result of his making a law of it. For in order to make this law compelling he isolates each epoch within itself absolutely. He asserts for instance that our mathematics have nothing to do with the Graeco-Roman world – which however not only contradicts the facts but is also false in a wider sense – the mysterious way of effect does not admit of being taken in at a glance! We are not in any wise able to determine accurately how far, for instance, the Classical writers continue to exert an effect in the basic elements of our lives, and as a result, how far again, through the Graeco-Roman world and through Christianity long-extinct civilizations are still effective in our own. And because Spengler thinks he knows the law he prophesies to us that our own civilization will before long become extinct – but as contemporaries we again have no possibility of judging how deep the epoch goes which we are co-experiencing. Naturally our own experience seems more powerful and significant to us, but how are we to decide whether this epoch corresponds to the changes of the Baroque period which were attended by the Thirty Years War, or to the more profoundly affective change of direction between Middle Ages and Renaissance, or even to that most profound upheaval between Classical world and Christianity? The far-reaching conclusions devalue Spengler's fine *per se* knowledge almost completely.

It can however become productive if we examine the individual changes of direction as closely as possible. We can establish the difference between medieval and modern thought, follow how the breakthrough of the Renaissance came about, and how Reformation and Baroque, Enlightenment and Rococo developed out of it. A comparison of Gothic and Renaissance makes it possible to determine how at a definite peak of development in every style, a time of overloading and apparent withering away sets in, and how it is that very time that gives rise to Baroque. And in all styles there is a repeated up-and-down, a constant withering away and a constant renewal. With the plant too the leaves fade, the blooms fade, and only then does the fruit ripen which is again at the same time seed. If we apprehend these isolated processes more closely we shall, it is true, still not be able to pass any prophetic judgement concerning our time but we shall stand more securely in it, broaden our experience, extend our lives and be better able to develop our powers.

1 December 1939

So now the Russians have started their war with Finland. They have been preparing for it using the same allegations, indeed, words, as the Nazis used for the war against Poland – the only innovation being that a few hours before the attack, Molotov was assuring us that it would be a most wicked slander to ascribe such an intention to Russia. And so now the Russian lamb is defending itself against the Finnish wolf . . . What is to become of a world in which such perversions are possible and perhaps even effective?

The day before yesterday it was still being announced that Britain was asking Russia why there had been no reply to her proposals for extending trade relations. Today Britain is bound to disassociate herself from Russia – did she *have* to collect another snub in advance? Was the situation not equally clear weeks ago? What is to become of a world where *Realpolitik* assumes such forms? And where the deeply and truly disgraced authors of the Munich Agreement simply remain in power, and where confidence in them is increased by their failure? How too are those men to appreciate any clear sort of situation properly?

185

2 December 1939

The Russians seem to have very radical plans for Finland – a *People's Government* has been formed, and the Finnish Communists expelled to Russia during the Civil War, are now going back as a *Legion*. Perhaps it is just 'many thousands' – as the British press writes – but with such a small people and supported by Russian might, even a few thousand can play a decisive part. I am afraid that brave resistance will be of as little help to Finland as timely surrender would have been. If the Russians have the possibility of Bolshevizing the country – and what is to prevent them? – we can close the independent-Finland file for good, regardless of how the war goes.

The British are emphasizing of necessity that they must first win the war against Germany, then many things will be possible – until then, nothing is. It is hard to object to that. America's informal indignation is plainer than it was over Poland, but even so is of no help. Still, won't *after* the war be too late for it? The advance of Russia bears the fishy hallmarks of an irresistible development – East Poland is lost for good, a Bolshevik Finland is also likely, and who is going to save Romania whose turn it then seems to be? And how far will Russia have advanced by the end of the war? And how will one call a halt to communism advancing in that fashion?

3 December 1939

Oh these neutrals! True, the British press is today styling the news as if this time there were hope of their indignation assuming more concrete forms than in the case of Poland. But meanwhile the Russian invasion is taking place under the protection of Swedish and Norwegian neutrality. And the British press is also itself making its news painful by laying heaviest stress on the indignation felt in Rome. Shall we ever get used to this complete non-dependence on truth? One can hardly believe one's own eyes at reading extracts from the Rome press declaring emphatically that a stop must at last be put to attacks on small states.

Finland herself is going to appeal to the League of Nations. What a chance for the dreamt-of federation! But at the same time in the paper I find the following, 'For the first time since the outbreak of war the League of Nations is meeting again in session to discuss financial and administrative questions.' It is hoped to dispose of these purely technical questions in the course of a week and 'to avoid any split, although there is a fear of political incidents as all members will be sending delegates'. That is to say not only Russia and the neutrals but also Finland, Poland and the old Czechoslovakia. What an opportunity to clarify things and do something. But no – there is a fear of incidents 'and Great Britain and France are anxious to see the League preserved as an institution even if not used'. It's really not worth the mental bother.

It is merely bitter to keep discovering this in Britain of all places. Hardly a day passes without our experiencing some kindness from British people. Everyone takes pains to lead us slowly back again to an ordered life and make us forget foreign lands. Never before have I had as I have here the sense of an old civilization's having to a large degree transformed itself into a human attitude! In France I had to admire the high degree of independence of the individual, his interest in things of the mind, but his human attitude remained inscrutable. But here the overwhelming thing is the powerful humanity. Of course, the old university city of Cambridge provides a too favourable image of Britain – the picture in the industrial towns will be different. But that is something the British appreciate – their ideal is to have their sons educated here. The grim battle for every particular of the rights of Parliament and the individual reveals a living sense of justice. How glad I would be to express the gratitude I owe this country in unreserved approval. But it is not possible. This England has still not understood the signs of the times, for where, except Utopia, is Democracy setting its feet firmly upon the new that is bound to come?

6 December 1939

Modern architecture – a memoir. That really was the plainest and most perfect realization of that better world which we believed to be on its way. Here the old confused forms were finally eliminated and the true basic form liberated in perfect clarity. What was eliminated was the general dominance of the lordly vertical which no longer really dominates the modern house because, thanks to technology, it does not need walls any more. What was liberated was the clear horizontal pointing into the distance at the beauty of this world and opening the horizon. The vertical retained power only as height, merely as an isolated counter-weight – it was an upward swing in the released spaciousness.

A new element intrudes into building – glass. The outer walls of the building, for centuries the most real and solid part, are suddenly no longer necessary. The window can be enlarged into a wall, and behold, the wall thereby acquires a new life, and is, according to the light, hardly visible at all, or transparent, or a mirror of the surroundings, and only suddenly does it sometimes still consolidate itself into a wall. These buildings allowed a sense of freedom and lightness, a playful merriment that really seemed to promise a counter-weight to and an unsuspected human fulfilment of this at first menacing development. Still technology seemed to be enslaving man – and yet already his second victory, his new resurrection was proclaiming itself.

And what was it like to enter such a house, say in Grunewald? Gone was the breathtaking magnificence of the nineties, the hideous nightmares of the Makart period, the confused abnormalities of the *Jugendstil* – gone too the tastefully subdued ponderousness of inner perplexity that usually fills rooms still today. Instead, the room was suddenly a space opened wide to the landscape, with only simple furniture and little of it standing freely and correctly in place, the walls bright and plain, the floor in colours that showed well. Suddenly you could move – and in such rooms it was the person who mattered – the inadequacy of owners who had no relationship with their houses was mercilessly revealed. The house served the person, and so there had to be a person there who was worthy of that service.

I do not know whether it is right to be writing an obituary to this architecture already.

My thoughts range back to the Renaissance in Italy. The process was similar to that of today. The first trend-setting buildings were brutal naked boxes which, to begin with, were a restoration of pure form. The great mass of contemporaries must have raised an outcry about them in the same way as about the ultra-modern ones yesterday – for were they not poor and tasteless compared to the carved buildings of the late Gothic period and the Moorish windows? It is no accident that wealthy Venice does not go over to Renaissance until the latter has been debased into showy baroque! Indeed we must, I think, imagine the beginning of Renaissance painting to be exactly like that of any modern painting – certainly the majority were appalled when, for instance, Fabriano who reproduced magnificent garments almost physically in the most sumptuous colours, setting them with precious stones, was ousted by Masaccio who *daubed* swiftly and sketchily using only ordinary colours! And are the first Renaissance chapels whose effect is produced merely by the clear arrangement of unadorned walls, to be compared with the Gothic churches?

But the new art is very rapidly transformed – out of the material of the door-frames and the pillars grows a delicate new form of ornamentation. The windows are strengthened by means of plain projections and roof-

188

ings, the pillars become more solid as flat, and then round, columns. The old, external magnificence is disposed of, but out of the inner strength of the new style grows a new prosperity – the inner wealth liberated by the new form has an urge for ornament and there too creates a new world. And how clear and new the colours which very soon dominate painting!

But where is this transformation at work in our modern architecture? Am I too impatient, is it still too early? But twenty or thirty years is not exactly a short time in this regard – and the need for this transformation can be felt everywhere also.

The signs in the realm of these arts coincide with those in the realm of the idea. Yet modern architecture is the very thing to increase confidence – so great is the degree of perfection here that it is hardly conceivable that this, the earliest art of every nascent civilization, should not be an early sign. Already growing underground perhaps is the idea that will guarantee the liberation of a humanly rich life and thereby preserve even modern architecture from being suffocated in jejuneness.

8 December 1939

Every day as I read the paper a dreadful weariness comes over me. Indolently and imperfectly Grand Politics are at work, the League of Nations is now supposed to be doing something against Russia, but will it be any more than a useless protest? But even if politics worked better what could be directly achieved? Terrible things must be happening in Poland if even only a fraction of the news is true – and it sounds likely that most of it is – and now, fighting in Finland, terror in the Czech territories! And passing over those more striking instances in silence, how much suffering life will contain daily for a tolerably decent, tolerably warm-hearted person in Germany, and how much suffering is involved by the so far truly slight losses in the West and at sea! And things are bound to be very different of course.

That is the paralysing thing – that one can devise nothing which is not powerless in the face of this suffering. Allied victory – it can hardly come quickly, and will it not assist the breakthrough of another terror, and with it, revenge? Sudden peace – it might perhaps create new conditions for the growth of the idea, but only by increasing the area of suffering. A terrible vengeance is being exacted for the fact that the mortal sin of the Germans, the sin against the spirit, should not have roused the spirit of others in time, and that they should over the years have remained idle.

Perhaps it is this weary emptiness which today brings the baroque so close to us. Think of the wonderful late Tintorettos – especially his *Last Supper* in San Rocco, Venice. In the centre and in the foreground of the picture is desolate emptiness, the great scene is pushed wholly to the side. The humans sit, shadowy figures, around the great, and again empty, table, even Christ hardly stands out from them. They are full of life, in great agitation, but even that remains shadowy, a self-deception, a self-deadening that does not prevail against the emptiness and darkness. But on the other side this very displacement of the human makes room for a broad stream of light, the flooding divine light, to break in – but this stream of light remains an intrusion – it does not wholly penetrate the darkness, it lights it only a little, it does not find its way to the humans. A hovering angel creates the transition forcibly, and yet this very angel, a master achievement of Tintoretto's baroque technique, hovers only with difficulty, only as we ourselves hover in dark dreams, as if fascinated by the void he is supposed to bridge and remains banished to.

Later, when the humans have sunk wholly into shadow, into Rembrandt's half-darkness – when they no longer strive to free themselves but surrender, the light becomes a new message. Now it no longer forces its way in front outside but breaks mysteriously from within. The room remains dark, but the man Christ is illuminated.

Remember Rembrandt's *Christ at Emmaus* – Christ and the two disciples are lost in the dark, and yet they are not lost, for the inner light makes them stand out from the dark. This and the pictures related to it are the true completion of the Renaissance, for while in the Renaissance the triangular arrangement of heads was still flexible, still leaving many possibilities open, here it is unshakeably fixed, for any movement would shift the heads – again arranged strictly in a triangle – out of the light into the dark. But that is to say that the light is no longer a fortuitous, no longer a deliberate subterfuge – it has become compelling – if you recognize the inner compulsion and entrust yourself to it, it raises you into the light. The light does not again break from heaven until the way of suffering is completed in the Crucifixion – but now it is reaching man, now it is creating a link with heaven.

Must we too go down wholly into the dark – walk the road of suffering to the end, before we again partake of the light?

9 December 1939

At the International Club we meet many Britons, Indians, Canadians and South Africans. Communists excepted, they take the superficially

190

correct view of the political situation, and they are clearly and semi-adequately aware of what is involved. Most clearly aware are the Indians, but they are busy with their own worries. The others however show how little this relative clarity today suffices. Up to last summer they went often to Germany and liked going there. From their superficial impressions they are, as they know, unable to judge the Third Reich – but it is impossible to get them to understand that by these journeys they have helped the Nazis nevertheless, and how wrong it was to leave the Germans to think that even the Third Reich was still an integral part of the civilized world, instead of ostracizing it. Again and again one is forced to see that the danger is that the British are still not grasping even today how absolute a decision is involved.

10 December 1939

The paintings have put me in mind of the Eucharist which must in these days be being received at church by countless people. Is there not here also a rigid convention which is accepted without a thought therefore endangering real Christianity?

The Last Supper of the Bible is unique, and no work of art is capable of reproducing it. The shadow of death is descending upon Christ, his soul is troubled unto death, for he sees the fearful way which he now has to go. Yet out of this deep sorrow, out of the despondency that threatens even him, he composes himself for the last celebration. On the high Jewish feast day he gathers his disciples about him to tell them of the agony awaiting him, and show them the way through this agony to joy – to the certainty of the good tidings which they will only be able fully to apprehend and make their own as a result of his death and terrible suffering. Supreme artistry is employed to make the significance of this farewell which is at the same time a most intimate union, stand out in the simple narrative.

Above is not the sky under which Christ usually makes his teaching known to men – this time his friends, his children, his disciples are involved. But the Son of Man has nowhere to lay his head, the roof that shall shelter him and his disciples has to be found by approaching someone who lets them have a bare room. Then supper begins with the bewildering and disturbing marking out of Judas as traitor – it is a question of startling the disciples deeply so that they shall be certain to hear what they – who are again soon to forget their vigil – should listen to with the utmost attention. And only then does Jesus break the bread and give it to

191

them as his body, and hand them the cup of wine that is the blood of the New Testament that is being shed. It is an extraordinary metaphor that he gives: what must be its meaning for us?

Certainly not that a new celebration is being instituted. For he passes them not the Easter Lamb that disciples have prepared for the Jewish feast, not unleavened bread which is prescribed for this day, but ordinary bread which breaks the tradition. And he does not read the old prescribed prayers but proclaims a new future, a new teaching.

The fact that it is plain bread that he hands them seems to me to say that they are not to cling to his body – not to cling to him who is going to die and go from them, and that it is not he, the teacher, not the exceptional phenomenon or unique manifestation of genius that matters, but simple, everyday, ever-present life, and the indispensable daily nourishment of this life. Only if we succeed in incorporating this teaching wholly into our lives – only if we build ourselves up spiritually upon it as we nourish ourselves physically with bread, in the most natural and compelling fashion – only if we live always in it and through it, day after day – only then is Christ really present – only then do we understand and experience his example in which this teaching has embodied itself. It is only as bread nourishes the body that this teaching leads us to the living life.

And wine in the Bible stands constantly for joy. The blood which is shed becomes, as the blood of the New Testament, wine, and with that, joy. Christ offers it to the disciples in the chalice, the chalice of suffering which he is preparing for them and which God will not let pass from him – yet it is precisely as a result of this suffering that it becomes the wine that brings joy. His teaching is not only bread, not only harsh, self-evident necessity – the indispensable; it is also wine – superfluity; pure bliss released from the physical dreariness of bread – riches and joy. By virtue of a mysterious transformation process, the body derives from the bread nourishment for the blood, by virtue of which the heart preserves and rules the body; and Christianity which is what first makes us wholly receptive to suffering, which is what first teaches us also to feel the agony as powerfully as if our own blood were being shed – Christianity, by a similar transformation process, leads out of suffering and into joy, waking, out of the most powerful and violent tension, a sense of the divine. But again it is not to a life beyond life that Christ points, but blood and wine, things of daily, of real, life – and the bliss too must stream from real, lived life.

192

12 December 1939

The League of Nations does seem now to be deciding in favour of positive action. Russia, within twenty-four hours, is supposed to declare herself ready for peace negotiations. But what will happen when, as is certain, she refuses? Shall we content ourselves with the ineffectual expulsion of Russia? The Finns are announcing successes non-stop, but I am afraid they are of no great significance.

The British are now removing the mystery hitherto surrounding the Anglo-Russian negotiations. They declined to surrender the Baltic states and Finland – and also allowed negotiations to break down because they considered the *ramshackle* Russian Army incapable of fighting beyond Russia's frontiers. So what was impending had been known long in advance, and what to think of the Russian Army – and yet economic negotiations were being carried on!

But as long as Russia is regarded as neutral, the enormous power of communist ideology remains Germany's ally, and defeat of Germany will not be victory by a long way, for only in Russia will the system of terror be struck at where it can be beaten. And as the world is now for once more outraged by Russia than by Germany, would not battle with Russia provide the one opportunity of rallying the world against terror systems?

Oh, but strategic considerations really make no sense. It simply is not possible to assent to war in any way. For in order to chance that most perilous of blows we would have to know what we wanted, and even to work towards revolution in Russia we would have to have a living idea that was better than the communist! But democracy is of course ideologically so weak that there is not even any hope of accomplishing anything in Germany which has only wretched substitutes for ideas, or in India, which would seem essential for this struggle, or of convincing the young people in its own country. For these young people argue that terror is vile, but the capitalists will not give way, therefore terror is necessary.

In fact of course, the more we simply let things slide, another bogey also rears its head, that of a world united with Germany – a superficially altered Germany perhaps – against Russia. For the indignation concerning Russia is of course of mixed origin – what people are afraid of is not dictatorship but communism. It is no accident that the indignation felt by Mussolini and Franco should be so very much welcomed by the British press. My belief, as ever, is that the Nazis and Stalin have far-reaching joint plans, but what is to prevent the Nazis from veering around once again if they find it more favourable? But that would mean making the world Fascist to an appalling extent.

So are the young people of Britain right? No! For they want to get rid of misery, they do not see that the misery they are combating within the Democracies is infinitesimally small compared to the misery within the realm of terror! They do not see that they are combating the lesser evil with the greater – minor, relative injustice – with absolute injustice. They intervene naturally in the question of war and peace and become subject to the falsifications which confuse the fronts. The vast majority seem to see only the choice between capitalism and communism. They do not see that the important thing above all is to preserve the enormous good of relative freedom and gradually transform this freedom into relative social justice. That is the only way that makes any sense.

13 December 1939

Yes, but didn't I too approve of the Russian Revolution? Didn't I too, in spite of many sad experiences, attach myself to this Russia? Was not my attitude to Russia uncertain? How, then, can I demand of the young people of Britain that *they* should see clearly?

I think I can absolve myself from this reproach, and many Germans also. News of Russia was always unreliable and obscure, and it is no wonder that the attitude to Russia remained uncertain. But pondering the work of Marx and despairing at the thoughts and deeds of the two socialist parties in Germany, we saw what was necessary. I can say *we*, for both parties kept losing their best forces because it was simply impossible to go ahead with them uncritically and because criticism was forbidden. That happened years before Hitler – so how, here and now is it possible not to make such a demand of young people, everything having since become so much plainer as a result of the Nazis and Russia's faithful imitation of Nazi methods! And when here too the socialist parties are making the old mistakes.

The fateful thing was simply that these people did not prevail against the parties' might, and that their voices were suppressed by the party and not heard outside the parties. This impotence drove many back into the parties against their better knowledge, or they dissipated their energies outside in a vain striving after practical effect. In any case they destroyed themselves without accomplishing anything. Is the fault in this country too that young people have no opportunity inside or outside the parties

194

to help divergent opinions achieve some effect? A government composed of old men seems to speak in favour of it.

But probably too little power is expended on the third possibility because it is simply not recognized and correctly evaluated. But it is probably here too that the fundamental mistake of our age is made: we concentrate strictly on external effect. We do not have confidence in what is within us, and are therefore consumed with impatience for result. The human quality is not being embodied in an idea – how, in that case, can we build on the idea?

14 December 1939

Slowly delving into modern English literature I have now come across a book I cannot get out of my mind – it is Hutchinson's *Testament*.

The most stimulating thing about this novel, which is set in the Russian Revolution and impresses me as entirely trustworthy, is that it reveals how very much in basic features the Bolshevik Revolution resembles the National Socialist. There are not, it is true, the orgies of sadism, but only because the Russians, fighting a hard civil war, have no time for them, and this civil war, although bloodier and costlier, being an open battle dangerous for both sides, seems the fairer. But that apart, it is all there – the absolute powerlessness of the individual, the dastardly annihilation of the best people, the senseless destruction of cultural and spiritual values, and above all, the dreadful domination of the secret police who turn everyone into hunted animals, stab in the back and murder in prison, render people defenceless and destroy them, degrade man and then exploit that degradation for most abominable purposes. All the features we know so well are there: not sleeping at home because they are looking for you; being caught and shipped from one prison to another without knowing what you have in fact done wrong, or what awaits you; farcical judicial hearings which pass predetermined judgement without considering counter-arguments. And no place in the whole world to protect yourself against this fearful injustice, no place to find justice or even simply mercy. And among these outlaws are the best people, those very ones with some knowledge of man who, at the risk of their freedom, have fought for true human rights. The party, pretending alone to know what is necessary, triumphs over all freedom, justice and humanity, and does so simply by employing violence, bloodshed, and extreme injustice, cruelty and inflexibility to enforce a programme in which all these features gradually become

195

indelibly imprinted. Lenin is followed by Stalin, and how could that be otherwise?

But that distinction which I too am inclining to, is false! Lenin's example is impressive by reason of the path he follows, and because not only is he an outstanding theoretician but he also possesses the rare ability to transform this theory, with the aid of necessary limitations, into imposing practice. But what is the use of that if at the same time he inoculates it with the deadly germ that is bound to produce Stalin? And Trotsky is certainly a splendid strategist, but what is the use of that when he it is who invents the method of fighting that enables his opponents to topple him, and root out his supporters by the same skilful use of terror? That is the method by which all forms of Fascism have come to power. Have these results been worth the millions of human victims they have cost? Is not 'by their fruits ye shall know them' again applicable here? It may well be said that Lenin and Trotsky were executors of an inevitable development – but they must not be regarded as brilliant models!

It is over this very point that the book makes a very crucial distinction between Russia and the rest of the world. Very movingly it depicts the unimaginable misery Russia plunges into as a result of Tsarism and war – here revolution really is an inevitable development. It is not a black-and-white picture that Hutchinson paints: he shows how the party leaders are moved, and hardened, by the misery of the vast masses, and how even the most human of them are compelled towards cruelty because it seems the final and only way out. It is only through this compulsion that also to power come those whose driving urge is a delight in cruelty. But here in Britain, on the other hand, the movement does not emanate from those reduced to misery. The lot of the unemployed figures in argument, it is true, but they play no essential part and may still be much better off than workers in Russia. Young people are just simply led astray by a false picture of the Russian Revolution. There misery was a misfortune that forced the Revolution on to the wrong track; here the party leaders are pleased at any extension of misery and exaggerate it in order to arrive as quickly as possible at violent revolution. Prematurely and of their own free will, they are opening the gates to cruelty.

In Germany millions of unemployed were in fact driven to despair, and yet even there it was apparent that the misery argument was false and that the moving forces lay elsewhere. Will not the same thing have even more to be proved here?

That is that the true moving forces lie in the *petit-bourgeois* class which does not as yet know any real need, but which, as a result of the capitalist

196

development process, has been impoverished and is therefore eaten up with envy and ambition. It presses for revolution not because it wishes to create a better world, but because it is internally empty, having become paralysed in Philistinism and *slavery to things and customs,* and is desirous of saving its external worth at any price. My fear is that the intellectuals of the Left, exaggerating the significance and the misery of the unemployed, are merely furthering the concerns of the *petit-bourgeois* Fascists. Today, after the change of direction in Russia, is not every revolution bound to lead directly to Fascist terror?

At the moment the intellectuals of the Left do, it is true, have a new and weighty argument at their disposal – is not *war* terrible enough? War is a dreadful misfortune, but has not *it* more than anything made the mistakes of the Russian Revolution abundantly plain?

We must all, I think, relearn our lesson more thoroughly. We are accustomed simply to glorify revolution, and are all too loth to believe that every revolution is a terrible catastrophe. And for that reason the one important thing would seem to be to render, by gradual evolution, any sudden revolution superfluous. Blinded by the supposed glory of ever-terrible revolution, we devote too little energy to making possible that evolution which is solely worthy of man.

Evening

Matthias Claudius wrote in 1793:

Sie dünkten sich die Herren aller Herr'n,
Zertraten alle Ordnung, Sitt' und Weise,
Und gingen übermütig neue Gleise
Von aller wahren Weisheit fern,
Und trieben ohne Glück und Stern
Im Dunkeln hin, nach ihres Herzens G'lüste,
Und machten elend nah und fern.
Sie mordeten den König, ihren Herrn,
Sie morden sich einander, morden gern,
Und tanzen um das Blutgerüste.
            Erbarm dich ihrer!

Sie wollten ohne Gott sein, ohn' ihn leben
In ihrem tollen Sinn;
Und sind nun auch dahin gegeben,
Zu leben ohne ihn.

Der Keim des Lichtes und der Liebe,
Den Gott in unsere Brust gelegt,
Der seines Wesens Stempel trägt,
Und sich in allen Menschen regt,
Und der, wenn man ihn hegt und pflegt,
Zu unserem Glücke freier schlägt,
Als ob er aus dem Grabe sich erhübe –
Der Keim des Lichtes und der Liebe,
Der ist in ihnen stumm und tot;
Sie haben alles Große, alles Gute Spott.
Sie beten Unsinn an und tun dem Teufel Ehre,
Sie stellen Greuel auf Altäre.
                    Erbarm dich ihrer!

[Lords of lords they thought themselves,
trampled all order, morals, custom,
and haughtily they went new ways
remote from all true wisdom,
and drifted luckless, starless,
in darkness, as their hearts desired,
and created misery near and far.
The King, their Lord, they murdered,
they murder one another, murder gladly,
and they dance about the bloody scaffold.
                    Have mercy on them!

Godless they would be, and Godless live
in their crazed sense;
and now too are delivered up
to Godless life.
The seed of light and love
that God sowed in our breasts
that bears the imprint of his being
and stirs in all men,
and when it is tended and is cherished
shoots more freely forth to our good fortune,
as though it were rising from the grave –
the seed of light and love
in them is mute and dead;
all that is great and good they mock.

198

They worship nonsense, do the devil honour,
and set up on altars monstrous things.
                    Have mercy on them!]

It was possible, then, in those days to see through a revolution at once –
why should it be impossible today? Certainly it was easier for Claudius,
for he believed in God. But cannot *we* tend and cherish that 'seed of light
and love' so that it does rise from the grave?

15 December 1939

Nothing but wrong paths, dead ends! Whatever you reach out to in this
reality – war or peace, democracy or dictatorship, capitalism and communism, fascism or semi-freedom – always you reach out into the void
without grasping so much as a straw! What a part the church could play
there, yet does not even dare consider the step that would be the essential precondition. And amidst this chaos, the idea – hardly conceivable,
powerless, helpless – perhaps a shoot that has had a hard job forcing its
way through the earth, and now, too early and unprotected, threatened
by harsh weather, is again covered, by snow. Can it withstand the frost
and wind?

But has it not always been so? Poor, naked, weaponless, powerless,
every idea emerges from deepest solitude to do battle with a world having
at its disposal all wealth and means of power. Christ too had nowhere to
lay his head, and between Last Supper and cockcrow even Peter betrayed
him thrice. Is it not then all the more wonderful that the human spirit,
alone, but nourished by the secret forces of the Absolute, and emanating
from the tiny sand-grain that is man, should attempt to overcome and
transform the immense and over-mighty world. And is not this greatest
of miracles destroyed if Christ is made only into God?

16 December 1939

Every new epoch needs a new style, and to contemporaries this new
style will always seem a repulsive trend, they being too bound up in the
old or too dull to join in experiencing it.

I think back to Expressionism constantly, with the deepest gratitude.
It failed, but not because it was too bold or too violent or too new. Its
exponents, too much involved in the horrors of the war, had been cut off
by those horrors from the positive force and liberating beauty at the heart

199

of human nature. They may have been able to see them but were not able to reach them, only suggest, imagine and abstractly paraphrase them, and it was for that very reason that their form got stuck at the suggestion stage and failed to become a productive technique. With horror as their driving force, they did not find the inner peace to push forward slowly towards their goal, they tried to jump obstacles and rush at it, because they needed escape. They knew what was needed – it was no accident that one of the most important German groups of painters should have called themselves *The Bridge* – they were struggling for a fundamentally different, for a new, for a perplexing technique, but their inner stress left them no time really to build that bridge and so they plunged into the abyss. Who could condemn them for that? It was nevertheless the last great attempt to usher in a new epoch! The unfortunate thing was that the new technique failed to be achieved or adequately realized technically, that it was deflected too much towards the abstract – but it is precisely the manifestations of technical violence that testify to the genuineness of this experiment.

18 December 1939

The German battleship *Graf Spee* has been scuttled. It is difficult to judge the situation which led to this decision, and difficult too to judge the decision itself. Nevertheless I cannot help feeling that it reveals the Nibelung fondness for glorious destruction. Hitler himself is supposed to have ordered the scuttling. How many men have been sacrificed for an effect that is all too tempting for all too many Germans? Is this destruction for effect now being praised in exalted tones in Germany, and perhaps not only there, also really worth a single human life?

It would have seemed to me better policy to acknowledge defeat and save first and foremost the men, and then the ship as well, for the future. But the power-addicted group dominant in Germany today is not, and never has been, capable of bearing defeat manfully. For a necessary part of doing that is to have a belief in life and the strength to fulfil life for its own sake without clinging to the prop of deceptive external aims. They distrust life – only that which receives the seal of death seems honourable. Is not here too again revealed that dreadful readiness, for destruction's sake, to sever oneself from the entire future?

19 December 1939

Fortunately the crew have been saved. And the effect does not seem to have succeeded, at least not outside Germany. Germany's enemies are arguing convincingly that if the ship *had* to sink, it would have been more admirable, would it not, to seek destruction in open battle. The opposing British forces were not all that considerable, quite a lot of damage could have been done – to avoid battle by suicide was simply dishonourable and cowardly! To which the Nazi answer is that Uruguay is to blame! The ship could not be made ready for sea, she would not have been able to fight. That sounds less convincing. The Nazis are obviously merely looking for a scapegoat, as they always do, not having the courage to take each other to task.

A conflict of opinions all determined by the heroic ideal always has a seductive ring. The long dominance of an ideal always results in familiarity with that ideal down to the last detail, and everyone knows what to say in every situation. The British press is bound, after all, to present the matter in the manner most unfavourable to the Nazis. But am I not letting myself be carried away too quickly into passing judgement – will not the affair very likely sound just as plausible from the other side?

But it is wrong to let oneself be misled into passing judgement on this conflict of opinion! Heroism is the criterion employed on both sides – what matters is to have a new criterion!

21 December 1939

The drama of the *Graf Spee* has today come to a moving end that sheds a shocking light upon the affair – the captain has committed suicide. By this act he confirms the British opinion – he too thought it dishonourable not to give battle and has made his protest against Hitler's will for self-destruction. Within the meaning of heroism all now seems clear. But this final point does, I think, point to other depths.

The Nibelung mania of Hitler, the Wagnerite, has meanwhile manifested itself in another way too. The *Columbus*, Germany's third-largest passenger liner has also been scuttled. Of course, with a vessel of that sort it is a different matter – she was not able to defend herself and would have been a prize for the enemy. But that she was the twenty-third ship to be dispatched on this death voyage by the Nazis does show how very much they stake on a last card – and also that they do not face up to the real situation. The *Bremen* has of course got back to Germany, but will she not be just as much sentenced to inactivity in her German port as other ships have been in neutral ones? It is merely a question of effect all the time, never of real sense, never of the living future!

But other depths are illuminated by the figure of the captain. In the

British papers – and could such a thing be possible in the German? – he is depicted as chivalrous and noble, as concerned for his British prisoners as for his German crew, putting off suicide, which, by the code of conduct, would have been finer on the sinking ship, in order to see all his men to safety. Obviously he was the embodiment of the old humane Germany. His telephone conversation with Hitler seems to have shaken him profoundly. But what was his response? Self destruction!

He did his duty – but what a terrible duty it was! Why did he obey a command he rejected as senseless, why not use his life to serve sense, instead of destroying his life after a senseless deed? And even if, which I cannot imagine, there were reasons which made carrying out the order inevitable, had not such a man then really for the first time the possibility – and with it the deeper duty even after an enforced act of just this sort – of fighting against Hitler and of serving the German, and the human, future? How is there ever to be a revolution against Hitler if the best know only self-destruction as the one way out: if they, exactly as Hitler, do not answer for themselves but remove themselves from the consequences of their conviction by death? For what I have said here against revolution is not applicable to Germany: there most terrible violence reigns already; there evolution has already been violently discontinued; there even evolution can only again be made possible by revolution! For a man of humanity who has the possibility of influencing the course of development in Germany, the revolutionary struggle against Hitler should be his whole life! Does not heroism, in spite of noble personal qualities, in spite of courage and defiance of death, here lead simply to cowardice?

The captain knew only two ideals – heroism and performance of duty – and when they came into conflict, he shot himself. But his very heroism provides a remarkable contradiction: concern of a high order for his crew whom in battle he would have sacrificed without a moment's hesitation! We assent to war and are powerless in the face of its real horrors but would still like somehow to help humanity into its own. The heroic ideal is no longer sufficient for men who have become human, and for that very reason it is subordinated to duty. But why does the knowledge of having fulfilled his duty still not save the captain?

Duty is one of the most dangerous of concepts. It is the form given to an activity – it says nothing at all concerning the nature of the activity; any activity can become the performance of duty. Duty, when its content is good, may be a very fine thing, and it may justify the worst of crimes – murder may be done as a duty too. But thus duty, as an ideal, is a fateful thing appealing to man's best powers, overcoming his egoism in favour of

202

sacrifice, but, having no definite content, depriving him of any criterion as to whether he is risking his life to good purpose or wasting it on what is futile and bad. In most cases it even misleads people into abusing their best powers in this way – a living ideal rich in content has no need to appeal to duty – it works through the enthusiasms that it engenders. Only when the ideal becomes empty and at the same time a mask for all the bad urges, does it require duty to keep the better men under its spell. It is to the captain's credit that performance of duty did not blind him concerning his act.

Nevertheless this linking of performance of duty to an ideal that has become empty does in fact mean cowardice. We must finally break ourselves of the habit of seeing, in conformity with the idea of heroism, courage wherever life is risked. A certain degree of courage is required for that, to be sure, but even life can be risked lightly and not lightly, and that alone is the crucial criterion for courage! It is easy to stay on the beaten paths of the customary, in harmony with comrades, government and the people we live with – difficult to stand up for something new which the world is throwing stones at, and which also cannot yet be built upon simply and unambiguously, but has first to be struggled for. It is easy to follow adopted concepts – difficult, at the price of moral ostracism, to struggle for new. Were not the true heroes in the last war the conscientious objectors? And yet they exposed themselves to no greater danger than the men at the front. It is never the sacrifice that is important but what the sacrifice is for, and the spiritual act that that sacrifice represents.

But cowardly or not cowardly is not a criterion. Fear too can bring forth great acts. The crucial thing is the captain's staggering from one void to another, and thus illustrating the dreadful drama that is being played out in Germany, the best simply wasting themselves in heroism and performance of duty. What lofty human powers are here at work, what wonderful humanity if that is the kind of sacrifice they are prepared for, albeit from a deeper fear. But these glorious powers are wasting themselves senselessly because of the lack of the new ideal that could sweep them from confusion into clarity, from void into life, from past into future.

And to my surprise, the heroic point of view is even receding here in Britain, many papers being today of the opinion that internment is the more honourable and meaningful course, there being no sense in hazarding lives for the sake of glorious defeat. They take above all account of the future – belief in the future would make internment meaningful. They are beginning to understand Hitler's will for self-destruction – do they also understand the danger it represents for our whole civilization?

203

We can still perhaps split hairs concerning this realistic attitude, and say the new standpoint should enable them to do all the more towards unmasking Hitler. But any doubts we may have are removed by the discussion there is concerning the future of Europe. To this there is no end – day after day the papers are full of letters testifying to a most honest concern about the new Europe, the whole nation seeming seized with impassioned reflections concerning federation, and the rebuilding of the world and practical Christianity. It feels a deep, living responsibility for the civilization which it is protecting – a proof that it is not merely pretending to protect it – and has constantly to be reminded that the war has got to be won first before such plans can be made reality. And however much Hitler may demonstrate his lack of any right to attack the Treaty of Versailles, which, bad as it is, is made to appear a work of supreme humanity by his treatment of the Czechs and Poles, the feeling of guilt about this treaty has penetrated deep into British hearts. The British are not letting any argument dissuade them from their reflections, and will not be put off in their endeavours.

But how the reality looks in fact is revealed with unsurpassable clarity by a brief paragraph from a report by the *Sunday Times* Paris correspondent.[9] I must quote word for word, for every word is a revelation:

> A week ago the *Temps* declared that the Allies ought to declare war on her [Russia] . . . The deliberations at Geneva have somewhat damped this anti-Russian ardour, for they revealed a dangerous tendency among certain neutrals to treat Stalin as enemy no. 1 and Hitler as something subsidiary or, worse still, as a potential leader of a European crusade against Bolshevism. The prevalent tendency therefore is to regard Hitler as an accomplice of Stalin, but still as enemy no. 1.

That is how the situation looks to the neutrals – one could almost wish them joy of Hitler – but how it looks too to the powerful *Sunday Times* circles of Britain. This face of capitalism is hidden in Britain by the splendid human attitude of the people. Here one can even overlook that the communists, the British ones too, are today celebrating Stalin's sixtieth birthday with praise and panegyric, and are obviously sorry that the Liberation of Finland has still not succeeded. But the posture between capitalism and communism, and still more against Hitler, really does involve the very greatest of difficulties. Can they really be overcome by means of

9. *The Sunday Times* of 17 December 1939, in an article headed 'French War Finance'.

external plans? The League of Nations, following the expulsion of Russia, has dropped gently off to sleep again – is that how to find a way of replacing this still-birth of a splendid idea by a living institution?

One cannot help thinking how easy it would all be if the German capacity for self-sacrifice could be combined with the British sense of reality and responsibility! How then is European civilization to be perfected if not by co-operation on the part of the European nations? But whenever one nation happily gets to the point of renouncing the old plans for conquest, another reverts to the old madness. Does Europe really have to slaughter itself? Is the idea really only able to rise up out of rubble, or will rubble finally bury all these magnificent human powers? Seeing what powers are still effective in Germany beneath the surface, one has hope. Experiencing the human attitude of the British one has hope. And at the same time it is impossible not to despair at these powers being dissipated in duty and Utopia. The hour would seem favourable. The old outlived ideas are obviously no longer able to bind these powers. But aimless power is bound to remain inferior to purposeful destruction. It is difficult in this burning need to put trust in bridge-building, which in any case takes a long time.

22 December 1939

Here in Britain where Christianity is so much livelier, these questions lead willy-nilly to the church. In order to judge it better I have now read a theological book that was recommended to me as good and characteristic, *The Way, the Truth, the Life*, by Fenton Hort.

The book employs the old method of theology which assumes the truth to be provided completely by the Scriptures, and the task of scholarship to be therefore to discover this truth by interpreting the Scriptures, and to make it comprehensible. In Scholasticism this method led to extraordinary results, paving the way from barbarism to highest civilization. People were convinced that the Scriptures and the works of the early fathers of the church could contain no contradictions – the fact that such contradictions *did* arise, in any number and in crucial places, was the fault of the human spirit which was unable to grasp their sense. The solution of the contradictions was therefore a burning, indeed *the* most vital problem, for only here did access to truth open, and only here did the human spirit encounter divine grace. And this problem, possessing this living strength, led to the heights of heaven and to the depths of hell, deeply entering the whole of human life, the opposites in this case too proving an unusually fruitful starting point. However, the few examples of Scho-

205

lastic thinking cited here, already show this way no longer to be accessible to us. We are no longer able passionately to immerse ourselves in these contradictions because they are being solved by our historical understanding and deprived of their force. Even powerful belief in the Revelation will today no longer adhere to the letter but will have recourse to the aid of historical interpretation, just as Fenton Hort has. Can the old method of theology then still stand the test at our present time?

The natural sciences have freed men from all the old obligations without having been able to create a new internal obligation. For that reason the external is bound to rule the internal by compulsion. To these imposed injunctions man may bow reluctantly or voluntarily, enthusiastically or despairingly – there remains nevertheless accessible to him, whenever he wishes, a mind freed of all fetters, a mind by whose aid he can recognize every external injunction as internally untrue. It is thanks to the natural sciences that man stands and confronts the world alone. He has at his disposal the mental capacities internally to free himself from everything that has been set over him from outside, even if externally he is obliged to bow. That is the curse and the blessing of our time, its weakness and its greatness – its *curse* and *weakness,* whenever we cling to the external notwithstanding, and get stuck in so doing in the formal which, creating no internal obligation, drives the internal to devastating and destructive outbreaks; its *blessing* and *greatness,* whenever we find an internal principle corresponding to the new range of the mind, and thereby binding opposites into a living force again that creates new mental life.

Hort himself says, in perhaps the finest passage of his book,

> It is not a loosening off that we need but tension and obligation. We are all in a foreign land, never at home. We must live with loins girt and lamps burning, instantly prepared to apply ourselves wherever necessary. But the time is past when concentration could be acquired as a result of the narrowness of our aims.

But it is not enough to shake off the restrictions, it is not enough to be prepared. Man is finally dependent on himself to discover God within, and at the same time the way to his own most perfect realization.

23 December 1939

Hort's book has raised in my mind a whole number of questions which I have not really wanted to mention because to me they seem in essence already answered. But not being able to get away from them, I will briefly consider them – maybe they will in fact lead further.

'Man is finally dependent on himself' I wrote yesterday; is not any pleasure taken in that somewhat overbold? The books of all times, from the prophets to Dostoyevsky, have depicted the appalling horrors bound to assail men whenever they fall away from God – do not our own times prove them to be right?

> Godless they would be, and Godless live
> in their crazed sense;
> and now too are delivered up
> to Godless life.

That may well be right, but did not faith in God lead to that for precisely the reason that it was not yet the right faith, too external, and thereby conditioned by time? An English parson recently received the reproach:

> We've known the Gospel now for some two thousand years but it has not been able to change man and it has not been able to make itself a reality. Does that not prove that it is after all too weak, not appropriate to man, a false path?

The parson's answer was very fine:

> The Gospel has been offered to us for two thousand years, but we have still not yet accepted it – how can we judge it? But has not our failure to accept it been by reason of the very fact that God is still enthroned above the clouds and we have not been able to make him a reality within ourselves?

The development of any ethic consists in eliminating ever more powerfully the external rewards which initially are supposed to facilitate and bring about adherence to moral laws, its aim being to achieve adherence to these laws for their own sake. Is not the external God still he who bestows rewards? We ought, I believe, first to bow to the absolute in ourselves for its own sake because in so doing we discover so rich a content that we are no longer able to think of reward at all.

The aim of ethic and of faith is not even of course good works. The success of these is not within our power, and if we ascribe it to ourselves we are led from faith to pride and arrogance. Whether good works succeed depends on grace, and for that reason we should not believe either that we can be redeemed by our striving alone – we must of course strive,

207

but must retain an awareness of grace so that our feeling should not expend itself on the external. Thus the great importance of the internal.

That basic idea of prayer – that success is something that must be bestowed upon us, is very fine, but does not it too, as we are no longer able wholly to immerse ourselves in God, lead nowadays to the external, to result? Does anyone, repeating the Lord's Prayer today, still bring alive within him a full response of feeling? This prayer is perhaps one of the most difficult passages of the Gospel to understand, and this is precisely the one which is repeated so incessantly and unthinkingly and thus destroyed. I am, I believe, slowly beginning to understand it, and want, later, to attempt an interpretation.

Besides, the view I have expressed here concerning prayer now seems incomplete, in its basis especially. I was wrong to quote Christ's 'use not vain repetitions, as the Gentiles do', against prayer in general, for Christ too prays. But his prayer, especially on the Mount of Olives, is not so much an immersing in, as a wrestling with, God and for God, and that to me seems also the deepest sense that prayer can have. But this wrestling for the true and the good, for faith and for the ideal, for affirmation of the whole, for that feeling of the divine – is it not always a wrestling with ourselves? Are we today still able to wrestle with the angel, or is this struggle with the angel not today a symbol for the opposing forces and urges within our own breast?

Today, from those very people who are honestly tormented, we often hear reproaches against God for arranging this human world in such a way as constantly to drive people to destruction. Does not the thought suggest itself, especially when we are truly suffering from this world, that God is playing a game with us, that he is cruel and imbued with a delight in evil? It almost seems sometimes that belief in God has been outlived by belief in the devil, although already he too is disguised, paler and more colourless. All of which only makes clear the dangers conjured up today by a belief in God in a world beyond.

Evening

Some time ago a poem by a nameless prisoner in a concentration camp came into my hands. Here, wrestling with and for God has been realized most movingly. A cry from the depths of suffering, captured in the strict form of the sonnet:

208

Ja, wärst du nicht mein Gott, wie könnt' die Qualen
der armen Schöpfung ich dir je verzeihen!
Ja, wärst du nicht mein Gott, ich wollte speien
und Not mit Haß und Schmerz mit Bosheit zahlen.

Da wir uns deinem Schutze anbefahlen,
gabst du uns preis, und da wir aufwärts schreien,
bleibst du uns taub, und da wir uns kasteien,
verbirgst du dich in ungewissen Strahlen.

Ja, wärst du nicht mein Gott! wärst Herr von Knechten,
wärst Kirchenbild und Spielzeug für die Dummen,
ich wäre mir zu gut nur dein zu denken.

Du *bist* mein Gott! und darum muß ich rechten,
und darum zweifeln, spotten und dich kränken –
und darum an dich glauben und verstummen.

[Yes, were you not my God how could I ever
forgive you all that poor creation suffers!
Yes, if you were not my God I'd spit,
repay distress with hate, and pain with malice.

When we commended us into your care
you sacrificed us; when we cry to you on high
you do not hear; when we chastise ourselves
you hide in uncertain rays of light.

Yes, were you not my God you'd be a lord of slaves,
church image and a plaything for the foolish,
I'd love myself too well to think of you.

You *are* my God! And that's why I must argue,
and that's why doubt and mock and injure you –
that's why believe in you and hold my peace.]

Here is faith which has passed through accusation. But can this prayer be
re-experienced by anyone who has not yet traversed the uttermost depths
of despair? And does not the way to its understanding even then again
lead via the voice of that within us which is divine?

Night

In Hort I have found another fine and clear opposition which he rightly reads into the Gospel. Christianity, properly understood, is to free man from the restrictions of family and nation, and set him in the extreme opposition existing between individual and human community. The rightness of that has already become clear here. Family, nation, are specific natural assumptions which, because we are unable to contribute anything to their realization, must not become ends. Human community, humanity, we translate into reality by the very means of our own improvement, which we, on the other hand, also find our way to only when we see ourselves not as individuals having broken away, but when we see within us the opposition between ego and humanity.

24 December 1939

The days have grown dark and short – light sometimes hardly breaking through at all. Today the streets are in the grip not of snow but of fog. Before the fog disperses darkness falls again, and today's moon diffuses a lustreless light that seems only to make you notice the cold. It is difficult to visualize in any clear, firm way that summer has been and will be. It is still not long since we were able, without turning in on ourselves, without fear or defences, freely and easily to stride out into the ripening countryside amongst greening hedges and blooming flowers in blinding light and relaxing warmth. Shall we be able to again?

It is a beautiful thing that to this longing for light and warmth and to the certainty of their returning to us, Christmas should attach the deeper interpretation – that true light, a security we cannot lose, is today bestowed upon us. In darkest, most oppressive night, the shining star that cannot lighten the darkness or provide warmth, points to the light that cannot be extinguished, the light that more profoundly illumines us and more richly showers us with gifts than any suns can.

Not, like Easter, the reality of Christ, Christmas is merely legend nourished by the many sources of many traditions. Linked to the story of Moses, it holds out for Jews the promise of their hopes of the Messiah being fulfilled by the House of David; the Kings from the Orient follow the star which there today still leads to the discovery of the Highest of Priests; and most beautifully of all perhaps, the German Christmas tree gathers the light of which this feast holds the promise. It does not plunge

210

us into ultimate depths or raise us to ultimate heights, but calls us to celebration, to joy and gratitude. Only the crib of poverty embodies an essential feature of Christian teaching, but it too in delightful fashion. If this feast is to present us with gifts, we must previously have been presented with the gift of the reality of Christ.

Yet while Christmas restricts us and makes the more easily fulfilled demand first and foremost of the family, it loosens these all too rigid bonds. In giving presents first and foremost to the children it raises us into a purer world. Today people are unconstrainedly concerned and honestly prepared to love each other – for a moment it may seem that they are really prepared and able to bring and keep peace. Indeed, in the midst of war I am prepared to believe that this semblance is more than semblance. Each Christmas men are again shown that they are capable of making peace a reality – that all is provided that can provide peace. They are shown what they must realize within themselves in order to create peace. That is no semblance – that is human reality. And it is only by submitting themselves to the external semblance-world that they lose the peace that would be profoundly appropriate to them.

When will that message at last be understood?

27 December 1939

Despite the fact that we were not in our own country, which makes Christmas a doubly painful experience the festivity turned out well. Touching concern on the part of the British provided us with that security within a small circle of friends and relatives which makes Christmas what it is. Our pain at being in a foreign land also made us doubly glad in our gratitude for the gift of Christ and for the goodness of men.

But all the time I have been dogged by a memory from the last war. Amidst the bloody reality of that time and of the present too, this little episode may seem almost like an idyll. All the same I am more deeply affected by it than by many of the more bloody experiences because it reveals much that has retained its validity way beyond the war, and much that ought not to have been allowed to.

Christmas 1917 was over. We were comparatively well off – housed on a sheltered hillside above a shell-battered Italian village some distance from the front. The village had supplied the materials from which we had built ourselves proper huts in which, if we could not stand, we could sit and lie and – above all! – get some proper heating going for once. We had to patrol regularly, but that, given the protection of the broad Piave river, involved no extra danger; and again and again we were able to look forward to returning *home*. After our endless dangers and hardships we did indeed have something of a feeling of being *at home* in our warm huts.

Christmas had merely dragged us out of our dull repose. Its tidings of peace we received as a mockery – the peace which we were longing for with all our hearts, seemed just as far away as ever. Only a few honestly believed that they would ever live to see it – we seemed sentenced to this never-ending cruel senselessness for the rest of our lives. And then to be supposed to celebrate a feast of peace!

All our expectations were concentrated on New Year's Eve. We had discovered a wine-cellar in the village, and had it under anxious guard. On New Year's Eve we were going to seek total oblivion, bear this dreadful, infinitely long, old year fittingly to its grave, and sleep, oblivious, long into the New Year which, though it raised so little hope was the only hope we had, so as to wake as late as humanly possible to consciousness and senselessness again. It was to be a fitting climax to those crippling festivities in which we had sought oblivion at every opportunity.

At 4 p.m. on 31 December, when preparations for the feast were already under way, there was a sudden alert. The Italians had taken an important mountain on our flank, there were fears of a breakthrough, and we were to be sent into action. Had we marched off there and then nothing would have happened. But as so often in war, senseless haste was followed by senseless hesitation. Again and again the order was for instant readiness, but hour after hour went by without further orders coming. Furious and freezing, the men were standing not far from the huts where they could have been celebrating in the warm. And then, all of a sudden, wine was circulating. Who had brought it nobody knew. The officers tried at first to stop the men drinking, but in vain. Soon they were drinking too. Out of cold, anger, despair and defiance blazed an eerily silent orgy.

At 10 p.m. the order at last came – we were to occupy a village further to the rear. So the Italians had not broken through after all and all the hanging about had been senseless. There was no tension to jerk the men back into a state of vigilance and the column set off at a sluggish stagger. Two officers only were dependably sober, myself and a friend, so we two had to see what we could do with the drunken men. First we tried splitting the task – I was to go ahead and find the route, he was to keep a look out at the rear to see no one got left behind. But this soon proved impracticable – too many fell down in the snow, too many tried to slip off. If we were ever to get them where they were supposed to go, there

212

was nothing for it but to keep running up and down the column that was getting more and more strung out.

That night will stay forever in my mind as clearly as it does now after twenty-two years. Many hundreds of times I ran up and down that endless column panting and sweating, knocking wine bottles out of the men's hands with a stick, but fresh ones kept mysteriously appearing. Any who were lying down I belaboured desperately with my stick, for to remain like that meant freezing to death. And hardly had I managed to get a couple of them going than I had to rush to the head again to keep the column moving and on the right course. I was responsible for a whole number of companies, and had to be everywhere at once over a distance of about half a kilometer. We took a seemingly endless four hours for what later proved a march of some thirty minutes at normal pace.

After a vast amount of trouble, with men collapsing like sacks when allowed to halt and with the infinite complication of darkness, we had no sooner got the men accommodated in the village than the order came for two officers to go forward with a patrol to take over the position.

We were dog-tired, but there was nothing for it except simply to carry straight on. This time it really was an hour's march and taking over the position was not so easy, as the others had been celebrating too, and had to be pommelled out of their slumbers. There was no position to speak of, anyway – we were supposed to lie up on a sheltered but bare slope and await further orders. That happy discovery made, I had to go back to meet the column half-way and lead it in. My only help in this was a hot coffee that I grabbed somewhere.

We then spent New Year's Day on the slope. It was freezing. We were not allowed to make a fire and were scarcely allowed to move, the slope being under observation, and it was too cold for sleep. We kept a keen eye on the artillery fire descending all round us and longed for it to close in so that we should at last be allowed to move. Somehow this day too came finally to an end, and that night we returned to the village and there even had a couple of days rest.

Nothing on the whole had happened – an unimportant episode involving little danger and no losses. But is it not an allegory of the role of the vigilant, aware man in our time? A tiny stretch of track that he knows well and can cover quickly, and he is obliged to run to and fro on it hundreds, thousands of times, using his last resources of strength, to take just a few men that tiny way with him also. And no sooner does he get them there than he is driven out again, without help, alone, into the cold void. And then, having again found a way to take them, he is again forced to lead

213

them that way twice, three times, and then again, at the end, finds the helpless mob clinging to him, and is paralysed with them in the cold and void, having neither improved the general fate, nor broken through it. Can it then be held against him if, finally, he resigns himself with them to the senseless that does at least afford a little warmth, a little human presence, a moment of peace?

I can remember it as if it were today. Occasionally, even on that New Year's Day, the sun broke through, and as it played on the bare branches, the patches of snow and the still green grass, gave minutes of joy. But that joy was numbed as we looked back at the past year and ahead at the year to come. Today too, in this wonderful lull that we have been granted, is not the same almost superhuman strength required to counter that numbing effect?

28 December 1939

The Pope has issued a Christmas message which is a colourless repeat of what most people are saying anyway. But there appears to be satisfaction at his condemning not only the attack on Finland, but also the attack on Poland. And in the next few days too he is going to receive Mussolini, an event which, I am sorry to say, is getting a very good press here in England.

The Finns have even advanced across the Russian frontier. They are doing admirably and are receiving the eager admiration of the whole world. But what is *it* doing, that world which is being fought for there in Finland? Sending a little war material, a few volunteers. Even the neutrals directly threatened are sitting tight. What sense is this battle to have then in the long run? And what fate will this world then justly deserve?

29 December 1939

The Christmas period has swamped me with newspapers, and I have been glad to have something different to read for once. But they make me none the wiser, merely uneasy.

A remarkable thing is that here we hear hardly anything from France, apart from ministerial speeches. I was therefore curious to see the French periodicals amongst them. But they show no sign of that internal struggle on the part of the people that is immediately plain in every paper here. So powerfully tuned are they to disparaging the enemy that they might almost date from the last war. They all seem to me too interested in listening to any rumour emanating from Nazi Germany, even the most senseless, and they cling to the illusion that Hitler is doing Stalin's dirty work for him. France's standpoint is being strikingly simplified, 'We have got to fight in order not to suffer the fate of the Czechs and the Poles.' But what the mood of the people really is, we do not discover. Almost all leading articles in the Christmas numbers have fallen victim to the censor. The *parlement* has been virtually eliminated, and yet in the last war it was by virtue of the *parlement* that France won. These not altogether pleasing indications are, I hope, deceptive – the literary articles are, as ever, of an amazingly high standard.

With high expectations I tackled the refugee papers. The Czechs publish a periodical here – *The Czechoslovak in England*. The first thing to make itself felt was the hostility of the reactionary Osuský towards Beneš – still, this conflict seems to have been settled, and probably largely in favor of Osuský who is backed by France. Then, for a long time, there was no mention of the Sudeten Germans; now, with a certain amount of embarrassment, their aid is being accepted and a tiny article has even been printed in German. But so far not a word about the Jews, although the Czech Army must be roughly 70 per cent Jewish. Well, it would certainly be fine if this doubtful problem were recognized to be no problem – but that won't be achieved by silence alone, and that is what ought to be said! Silence is more a sign of further embarrassment. It is probably a good thing that the paper appears in Czech. It would not, I think, be to the good of the Czech cause for the British to read it.

A left-wing anti-Nazi periodical *Inside Germany* is being published, unfortunately in English. It is still lumping the German capitalists together with the Nazis. Even the flight of Thyssen – who now has a warrant out for him, and has for that reason left Switzerland for South America – does not teach them any better. Now it is right of course that the periodical should warn against crediting the German generals with a will of their own – but many generals may today be more inclined to yield to the will of important reactionary forces than to the will of the Nazis. At any rate it is dangerous and suspicious that there should not, in the whole number, be a single word about Russia or any mention of Poland or of the deportation of the minorities and of the Jews, who must, after all, be suffering the very worst that the Nazis are at present inflicting. With brief obeisances to the churches and the *petit bourgeois*, the talk is almost exclusively of the workers' dissatisfaction which is already being regarded as revolutionary, although from reading all these leaflets since 1933 it is

215

simply impossible to understand how the Nazis have ever been able to stay in power. And so it is then that the leading article ends with the senseless and dangerous sentence: 'The German people wants no war and needs no war in order to settle its account with the Hitlerite military regime.'

Neither is it elevating to see the leading article expressly opposing itself to the other German committee, that of Rauschning, Strasser, Brüning etc. This committee does, it is true, expressly exclude socialists of all complexions as having demonstrated their incompetence. The exasperation is therefore understandable, and until now this exclusion has seemed unjust to me too. But reading this periodical I am forced to admit that this standpoint is broadly justified. How would it be if, instead of glossing over their errors and repeating them, the socialists were to learn a thing or two – from Rauschning's book for instance?

I am glad to return to the British papers. Admittedly there are at the moment some friendly notices concerning Goering which strike me as suspect. Nevertheless, in every single issue can be felt an honest sense of responsibility and a vigorous struggle to be self-critical.

30 December 1939

The British and French troops are having from time to time to be consoled that boredom is better than drum fire. This standstill war is really sinister in so far as we are still and constantly awaiting terrible surprises, its horrors are all the time descending upon the defenceless – the Poles, the Finns, and groups within Germany – and it is not being staged where real fighting can be done and a decisive result achieved. But boredom – a hazard for troops? Is human imagination really so feeble that it cannot see what a blessing this lull is?

Experience confirms that boredom *is* in fact a hazard for troops. And this lack of imagination and feeling seems to me again and again to be one of the greatest dangers which we face. So overwhelming is the suffering in the world that we dare not become conscious of it all if we do not want it to break us, if we want to achieve *anything* – to be a little happy, which is after all absolutely necessary and a thing we should approve of. But do we not, by this constant suppression of our feelings, so greatly steel ourselves as to kill off all our feeling and falsify our awareness?

Let us be honest. How coolly we read the news of the terrible earthquake in Anatolia with a death-toll of thousands. In Goethe's youth, the Lisbon earthquake was, for the best people, a spiritual shock and brought

216

as a consequence great spiritual clarification. Today the destruction being wantonly provoked by man overshadows any natural catastrophe. And whereas we face nature unaffected and can therefore give full vent to our feelings towards it, we are obliged to close our minds to man-created suffering because we cannot bear the disfigurement of the human image, and the guilt!

31 December 1939, Midnight

As 1938, which brought the occupation of Vienna and the Czech crisis and mobilization, was drawing to a close, our wish for the New Year was that it should not prove such as to make 1938 seem idyllic. This wish has not been fulfilled. The past year has brought the occupation of Prague, the new emigration and war. And so today we repeat our wish, but the probability that the New Year will not again prove more terrible, is slight.

Today's sermon produced a very fine thought – the Christian does not ask about the future, and gazes into the New Year undismayed, for he knows what the future must finally bring. In any human sense it is right to live trustingly for the present without destroying it by expectation of the future, and true Christianity makes it possible. But who, indeed, can today look forward to the New Year without fear and horror. Ought we not, as real Christians, to affirm even suffering as the only way of again undoing the hardening of man?

1 January 1940

I keep thinking of the danger of becoming hardened, and must, for his especial sake, begin the New Year again in the sign of Dostoyevsky. His works are amongst the most powerful impressions of my youth, and one which has endured with me all these years, not only because Dostoyevsky lived through, and portrayed, the ultimate depths of chaos – that chaos which at that time, after the war, was deeply affecting us – but because he found his way to a pure and clear wisdom that endures in the face of all life's questions, and shows us the way out of chaos. Here is one of the major summits of our civilization, and as, widespread familiarity with Dostoyevsky's works notwithstanding, his wisdom is almost unknown, I feel a constant urge to renew my own profession of it.

I resist the affirmation of suffering that keeps waiting for fresh suffering. Suffering is certainly one particularly clear way to depth. But the world contains an excess of suffering – do we have really to wait for special

217

personal suffering all the time in order to experience it fully? And can, in general too, an increase in suffering ever produce anything other than a hardening of the self against it? The fact that we wait for suffering only betrays again our lack of feeling and imagination! Are we not here again making an assumption into an end and thereby depriving it of its fruitfulness? If we were caught up in suffering we would realize too that Christ has indicated the way out of suffering – its meaning and its removal. For it is in the very midst of suffering that we ought to understand the joyous tidings. But as our lack of feeling and of conscious imagination still does not allow us rightly to apprehend suffering, we, in elevating it into an end, merely harden ourselves further.

And I also resist the overemphasis of the penitent sinner which to me seems to emanate from the same sources. How often today emphasis is laid in the Gospel on the fact that Christ came not to the righteous but to the publicans and sinners. There is a hankering after a major sin of our own in order to partake of repentance and mercy. Now repentance is certainly also a way to mercy, but are we not all sinful, and do we need to commit a special, colourful sin to be aware of it? And is it not turning Christ's example into its opposite to begin by praising sin? Has not Christ removed original sin, showing the way for every man – for the sinners and the righteous?

Dostoyevsky is so often misunderstood as the advocate of this false praising of sin. But he, it seems to me, is the very one to have found an escape from the excessive affirmation of sin and suffering in announcing and claiming, 'Everyone is guilty for all things.'[10] We resist this claim first of all because it seems oppressive and paralysing. But it is not, for Dostoyevsky is speaking, of course, not of sin but of guilt, and in replacing the lower concept by the higher he is pointing towards the positive. Once again it is the clarifying of terms that is important.

Sin leads to repentance – that is a simple and obvious opposition, but one which in reality paralyses. The final evil, once happened, cannot be made to un-happen again – if repentance is directed towards extinguishing sin, we are condemned to impotence and endless penitence. The concept of sin leads of necessity to that of original sin, from which we cannot extricate ourselves at all. But, then, what human act *is* unambiguous, and what human act *can* be dismissed in such simple terms as *radically evil?* Sin separates man from God, but is it at all within our power to separate ourselves from God, as we, after all, carry the absolute within us?

10. A telescoping, attributable to the translation relied on, of Dostoyevsky's: 'every man is guilty for all and for all things'.

Christ has delivered us from original sin, not by acknowledging and atoning for it, but by simply destroying the concept. Again and again he comforts sinners by assuring them that their sins are already forgiven, and freeing them from the intolerable burden of sin. In one of the most beautiful Gospel passages, he drives away the sinning woman's accusers with the words: 'He that is without sin among you, let him first cast a stone at her', and the men he is driving away are those who are clinging to the unequivocally evil in order to turn their dubious purity into that which is unequivocally good. But that is in truth the purpose and danger of the concept of sin – the unequivocal establishment of evil being supposed to make good tangible – we, in isolating the sin, believe we are making the good so tangible as to be able to find comfort in it ourselves. But Christ, in shaking the all too simple concepts of the accusers forces them to take stock of themselves. He brings alive in them that simultaneity of evil feelings and good, which makes us all partakers of sinfulness, and which at the same time, amidst evil, nevertheless points the way to good. The repentent sinner is saved by Christ only because he is extricated from the fruitless conflict of sin and repentance. If the sin awakes pain then it does not need to be atoned for through repentance. The pain has merely to be understood, for in it the good is already alive.

Christ does not speak of repentance. He says to one sinner, 'thy faith hath made thee whole; go in peace', and to another, 'he that followeth me shall not walk in darkness, but shall have the light of life'. He diverts them from their act, using the act simply as a means of pointing them in a different, positive direction, using the discordant act simply to release light from the opposition. We are not to remain in the past, we are not endlessly to expect the future to extinguish the past, in every act – and even though that act be a sin – we are to make real that opposition that releases light, thereby fulfilling present and future.

But that is precisely the meaning of the concept of guilt. Dostoyevsky's *Guilt and Atonement*[11] tells of a murderer who again and again finds grounds to justify himself, and of the long road he has to travel in order finally to realize his guilt. Nevertheless the title is appropriate, for with the awakening consciousness of guilt the act is in fact atoned for. He cannot undo the deed – he is not to atone for it in endless repentance – the important thing is the awakening of the consciousness of guilt, for the consciousness of guilt awakens the sense of responsibility, and with that

11. Here, *Schuld und Sühne*, a retitling on the part of a German translator. *Crime and Punishment* is the more accurate, and appropriate, rendering of the Russian.

sense which corresponds to the voice of the absolute in us, his human powers are released, are again able to develop – he can again become man – he walks in light! In leading to a sense of responsibility the sense of guilt opens the way for the absolute to unfold, and that is what is important. In the pain of our sense of guilt we atone for that guilt, and in so doing no longer require any direct connection with the sin. Further life must not be any further overshadowed by the deed, it can only be made productive by it. The sense of responsibility guides us from the wrong use of our powers, which has found expression in the wrong act, into that area in which we can employ our powers for the fulfilment of our lives.

Guilt and responsibility is the productive, aim-indicating opposite, which slows the way to the goal. Guilt may well be a fearful experience that oppresses us, but where there is guilt, there too is responsibility, and our feeling of responsibility shows us a way of being able to face, set aside and truly expiate guilt. While guilt oppresses us, our feeling of responsibility simultaneously raises us up from our abasement. By taking guilt upon ourselves we are freed from it – we can breathe again – we open up a world that is humanly accessible and comprehensible, we can again work, act and develop. And sin too is a to that extent externally unjust event – why did God make us so that we sin – if he condemns sin he ought not to have imposed it on us. What a devaluing of grace for it to be necessitated only in this fashion! But consciousness of guilt also already, in the form of contrition, contains grace; responsibility, in teaching us to relate the external to our innermost selves, is already consoling us. We must not deflect the concept of grace into a false sphere. Our talents and works, effect and result, are enigmatic and inexplicable. Success becomes ours only through grace. Here we must not let our powers be destroyed by failure, for consequences do not lie within our power. But grace is also not a reward for good behaviour — grace is something we partake of in our innermost selves, the reduction to an *ultimately evil* being just as false as the reduction of God to the *humanly paltry good*. By abasing ourselves, we are raised, whenever, seemingly broken, we take our guilt upon us, we awake the power of the absolute within us, and that alone is of importance. That absolute within us is grace, we cannot force it to descend from without, we simply must do everything to fulfil our lives in the true sense. Only then can we hope for the absolute to come alive within us and to be granted grace.

It is in this sense only that Christ takes our guilt upon himself, freeing us from the crushing concept of sin and showing us that grace is already

220

alive in the active consciousness of guilt. It is for that reason alone that he is destroyed by guilt, that he chooses death on the cross – not to atone, but to make his example plain and to preserve it. By willed suffering, by intended sin we simply keep forcing that crucifixion anew. Not until we recognize that we ourselves are to blame for it, because we have failed to understand Christ, misjudged him and been unable to live his example, does he become so alive within us that the crucifixion is no longer necessary. Only in this most deeply moving of experiences do we find our way to the uncrucified Christ, and again that is the only thing that matters.

But Dostoyevsky's challenge shows us that to find this way, we do not need first to become specially sinful and guilty. 'Everyone is guilty for all things' – the consequences and effects of our actions are mysterious. We cannot calculate at all how far they will extend. 'You touch the world at one end and there is a reverberation at the other.' And even believing ourselves free of any share in the blame, we would not, would we, be able to take the lead before all other men as the solely righteous ones? 'Everyone is guilty for all', we are involved in the human community and the effect of the absolute is incalculable – have we used our powers sufficiently in this sense – given such shape and form to the absolute within us as was practicable to make this incalculable effect possible? Have we also felt responsibility only to the extent that we obviously bear it?

But does that not again exceed the measure of human powers? Abstractly it may be possible to see this guilt, but we saw that war was bound to come, and for years, for as long as we had voice, warned against all the false paths – in what way are we to blame? And even if we should succeed in it all, do we not go to pieces if we take upon ourselves too much guilt? Does not this intensification of our powers of feeling and imagination threaten to break us too? Does this not bring me back to where I started – we have to cut ourselves off in order to live!

We do, and yet we don't – this challenge shows a way. Only where we experience guilt, do we feel responsible and with that are alive internally. This challenge diverts us from the unattainably large circle of the external which we can do no more than contend with. It shows us the circle in which we can and must live. By heightening and projecting our sense of guilt from ourselves into the life circle accessible to us, we make the world our own, and it is only by making it our own in this way that we do not founder but accomplish what lies within our circle. On our talents, our mental powers and on grace will depend to what extent we are thus able to penetrate the world – but it is not quantity that matters – in any real sense of guilt, suffering and sin are realized and overcome, and we

221

are saved by virtue of that joy without which we are unable to arrive at the meaning of our lives.

This challenge is, I know, infinitely difficult. There are sufferings which break us, there is guilt which we are unable to bear, external happenings which we can see no means of access to, and which therefore drive us to rebellion. For our own fate, we may still succeed in locating the guilt: we warned against the Nazis, against wrong means of preventing war, but were we not struggling too much for external effect, were we concentrating all our powers on the task we thought we were there for? Yet as a result of these political events, our friends are in danger – how could we bear not being able to help if obliged to adjudge ourselves guilty for that? And even if we were ready to do that – did we not do all that we could – where then is our guilt to be found in that?

Nevertheless, the sense of guilt encourages us to start first of all with ourselves. It has the wonderful quality of releasing us from the immediate cause, leads us away to the absolute, and awakens within us quite different, undreamt-of powers. Dostoyevsky's challenge is a way – we must try it first in the smallest circle we can – that which we are not broken by – we cannot foresee the consequences – we can have trust – must let ourselves be led. And where should we begin if not with outselves?

Our most earnest hope is that we shall meet our friends again one day. They will have suffered grievously. How shall we be able to face them if we have dissipated ourselves in unproductive hatred, in vain external attempts, in a struggle for external results which will be bound to lead them to envy us this period. But if we have begun with ourselves – can we not then hope to be able to face them – to be able to give them fresh heart again?

We have found considerable favour from life, new friends. We have done so only because of beginning with ourselves. Does that not show that we get on the right path by beginning with ourselves – does that not build the bridge to all those friends with whom we already know ourselves to be one in spirit?

2 January 1940

Bitterly cold days have come. No snow. Clear sky. The frost penetrates to our very room, and we are freezing with the British.

How simple it would be to take over a sensible form of heating from the continent! But no, they find a thousand reasons for defending the expensive and unsuitable open fire. None of them are valid. It does not

222

prevent colds – the British are, it is true, somewhat more inured, but they too get their colds, and above all there is much more rheumatism here than elsewhere. Neither is this cold winter really an exception, otherwise the papers would unfailingly have come out with the news they are so fond of coming out with so often 'Coldest winter for sixteen years, temperature in places lowest since 1867.' All that I have been able to discover so far is that Rome has had its heaviest snowfall for ten years. Therefore it is always, or at least often, as cold as this in Britain in winter. And why then do they not have proper heating? They are simply clinging conservatively to a beloved tradition.

Now traditions are a fine thing, certainly, a must. But there is no need to keep and preserve the earlier existence entire. One must select what is essential and can also, amidst necessary change, remain as the core. And does one not endanger the whole tradition by the very act of clinging to a false external that is obviously senseless and will have sooner or later to be thrown overboard? It is in this country more than any that one learns to appreciate conservatism, but I am afraid that by also preserving here what cannot be preserved, that which ought to be preserved is being endangered.

Evening

The reason for my thoughts today, my anger at forever freezing in our room and at the gas fire which costs much and heats little, may be childish and of little validity, but the conclusion seems worth detaching from this assumption.

I have, in recent times, learnt to appreciate political conservatism. Evolution means connection with tradition and its organic continuation, and the fight for freedom and democracy is today already conservative. But first and foremost the conservative parties want capitalism and to preserve the privileges of the ruling classes. Are they not, by the very act of so doing, endangering that conservatism which is of importance? Self-centredly they select from tradition that which is unjust and identify tradition with their own advantage, thereby turning the fight against injustice into a fight against tradition. And so as a result of conservatism, which ought, as such, to be approved of, but gets wrongly understood, the tradition which would seem to matter gets destroyed. For capitalism, while provoking the battle against tradition because it, capitalism, makes look like tradition what is not at all the essence worth preserving, is the very thing that leads to the destruction of freedom and culture.

223

We can see it in many of the representatives of the generation decisively determined by the pre-war period, i.e., prior to 1914 – though in more recent times many of them seem to be changing. This period liberated human powers in a playful fashion: the passions, the tumult of the heart were a spectacle for it, religion – an aesthetic pleasure, the function of the intellect – a delight, and art, its holy of holies – a world beyond the everyday, that imposed no obligations. Their intellectual capabilities are admirable, life in that detached world often conferring great powers upon them. But it is always a world whose relationship to the everyday and to reality is only a loose one which – unless life assumes the shape of the Third Reich – seldom even finds itself at variance with life because it simply marches along beside it. It promotes an extreme individualism incapable of influencing the human community because it distances itself from any relationship with it. This generation is liberal in the best sense – everyone frees himself from external obligations in order to live his own life, and as he succeeds in that, demands above all this liberation from obligations, considering it sufficient. Nevertheless, in so far as real life requires obligations, he strives for the compromise that creates a tolerable middle course for everyday life and influences him as little as possible beyond the everyday. Compared to today's reality, this solution may seem to us almost ideal. But workaday routine, real life are today so predominant as to be bound to destroy this division between the general and a personally isolated better life, and the basis for Liberalism. If we want to find our way to a better world, then it must be to a profoundly real world, and that also is justified and rightly so. Compromise is never what matters, anywhere, what does, is to recognize the right and the true and the good, and to stand by them absolutely. Once we have recognized the right, there can no longer be any compromise. The highest goods must not be a game, a spectacle and an aesthetic pleasure. They must become the foundation of our lives.

Is the creation of such a world really to come only from God and not from man? Expressionism was a revolt against the non-binding nature of this kind of humanity. It wanted the whole and the ultimate. It failed. Is a human experiment of this sort bound to fail?

I believe that what I am seeking here, and certainly not only I, differs radically from this humanity. The opposites which matter to me are destroyed by any compromise, by any premature forming of a unity, any resting content with a mere middle course – thought is supposed to be dispersed into the opposites and to realize them as purely and clearly as possible, for it is only by this means that the third thing of importance to

224

me can arise – form, the uniform sense – that is to say, the interconnection which does not in simplifying and disclaiming fashion remove the opposites, but awakens a binding response of feeling. Is true human community any different? What concerns me is not, of course, a non-binding liberation of spiritual powers – spirit must not be a fine game that proves to be a delusion when confronted by reality – it is nurtured by passion and by composure – joy flows into it and despair, it is most profound seriousness and supreme liberation, and for me, not spirit if all of human life with all its heights and depths is not expressed in it, and if it has not passed through the entirety of them. And by virtue of that I also discover by its aid the most powerful obligation – the perfectly realized, correctly understood human spirit causes moral laws to be recognized as inviolable facts, and it is by this very means that the firmest absolute accessible to us, the absolute within us, is made a reality. What stronger obligation, what firmer foundation for human life and human community can be conceived?

I believe that humanism of that sort dare even confront the church, and that I can regard this objection as refuted so far as I am concerned. Here, writing away at this diary, I keep asking myself – is not everything I am writing down here still formal – isn't it again only the *how* and not the *what?* I know that my attempt is still broadly inadequate. I know how terribly much further I still have to go in my philosophical work – nevertheless I believe that here too the content of that human attitude which I have in mind as my aim, has already become largely clear.

But the more I ponder what I have written so far, the more obtrusive I find the gaps arising from my simply giving free vent to my thoughts. But now, having for once been forced onto this personal path, ought I then not also to attempt to clarify for myself how I have arrived at this thinking and this life. Many of the gaps would then, I think, be closed and the whole ought to become clearer. Yes, of course, but . . .

I can date the beginning of my path very accurately – it was on 26 May 1917, and even today I still shrink from reliving what were for me the most terrible days of the war. Often, when unable to sleep, I see details before me – a circle of sitting men, a large circle, sixty men perhaps – I touch one to ask something, he topples over without a sound, and in a flash I realize that they are all dead. Or myself, grenade in hand, behind the low stone wall which in the karst so often took the place of trenches – the Italians charging nearer and nearer – and between me and the wall, face eaten away by decay, a bloated corpse divided into two hideous balls by its leather belt, and a stench that threatens to stupefy the senses . . .

Are these the images that I am to revive in their entirety of my own free will?

But millions will be experiencing the same today, today and tomorrow and the day after tomorrow, am I in that case not bound to use the encouragement this diary offers me, to re-descend into that deep place?

For that hell too was in every sense a deep place, it was there that the spring of life flowed, shall I not increase its power for others by myself re-descending into death? Shall I? Must I?

3 January 1940

In condemning compromise we ought probably to be more careful than I was yesterday. This condemnation may, in an absolute sense be correct, but have I not been obliged to stress again and again that fulfilment of life is what matters, not rigid absolute demands? And this fulfilment will necessitate compromises both in practical matters and also in the life of the individual attempting to approximate to the Absolute in the way that he can.

The liberating solution of this contradiction seems to me again and again to be Goethe's call for *flexible inflexibility.* We must know essentially what we want, and never give way over it, but we must not endanger this essential by being non-essentially inflexible, and where, *en route* to the essential, obstacles present themselves, we must not charge at them like a bull at a gate, we must give way flexibly so as to be able to head towards our goal again and the better. Only by giving way whenever necessary in the sense of the Absolute, can we remain essentially inflexible.

It is in the light of that call that we must see the rejection of compromise, for then only is it right. Compromises may be inevitable – they may, *en route* to the idea, even be necessary and promotive – we can never take them as results and ends, we can never rest content with them, we have constantly to take them again as starting points for the way to the idea. We are entitled to give way only in order to remain inflexible. And it is for that very reason that condemnation of compromise in the intellectual sphere seems to me absolutely right. We must know what we want and we cannot allow this knowledge to be veiled for us in any way. How can flexibility become a means of inflexibility if we make compromises with ourselves – if we rest content in our knowledge with a middle course? Between opposites there must be no compromise, only if, simultaneously with the relativity of all knowledge, we possess the certainty of the Absolute, will we also strive inflexibly towards the Absolute through all the

226

relative compromises. As long as we are in the sphere of the relative we must not destroy our lives by means of absolute demands. We must constantly adapt ourselves to the possible way to the Absolute – but this way must not become an end in itself, it must not conceal, and destroy, the Absolute, the moment we confront the Absolute direct, there must be no more compromises. And to be able to recognize that we must, through all that is relative and through all the compromises, keep our minds uncompromisingly clear and pure.

4 January 1940

I keep hesitating to start *The Way Back*. And also I must, before I force myself to, and because it clarifies from a different side many of the problems I have just touched on, go into another book that I read recently. It is Peter Mendelssohn's *Across the Dark River*, which deals with the expulsion of the Bürgenland Jews by the Nazis.

The author is a friend of mine, and using this novel we considered and discussed at length whether it was right to write novels-with-a-purpose. And that really is an essential question.

This book provides a particularly valuable criterion for this literary genre on two scores. Firstly, the purpose of this novel is undoubtedly worthy of approbation. Here in England, the nature of National Socialism is still too little understood. People still do not wholly believe the Nazis capable of the evil which for the Nazis is routine – how often still I get asked if I believe the reports coming out of the concentration camps! It may be very important for the future, for the sake of Europe and of the better Germany, for everyone in Britain to understand what is happening there. Since it was written, the book has become topical once again, and in a manner unforeseen and terrible, as a result of the deportation of the Jews to Poland – what better confirmation could there be of the extraordinary value of its purpose? Secondly, the book is unusually successful as regards artistry. Its people are alive, not one dead passage in the whole book – the construction austere and clear – not once does it let itself be carried away by its purpose into simply painting in black and white; the narrative is dispassionately clear and for that reason gripping. Natural beauty is alive in this book, and the greatness of the human heart – real life makes its indictment. Most novels-with-a-purpose are bad novels, but it is not until a good one like this that we are able to judge their worth reliably.

As long as it is conveying experiences of lawlessness the book is stirring and shocking. These Jews are respected, established citizens and farmers

227

– they have never done any kind of civil wrong – they live in the dependable security that a state founded on law and justice guarantees its children. Out of this they are dragged by the Nazis – are, without the slightest conceivable cause, stripped of all they possess, and smuggled over the frontier at dead of night, wretched, outlawed beggars. Man is turned suddenly into a lifeless rag which people can do what they like with. His life is worthless, his rights are extinguished, his property is stolen, his ties with loved ones are trampled underfoot, and he himself is put out into the void, and in the whole wide world there is no authority to protect him against this dreadful injustice, or for him to appeal to against this vileness. Amongst these Jews chances to be a non-Jew who, merely for showing gratitude to Jews, is considered to be one. The way simply no one believes his *I am not a Jew* – the way the most positive truth remains impotent and is even mocked – the way there is simply no means of helping the truth to recognition – this reproduces the essence of life under a dictatorship movingly and unsurpassably. This effect could not be achieved by a bald report – ordinary imagination is not sufficient to select this essence from the facts, human imagination – too poor to evoke this feeling without the aid of the creative writer. Seldom has the enormous value, vitally essential sense and indispensibility of justice been made so clear to me as by this derisive denial.

But then, when the adventures of these people are depicted, the shunting across frontiers, the dangers of being constantly on the run, the lives claimed in the process, and all the appalling distress, we have second thoughts. We know this novel to be founded on documents – know that these people really fared in this way, were, as the book narrates, finally accommodated on a Danube barge between Hungary and Czechoslovakia – know that many perished, many were saved, and that all had terrible experiences . . . – but into this knowledge creeps something else – suspense as to how the story will continue, and pleasure – a strange word in this context, but it really is, I think, a kind of sombre pleasure – in the adventure, the story, its development and the individual characters. We lay the book down with a strangely mixed feeling of satisfaction which most will not admit to, but which will, I am convinced, be unconsciously present all the same – we are partly glad at being released from this experience of horror, and have partly that sense of satisfaction produced by the end of the story and the relaxing of the suspense.

With every novel-with-a-purpose the question is – would the subject have been better served by a simple report, or was the art form essential? And while, in the first parts, I am prepared to give preference to the novel, the later development would, I believe, have been more impressive in a bald report. But to me that seems decisive for the whole novel, for the feeling awakened initially is imperceptibly weakened by the further development. I know that there are any number of such reports available which have had no effect, and fear that the ears of the deaf and the eyes of the blind will not be opened by this transformation of the report either.

The intention, I'm afraid, falsifies the form, and the form the intention. As Mendelssohn's novel proceeds, the laws of the novel form assert themselves. By very reason of the fact that the novel is good, the portrayal of people and nature, of events and story becomes an end in itself, and is bound to whenever a real writer is at work, but being prefixed with a purpose expressed in the very choice of title, they are unable to integrate themselves in conformity with their nature, and cannot lead to that depth and living interconnection to which they ought. By virtue of having a life of its own, the form weakens the intention it ought to serve and cannot serve completely because that service is contradictory to its nature. I have always been disturbed by something similar with good war films – they ought to make the horror plain and tangible – they ought to serve peace, but by imposing a plot upon this horror they again also reduce its effect. Instead of exposing the horror they make it into a background which we simply accept. The plot itself cannot lead to any depth because it is not an end in itself, its sense being destroyed by its being played out not amidst the generally human but amidst special exceptional circumstances imposed by the novel's purpose. So here too the struggle against injustice does not attain its full force because it takes place under circumstances which we can push aside as unique and accidental – a thing we are inclined to do because the horror threatens to overwhelm us – and the terrible circumstances themselves do not achieve their full weight because, contrary to the author's will, they become background to a plot claiming attention as an end in itself.

I cannot and will not deny that novels-with-a-purpose have often played an important role and one certainly deserving of approval. We have only to think of *Uncle Tom's Cabin*. But it is probably no accident that those having this effect were mostly mediocre novels! Their effect was due only to the maturity of the time – the author being so far on the way to depth as to give expression to an existent movement and thereby make it visible and effective. His ability to penetrate deeply was limited, but he gave expression to it by his very purpose. But is it possible, on the way to depth, to discover such a movement today? Must not any true artist today

229

be bound to feel that the time is not ripe – that it is a question of saving, reviving, resurrecting the human being, before being able to reckon on any general effect? But this resurrection is not to be achieved by means of a superimposed purpose. By those means we merely subordinate our-selves to the time, so running the danger of achieving the opposite effect. Have not all the anti-war books in Germany had a disastrously inspiring effect upon a perplexed rising generation, and by very reason of their adventurous tension. 'You have at least *had* experiences!' was the answer I got from many young people, on my failing to understand how they could be misled by Remarque's book into an affirmation of war. Sense can only be preserved within the living form; the sole thing of importance today – the slow, invisible but lasting effect that can prepare what is need-ful – is sacrificed for the sake of purpose.

Let the reports preserve the horrors of our time. If form promotes the development of man, then that shock which all ought to be experiencing today, will be experienced by the people of later, not at all distant, times. It would be a misfortune if as a result of a renunciation of art, which is what purpose always implies, even just one small brick were to be removed from the new edifice that has to be erected.

5 January 1940

Strange how empty the newspapers now are. Reports of the Finnish war are receiving maximum splash because there is apparently nothing else to report – or maybe too to mask the faint signs of peace efforts – the Papal Nuncio has been daily at the Wilhelmstrasse, Mussolini has still not been to the Pope. Apart from that there are tendentious reports of inter-nal movements in Germany which to me seem neither reliable nor prom-ising. One has the feeling that a very great deal is going on behind the scenes and that not much good can come of it.

For this reason I shall hesitate no longer – what was it like in the last war? But once again I *do* hesitate. Am I not, after just condemning ten-dentious portrayals of war, about to portray war myself? But this objec-tion, while welcome, does not strike me as valid – I, after all, am not going to attempt a novelish, action-packed account, the desired object of which is not mentioned – I am going to recall my own experience and express its mental and emotional consequences as clearly as possible, as a result of which our experiences will probably become plain. I want to descend into the days of my awakening, to the beginning of my own conscious way in order once more to find the way from there, and more clearly and plainly.

My reminiscence begins with horror – as we were moving off a hand-grenade exploded in a rucksack, fearfully dismembering a man I knew well and wounding others severely or slightly. But all thoughts were soon obliterated by a never-ending march in scorching sun. That evening, dog-tired, we fell asleep in a field. Just before midnight we had to move on, but we were at least glad to be able to march in the cool of the night. It was a clear night, no doubt with those southern stars again in the sky whose seemingly physical light had been a source of delight always at other times. But who had the strength now to look at the stars? We were now practically ignoring the perpetual roar of the gunfire, only there were many moments when it occurred to us how much closer it had got.

The first impression of 26 May 1917 is of the chill of the early hours. We had been longing for them to come but now the cold had us in its grip – everyone was trembling slightly – or was it unconscious fear at going up to the front for the first time? The conscious feeling with everyone was probably only of dull weariness. Night had yielded. A pale, greenish grey light was preceding the sunrise. It was a remarkable light, which we grew used to during the war, and I was deeply moved to see it again, after many long years, in Jessner's Berlin production of *Faust*. He employed it in *The Prologue* at the point where Heaven closes and Mephistopheles remains alone. Radiant brightness was followed by that pre-morning light, and you knew, from the very fact of its no longer being dark, that Heaven had closed. We could not have said as much then, but we sensed the same thing – heaven was now shut – our way led finally and utterly to hell.

At that time we were fond of symbols that made the intangible some-how tangible – we were fond of strong words to drown the sound of gross reality with. In the broad daylight we could clearly see the road we were marching along – now and again on either side were telegraph poles between which, high up, straw mats were slung to obstruct airmen's vision. These narrow straw mats did in fact fulfil their purpose – concealing the road from pilots flying over at speed and preventing observation. The image of that road is inseparable from my image of the war, but it remains a somewhat uncanny one. From below it was possible to see the sky clearly. Were we really covered and concealed from sight from above? Not until later did I realize why these roads made such a powerful impression on us all – the straw mats covered nothing – we could see the sky, see air and space and sun and life, but in a mysterious way were cut off from them all the same, a couple of straw mats, a few scraps of paper bearing orders, and we were covered, concealed, banished to an unreal subterranean world. We were not allowed to stick our heads out – that was death – we had to duck, dig in – the deepest burrow was not safe enough – air and sky and sun, *they* were for other times and other people. Us they were merely mocking, giving a feeling of what we had got ourselves into. We, yes, we were allowed to see them but they were not allowed to find us! While yearning for them with all our powers, we still had to cover ourselves against them, obstruct our access to them.

But I must not dwell on the old symbols either, I must, if I am to penetrate it, grasp truth as much as possible in the raw. We did not continue along the road for long – soon it was under observation and fire. Where it emerged from a half-destroyed village, it was packed with men and wagons and horses and guns which we had to thread through with difficulty, then suddenly deserted – not a soul. But even then we kept going as we had learnt on the drill-ground on the barrack square, charging in open order down a meadow and up the other side of the valley again. There the road skirted forest and we went in straggling single file. A short time after, when we came this way again, not much was left of the forest, but for the time being it still afforded cover and the illusion that the shrapnel shells and grenades exploding ever more frequently above and on the road were nothing at all to do with us. It was not until we entered the roaring zone of our own artillery that we became more clearly conscious of where we were. But there it was that we spread out in a shallow trench along the edge of a deep gorge to form a skirmish line, and became enthralled.

It is impossible to describe that first glimpse of hell. Before us lay the deep valley of the Isonzo where the Tenth Battle of the Isonzo was raging. Leaping constantly far below were most glorious cascades of smoke and dust, volcanic eruptions of fantastic shapes, towers of dust which concealed, and then suddenly revealed, the view over the hot, desolate karst valley that really did resemble a landscape out of hell. No play of waters could reproduce that monstrous spectacle of spraying earth, those savage geysers and fountains! Evening, which was what we had to wait for here, soon fell. Searchlights blazed, veiling everything in white, and then again isolated stabbing beams gave way to an ever-deeper darkness. Interspersed with the searchlights were signal rockets of many shapes and colours, the blazing and dying fire of the separate guns, the sometimes visible dust fountains – never had we seen such a gigantic and fantastic

232

firework display! Impossible to imagine that those were guns spewing death and destruction, that every searchlight beam was pointing the way for the mowing machine-guns, that the rockets were orders to kill, or pleas for aid in extreme distress. Impossible to duck our heads down into the safety of the trench – we learnt to later all right, but this first time we were spellbound.

It was not until we were climbing down, with the view concealed to us and the fire passing over our heads, that we became conscious of the noise around. But noise is a feeble word for that unreproducible symphony of sounds. Represented there was every sound that there is, from the soft whistle of rifle bullets to the sharp rat-tat-tat of machine-guns, the soughing, blustering and storming of the heavy shells and the dullish piping of the light, the ponderous howl of the mines, the harsh crack of firing, and the gentler pop of bursting shrapnel shells – from chirruping, singing and ringing to booming, banging and thundering. Do you know the hum of a telegraph wire? The sound of a spade hitting a stone in earth? The noise a glass makes scraped by a fingernail? Do you know the different twitterings of birds – the many kinds of thunder? It was an unimaginable sounding together of well nigh all the sounds that exist, only without melody. Later those sounds filled us with horror, but this first time we were simply intoxicated – later too we learnt to know and distinguish them, and they taught us how to protect and save ourselves – this time we were at their mercy.

Beneath the weight of these impressions the next hours are a blur, and even the first wounds I remember only because of a friend saved as a result of being wounded early. I myself was hit by a splinter, but the wound was not deep – it was dressed and I scarcely noticed it. When next I see myself it is under fire, in the thick of spraying earth, landing shells, whistling bullets, running, screaming, crouching and falling men. It must have been after midnight, and the darkness, which we were slow at learning to see in, was making the horror and confusion more intense. And then the war took on a different aspect.

6 January 1940

The terrible thing was that I was immediately given a burden of responsibility which, aged eighteen and a half, and going up to the front for the first time, I was quite unable to carry. A few days later, vastly more experienced and years older, I would not have given it a thought. But by

233

virtue of that responsibility those first hours assume an enormous importance.

Our company had a captain and three lieutenants – the captain had been left behind, severely wounded – one lieutenant had been sent forward to reconnoitre, and one lieutenant went back to the captain again – for we had been supposed to pass through six of our own lines, and so be able constantly to get our bearings, but no trace of those lines could be discovered. They had been wiped out by drumfire and only the most forward was still holding. It was hopeless confusion. We were advancing in single file or extended order, depending on the fire, when the lieutenant, thinking all of a sudden that he had lost control of us, ordered us to fall in on the road! That was plain insanity – the road was under a creeping barrage and we had just got to a village which the Italians had the range of – to assemble on the road was certain death. But he chased every man of us, his revolver drawn, firing into the air, and to cap everything drove us into a barbed wire entanglement. We extricated ourselves only with extreme difficulty, slowly and with painful wounds, every instant under the threat of the reloaded revolver. Madness seemed to endow the lieutenant with immense powers. All the time he was everywhere. At last – and how, nobody knew – we were indeed all standing on the road, and that we came to no harm as we stood there is a miracle that will never be accounted for – although later we grew accustomed to such miracles, for how else to account for men coming out of drumfire alive. The lieutenant got us to stand up straight, dressed us off as if on the barrack square, brandished his revolver and fired again, but when it was again empty, he became conscious for a moment of the mess he was in process of making. He called me to him. 'I'm handing over command to you. I can't take it any more. I'm going mad. I must go back,' he said, and disappeared into the darkness. Not many days later, on 6 June, he was killed.

So there I was, responsible for 236 men, or what was left of them, with no precise knowledge of our orders, which were inadequate anyway. First I got the men off the road. There was another one-year volunteer there. He, together with the NCOs of whom, unfortunately, not one had battle experience, was to keep order. Everyone was to follow in single file, while I, in front, would try to re-establish contact with the other company. In fact it all worked out – after a terrible time – just how long I cannot say. How, in spite of darkness and drumfire and being constantly driven off the line of march by bursting grenades, I found the other company, I cannot remember and have never known, but suddenly there were our troops ahead of me. For a while I had the feeling that there was such a thing again as reassuring order. I even sent forward for an officer – but. . .

The company ahead of us had got into a dolina, one of those circular hollows so frequent in the karst. I was following. I was still climbing down the side when a shell landed in the middle of it. Artillery and horses had strayed into this dolina somehow – the thunder of the guns was drowned by the screaming of men and horses. The scream of a wounded horse is something you need to have heard for yourself – it goes beyond that of a man in a way that is unimaginably heartrending. Seeing already, entangled in the wreckage of the wagons, a gigantic quivering heap of men and animals writhing and lashing, I was dimly aware of a dreadful mass in its death agony. With all the strength at my command I tried to get out of the dolina, shouting at the top of my voice to attract the attention of my men, but they were following already. Then the second shell landed.

Three men behind me were blown to bits. I do not know whether I took that in somehow at the time or realized it after. I was hurled senseless some distance up the slope, but must have regained consciousness quickly. Once again, by a miracle, I had escaped unhurt. I rushed up the slope in search of my men. Somehow I caught up with the one-year volunteer and one man – no one else was to be found. As hard as we could we dashed off in the direction we thought likely.

Before us, distinct against the searchlight-illuminated sky, lay a broad, level field. We must have been fairly near the front line – that field was being subjected to drumfire of an intensity such as we had never dreamt of on the village road. We were alone in a veritable landscape of death – a glowing, spitting, exploding, raging field of lava ceaselessly rooted over by an inexorable iron rake that burst incessantly into thousands of death-dealing fragments. Then, as I ran, the thought flashed suddenly through my mind: 'What are you running for? Have you perhaps some idea of saving yourself? You are not going to come out of this. It's all over, finished.' So powerfully did the thought possess me that I stopped running, and rather slowly, wearily and casually I strolled in the thick of the drumfire, a dead man past harming. The other one-year volunteer, lacking any will of his own, suffered himself to be led, the other man ran on. I don't know how long I walked like that, later the time seemed endless, but it may have been only minutes or seconds. It dimly occurred to me that before death we review our whole life in a flash. I tried to take leave of the people I loved, but was incapable of forming a clear thought. Life lay unattainably far behind me, *when* death would strike seemed only a matter of seconds, and that it *would* do so was something that had long since been decided.

An eternity later I noted automatically that men were disappearing strangely on the horizon. Their silhouettes suggested that they were not falling but taking cover. Instinctively I doubled after them. It was a dolina they were disappearing into, on the slopes of which were a number of corrugated-iron shelters. Into one of them I forced my way, stumbling over furiously cursing men – I pushed them aside, I fell, and then I remember no more.

7 January 1940

Next morning when I awoke, I was lying on a heap of rifles. The bolt knobs had bored painfully into my back but I hadn't noticed. The hut was crammed with men who addressed each other only rarely, and what they said, I didn't understand. I think it was Slovene or Croat, but how could anyone ever know his way about the babel of tongues of the Austrian army? Beside me lay the other one-year-volunteer, still unconscious and talking incoherently to himself – presumably in a fever. The sun was blazing on the corrugated iron, the sweat was running off me, I had a terrible thirst. But there was nothing to drink, and hadn't been for days, as I managed to some extent to grasp. Beyond that I did not manage to make myself understood. I tried to get out of the corrugated-iron hut, but a man shoved me back roughly, and it was a long time before I could get up again. And during that time I realized my life had once again been saved – for after a heated argument a man did crawl to the exit, obviously intending to fetch water, hesitated there for a moment, then dropped without a sound. We had neither seen nor heard, but a rifle bullet had got him in the forehead.

Three days of gloomy brooding followed with no distinction between waking and sleeping for there was only the one incessant feeling of thirst. The days were mercilessly hot, the nights brought no relief to the tightly packed hut. There was nothing to eat, but we didn't mind – but there was nothing to drink either, and that was terrible. Often, though, our brooding was interrupted – the Italians attacked and we had to go out. We tried too to get out at night but were usually quickly driven back and could never get far. The torment of thirst remained, day and night, the background to a series of terrible scenes.

We were lying in a great flat dolina affording practically no protection. The corrugated-iron shelters dated from the time when this dolina was still situated well behind the front. They were no protection against artillery, only against rifle fire. That was our salvation, but many of the other shelters were destroyed by artillery fire and the corrugated-iron merely increased the effect of the shells. There were no trenches, only a few stone walls. Nor was it possible to dig in inside the hut. The floor was rock. There was one single burrow available, but that was packed with wounded. Again and again isolated attempts were made to fetch water but no one got over the lip of the dolina. Whenever we were outside we saw those who had tried, and I see them still today – drenched with blood, somersaulting helplessly down the slope – see the screaming that could only seldom be heard. Most of the wounded would then drag themselves laboriously to the burrow, many would stay where they lay, and sometimes we managed to get them into the burrow. But there were usually fresh casualties, for it was directly exposed to rifle fire. But one casualty was caught on a rock on the slope, and as soon as there was a break in the firing we could hear his monotonous screaming. Again and again there would be an attempt to get him in, but no one succeeded. All were wounded or killed. We heard him on and off for over two days.

Whenever the Italian artillery fire eased for a moment we would rush out, that being the signal that an assault was under way. The first casualties were always just outside the shelter – those who did actually get out of the riddled shelters became casualities later. I always got the position behind the bloated corpse. But who was going to risk his life retrieving bodies when we were hardly able to help the wounded? The most terrible thing – hand-to-hand fighting – we were spared. Our own artillery was so powerful that time and time again at the crucial moment fountains of bodies and rocks and arms and legs would be whirled up into the air, saving us. But then gradually it dawned on us that we were forward of our own front line. Our own lines obviously had been closed behind us, and we had been forgotten! That was why the bullets were coming from all sides. That was why we had nowhere to take cover. We could almost calculate when we should be finding ourselves under our own artillery fire – the shells were landing nearer all the time. The telephone lines had long since been shot to pieces, and there was no hope of runners getting through! Attempts were made of course, but only lost more lives.

Then, late on the evening of the third day, there was yet again one of those incomprehensible miracles – two men managed to fetch water. We threw ourselves upon it, and only when I had drained the second bottle did I notice that what I was drinking was thick brown mud. It was this miracle probably that gave me the courage to try to get back to my regiment. Why hang on in that death trap? The other one-year volunteer was

237

ready to come with me. He was half his old self again, but still not quite right, and it would probably be a good thing to take him back. So off we set into the pitch dark night. I would have liked to avoid the road by the village. The water-carriers claimed that it was still under a creeping barrage, and that was highly likely. But I was confused by the firing from our own lines in our rear – and when we came to a couple of men lying in a tiny trench and asked the way, they answered in Italian! I don't know if they guessed what was up – we just took blindly to our heels. I dimly remember the grenades falling incessantly, practically on top of us. Times without number another step to left or right, one second earlier or later, would have meant certain death. Again and again we were hurled to the ground, but again and again we managed to get up unhurt. Our lives were definitely saved by our following, with mathematical precision, the way which we could neither choose nor determine – that of blind chance.

At one point we came upon that great circle of dead men to which I have already referred – what happened has never been quite clear to me. We also arrived back in that village where, as we moved up, there had still been houses standing, and now just one corner wall was still to be seen poking spectrally towards the sky. Later on our way was blocked by a high wall, we scaled it easily – when had I ever done such a thing before? Slowly we were emerging from the area of heaviest fire, half-way through our breathless dash we suddenly became conscious that the grenade craters were becoming rarer, that fewer shells were falling, and that the worst of the din was behind us – but only later did I realize that we had escaped the greatest danger. Also there were men again of whom to ask the way, and before dawn we did in fact reach the regimental dressing station.

There, the other one-year-volunteer collapsed with nervous fever. As a result, we managed to get ourselves seen comparatively quickly, in spite of the many casualties thronging the tent. I was told to see my companion to the nearest field hospital, and then report to the field kitchens for a couple of days to get fit for action again. Somehow I dragged him as far as the road – it was getting light but one last lorry was racing back to be out of the shelled area by dawn – still, it picked us up. It was full of wounded and I dropped my companion at the field hospital with them. I got taken on a bit farther, and from there limped and stumbled to the kitchens. People stared at me like a ghost. One of the wounded had reported me killed.

Next morning our regiment came back. Of the 236 men in my company, thirty-six were left including the cooks and the sick who had remained at the kitchens and not been forward at all. Three days later the company was brought up to a hundred strong. Of those, again including the ten or so who did not have to go forward, twenty-five came back. With the other companies the picture was the same. I was amongst those survivors, but my participation in this second four-day period had been a much reduced one owing to a special assignment. But all the close friends I had been at Officers' Training School with had been killed, except for the one saved by being wounded as we were moving up. And normally too there were few wounded, mainly dead.

8 January 1940

It is difficult to free oneself from these memories – I should like to banish them but they hold me fast, there is a great deal more I could go on to tell. These days are the highlight only because they were the first. But that is enough, more than enough! What did all that experience in the face of death teach me?

Attempting to assess that today I am summing up a very long period of time. I did not think much – I did not really live – I was convinced that I should be killed. The scenes that I have described were repeated but I no longer experienced them so powerfully. Against that, I experienced more powerfully other terrors which had been concealed by new danger. There were hardships which brought me near to collapse, but I would also recover again whenever we moved back. A few quiet summer weeks near Trieste even had the luminosity of summer and the fragrance of the sea. But eating into me slowly and increasingly was the ever-powerful certainty of being killed – with seven days and nights of non-stop advance into Italy behind us, I grew careless and apathetic, failing to notice frost-bitten toes, forgetting to clean my teeth, hardly noticing the lice from which we suffered specially that winter. I did not even think any longer of my imminent death.

Then, somehow, I re-emerged from this state – I was made an officer, marches became easier for me as a result – an internal source of aid – the New Year's Eve already described threw me back again, but immediate danger being less at that time, I fell to wondering at my still being alive. I found strength to worry about leave, and not having had any for thirteen months, did in fact go home for four weeks at the end of January 1918 – and that leave made a decisive impression on me; my thoughts began to shake off the overwhelming effect of the front and death. But it is still a long way from that to even a tentative degree of clarity. Nevertheless it

239

was during these days that the way to clarity begun with the encounter with death, began to become clear. I am not however going to trace this way and its individual stages, but say merely what thoughts seem to have their basis in those days.

But I must here first of all counter an important misunderstanding. I do not believe such experience to be essential to this clarity – I even believed it to be pernicious – the fact of my having found a way to clarity out of it being a piece of special good fortune. Quite apart from the fact that this experience has usually not made life productive but destroyed it, a very great number who experienced the same thing were killed – if the effect of the experience had been obviously productive, it would not be necessary to conclude how small its contribution has been to preventing a new war.

I cannot judge how it is here or in France – in Germany a constantly oppressive problem has in fact been how it is that the appalling horrors of war should have deprived war of so little of its glory. To some extent the problem can be disposed of arithmetically. War calls for an enormous machine located in relative security; and of the fighting troops, batallion and divisional headquarters and the heavy artillery still only seldom experience the full fury of battle. On the other hand, of those who are at the front, a disproportionately high percentage are killed, the losses falling almost exclusively upon the front-line troops. Indeed, what is more, even of those actually at the front, very many do not experience war at all. My friend who was wounded as we moved up, did not return until the winter when there was hardly any fighting, and happened to be detached for duty before the spring offensive. He was months at the front, and yet does not know what war is. I myself was sixteen months at the front, which for my age was unusually long. But if out of these sixteen months the thirty or at most forty days are taken on which the worst experiences occurred, then *I* do not know anything of the true horrors of the front either. Of course, these days were spread out over the sixteen months, but many, as a result of special tasks, light wounds or illness, or by chance, escaped such days altogether.

But this external explanation is not sufficient. The number of men called up was so enormous that there are still an enormous number left who were clearly aware of everything, yet still remained uninfluential. But just look at those men and the state they came back in! It was years before I was able to talk of the war at all – I had first to forget – and it is no accident either that the retrospective war novels should have appeared ten years after the war! All had first to suppress what they had experienced in order to go on living at all. Many, especially the older ones who were able to resume their old lives, managed so well that they even accepted the old concepts too, or at least did not find the courage to go against convention – or at least so far suppressed their opinions as not to be forced to. Of the younger ones, many failed to find their way back to normal life at all, for they were internally destroyed, and out of that destruction sought that form of life that accorded with that experience – mercenary service, which has never, since the war, been extinct in Germany. Or they did not, for a very long time, find a way out of that destruction, many remaining half mad and many having to turn night into day, or take to drink in order to forget. For years I was unable to resume the night walks I loved, and now, over the years, have come to love again, in the country and through the woods. Then, by the time they were finally capable of returning to real life, their places had been taken by a different generation, and they no longer achieved the influence that would have been necessary to make their war experience productive for others. Their position, at least ideally, was a lost one. Now, horrified by the older generation's military notions, which they had seen through, and by the young people's new thirst for war, they cried out what they had been through, but their cry was bound to be lost upon the air. The ranks behind them had closed and they were outside, forgotten. They, knowing the mental changes brought about by the war, might perhaps have lent persuasive power to pacifism, but the cause of pacifism had already been lost. Was it to be wondered at that many subsequently found their way into mercenary service and even began to idealize this mechanical war?

That I should be obliged nevertheless to ascribe particular importance, at least for myself, to experience of death, is simply to do with the general lack of imagination. Are we not all aware that we must die – do we not experience death countless times even in our own intimate circle? But for all that, it is the minority who live conscious of the fact that death may overtake them hourly, or that their mortal path which they are in fact walking may at any instant come to an end. The Crucifixion ought to force us to face death – that is one of its many profound meanings, but one which for the majority has long since been lost. And it has been lost because in essentials we no longer understand how to live fully, and for that reason cannot bear the thought of death. If life were lived wholly and properly then, it would by virtue of the very certainty of death, acquire its supreme splendour and ultimate power.

But I am anticipating. I want to try to put my thoughts in the face of death into some sort of order.

Evening

But first another interpolation – since writing down these memoirs I have been tormented by the thought that I may still have learnt too little from them.

Anxiously and mistrustfully I am following news that seems to point to the possibility of peace with a modified form of Fascism. Now the War Minister, Hore-Belisha, has resigned again – why, we are not told – is it that they are breaking off the democratic development of the army for the sake of right-wing unity, or – and this I do not believe – is it an attempt to relieve the Cabinet of the Jew who is under attack in Germany? Such thoughts, I cannot deny, fill me with great uneasiness. Does it not seem as if, as a result, possibilities are again being discarded which have, after all, been created by the war?

9 January 1940

It was natural at first of course to see my unexpected and miraculous deliverance as a special singling out by fate. Belief in some kind of recognizable causality could no longer keep pace with that. Every step I took, every time I hesitated or hurried had been my salvation – had I stumbled once more or once less in the darkness, had I fallen or got up again seconds faster or slower, or had I in my blindness run so many inches this way or that, I should have been no more. Of course, given an exact knowledge of all the circumstances, it seemed conceivable to calculate my entire course, but quite apart from the impossibility of that knowledge, *I* had been involved too, *I* had not been able to choose my path – had not had the slightest possibility of any knowledge or calculation – from my point of view any such explanation was simply senseless. The fact of my having, innumerable times, run the very way that saved me from being hit was obviously due to a host of coincidences. But so gigantic an accumulation of coincidences all working in the same direction could not simply be chance – that was inconceivable – they *must* be based upon an unrecognizable necessity – they *must* be fate.

But set against the number of the dead, the idea of being singled out was again impossible. Why just me? Why not the others? It was outrageous arrogance to believe that I was special, whether by reason of some kind of – certainly non-existent – merits, or by reason of some special task. Those killed were the men of greatest value. I, on the other hand, was no more than one amongst many. My youthful exuberance had been broken, but not even that would have deluded me that I, of all people, represented any particular value. I could see myself neither as specially gifted, nor as strong and pure in the human sense. Amongst the friends killed were many I had to acknowledge superior to myself – and I was above all attached to them – I could not feel my saving fate to be a special singling out, but only resent it on account of the dead – at the same time, the fact of my still being alive was a reproach to fate.

Whether my faith in opposites is rooted in those hours, I do not know, but it seems so to me today. There were two mutually exclusive thoughts thrusting themselves upon me with equal force, and any attempt to force them into a unified channel failed. I could probably simply have let the coincidences exist as coincidences and said, 'I do not know the preconditions but that does not mean that no causal, scientifically plainly recognizable correlation existed, and were my knowledge more comprehensive I would recognize the ever-present conformity to law.' But that conclusion visibly deprived the experience of its force. For of what use is that subsequent knowledge of causes? I had acted without it and, had I been entirely dependent on it, it would not have helped me then in the slightest – I should have been dead and buried – and similarly it seemed, and seems to me, life would be deprived of its sense, breadth, depth and truth if we were to try to ignore the endless number of events which appear absolute coincidence, and simply trust that that extension of knowledge will some time come about which explains even these coincidences causally. But that would mean deferring full life entirely until the future, and simplifying and impoverishing the present in an inadmissible fashion – all causal laws do, after all, explain only the external happening. Also we may have an external understanding of our dash through bursting shells, but why it fell to us to make this blind, unconscious dash, why we are as we are, although the very exact laws of heredity – which we do not yet know – admit of countless possible combinations of the genes that formed us, why what we experience has precisely the effect on us that it does, and not another, although the most varied effects are possible and we ourselves experience the most varied effects, why our thoughts and feelings go *this* way and not one of the infinitely many others which admit just as well of a causal explanation, and which are probable to precisely the same degree – these causes simply cannot be identified. I, inconceivably supreme perfection of causality, may also one day be able to say precisely what path is followed at every thought by the atoms of my brain, but as a result, I shall still learn absolutely nothing concerning the content of the thought and the feeling. I experience the unity of the world, certainly, but one tiny bullet in my head, and I cannot think anything any more – not only my external but also my internal life is extinguished – nevertheless, two worlds, two realities do exist for my knowledge, and I merely flatten the world and block my access to it whenever I try to force these two realities into the realm of a unified explanation.

Neither does it work from the other approach. Even if we call fate by the name of God – why did God select us and destroy the others? Why did he send this stream of destruction into the world? Why did he so make men as to necessitate a Deluge time and time again? Did he then *not* form them after his own image? To whatever heights of ecstasy we may intensify our feeling, we shall not, in so doing, rid the world of the reality which we have experienced. It will come upon us again at moments of weariness, and also destroy again the unity which we believe by living thus, thus to have won. And is not life rendered the poorer and flatter again as a result of this unity? Do we not thereby deprive ourselves of the possibility of passing through this life with eyes open and senses wide-awake; do we not thereby work ourselves up into a state of ecstasy which again is destructive – for the very reason of our wanting to forget and not heed what we cannot forget? It is when we affirm fate, give it the supreme name of *God* that we are then obliged to regard this world as God-created, that it is then our task – the sense of this life – not to ignore the world, but to experience it in full, grasping it with the senses, that we must then be ready to say yes even to the most terrible experiences that shake us out of any ecstasy. No, this way fails too – our thinking does not suffice to apprehend directly as unity the unity we experience.

There was nothing for it but to let the two thoughts stand side by side. And as soon as I was no longer fighting feverishly and vainly to reconcile them, a clear, powerful feeling developed: that I must show myself worthy of the fate that had, for inexplicable reasons, befallen me, and make it my fate – not fritter away my energies in irrelevant things – in practical result, but do what I consider essential, live in the essential! Out of the conventionally commercial education that might have determined my life, a way to freedom and spaciousness – a way to vital life suddenly opened to me, and other, more genuine values appeared, which it was my task to devote my life to – externally I was taking the step from security into uncertainty, and in so doing encountering a certainty corresponding to the feeling which the conflicting and incompatible thoughts had aroused in me. For the freedom and spaciousness I arrived at, were not licence – here too I could not arbitrarily determine my path – another, deeper compulsion was taking possession of me, in which gradually I recognized the voice of the Absolute.

But with that, the opposites guiding me also acquired more definite shape. They had been very unclear – throughout the coincidence a needful fate had emerged, but this again had been no special singling out, but, in a remarkable way, coincidental itself. I now saw that I must not read fate into the external – this external was relatively comprehensible with the aid of causality, and causality alone, but this knowledge was, after all, relative – within us, on the other hand, lives and speaks the Absolute that no absolute external knowledge can impart but which nevertheless imposes on our lives compelling moral laws. As long as we struggle for absolute unified knowledge we shall always get into hopeless confusion and become helpless and at a loss – we must let the opposition stand, recognize the reality and follow the moral laws nevertheless, then we achieve harmony with that compelling feeling which opposites engender in us, thereby obtaining a certainty that extends beyond all knowledge. We have an externally needful fate that is internally coincidental – we must recognize external necessity, but live in the essential, then we shall make fate our fate, and live off that essence which makes external compulsion our servant. Any external tilting against the compulsion of our fate is futile – we are bound – we must let it endure, live off the essential, obey the voice of the Absolute – then perhaps we shall manage that genuine act which creates a new reality. It is definitely only then that we *can* manage it – only proceeding from that Absolute provided within us for us alone, that the enigmatic, the inexplicable and unnameable, the divine, or mercy, can appear creating from opposites a new unity.

But I had experienced life too powerfully to be able simply to rest content with this knowledge. Life was not so simple as to be a question of obeying a rule! Had it not been right for me to attempt to escape from the dolina of death? How could my fate have been accomplished without that attempt? Had I not in the process saved at least one other person? Where does the borderline lie between acting and surrendering oneself to fate, between inertia and recklessness, ease and fate? How am I to turn a fate into my fate if I do not recognize it – and how am I to recognize its binding compulsion if I do not resist it?

There was a simple answer to that too – 'Obey the moral laws.' But where were the moral laws when I escaped from the dolina? I could have stuck to my duty, but that, at that time, was very ambiguous too: was it my duty to hold out, or to find my way back to my regiment during the actual battle? At the time I acted without thinking – yet it was that very experience which at a later time deprived me of the ability of acting simply without thinking. And I had learnt to prize life too highly to see its destruction as an end, albeit for the sake of moral laws – life seemed to me to stand every bit as high as these laws – fulfilment of life seemed to me to be the sense of them! But if we are going to fulfil life, we cannot simply live in the essential and the Absolute – that all too easily turns merely into a destructive ecstasy again – we have also to get on with the relative – the external!

No, there is no absolute rule – as our thinking is bound to opposites we must not rely on so simple a process of unification here either. We must attempt to fashion our path externally also, we must tilt at our fate to recognize at what point it is really binding, and we must nevertheless at the same time obey the internal compulsion. Then we may manage to employ all our powers without breaking them; then we shall recognize at what point our fate is compulsion, and from that point, unbroken, find a new way; then external and internal compulsion will let themselves be weighed against, or balanced with, each other in a manner surprising perhaps to ourselves. Then the external will lead us to ever clearer knowledge of the internal, and experience of the internal will point the way in the external. We must let the opposites stand in their full force, but, in our own lives, that means above all that we, having a clear knowledge of external necessity, must nevertheless experience the Absolute in its full force and stand by it. We must not attempt to stand aside from this opposition – that is probably the only rule that we can clearly recognize.

And that may well be good thus also – for it is by those means only that life comes fully into its own. But what this life means to us – that too I learnt only when confronted by death.

10 January 1940

Once I had wrenched myself free of the certainty of being killed, life lay before me in a completely new light – seeming to me a thing of enormous value – seeming, content apart, the thing of greatest value *per se*. When I got back to the front after leave, i.e. at a time of no longer believing in my death absolutely, but fearing it all the more instead, an unbounded longing for life awoke within me. I simply wanted to live. How didn't matter. Every moment seemed to me a new gift – however empty it might be, that moment, I *was* conscious of being alive, conscious of the pulse-beat of my blood – of the circulation of my thoughts, and however

246

dark the days and fearful my thoughts might still be, that was an immense gift, for that was life. The thought that I might therefore perhaps go on living was a quite new and overwhelming thing – a wholly new infinity opened, an eternity, of which I knew, it is true, that it must also conceal misfortune and suffering but which nevertheless seemed to me new bliss, for even misfortune and suffering were after all yet another confirmation of being alive. I no longer needed to count the moments – but how I tried to use them all the same – how I tried not to forget for an instant that always, throughout all the dark things, there would be the supreme happiness of being alive.

Years later when I came across the works of Dostoyevsky I was moved deeply and again and again to the point of tears by the hymn to life into which he so often breaks. I was ready to cry out with him, *'There is no end for which man is entitled to ruin his life'* – and my feeling was reproduced by Dmitry Karamazov, when, out of the deepest and darkest abyss, in face of the most fearful fate and in defiance of all torments, he still exclaims,

> And there seems to be so much of this power in me now that
> I shall overcome all, overcome all sufferings, just so as to be
> able to tell and keep on telling myself every minute that I *am!*
> Amidst a thousand torments, I *am.* I writhe under torture, but
> I *am!* I sit in a tower, but I too exist – I see the sun, and if I
> don't, I know that the sun *is* – that is the whole of life![12]

I shall not speak now of how often this power nevertheless later deserted me or of how many moments and, indeed, long periods of time, passed without my feeling suffering to be a confirmation of the happiness of living. But soon another objection presented itself – if we want to live in the essential and obey the Absolute – do not these values then stand above the value of life? Is not the important thing the content which we are able to give our lives, and do we not have to follow our ideals even at the price of life? Do we not, for the sake of the supreme values, have to be ready for the sacrifice of life – is it not that we are only actually entitled to believe we are standing by the Absolute when we are risking our lives for it? And do we not find our way to a full life and to the sense of life only when thus, with all our power, and so at the price of life too, we strive for a higher end?

Again two thoughts stood opposed which did not admit of being reconciled or eliminated. Again, my effort to bridge the abyss notwithstand-

12. *The Brothers Karamazov*, book 11, chapter 4.

ing was merely threatening to confuse me – life as such did not admit of elevation to the highest level without the voice of the Absolute being choked, nor was the Absolute able to raise the value of life. And from the ecstasy which can really turn the hymn to life into an overpowering feeling, I was restrained by life itself which, as earthly life, had favoured me, and had therefore to be fulfilled in an earthly sense in the same manner. I could not make heaven come on earth, nor would heaven let me forget earth. I was ready to take pleasure in life where that proved possible, and to subordinate love of life to higher ideals. But my experience had been too powerful for that, and I was restrained too by the profoundest of my formative experiences, Dostoyevsky, *he* had taught me to apprehend the world so much better, *he* had led me to a life that I felt to be my true life, and *he* demanded love of life as an absolute precondition – a demand as important as that, the message of his whole work, and one that had awoken a response in me, was not one that I could simply pass by.

What taught me to understand this contradiction was the figure of Christ. Encountering the figure of Christ late in life, I apprehend it the more purely by reason of its not having been familiar to me from childhood, so that it has not been effaced, and weakened or distorted by habit, school and convention – or is it that I am not *sufficiently* familiar with it? The hymn to life is something I have always read into the Gospel – that purest of realizations of supreme joy – but I have learnt to understand also that it is one that can be sung only out of a readiness for death.

Again we have to let the opposites stand. God is the whole. Only when we feel the glorious and the terrible, supreme happiness and most profound suffering, can we hope to experience a sense of the divine. But how can we feel suffering, mortal danger, the terrible, powerfully enough if we do not love this life? If we do not cling to this life in an obsessive and unbounded way, what *can* impress us with full force? Take love of life away and everything is again impoverished and levelled. There is no longer any supreme price for us to pay for the supreme. For life is our whole and most original possession – only if we love it as such can we fully engage ourselves at all! But we cannot feel this love of life wholly if we are not aware of death. It is precisely because life is incessantly in danger that it is so valuable. Only because we may at any moment be called away does every moment count. Through consciousness of death we learn to experience the moment, and it is only in the moment that we love life wholly. Any activity, any thought, any striving towards an end calls for a long series of moments, and as a result masks life as such, but it is only

248

and solely in this – the shortest – time span that nothing is present but life itself, and it is only here that we grasp what life is, detached from all its content.

Indeed, more than that. This opposite reaches its full power only when we know that we have to stake this life, and when death is not only in store for us at some time or other, but when, in spite of our unbounded love of life we are ready to take death upon ourselves. For to begin with, death has the appearance of blind chance merely destroying life – and death being indissolubly bound up with life, such absurdity devalues life also.

How can we love life if it is conditioned by the nonsensical! We cannot wholly apprehend the enormous value of life until we wholly apprehend the value of the Absolute too, but we do not do that until we are aware that the Absolute counterbalances even death, until, therefore, we are prepared, for the sake of the Absolute, voluntarily to suffer death. But then we are aware too that there is a Something – which we cannot or will not name – in our lives that extends beyond our lives – that there is an Eternal Something alive in our temporal lives. Blind chance, which threatened love of life, is in fact done away with – death is delivered of its lack of meaning – however hard we may have exerted ourselves to make the Absolute a reality, we shall never arrive at our goal; we live conscious of the fact that the ultimate thing still remains for us to do – we live ready to intensify our devotion to the point of self-sacrifice – and thereby even natural death still becomes the sacrifice that we make to the Absolute. Full experience of the Absolute intensifies and safeguards love of life – but at the same time death, destroying the life that is loved in an unbounded way, will occur for the sake of the Absolute, and thereby meaningfully.

We have to live the opposition as powerfully as possible – death, because we love life deeply, may be a terrible annihilation, but as, at the same time, it occurs for the sake of the Absolute, we are entitled to hope that the deepest pain will also become the realization of the Absolute – the realization of that which extends beyond our lives. Death no longer devalues life but enhances it – the fulfilment of life leads to the fulfilment of death. The Crucifixion, by very reason of the fact of not breaking the force of death by means of a miracle, but of making it a terrible reality, has shown me the fulfilment of death – and it is only in that fulfilment that the hymn to life is accomplished.

11 January 1940

I am shocked to be speaking so definitely and plainly here but I am speaking of my experience, and that experience has been very definite. But that is not to imply that I know, or am able to do, better, or that what I say here is absolutely and exclusively correct. I have already said how far I have departed from my intentions – and is anyone able to accomplish the ultimate? Again, no rule shall or can be given! I realize today that people may lack the strength to endure this life, and may do what they should not do – throw their lives away. And I know too that my experience has been one-sided – after a fulfilled life, the fulfilment of death may come about in pure serenity – in blessed peace – and that fulfilment I must set even higher as a premonition of the uncrucified Christ. I feel it to be a final slur upon our times that they should again be threatening to make that peaceful fulfilment impossible.

13 January 1940

I am again in danger of getting lost in the boundless, and I am touching on areas where my philosophical work has first to be taken further before I can speak of them simply and clearly. But there is another important element of my experience that I must mention, for it explains another essential basic feature of my philosophical work which I have only hinted at – explains how it is that the abstract basic concepts leading to extreme opposites do provide a wholly concrete illustration of the content of the moral laws. I have mentioned that these basic concepts have a double aspect – as regards external reality they are abstract – for man on the other hand, they represent the most important realities. The meaning of that again became clear to me through my war experience. For this was also a particularly clear, deeply moving experience of the time.

But how was that? My dash on that level field through the drumfire seems like an eternity to me in the literal sense, and yet was perhaps of only a few minutes' duration. The three days in the dolina of death and the way back seemed never-ending, and still seem never-endingly long to me even today, but not as eternal as the minutes in that field. Then, when I believed in life again and feared death, I counted the moments and experienced them – every one was a long distinct time span, yet many of the subsequent years merge in the memory into a short time span and seem shorter than those fully experienced moments. And though many of the important subsequent years still seem full long years even

250

today, experience of eternity has again and again been possible only at moments whose time content plainly exceeds the time magnitude of years.

Time is purely a form of perception, and as such completely abstract – something which we ourselves add to our apprehension of reality. We are able to measure this time – we count the years, and each year has months and days, hours, minutes, seconds. But the measurement is artificial – we select what ever years we like – solar, lunar or light years – they do not correspond completely with reality and have from time to time to be corrected. Time is also something that we read forcibly into reality, a body falls – *that* we can see – that it takes time to do so is something that we add. The unalterable course of seconds that continues uninterrupted before, during and after the fall, has obviously nothing at all to do with the fall we measure against time. Similarly we ingeniously calculate the elliptical orbit of the earth, but it is conceivable for a superior *Organon* to see this ellipsis as an unbroken line at rest – although not easily so, for what is to us a second would have, to this superior *Organon* to be a year. But does not our brief day comprise, for many living creatures, a whole lifetime – by virtue of which has not a whole lifetime become almost present time for us too? And do we know what a second means to microscopically small living creatures? This exactly measurable, regularly expiring time is an abstraction which we add to things to enable us to apprehend them – time, set against external reality, is in itself void.

But we cannot help ourselves – we are obliged to think with the aid of this abstract intuitive form – everything we perceive or experience takes place in time! But as a result, time becomes one of the most important realities for us that there is – for there is of course no experience in which time is not contained – we experience it uninterruptedly and without exception, and we experience virtually no other thing so powerfully and incessantly. But *this* time, which is a human reality, has a quite different aspect. It is abstract form no longer, it is itself already a substance.

We do something, experience something – time passes as if on the wing, but later we can remember everything exactly and in memory time seems long. We have to wait, we are bored – time refuses to come to an end, but in memory it simply disappears. Or for years we do something that gives us pleasure – the years pass quickly, it is true, but to us they seem rich and filled with activity and result – later we recognize that our activity was senseless, that our industry was in vain, and in memory the years shrink – not only in conversation but in our memory too we pass over them in a couple of sentences – 'At that time I was doing this and that and earning such and such an amount.' The details elude us, and

251

finally we are quite unable to understand any more what those years were actually filled with, or that they were many. But if, in these years, we have had a powerful experience or a powerful artistic impression or a powerful feeling, we remember these hours in all their details, and they seem to us as long as they were or even longer – longer at any rate than the days and weeks and months incessantly filled with the same activity. Looking back, we know that we have lived forty years, and that these were forty equally long years, each having twelve months. But we cannot make much of that in reality, for that measurement has become abstract and meaningless. Our memory has a wholly different time reckoning, in which moments and years have become completely mixed up in their relative magnitudes. And the same thing happens while we are still experiencing time – if we did not know that the hours were of equal duration, we should never guess that an empty hour and one filled with external activity or become important internally were of equal length.

But it is with this that time as a human reality does in fact become a direct elucidation of moral precepts. For man, time has on the one hand the appearance of expiry, a constant unbroken flow; on the other hand, the appearance of duration, a self-contained portion of time as day, year and human life. Expiry of time is an urgent, compelling precept – time has to be filled – man experiences time only when able to give it content – gains and realizes it only to that extent – time not experienced remains unreal and becomes irrevocably lost to man. Time is itself a moral precept – to conquer and realize time is what matters – boredom is a torment, indeed, bad conscience. *To kill time* is an apt expression – if we do not know how to fill time, any absurdity is welcome merely to prevent our hearing this eternal admonition – to deaden the tormenting inner voice, – and time really does get killed – for absurdity obliterates rather than realizes it. For time is also duration, empty activity, senseless industry still fail to satisfy this inner voice, for what fills it must also have a lasting quality, only when portions of time are filled with valuable content is time in fact realised and snatched from the irretrievable. Time requires not only to be filled, but filled meaningfully. And as duration, time also reveals itself not only as a powerful internal compulsion but directly as a moral precept. Human time is distinguished from the abstract form of perception by the fact that nothing is repeatable: the past is irrevocable and final; what has been done, cannot be undone; what has been missed stays missed; there is no way in which we can withdraw from the past and its consequences. But time is thus responsibility also. Only what meaningfully fills time can be answered for, and only that which can be

252

answered for, will fill time in such a way that it becomes the past, and we resign ourselves to it and are able to build on it. What cannot be answered for, turns into a burden that we are obliged to drag through time with us – and, simultaneously, into an inexorable admonition to responsibility.

Again, we shall not succeed in achieving an uninterrupted realization of time, it will not be possible for everything we do to be meaningful. But against this inevitable weakness and pliability, time itself provides a counterbalance, leaving room for the necessary wrong path and the superfluous devious one – its duration in human terms is not fixed. Eighty years can be empty and brief; a single year – rich and full and, on account of its content, as good as infinite. Looked at from the Absolute, nothing depends on the duration of our lives. We may, after a long and empty life, face death blindly and impotently, but even then a single moment can still suddenly raise us up for the fulfilment of death; whereas a brief life can be so filled as to lead naturally and inevitably to that fulfilment. How perfect often seem the lives of artists who die young – and how else to understand the infinite fullness and effect of that one year that very likely contains the whole way of Christ? Time is the very thing that shows us how little we depend on the external – the external is important, and that importance may lead us on to wrong paths upon which we shall lose time externally to no purpose – Christ's way, if it teaches us to fulfil our time, nevertheless deprives us of none of the time allotted to us. Eternity itself *is* of course in any case something that we can experience in only a moment! For eternity is not only infinity of time, it is something else: it is time itself detached from infinite expiry – it is rest – but that detachment is only possible for us in the moment, for only there do we experience the lifting of the expiry of time to which we are otherwise bound. And it is for that very reason that the fulfilled moment is able to counterbalance a whole life. A sense of unity is also something that we can of course realize only in the moment – and it is precisely in the moment that we experience the whole which is also eternity.

The important thing above all seems to me that my experience has taught me the great extent to which we can commit ourselves to thinking in opposites. It may, it is true, deprive us of the premature comfort of a unity, logical in itself, that we rediscover always and everywhere. But as all our thinking and perceiving, feeling and knowing are determined by the laws of thought, they are the most certain thing we are able to assert concerning man, and also in fact teach us most clearly and surely to apprehend his true nature, the moral laws profoundly appropriate to him, and the Absolute alive within him. The content of morality becomes – it

253

seems to me for the first time – a scientifically apprehensible fact. And that, at this time of lost faith, is bound to be of very great, indeed, exceptional importance! Faith, once lost, is almost impossible to win back, but our time teaches with abundant clarity that, without faith, it is impossible to manage human life. The way I have found may still not be the right one, but the attempt to find such a way is, at all events, worth the trouble – to pave a compelling way to faith, beginning at man, should prove a decisive advance. And already a great deal of evidence suggests my way to be one of the correct ones.

16 January 1940

And now at this point I may as well mention also something I ought to have mentioned long ago. A Czech National Committee has received recognition by the British Government, and consequently is able to call up Czechs living in Britain. I being over forty, this call-up will probably not affect me at once, but there is little doubt that it will get to me sooner or later. The undeserved quiet I have been permitted to enjoy in the midst of war, will soon be over – I must make up my mind.

This brings me back to the question this diary opened with. Have I any right to keep out of the war – out of the armed struggle, when the fight is against the Nazis? It is over this concrete and decisive vital question where life is at stake, literally and figuratively, that must be shown whether my thoughts are of such moment and vitality as to be really capable of helping me, or whether they are merely formal and lead away from life and into the void.

What is certain is that the Nazis have to be fought. But that is because in them we are bound to recognize all that we fight in ourselves when struggling for a breakthrough of the human element – unbridled animal urges and destructive passions, presumption, contempt for others, the arrogance of allowing the validity only of our own opinions – not because they are right but to justify injustice to our own advantage – and a joy in destruction and self-annihilation. We have to recognize in them what we fight in ourselves, for only by so doing do we also recognize that we all are guilty of everything. And only in being destroyed by that sense of guilt do we experience the Absolute which can at the same time save us.

This opposition between the damning of others and our own guilt is one which we must not remove. If we carry the damning to the extent of concealing our own guilt we enter the realm of convenience – today it is clearly simpler to obey the command and fit in with the rest without giving it a thought, instead of singling ourselves out for an uncertain fate for which we have to assume our own responsibility. If we are too quick to take comfort in the idea, we find ourselves in the realm of anxiety – danger to life being after all probably excluded – prison too being, presumably, safer than the front. It is only when we experience the opposites equally powerfully that we have the certainty of not hiding behind evasions, but of wholly and unreservedly involving ourselves in every decision that we take. And only when *we* are wholly involved can the Absolute also be made a reality.

For months now I have lived confronted by this decision. So strongly do I feel the necessity of fighting the Nazis that any reassurance at the idea of a future Europe seems to me like Utopia. I know that the sacrifice demanded of a refugee by conscientious objection is greater than that demanded of ordinary British citizens, for he will, as a result, forfeit the right to a home anywhere, in which case he will be hounded still further through the world by the peace. Fulfilment of life calls, I know, for consideration of these apprehensions – only in extreme distress are we allowed to take a decision that may destroy the real foundation of life. I understand the two pleas of the 'Our Father' – 'Give us this day our daily bread', and 'Lead us not into temptation', we *can*, for the sake of daily bread and of building up life, be tempted to be disloyal to the idea. Both ways can be right and can be a temptation – we need daily bread, and we need the aid of the Absolute to be able to distinguish between volition and compulsion.

It is for that very reason that the decision cannot be prepared. It is extraordinarily difficult to distinguish between the admissible escape and the inadmissible wrong way – between the necessary and the superfluous act – any preconceived opinion can trouble the clear view. We cannot withdraw from the opposites, we must let the decisive moment come to us. Only then can we hope at the crucial moment to remain true to ourselves in the deepest sense.

How to endure in the face of this test?

17 January 1940

The opposites that determine me I can formulate still more abstractly, and thus, in fact, more clearly. Kant requires, as supreme precept, that 'Thou shalt always regard man as an end in himself, and never as a means.' That sounds very much like a mere, and all too general, idea, yet it leads deeply into the reality of our lives.

If man is a vessel of the Absolute, then it is also a degredation of the supreme to use man as a means for some external end, for there *is* no end that can be placed above the Absolute. But the social existence of men requires a structure, and in this structure it is unavoidable that men should serve – the organization of human society demands inexorably that men should be employed as means for definite ends. Men are not perfect, they do not serve voluntarily, they have to be compelled – it is when we love men that we have to see that they live together without friction – even love of our fellows requires man to be employed as an end!

But where is the line to be drawn in this in itself reprehensible, but nevertheless necessary, activity? Once it is permitted to use man as a means, the way is open to dominion over human life, to the inclusion of this incomprehensible treasure in rational calculations, and so to the totalitarian state, to war. Death is not where to draw it, for even abuse of the mind must remain inadmissible – Christianity is right to regard the sin against the spirit as the one deadly sin. If we once subordinate our thoughts to compulsion we are soon controlling them by means of untruth, and in so doing, paving the way for coercion by impulse and for every form of seduction. The very first step opens the way to final destruction.

Does that not again show the necessity of keeping the opposites alive, and does it not show them most clearly and powerfully? Only from equally strong knowledge of both demands can we decide in each individual case. The rule which Kant considered generally valid, is not sufficient, there is no absolutely unequivocal knowledge, any absolute rule must destroy either human society or man. We must experience both arguments equally strongly. Only then will our decision be sure. Only then do we know that we have done justice to the opposing claims as far as is ever possible in this relative life.

But it is good that that should be so. How can we love men without suffering? Love for our fellow men that does not cut into our hearts remains not lived and inadequate. But it is wrong to pine away in sympathy, for by so doing, we thrust ourselves onto the path of external result. Love for our fellows is bound to encounter suffering in the fact that we run up against duties towards man and duties towards ourselves. Only then it is not impaired by the external but made reality in fellow suffering – in fellow suffering that becomes profoundly painful for the very reason that we cannot simply follow it because we have to set our duties towards the absolute higher.

We cannot and must not draw a line – that is only to flatten life inadmissibly. The example we follow, the way which is thereby prescribed for us, consists in our engaging ourselves unreservedly and to the utmost; no rule suffices because the important thing is that we should find our own way, for that is the only way that can be experienced and suffered to the very utmost – it alone can therefore reveal the ultimate in us. We shall have to deviate often before we succeed in experiencing the opposites in full clarity simultaneously. But we must not let ourselves be deprived of this experience by any over-hasty, clear-cut conclusion – for only by ourselves experiencing the opposites can we advance towards certain clarity, to the Absolute within us. And it is precisely as a result of that that we first experience the profoundest certainty – that as we find the Absolute within us, we also possess it unlosably.

The result is not in our hands: we must have trust. But we can, because we are vessels of the supreme – and that supreme is also mercy.

23 February 1940

After my long break, a rough account of the state of the war.

Pre-war, the good and abundant chances were missed completely by the Chamberlain and Daladier governments – especially the final one in the autumn of 1938 when the Siegfried Line, today such an obstacle, is supposed to have been still incapable of being defended. The unprepared state of Britain at that time also represents lost chances: between the occupation of Austria and the crisis there were six months, in which time, with a bit of effort, it should have been possible to turn London's twenty anti-aircraft guns into two thousand, and produce large numbers of aircraft.

This missing of opportunities seems to be continuing in war. At any rate, all the other Democracies have missed *their* chance – if they had all come to Britain's aid *en bloc* the war would assuredly have been decided long since. Germany could not have invaded everywhere at once, and would have been cut off completely from the necessary raw materials. But alas, the Democracies have long failed to grasp what this war is about, and the aid which the Allies granted Poland was not in the end encouraging either.

I believe as ever that the Allies will win – not easily – but only when decisive German blows induce them to make a proper effort. For there seems to be any number of lost chances in this area also. There are still over a million unemployed in Britain, and nothing suggests that the months gained have been usefully given over to energetic rearmament.

257

But I believe too that those governments who have been missing all the chances time and time again, will not be capable of seeing chances in future. I am afraid that victory too will come as a missed chance, and when nothing can any longer be saved.

All these arguments could be used as arguments against the war, and they could be used to make the cause of pacifism, of the idea, outwardly convincing too. Only when we face reality, making ourselves conscious of the enormous necessity for and justification of this war, yet nevertheless feeling the dreadful, the inescapable necessity of being against war – only having bought that knowledge at the cost of very great horror and very great self conquest – only then can we be confident in the fact that we are not really employing evasions but obeying the voice of the Absolute.

Maybe that *is* the sense of rational thought – any acute thinking leads to recognition of the negative, of absurdity, of necessary destruction. But this negative, in which no comfort can be taken because it simply no longer has any content for the mind, and because the mind here comes up against an intolerable void in which it can no longer see its way, is the very thing that awakens positive feeling; the negative has a vital significance for feeling, being a component part, the other side, of a positive feeling arising simultaneously. And that feeling needs the acute, destructive conclusions of the mind in order not to get lost in the void in romantic exuberance or vague longing; only by that means will it be referred wholly to its own content, and only by that means will it really and unequivocally become the voice of the Absolute!

13 March 1940

Finland has made peace, buying, at the cost of enormous and terrible sacrifices, a far worse peace than she could have had without sacrifice.

But almost worse, I find further, is that peace should be concluded under suspicious circumstances. The very moment it was finally too late, the Allies announced what help they had made ready, saying they were only awaiting Finland's call for aid in order to begin supplying it! As if there were any need for another such cry to make Finland's position plainer! That claim only serves too to push all blame on to Sweden and Norway for not allowing the passage of Allied troops. Yet even if that is true, is it an excuse?

258

9 April 1940

The Germans have occupied Denmark and invaded Norway. I am ashamed to be German!

16 April 1940

A hectic week! The first reports of Allied successes were unfortunately not true. Still, half the German fleet has been sunk and the British have now landed in Norway. As they are claiming to be able to cut the Germans off at sea at the same time, the Nazis may perhaps suffer their first repulse. How important it will be for the Germans and the neutrals if the nimbus of Hitler's invincibility is finally destroyed!

The optimistic British speeches seem well-founded – it is to be hoped they have now realized the need to be quick and vigorous. I would be the more confident if it weren't for this government being so optimistic. Is really no other government possible here? French Democracy, which was said to be dead, has managed meanwhile to topple Daladier, and Reynaud has managed to talk even the opposing deputies round – what sort of a state is *British* Democracy in?

17 April 1940

The better political atmosphere has, for us personally, a dark side. As a result of these recent events, feelings towards the refugees are undergoing a clear change, it is no longer the Nazis people want to fight, but the Germans. Long articles are appearing to the effect that the Germans, since Frederick the Great and Bismarck, have always been war-minded aggressors, and so there is nothing for it but to destroy them utterly. And we, of course, are the first to feel the effects.

This change is, of course, very understandable. It is admirable how long the distinction between Nazis and Germans has been maintained, to say nothing of our treatment here for which we must be infinitely grateful. How would British refugees fare in Germany today? England is without doubt the only country in which such humanly pleasant things are today still possible. And, as always, a great number are resisting the flare-up of hatred.

But it would be fatal if hatred, however understandable, were to win the day here. The hope that a rational peace will be possible rests upon the human attitude of, above all, the British. If that fails to stand the test

259

then there will again be a peace that will merely supply the basis for the next war. Certainly it is difficult to defend the Germans – they are causing havoc, and this is not the first war they have unleashed in the last hundred years, and the true Prussian officer, I know, believes not in right but in might. I know that it is not only the Nazis who are now responsible for the war, but most German nationals, the army and the *petit bourgeois.* And I know that it is war that evokes the strongest response even in the hearts of countless reluctant anti-Nazi Germans.

Nevertheless, such dark hours as exist in the life of every nation must not be overestimated. How was it with Napoleon I and Napoleon III, and how did the British Empire come into being? Certainly the havoc has been made infinitely greater and more acute as a result of technical progress. The wars of the nineteenth century seem harmless compared with those of today. But it would be a betrayal of those fine first years of the Weimar Republic; it would be a betrayal of all the good friends in Germany whose suffering is greater than can yet be conceived in this relatively secure world, unless we make ourselves constantly conscious of it. There is another Germany, and everything depends on keeping the way clear for that Germany: only if that way stays open can we still have any hope for Europe!

Our fate as refugees may, against the great scale of things, be insignificant. But it is probably no accident that the campaign against us should emanate from the very papers that first defended Hitler. It is the lazy, bad, fatally shortsighted world that preaches hatred! And so it is gratifying, not only for us, but in a much deeper and more significant sense for us, that Britons should now too, at the risk of unpopularity, be standing up and standing by the refugees, and defending them, and attacking Britain for her mistakes. That this should still be possible here makes a good background to the Norwegian campaign.

I hope – hope hard – that *this* Britain will win!

18 April 1940

Am I merely disconcerted by the British inability to splash news of triumphs effectively? Have I already been so badly corrupted by Nazi propaganda? Or are we really not winning quickly enough?

It seems so clear that the theatre of war has now been found in which the Nazis can be defeated. But what is not so evident is that Germany is being left unmolested while the Norwegians are being made to suffer. Britain has wanted not to bomb German cities until the Germans bomb civilians. But are not Poles and Norwegians civilians? The reluctance to provoke air-raids on London is of course understandable, but can war be fought like that? Are we not this way granting the Germans freedom to commit with impunity any crime they wish?

It is a fiendish situation – the war can only be decided on the Western Front, yet it is there that it cannot be waged. The air-war alone would no longer seem likely to make sense today – and yet it is hypocritical not to be waging it, in spite of all its horror. So what more is to be hoped for beyond that a big success in Norway should produce a decisive shock to morale?

But will not the Nazis then wipe it out again with some other successful *Blitzkrieg*, and with impunity, for then too there will again be no civilians to seem in need of protection!

It is dreadful to have basically to approve of the air-war in this way. But how is Hitler's power ever to be undermined if the German people never come to feel the war?

It's no good. All thinking about war ends in ghastly absurdity. Even optimism assumes the appearance of a product of hell.

3 May 1940

Today the Allies have withdrawn from Southern Norway. I shall not venture an opinion as to whether their withdrawal was necessary or avoidable, the consequence of errors and tardiness, or, on the contrary, an expression of courage in bowing in time to the inevitable and not causing further needless casualties. Nevertheless it cannot be denied that it represents a defeat which will, first of all, be of quite decisive moment from the morale point of view in its effect on all neutrals, and the fear remains that it may be of strategic significance also.

The attitude of the British people and the British press is still admirable – how plain and factual the admission of defeat, and how calmly and surely it is being borne! All the hostile, reproachful, despairing, sneering voices of the neutral and the semi-hostile foreign press are simply reported, confidence being in fact rightly placed in an absence of panic.

The British Mediterranean Fleet has been reinforced. Was Italy going to strike, or merely helping the Germans by diverting British attention? All the same it is hard to escape the feeling that swift, resolute action would have been bound to have brought success in Norway! It is fine that human lives should be used carefully and sparingly, but can war be waged without some risk? And can a war be fought for freedom and democracy

261

and against dictatorship, if Reynaud is allowed to say that he would like to come to terms with Mussolini?

4 May 1940

There is a very important report in *The Spectator* by an Englishman just back from a journey through neutral countries. He speaks of the plain hatred everywhere for the Nazis. But we should beware of concluding from that, he says, that the mood is already pro-British. Quite the reverse – there is at the same time a profound mistrust of the Allies. Again and again in recent years, those under attack have been encouraged to resist, but again and again they have simply been abandoned. China, Abyssinia, Austria, Czechoslovakia, Albania, Poland, Finland, and now Norway too: how, after that fearful list, can people still believe the Allies to be serious about defending freedom? They are left to conclude that what is involved is selfish imperialism, and shortsighted imperialism at that.

I can easily imagine the feelings of the Norwegian troops and people at being abandoned! It is the same as in Prague after Munich. The British had been trusted and obeyed – the door had been opened to Lord Runciman, and all the mobilization measures ordered by Britain, carried out impeccably – for Britain's sake the Sudeten Germans had been left practically unmolested, and then, at the crucial moment, Britain jerked back and dropped the Czechs apparently cold-bloodedly. Chamberlain did not come back from Munich shamed and despondent, did not say 'I am sorry. We are not ready for war. We had to give way.' No, he allowed himself to be fêted, saying triumphantly that he had ensured peace in our time – every bit as satisfied as now with the retreat from Norway. At that time many Czechs were so embittered that they actually wanted to fight with Germany against Britain and France. That mood quickly vanished when the Nazis marched into Prague – but what will be the mood of the Norwegians abandoned on the battlefield? And of the Czechs in Prague, and of the anti-Nazis in Germany?

Certainly many British people think differently. At one meeting where Masaryk spoke, the deputy mayor of Cambridge said, 'We recall Munich with deep shame. It is a disgraceful chapter of British history.' Nevertheless Chamberlain obviously cannot be toppled, and that not because democracy is not working but because apparently there are many who have confidence in him because they approve of his policy. And above all because, seemingly, there is no one else to replace him. The decisive opposition ought to emanate from the Labour Party, but here too the incompetence of the social democrats seems likely to play its fatal role.

I am conscious of knowing too little to be able to judge, and am merely reproducing the impression made upon an unbiased observer who has, perhaps, on the basis of much experience, the advantage of being able to see from the outside. My one prejudice is a love of freedom and a wish for the Nazis to disappear, utterly and for good. But is there not the danger of seeing clearer this way than if I knew all the complicated reasons that lead to unclear decisions?

5 May 1940

The British constantly compel my deepest admiration. A German plane with a mine on board crashed near the coast and exploded killing two, apart from the crew, injuring many and destroying a row of houses. Today the Germans were buried. Wreaths were sent by British women, one inscribed: 'Love ye one another at all times. From a mother', another, 'Just a few flowers knowing you have left someone dear to you', and a third, 'With heartfelt sympathy from a mother.' And finally a wreath, 'With deepest sympathy, from the R.A.F., all ranks.' In what other country in the world would such a thing still be possible today?

At the same time, however, I cannot get rid of my fear. French newspapers are publishing letters written by Thyssen to Hitler and Goering and British papers are giving a great deal of space to them. And what does Thyssen, who was decisive in helping the Nazis to power, say?

> Remember the oath that you swore at Potsdam. Give the Reich back a free Parliament. Give the German people back freedom of speech and of conscience. Guarantee those rights which restore meaning to the words *law* and *justice* so that treaties and agreements can again be founded on good faith. Then, if it is not too late to prevent fresh disasters and useless sacrifices and bloodshed, Germany may still obtain an honourable peace that will preserve its unity.

That is the sort of thing that is simply printed without comment. Can no one see the appalling grotesqueness, the fearful ridiculousness of those letters? So it was just to support Parliament and defend justice and freedom that Thyssen helped Hitler into the saddle, and not because *any* measures against the workers were all right by him!

11 May 1940

The Germans have invaded Holland, Belgium and Luxemburg. I'm
sorry – not *invaded,* that, say the Nazis, is a grotesque distortion, they
are, of course, merely trying to protect the poor neutrals against the wicked
Allies. For a second time, non-involved Belgium is suffering all the horrors of war as a matter of strategic necessity. Do we really have to be
ashamed of being German? Is there really nothing for it but the constant
use of brutal force, the trampling of all rights, all decency, all humanity?
Or this shameless distortion, the absolute rule of the lie which is still also
supposed to engender the feeling that everything is just and fair?

How little sense there is in reflecting on the course of the war and
attempting to understand the external events! Was it then, after all, right
for the Allies not to commit themselves in Norway? Did they know they
would be needing their forces elsewhere? Has Chamberlain, at the point
of being forced to resign, for once been right?

His resignation speech was dignified and impressive, an expression of
a great democratic attitude. I only wish his concluding words had come a
few years earlier. If he had described Hitler as *a wild beast* three years
ago, there would have been no need for war at all.

I also cannot escape a certain uneasy feeling that there is no one apart
from Churchill in whom people can here and now put trust. At any rate,
for the past few days the working of British Democracy has been a grand
and invigorating spectacle. That it should be possible, in the middle of
war, to conduct a mercilessly public debate, that people should not let
themselves be influenced by what their opponents are going to say – a
point that has hindered all good endeavours in Germany, even in the
most peaceful of times! – and that people should, in the knowledge of
their own power, do what is right – that really does inspire confidence.
Again and again it becomes plain – the hope of the world rests on the
mature human attitude of the British.

In this sense it is, all misgivings apart, also a comfort that the Labour
Party should now be playing a part in the Government. It is sad that it
should be obviously incapable of itself forming a government, but its taking part in the Government will probably counterbalance the growing
hatred. As long as Labour is governing too, its programme and convictions will, when it comes to peace, secure a hearing for the voice of reason.

And that perhaps is the only good thing about the new turn of events –
it may not now need to be a long war. If the Nazis were really strong it

would have been more advantageous for them to wait – inactivity – had they been able to wait, would certainly have worked out in their favour. Are they, then, weaker than they seem from outside?

But this time will the Germans be capable after defeat of creating a viable government able to adapt itself to a New Europe? That the Nazis are internally weak is a conviction held in particular by Otto Strasser, and wide publicity is being given to his utterances by the British. Are we heading towards a Strasser government, and is this other form of National Socialism a desirable goal? I am afraid not. But so little, I suppose, can be anticipated in advance that there is as yet no need for uneasiness.

I hope the invasion of Holland and Belgium really is a fiasco as is being proclaimed at the moment.

13 May 1940

Is not the vicious circle being completed? The circle of hate from which there is no escape but war, and war, time and time again?

There are signs that the new Government is inclined to engender and nourish hatred. German and Austrian refugees have been interned. That may in itself be unavoidable, and it is only hard on individuals whose plans it interferes with, but no worse – for it is not, after all, Dachau or Buchenwald they are going to. But it is still disquieting all the same, that many of those who have escaped from Dachau or Buchenwald are now again being fetched by the police and sent to a camp. And it almost seems as if this measure is simply supposed in part to placate popular feeling and in part to supply a direction for anti-German sentiment. A further sign is that Duff Cooper has become Minister of Information. It was he who a short time ago made the most hateful speech so far delivered in this war and this admirable country. Was that what procured him his ministerial post? I was glad that most of the weeklies attacked this speech, nailing its untruths; declaring themselves freely and courageously for human clarity and rejecting the rise of Goebbels' methods. Are these methods now to be promoted officially – and will not even those in Britain who are mature in their humanity now be forced on to the defensive? Is it, even here, only by way of hatred that a vigorous and resolute attitude can be arrived at – is human generosity a product only of weakness?

Duff Cooper says in his speech, 'After the last war the German people came whining and weeping that it was not the people who were guilty, just the rulers. If, after this war, they come again, we are not going to believe them any more.' The British journals responded rightly – were not we too decidedly to blame for the undermining of Germany's republican governments, although their intentions were undoubtedly honourable? And is it not goodbye straightway to any hope of real peace if we finally condemn and damn the German people as early as this? Duff Cooper also says, 'According to Hitler, he and the German people are one, and we are going to take him at his word.' Why suddenly believe Hitler in this respect, after taking him at his word has proved so disastrous?

But happily and wonderfully at the same time, the other Britain is also asking permission to speak. Yesterday's Anglo-German Whitsun service was held in spite of all the difficulties. The German Pastor Hildebrand was allowed out of internment on parole, the English sermon preached by Professor Raven, was one of the finest I have ever heard. He is a convinced pacifist and knows that difficult days are now coming for him also. But, foretelling these difficult days, he entreated British and Germans to remember then this joint divine service which demonstrates that Christianity is above the nation, thereby makes the meaning of Christianity plain. Come what may, Germans should remember that there will be no hatred in the hearts of true British Christians, no contempt, no timid dissociation from that which had its beginning in easier days – they will remain faithful to the one Christ and to the one church that knows only man. That promise he gave in the name of the congregation, and just as with that deeply moving joint service on the day that war broke out, I had the feeling that here were people who would remain firm. The great act which has made these services possible, will stand the test in the bad days also.

18 May 1940

The news leaves one speechless. Holland has surrendered. The greater part of Belgium including Brussels has been captured. The French defensive positions have been broken through on a broad front, and the Germans have pushed deep into France. Is Hitler going to win after all?

The British, remembering the same news at the beginning of the last war, are cooler about it. Even greater successes did not help the Germans then. But isn't the situation different this time? Confronting each other then were two roughly equal worlds; today, a new, a terribly yet undeniably new world is confronting an old. It is developing what, in most wars has been decisive, a new war technique – strengthened by its new idea – it is very purposeful and very ruthless, while the old world remains at a loss. I still believe that the hollowness of this new idea will find expression in the fact that its external successes will remain apparent successes. On the other hand, the helplessness of the old world does go very deep – is it not also going to influence the conduct of the war?

Is it remarkable that it should be even, or precisely, at these terrible moments that the lack of the living idea should become especially manifest? I was talking yesterday to a student who does not think much for himself, and is therefore probably quoting what many are thinking. He is clear that capitalism has had its day, he even sees too that the national–socialist–communist form of socialism is wrong, and that the important thing is a new form of socialism. But it is, of course, precisely that clear recognition that puts him at a loss. For how can people today fight for this new socialism when even its outlines and basic features are unclear? And how can people create a new idea before they have really understood what is happening – i.e. before having experienced the nature of this false new world for themselves? That need not of necessity mean defeat, but it does mean a long and difficult war.

Certainly on the whole the capitalist world of ideas is still unbroken in this country and to begin with the war will be bound to strengthen nationalism and capitalism here, for the necessary strength can only be drawn from a return to the well proven, and not from that which is new and uncertain. But at the same time war urges towards socialist forms of economy, being bound to show that the old no longer stands the test, and the front line is the most intensive school there is for socialism and readiness for the new – thus new things can be slowly introduced by a long war. The terrible thing is merely that war simultaneously reinforces man's worst powers – that its fearful destruction blunts and destroys what is best – that therefore the probability of the new powers being guided into the right channel is slight.

20 May 1940

It is two years to the day since the May crisis in the Czechoslovak Republic, and it is difficult to avoid bitter thoughts. Two years has been time to prepare properly for war, for since that crisis there has no longer been any kind of excuse for good faith, indolence or negligence; but even during the final months time was clearly still not being made proper use of, nor has it been during the war to date. It was always said that British rearmament would reach its peak by spring 1940 – that it was foolish to expect the Nazis to wait that long – but now it is gradually emerging that the Allies do not possess enough aircraft, that the Maginot Line does not extend to the North Sea but has merely been supplemented by means of substantially lighter fortifications, and that there are probably not enough tanks or troops there either. In the bitter days after the September crisis, the claim in Prague was always that Chamberlain and Daladier had not rearmed deliberately, so as to render war against the Nazis impossible, and this out of fear of Russia – but may not criminal stupidity really have been involved, as well as negligence? The speeches of Reynaud and Churchill contain, if one wishes, dark hints that a great deal was not in order.

22 May 1940

The Germans are further already than they ever were in the last war. Amiens and Arras have fallen, and they are probably at the coast by now. According to Reynaud, these successes have been brought about as a result of most incredible errors, which are to be punished – but what is the use of that? It grows harder with every day to believe in Allied victory: not just because of the great German successes, but above all because it is still absolutely incredible that they should have been able to achieve them, that they should apparently be advancing without meeting serious opposition, and that they should be able, in France itself, to wage war exactly as they did in Poland! Soon the Allied army is going to be cut off in Belgium, and what then? Any inferences will be highly unreliable, of course, but is it premature to begin believing in a victory by Hitler, or culpably optimistic to believe in Allied victory?

In any case, what is sufficiently plain already is terrifying enough. The Germans have been helped by incredible blunders. They have marched through the continuation of the Maginot Line simply because it was not manned – the *continuation!* Up to now the story has always been that the Maginot Line extended right to the sea. Why, if that was not true, were not proper fortifications built in the eight months since the outbreak of war? But they, alas, would have been no good without any troops! And where there is a failure to blow up bridges, why are they not subsequently destroyed by suitably strong aircraft sorties? And why not, where the threat is greatest, bring in great numbers of aircraft? A thousand or two thousand planes ought to be able to halt the advance of single motorized columns! Have we really so few planes as to have been condemned to inactivity from the outset? But Czechoslovakia was surrendered so that they could be built – and the war has been on for eight months! Yesterday I was told by an Englishman that there are still aircraft factories lying idle

268

because rival firms will not release the licences, in order that they alone shall make the money! But even if that is not true, the capitalist system has obviously failed again. It is staggering when America is now beginning to step up aircraft production from 5,000 to 50,000, and that is certainly not propaganda – Roosevelt said it himself. We watch Hitler building his army, even supply it in so far as we make money in the process, but egoism and inability to plan overall prevents us from at the same time rearming to at least an equal extent. That is the dangerous thing. Even this German caricature of socialism supplies proof of how very much superior this system is to the capitalist already! Hitler's whole success from the very first day has been founded on other people's blunders – is he not now again being helped over all his own weakness by any number of incredible blunders?

Nevertheless it is wrong to assert, as people do again and again – a meaningful life on the basis of inner laws, redemption through suffering, the reinterpretation of fearful events for purposes of perfection – all of them are possible only for the individual and not for the totality – and therefore every internally founded ethic, the Christian ideal included, is false, for it remains egoistical. It is precisely for the sake of the highest ideals and for the sake of love of our fellows that it cannot be accepted. We cannot trust the voice of the Absolute within us because it is unsocial, because it cuts us off from the totality. We must find an external, generally practicable way that leads humanity to one goal – that is, we have to act contrary to the inner ethic, contrary to the Absolute within us, and contrary to Christianity – we have to put up with injustice and use of force, for only as a result of these violations can we hope to make general an at least relative improvement.

This assertion again overlooks the conditioned nature of our thinking. The Absolute is something we are endowed with only inside us, only by virtue of highly personal experience; we experience it in a sense of unity without being able to translate it clearly into words; it is bound therefore to remain inaccessible to rational thought applied from the outside. If we do nevertheless attempt to apprehend it from the outside, we come up against the *person*, which is a vessel of the Incomprehensible; the human quality within is something which, proceeding from without, we only can apprehend as the personal; inner experience is what teaches us that it is, nevertheless, the Universal – that which alone is valid.

Again we must let both ideas co-exist. Viewed intellectually, a decision for good, for Christianity and for the Absolute must mean a decision for the Incomprehensible. But the negative conclusions of the intellect are something we need: we have got to see the probability of a senseless continuation of the terrible quite clearly, in order not to be shattered by it; we must not weaken in our recognition of what is senseless, so that sense should not be falsified through external conclusions but fully thought out in its own fundamentally different fashion. For we must not, of course, be led astray by the term 'intellectual thinking': we need the intellect too in order to become conscious of the conclusions that correspond to the Absolute – we think with our intellect both intellectually and in accordance with our inner self – and it is only when we make ourselves wholly conscious of both spheres that we are not lost in a stupefying excess of feeling, but arrive at that sense of unity which allows us to hear the voice of the Absolute. It is wrong to read that which is inwardly certain, the Absolute, into external thinking: if we believe ourselves able to prove the increase of good, we must either be shattered by the counter-evidence of our experience, or become intoxicated by feeling in order to drown the voice of external experience. It is equally wrong to regard encouragement through suffering as egoistical – for it is in so doing that we suppress what is internally certain. It is only in the opposition of the two ideas that we experience the incomprehensibly enormous power of the positive.

The apparent narrowing down to the personal which we are bound to make when reflecting on the role of suffering, clearly has the same task as all negations of intellect. If we did not see our limits we should believe ourselves to be dominating a greater circle, thus we should merely be adjusting the view of the infinite for ourselves, and would then wrongly take this circle for the whole – in just the same way as the natural sciences narrow the world to external reality, and the ecstatics become blind to reality. Only by finding a firm footing within the limits of our person do we become at all capable of really experiencing the whole. The narrowing down to the personal, which, intellectually, deprives suffering of its sense, first gives it this sense at all. And can anyone, in the face of this experience, adhere to the conclusions of the intellect alone?

We can rely upon encouragement as a result of suffering! To us the ways of the world are obscure – from the uttermost distortions of the human image grow new civilizations bearing a more human countenance than those which have been destroyed, while at the same time, lofty perfections prepare the way for destruction. The laws of effect are incalculable and impenetrably mysterious – we cannot estimate how far personal suffering will take effect – even Christ's way of completion was, from a directly external point of view, only the personal completion of an insignificant man. Time is nothing but a human conception – it is nothing absolute, and therefore hell too can be no more than a human, all too human conception. But in experience of the whole, which we achieve at rare moments, we experience completion, and so there can also be no doubt that this whole completes itself in itself. How and where, it is not for us to ask – we cannot know it – it is wrong to reflect upon the end of the world, or indeed upon the future! If, in suffering, the suffering is contained within personal limits, and if what is being suffered for is not our own fate but the true values of humanity, then it cannot be egoistical either, and then it will and must lead us to that meaning which we cannot think out in advance.

It is perhaps in that that the most profound significance of Christ's example lies, indeed of the example pure and simple that distinguishes the Christian religion from the others: Christ does not give us the complete translation into ideas, or the moral code, or just the teaching; what he gives as well is the vessel of the person in which we can first comprehend the teaching; what he gives us are the unavoidable, essential limits of the person, by the aid of which we can progress towards the internal. There is no clearer confrontation of senseless personal suffering and supreme universal sense than the death on the cross.

We cannot know how far finally the suffering of the individual adds up. Of every individual is demanded the way to his own completion, but we cannot know how far the way is from each individual to all individuals. But who, faced with the death on the cross, can attach any decisive weight to that question?

Certainly it would be more easily comprehensible, more satisfactory and in many respects finer if we were not forced to make absolute decisions, if we could collaborate in manifestly building up a civilization, collaborate in a slow development process. But it does not rest with us when and where we are born – we have to accept the judgement of time for we cannot withdraw from it. We must not seek this suffering – that alone would be egoistic, that would be a premature struggle for our own completion. We must try constantly to carry out our own immediate task given us within the framework of society, as well as possible. But if all our activity is brought to nothing, and all else is prevented, and suffering is all that still remains, then it is right to derive encouragement even from the most terrible suffering. Then we must merely still hope and struggle to succeed in taking the suffering upon ourselves, for then it is no longer a question of us alone, then even our own apparently insignificant completion can and must increase the good in the world.

271

23 May 1940

A new law gives the British Government almost dictatorial powers over persons and property, but still without cutting out Parliament completely. Under the present circumstances, and after the sad experiences of the first eight months of war, all that can be said is 'At last!' and 'Let us hope it is not too late.' Let us hope. The general situation seems a little better.

Although I can appreciate all that, I have my misgivings which I cannot dispose of. As could be foreseen, the war appears to be pushing in the direction of socialization of the economy. But it is sad that we can do no better than copy Fascism. Once again it is becoming unlikely that anything different, special and new will develop.

Is that the fault of capitalism or Marxism? I find myself forced constantly to regret that Marxism should have hindered the development of individual socialized concerns. If development had continued in the sense of pre-Marxist socialism – if individual socialized workshops, factories and estates had developed within the framework of the capitalist economy, then under the pressure of keen and hostile competition, competent individual socialist bodies would have been trained and the new form of economy would have found trained leaders and trained followers. Rather as in the case of religious sects, the new form of society might have developed in living fashion. And if then, as now in war, the egoistical Capitalist economy had failed, then, if they had not already done so during the economic crisis, these new men could have taken over the whole economy, and without falling into the evil of state socialism. For state socialism is only the excessive extension of the capitalist economy. It does not alter people, and does not alter the fatal effect of mechanization – on the contrary, it is bound to make it more acute, for that gigantic structure needs compulsion in order to operate.

But now probably it is finally too late. All development is heading plainly towards the intensification of technology, the opposing movements serving the same end – communism and Fascism just as plainly as Americanization, and, as now, the Democracies' conduct of war. That is the common denominator of all opposites, and probably at the same time also the direction of general development in so far as one can determine such a thing at all. He who can best adapt himself to the demands of technology will win: only if there is timely success in completely mobilizing the wealth of the capitalist world in the Fascist–communist manner, will it be able to withstand the assault of the better-organized but internally poverty-stricken Fascist forerunners. And as a result of this process a large part of the world will be made over to state socialism.

27 May 1940

On the anniversary of my own crucial war experience I suddenly saw myself again as a soldier. It happened like this: a cinema newsreel was showing the full horror of Belgium – burning cities, smoking ruins, corpses in the streets, a stream of refugees dashing in terror to seek cover from machine-guns – and in the midst of these refugees, a soldier calmly going the opposite way. A solider stamped with all the unmistakable signs of the front – grey, faceless, utterly colourless, and with those animal-sure movements which tell how to avoid the roaring shells. Amongst the terrified refugees, he was the embodiment of calm and security, and, as a result perhaps, even more powerfully, of horror.

Suddenly it flashed upon me – *That's me!* That's how *we* went stalking through the horror – unconcerned, our account with life closed, it no longer being of importance whether we died today or tomorrow – faceless, being no longer alive – animal-sure by reason of having suffered the most terrible of experiences.

And at the same time I realized – once we are put in that position of horror, it's the easier life! The refugees are all still clinging to the belongings slipping away between their fingers – clinging to the people dying around them – hanging on to lives that can hardly be saved. The soldier no longer has any need to be afraid or to worry – *he* is concerned with the horror professionally – *he* knows only the burden involved in carrying out any difficult profession. Certainly his first experience, the one that deadens him, is unimaginably dreadful, and the life he then has to lead is still hideous – but by virtue of the deadening, the unconcern and the professional attitude, it *is* also relieved internally.

How – in an ordinary cinema, in the midst of our still ordinary, peaceful lives – can we bear to look at these pictures of horror? Can we look without being deadened to an extreme degree – and are we granted that in ordinary life?

Certainly, most people sit unmoved, in a way that is impossible to understand – they do not rush out – they simply put up with the newsreel, at every performance; but it is not they who are the subject of concern one way or the other; of course, the people who *are*, are those who are still able to feel – the subject of concern is human feeling itself!

In this is the touchstone for genuine pacifism – only when we see ourselves delivered up defenceless because it has not been granted to us to be deadened; only when we know that in spite of all the dangers and horrors, it is easier for the soldier than for us; only if what we fear is not the bombs but the very peace in which we still live and wish to continue living: only then do we have a right to stand up for peace. And only then can we also hope that these people will pass the ultimate test.

28 May 1940

For days it has been becoming clearer that the Allied counter-offensive to cut off the German breakthrough is not really succeeding. And now the Belgian Army has surrendered! Now the Anglo-French Northern Army must be completely cut off, and all that remains is to try to save whatever can be saved. The whole Channel coast will be wide open to the Germans – as soon as they are consolidated there, disaster may strike this island.

The terrifying thing is how the collapse goes on and on – for this after all is no ordinary defeat – this is total failure! Is it no longer possible to hold on? Is German technology so superior, are the sins of omission of the Allies, including Belgium, ostensibly so well prepared, so great?

If I were still over there on the other side I should probably be thinking that the Democracies were so hollow inside that a mere push would be enough to topple them. Seen from outside, the blunders of recent years and months and the absence of the idea might have become the sole criterion. But on the inside, we see that Britain is neither weak nor hollow. It is not weakness constantly to proclaim: 'We must fight the battle to the end, but we must not hate.' It is strength when all blunders are ruthlessly acknowledged; and when people still do not make Chamberlain the scapegoat for all the blame but say, 'We supported him, we ourselves are to blame.' And it is real, full of life, full of greatness for the Dean of St Paul's to call for full commitment with the words 'All depends on me, and I depend on God.'

It is to be hoped that there will, nevertheless, soon be a turn of events that will create time! For I am as ever convinced that Nazi Germany will not endure a stubborn battle, but that Britain, on the other hand, will.

3 June 1940

A great deal has changed in the course of this week. The British and French have been able to effect their evacuation from Dunkirk and convey the greater part of their army to Britain. So it *is* possible to resist the

Germans, and to fight better than they! For a retreat is always the most difficult of all operations, and embarkation under fire from enemy guns and aircraft must have been infinitely difficult – that that has been accomplished makes this fearful defeat seem in fact a victory. And I also have the feeling that now, in the country itself, everything needful will be done.

It is splendid that the evacuation from Belgium has been successful, and that so many men have been saved who, a week ago, seemed lost beyond all help. It is splendid that the Allies should be proving their superior morale. It is to be hoped that there will not be a price to pay for the fact that that morale should appear only in the jaws of destruction! Modern war is decided not by heroes, but by time-consuming technology . . .

4 June 1940

Paris has had its first air-raid, and has not, apparently, been sufficiently effective in beating it off. Italy seems finally bent on entering the war, and Spain keeps shouting that she wants Gibraltar. The relief which the last few days have brought, will soon be over.

Or is that just personal nervousness? Even while remaining conscious of the fact that what I personally have at stake are unimportant vanities which are ridiculous when set against all that is going on, it is hard not to feel on edge hearing one day that I am to be interned, the next that I am to leave Cambridge, and the next that none of it is true but I should be ready for any eventuality.

It is terrible what the Nazis manage to do. Firstly they ruin German emigration – if only the Left had been forced to emigrate, emigration might have made sense – as a result of the admixing of the, in itself senseless, Jewish question, people of all political shades, classes and degrees of fortune have been obliged to get out, and so even emigration has become hopeless confusion in which each group has brought the other into disrepute.

We are still not personally experiencing any hatred, and only occasionally hear stories, none of them verifiable. As ever, I cannot help admiring the British attitude. Even internment however many personal rigours it may entail, is not after all a significant evil compared with the front. Nevertheless, I am left with the impression that our fate is beginning to become symbolic of the fate of all who are well disposed – of all precursors of a new time – we were forced to flee because we were, in all honesty,

275

against Hitler, the first people to be that, although we were not understood, for which very reason we have been hounded from country to country – and soon nothing but the concentration camp will await us anywhere. Will the many who helped, but did not entirely understand us, and so decided too late to draw their own conclusions from our fate, be obliged to fare the same way before a new world can arise?

The all too frequent invocation of God which one encounters constantly here, is of real support to many, and to many more than elsewhere. It is real, and that is why I was so impressed by the words of the Dean of St Paul's. Nevertheless, one has the impression that for many the over-speedy taking of refuge in God is a diversion and not a help.

We must not be satisfied today with faith in God. If we are to become at all capable again of experiencing the divine sense, we have first to keep silent about God. 'Thou shalt not take the name of the Lord thy God in vain.' Indeed, we ought probably first to put back the clock of Christianity in order to become capable of seeing the human example of Christ, or to begin the now due Further Reformation – direct contemplation of the human life of Christ – contemplation of Christ as human being! But as, for the time being, there is no prospect whatsoever of this third Christian epoch being begun, it is above all and absolutely important to recognize, emphasize and live the simple human truths and simplest human principles. Only from this most simple and most modest point of human commitment can we have any hope of ever finding our way back to God.

5 June 1940

My concern of yesterday about all-too-ready faith in God has found rapid confirmation. Every day letters appear in the papers claiming that the rescue of the army from Flanders was due to the Day of Prayer held at the end of May at the King's request, and therefore calling for further services of thanksgiving and intercession. Is it not extremely dangerous to determine God's decision so directly? What will become of faith if the next Day of Prayer is followed by a clear defeat?

10 June 1940

For days the battle has been raging in France. Paris is at stake, and perhaps the final outcome. Will the French be able to withstand this assault? The gigantic superiority of the German Army is admitted openly.

The British Army has lost all its equipment in Flanders and is therefore not fit for action at the moment – America may well be stirring herself a little, but she also has little, and how long will be needed for even that to get to us? It is difficult to hope for successful resistance but it is also difficult to abandon this hope. On clear consideration we must be prepared for the worst, against that there is, as ever, a sense of the superior inner strength of the Allies.

Certainly Britain is still feeling remarkably little of the war, but I do not think that danger will bring any change of attitude. Meanwhile there are air-raid warnings, which are wearying, but in few places only are there any incidents – here, and no doubt in most parts of Britain, it has been hard to see why we have sat for a few hours in the cellar. There has not even been any gunfire.

Instead of this the papers are seriously discussing an invasion of Britain – and Ireland! Is the inconceivable really going to happen?

As I write, news comes that Italy has declared war. How is it possible to force a people into an unnecessary aggressive war against their will? And yet probably a large number of these people will feel this villainous policy to be splendidly adroit. Any firm foundation vanishes once the custom has been acquired of disregarding standards of justice and morality.

11 June 1940

Britain is always Britain – yesterday evening I went to an English acquaintance's to hear on the radio if Italy really had declared war. With him was a friend who had arrived some twenty minutes earlier. After the news he asked this friend if he had not known before that Italy was in the war. For twenty minutes they had been sitting, without saying a word about it! And that is absolutely typical – I have been told of similar instances on many other occasions. Is it strength or lack of spirit? The Englishman at whose house I heard the news suffers genuinely and greatly under the onslaught of bad news – how does he manage to keep silent?

Today the first rain, after weeks of the most glorious weather. The whole afternoon it has been as black as night. The clouds were from the east, from France, and black with the smoke of the guns and the reek of battle. The rain too, when it came, was black. So easy to imagine the world was coming to an end, an almost comforting thought!

After the rain I picked roses from the garden. They are speckled black. Now we have red roses dappled darkly by the terrible breath of war.

277

14 June 1940

The Germans have entered Paris. The thought is unbearable.

Into the capitals of Europe they march: Vienna and Prague; Warsaw and Copenhagen; Oslo, Amsterdam and Brussels; and now Paris! To the thud of their boots, the clatter of their tanks and the roar of their aircraft, Western Civilization is dying. For Paris, the metropolis of the world, ancient and yet lucidly and deliberately built as a whole, a work of art – Paris, however it is looked at, is its heart. Paris was not defended – or shelled – it was just empty – but is not that an even more terrible death?

For the terrible thing is the way this Western world is collapsing – the way that resistance no longer seems possible. Obviously there has been hardly any more fighting for days in spite of Franco-British war communiqués to the contrary – obviously the Nazis are gaining these victories not even at the cost of any more losses – they are simply marching, marching, marching. Where are they going to halt?

Paris is standing – the façade of that world which the Nazis purport to be protecting, is standing. Somewhere, somehow, normal life is still being preserved. It is a veiled, a false revolution. But, it is obviously a revolution; it is a war that will end not with victors and vanquished, but with the destruction of the existing and with the convulsions of a new birth which, to begin with, will bring to light all the fearful things concealed in man, and, since the Nazis, wholly concealed no longer. Will Europe still be capable of rising again, even after this great migration of peoples? For it *is* a migration of peoples, even though they are not Asiatics who are on the march, but barbarians newly spawned in the middle of Europe by technology. But, as in those days, the stream is rolling in from the East, inundating first Russia, then Central Europe – Germany and Italy – then Spain, and now swallowing France. Will it stop short at Britain?

15 June 1940

Two days in London. There the impression of a dying world is stronger. Half the city is to let. Alarmingly little life and traffic. But in the main streets, the exclusive shops, now, as ever, are offering for sale all the riches of the world. In the big hotels a life of luxury goes on as if nothing had happened. There is horse racing and the dogs – there is elegance, exaggerated elegance: banquets, drawing-room recitals; while France and Europe are dying next door; while Paris has been occupied and the Germans are parading in the Champs-Elysées. Can such a world survive barbarian assault?

The refugees who still have the money, are fleeing fantastic distances – to Panama, Shanghai, San Domingo. At first, for a moment, feelings rebel at their deserting Europe *now* – leaving the old world, *our* world in the lurch? But can they be blamed for that? We had friends in Copenhagen and Oslo, Amsterdam, Brussels and Paris – friends who had been through the hell of the concentration camps, active fighters for freedom and justice – where are they now? Dare we imagine their fate? They understood what had happened – they fought – they, it would seem, had a right at least to go on fighting honourably – haven't *they* been left in the lurch? Would it not have been better, more honest and more human if they had escaped? The one sad thing is that money is the only thing that can save anybody now. But as the capitalist world stands, and as the capitalist world is what is betraying us, can we scorn the means of salvation? The most we can do is deplore that it should not be at the disposal of everyone!

But this way of escape does at all events show very clearly the hell we live in on account of money. It is just the same as in Prague. You rush from one consulate to another – all the gates of this wide world are shut – you get kicked out and nowhere will let you in, although vast expanses of the earth are empty still and waiting for people! All these countries have expressed abhorrence of the Nazis. All deplore the fate of the refugees in high-sounding words. But the very moment they are supposed to do something, the fine words are replaced by flat and less than human rebuffs. Day after day you wait at closed doors in vain, to be chased away in the end like a troublesome dog, so that some effort is required to restore an awareness of your own human dignity.

You try the round-the-back approach with money, and lo, doors that stayed closed to every decent, honest, lawful attempt, are suddenly mysteriously opened. And now there is no longer any need for sweet-sounding words – now the way is clear for impropriety, things suddenly move. It is not easy – everyone is kept in suspense until the very last moment in order also to squeeze out of him the very highest sum that he is capable of paying – everyone is fleeced to the absolute limit. The consuls of fantastically remote minor states, their officials and middle men all grow fat on the misery of others, enriching themselves without shame or consideration, and you are lucky at the end of it all if you're not tricked too – if the wretched deal is at least carried through with some last shred of honesty! And even then there is another essential combination of assorted ruses – you need a false visa from some country or other to help obtain from another country a genuine transit visa which you intend to use to enable you to stay. And you need blackmarket foreign-exchange dealers in order to be able to pay abroad, for your noble rescuers want their money in the best currency. But in fact all that is the only way of achieving an escape which you are forced to seek through no fault of your own.

Here, in contrast to Prague, there is no Gestapo to bribe – British officials are incorruptible. That at least eliminates the dangerous part of this road through torment – with the Gestapo you never knew if negotiations were not just the first step towards the concentration camp – either because the official himself was trying to get *you*, or because he got discovered. The second danger was certainly the lesser, corruption being so general in the Gestapo that those involved were simply relieved, quickly and without any fuss; another factor being perhaps the desire to make as many rich as possible. But for all that, you could still get arrested at the frontier if they discovered a passport stamp to be a forgery.

The consuls, on the other hand, now manage to withhold the crucial visa until the very last moment to shatter your nerve completely and get you to put down anything you've got left. And not knowing whether they really will relent in the end, you have to make more fruitless journeys to other consulates to get something to materialize at the eleventh hour.

Every twelve hours the situation changes. One minute it seems to be working out here but not there, and then it's the other way round again, and for everything, again and again, you need different stamps and documents and forms, and so are perpetually short of something, and strong nerves are needed to withstand that truly infernal round!

And if you have no money, or it gives out at the crucial moment, or you are not good enough at deception, you can go to the dogs, even if your danger is greater than anyone's, even if you have been fighting the Nazis and have done, and can do, a thousand times more than anyone else. Blind fate simply becomes transformed into human swinishness.

The British officials do not torment you deliberately, but stick to formalities which you, as quarry in a hunt to the death, find hard to grasp. They ought to be grateful to anyone who is helping to ease the country's position by leaving it, but no – inviolable bureaucracy creates nonsensical difficulties. One stroke of the pen, a single second, would suffice to remove these difficulties, and without the slightest infringement of any right or law, but no – time and paper and nerves and money are wasted simply to maintain the nonsensical pace of the rusty machine!

And that too reduces you to despair – they simply do not understand what is going on. For individual refugees may be unimportant: yet they are plainly the writing on the wall which the world has failed to read. The Nazis employ Frenchmen, Britons, anyone they can find – using the word *national* in their talk and in their title, but having grasped that what is involved is no longer the nation but a battle between might and right, freedom and slavery, man and beast. The British, on the other hand, are interning refugees, giving notice to German nurses, and chasing Germans out of concerns essential to the war effort in which they could, and would, be of crucial assistance. Here in Cambridge one such factory is at a standstill because twenty-seven Germans who have been working here for years, cannot be got out of their camp. The British are suddenly becoming national – they are falling for the Germans' national propaganda – can any good come of that?

And I am almost afraid that they are falling for other Nazi slogans too. Military heroism has never been very highly respected here, people being aware that there are other things of importance. But the longer the war goes on, the more people parrot the Germans in this respect also. Yet the Germans have obviously long since ceased to believe in it – they are producing the machines which make it possible for cowards to wage war, having found in the last one that heroism is a legend from the remote past but not a useful modern instrument of war. The whole Nazi Revolution was of course a cowardly revolution, which led us wrongly to conclude that it was not a revolution at all.

16 June 1940

Quietly, as if in passing, the Russians have occupied Lithuania – the other two border states may well soon be next. Curiously enough, this is reviving here the long-smouldering hope that *now* the Russians will move against Germany.

17 June 1940

The Reynaud Government has resigned. The disengagement of France is probably now only a question of days or hours. The Maginot Line has been evacuated, and the army that was holding it, probably cut off. Is any real fighting still being done?

The British Government is cautiously preparing for French disengagement and announcing at the same time that Britain will fight on to victory. But there have been so many announcements recently – that Norway was

281

being defended, that Holland's water defences were impenetrable, that the Maginot Line extended to the sea, that Paris was being defended street by street – how can we believe any announcements any more?

Afternoon

The tempo is uncanny – while I was writing this morning, France had already ceased hostilities, having ceased fighting at three a.m. today. And it has done so in an ominous way – the new government, being of the extreme right, wants to make its own peace, leaving Britain in the lurch. Pétain is appealing to the Germans, as a soldier to soldiers, in the hope of obtaining an honourable peace – which sounds very hollow, and is now just words to no purpose. Mussolini and Hitler are meeting today to lay down conditions probably long since laid down already – what they will be like can be roughly imagined, and they may very well put the worst that can be imagined into the shade. But if they don't, it will only be a new trick.

Meanwhile Russia has occupied all three Baltic States, they having allegedly concluded a military alliance that was a threat to poor little Russia. Fine stuff here for a farce on the period a hundred years hence.

And now Japan seems bent on becoming one of the marauders also. Is the world being parcelled up anew? That, in itself would not be so bad, were it not that what belongs to the relatively decent is being distributed to the criminals. Once again Hitler has got the better of the better Germany by these means – and now very likely in every country they will be used to defeat the better section of the people . . .

18 June 1940

Also announced today was a British proposal to France that the two countries be merged into one to give ultimate power and inner assurance to the common struggle. Dreadful that anything good that happens, should happen too late. Why was that not done at the outbreak of war, or when Churchill's Government came to power, or after the collapse of Belgium? Then there might still have been time for such an arrangement – but no – it happens the very day it is finally too late!

And besides, even that was only a very first step! Developments will show that even what has happened to the Chinese, has happened quite directly to our own selves – and many obviously do not even yet understand that what is happening in France quite directly concerns them.

The world has become uniform to a degree inconceivable at any earlier period, but man's intellectual development has here too failed to keep pace with technical development. But does not, in this new uniformity of the world, also lie great hope? Even the destruction of Europe need not yet mean the destruction of our ideals!

19 June 1940

Churchill has spoken, calmly and steadfastly, painting all the impending dangers in most sombre colours, and yet firmly expressing his will to fight and his faith in victory. His speech creates the impression of a man who knows what he wants and is able to do it, of a man you can trust. But all the same, why does that faith not come to me? So many promises have been made in recent times and so few kept, and so many rock-firm declarations have turned out to be false – have I now, as a result, become even too mistrustful? Am I too falling into the error people are now being generally warned against – that of overestimating Hitler, having previously underestimated him?

My faith is shaken on many grounds. Certainly, if people had listened to Churchill everything would have been different. For years he has been untiring in his warnings – the one man to have seen most things clearly and correctly. But Churchill is not, I fear, in a position to withstand a major capitalist clique, should one appear, and I am afraid that in spite of all the dismal experiences, the problems of defence are still not being properly grasped. The complacency that destroyed France is, I am afraid, still operative. Certainly for the long term the Nazis are weak – but even in Germany they won at the very moment they could not get any further, and their victory was deprived of none of its significance by that. I hope that I am not being too greatly alarmed by that experience, and that this time those in power really do understand better than I. True, I have been vainly consoling myself with this for seven years, but even that is not, in the end, any guarantee of the validity of the argument. The Nazis, having lived for so long off other people's blunders may, in the end, even save other people by making a blunder of their own. These successes ought really, of course, to make them megalomaniacs.

Midday

I've just heard that last night's air-raid was Cambridge's first. Eleven dead, some injured, one German plane shot down, which means two more dead, and two prisoners. So now it's beginning here too.

Are we prepared? Hearing the two or three bombs fall I was not conscious of lives being involved. And yet I live in constant awareness of what is going on, and with the last war before my eyes. How feeble human imagination is!

20 June 1940

At night in the shelter I try to remember what it was like in the last war, sitting in some burrow waiting for shells to land. Particularly clearly I recall the eleventh battle of the Isonzo round about 11 August 1917.

Night

We were sitting in a kind of shelter waiting for shells to land, just as we shall soon be waiting for bombs to fall here.

Our animal instinct was super-vigilant, having meanwhile learnt to distinguish between heavy shells and light, mines and shrapnels, and, so far as possible, to avoid them. It was vigilant too in the burrow, where it could not greatly help us. We knew, seconds before it landed, that that shell was for us. And when it came to digging out, we all set to work without a word and with absolute efficiency.

Conversation had long become a thing of the past. If we were in the rear, soulful Czech songs sung deep into the night were a help.

> Drink, brother, drink,
> long let your gullet burn!
> Nothing does a scrap of good,
> we shall not return.

> Drink, brother, drink,
> put this lot away,
> you may very well be dead
> before the light of day.

In quiet positions the ultimate things could be discussed at length and in detail with the simplest people. Almost always, conversations that began with politics, memories and plans for the future led to a violent discussion of absolute essentials. But in the face of danger, conversation became sarcastic and cynical, for beneath the crust of habit and indifference still slumbered the fear – which had disappeared completely from our consciousness. But these conversations, artificially kindled, never lasted very long. As the shells got closer, there was silence.

284

Time and time again that silence may have been death. None of us believed of course that we would come back, and so it seemed a matter of fair indifference to us whether we had to believe it this time or the next. I think it was simply a void. Instinct was working, but feeling and thinking had ceased. We were all ears, and in that listening was no room for the memories that are supposed to go through heads at the last moment. The very moments of greatest danger were, at bottom, devoid of impression – dull routine, empty indifference. Or maybe even *indifference* is too clear a word – these moments were nothingness.

Against that, time and time again, the decisive impression was that of first moving up to the trenches – of crawling on all fours, and over corpses, fearful, old, decaying corpses whose stench, even after months of it, was still utterly unbearable, and the fresh ones, amongst them our friends. We were seized with dismay and horror at the appalling mutilations – with desperate sorrow at the fresh losses. The dreadful screaming, whimpering and groaning of the severely wounded never ceased. Often we could do nothing for them, and often there were fresh dead and wounded amongst those unable to bear doing nothing for them. All around, whirring rifle bullets – the most dangerous of all – forcing us onto all fours, and above all, the infernal tack-tack-tack of machine guns. Spraying earth, raining rocks, flying metal, streaming blood, ripped flesh – apathy was impossible. The protective skin of habit was rent again and again.

But by the very fact of its being rent, another feeling was aroused. There I was, crawling on all fours, shaken to the core with terror, churned up with horror and sorrow, in the thick of the most perfect realization of hell ever, clearly aware that I might, any moment, be the next – not just to die – but to be made into an unrecognizable, bleeding, roaring, whimpering lump of flesh. And yet it was at these very moments that the embracing certainty of death would disappear, and an ardent, rearing, painful love of life awaken. For a brief moment – triumph – there I still was, still moving, breathing, feeling the earth beneath me and knowing a sky full of stars to be above me, even if not daring to glance up at it. One hand being scratched by rock, the other – feeling its way over a corpse. I can see nothing ahead but a tiny patch of defiled earth over which I have got to go on crawling – but once again, I have escaped, I still belong to it, this earth and this life, for a moment breath is still being inhaled and exhaled, blood coursing through my veins, shapeless thoughts revolving in my brain. For one moment I am still a living part of that gigantic horizon which I would see if I could straighten up. Out of the deepest abasement, out of the greatest of all terrors, joy has soared high for the space of a moment.

For a moment only – the horror was too great, the protective skin of indifference closed quickly over again. That overwhelming feeling had been only a very indistinct one – the words I have just used are much too precise, but what was predominant was that ardent bond with heaven and earth, with life in general, and that feeling was love of life, joy at still being alive. For a moment it cost an effort not to raise my head out of the trench, and that moment was filled always with the idea of the horizon of which my knowledge had, even at night, to be unclear.

Was it right to feel joy? I believe it was. What was wrong was that we could not carry this awareness over into the expectation of death, and that, awaiting death, we should be apathetic and empty. But that was perhaps attributable to the oppressive weight of a senseless life that offended against all human laws. But being now granted to lead a meaningful life, albeit once again amidst horror, ought I then not be able to await death consciously and calmly?

21 June 1940

Joy amidst most awful destruction, affirmation of life amidst senseless horror – are they really allowed, admissible, affirmable – are they not a terrible degeneration, again a lack of thought and imagination?

We are living here amongst a small circle of Germans who are concerned to maintain a connection with spiritual things and above all to understand Christianity proper. Not long ago we were reading the Marriage of Cana in the Bible. Does that not contain the answer to my questions?

The changing of water into wine – one of the most delightful of the acts performed by Jesus. Yet we were all dismayed by the harsh words with which he dismisses his mother at the opening of the story, 'Woman, what have I to do with thee? Mine hour is not yet come.' We were at a loss to explain them. But now, in view of my experience at the front, I find them clear and intelligible.

Dominating Christ here is the impression of his baptism. His decision to be baptised cannot have been an easy one, since by baptism he is cut off from the majority of Jews, and above all from their rabbis, who reject it. And baptism was not the pale symbol it is now, but a living experience – he was immersed in the waters of the Jordan until they closed above his head – was even, for a moment, cut off from life – it was an experience of

286

death. When he rose up again out of death, heaven opened for him – a sign which, amongst the momentous impressions of that hour, told him not only that he had from now on to follow a difficult and perilous way of his own, but also that he must now see before him that other hour for which this death-baptism had prepared him, the necessity of a terrible death. He will open heaven for others – but this he has got to do by way of a full realization of futility – by suffering every horror that is possible, and, indeed, is the overwhelming reality upon this earth.

Nevertheless he goes to the wedding to which he is invited. But so dominant are the impressions of baptism that he abruptly repulses his mother's attempt to jerk him back into real life. His previous human life has been removed by his death in baptism – he no longer has a mother – it is solely with things of the deepest gravity that he has to concern himself now. Every minute stolen from his essential task is a betrayal of his mission.

Most people dragged from serious conversation for the sake of a trifle, *are* offhand. Jesus must be deep in conversation with his disciples – he is living in sight of that hour whose coming he now knows of, and is preparing, in talk with his disciples, to meet it. Of what concern to him are the minor worries of others?

But more than that. I remember coming on leave from the front and wanting to shout out what we had been through, to make people understand what was happening out there – not a minute must be lost in carrying out our mission. We had been living face to face with death – how could we think of anything else any more? Were we entitled ever to feel happy again? Was that not treachery to those at the front? Christ is struggling against real every-day life that does not withstand the test of absolute standards.

Yet then, just as bewildering as the startlingly hard words is the transition to the cheerfully simple, seemingly so superfluous miracle. His mother acts as if she has not heard those words at all and tells the servants, 'Whatsoever he saith unto you, do it.' And he really does do it – change water into wine, exactly as if the sharp words had never been spoken.

But didn't we do the same? *Fight* real life at first? Today I can still hear myself, during the first days of leave, saying over and over again – 'War is terrible, absurd, of course, but the front is the place for any decent man to be.' But then we let real life take us captive, even enjoyed it to the full, and for that very reason came to ourselves again, finding the right attitude to the war, and the strength to give expression to it. We did it with a bad conscience, and yet the consequences showed it to be precisely the right thing.

Does not Jesus fare similarly? With real life all around him again, he imagines himself still lingering in death. There is his mother whom he has just been trying to disown, and a crowd of people enjoyably removed from their wretched every-day lives, and yet at that very moment their joy is threatened by their poverty – they need wine but there is none. Seen against death, it is a minor affliction – but this is real life, without which death is not possible.

We, for as long as we are alive, cannot shut ourselves off from it – how can Christ, who has apprehended real life more profoundly than any man?

He does not. What he does do, he does not with the bad conscience that we who are never certain of our own death, have: *he,* being certain of his end, endows this change with meaning. He frees himself from the all too rigid bonds of his encounter with death – he changes the water into wine to add to the people's pleasure.

He must at that moment have realized that it was not solely a question of the seriousness of death, but, for the seriousness of death's sake, of life, and, with life, of its joy. And it is by very reason of seeing most terrible things ahead and knowing them to be inevitable that he is so open to this life that his first, very first, sign is a joyful one. It is because he is emerging from death, into life, that he affirms the joy of life! It is no coincidence but of most profound significance, that his first step upon his, in itself terrible, road should stamp his Gospel as a joyous one – joyous in the earthly sense and in the sense of life. For him who is certain of his end, it is death that reveals the enormous value of life, pointing at the same time to the way, through all needful seriousness and the inevitable ordeal, to joy. We need never ever be ashamed of our joy – it is what matters first!

It is to Dostoyevsky that I am indebted for this interpretation of the Marriage at Cana. And Dostoyevsky takes us a step further. He explains too the meaning of this joy, touching once again upon my front-line experiences with remarkable directness.

Alyosha Karamazov grasps this interpretation of the Wedding at Cana at the very moment that his world is threatening to crack. Profound horror and intolerable suffering show him the way to joy. But then, under the impression of that experience, he flings himself upon the ground.

> He did not know . . . why he felt such an irresistible desire to
> kiss it, kiss it all, but he did kiss it, weeping, sobbing and

288

watering it with his tears, and swearing ecstatically to love it
for ever and ever . . . Oh, he was weeping, in his delight,
even for those stars shining at him out of the endless depths
. . . It was as if threads from all God's innumerable worlds had
all at once come together in his soul, and his whole soul was
trembling at coming in touch with other worlds.[13]

Does that not explain why I, even in the face of most terrible death,
could not renounce that joy? It is in the very joy that signifies most powerful community with life as such, indeed, with earth and horizon and
stars, that experience of the whole, that 'coming in touch with other
worlds', becomes manifest. It is from joy that that positive experience of
death arises which elevates us above life and into the whole. It is in this
all too personal, indeed, egoistical experience that access to the super-
personal lies.

The only strange thing is that Dostoyevsky should pass unheedingly,
indeed, awkwardly over Jesus' disconcertingly sharp words to his mother,
although in Alyosha's experience he does recreate the personal situation
in which these words are spoken. Usually, Dostoyevsky above all has a
most profound understanding for startling words of that sort, which are
not uncommon in the Gospels and seem to accord so ill with the image of
a gentle Jesus. This time he ignores them, and at once there is a dead
spot in his interpretation.

Does that not show how essential it is to be constantly aware of Jesus'
personal experience? The words that startle are always traces of the personal experience, and we must listen to them to prevent the conventionally false image of the gentle Redeemer from gaining power over us. It is
only when we look into these words and understand them from our own
experience that Christ's example becomes wholly intelligible. It is essential constantly to have clear in one's mind the image of Christ the man in
all his human limitation; only thus is the way found to a living, unconven-
tionally real super-personal being of whom it is possible to have actual

13. *The Brothers Karamazov*, book 7, chapter 4, the full passage reads: 'He did
not know why he embraced it, was not clear why he felt such an irresistible
desire to kiss it, kiss it all, but he did kiss it, weeping, sobbing and watering
it with his tears, and swearing ecstatically to love it for ever and ever. *Water
the earth with the tears of thy joy, and love these thy tears* . . . – the words
rang out in his soul. At what was he weeping? Oh, he was weeping, in his
delight, even for those stars shining at him out of the endless depths, and
was not ashamed of this ecstasy. It was as if threads from all God's innumerable worlds had all at once come together in his soul, and his whole
soul was trembling at coming in touch with other worlds.'

experience. Again, it is only from opposition that the way to the whole opens: the limited *person* is the vessel of the supreme being. Only when we recognize the person with and within its limits, can we hope to apprehend the super-personal with such certainty as to be liberated by it when the limits of the person finally crumble.

23 June 1940

It is slowly being admitted that France has signed an armistice with Germany, the meaning of which seems to be that she is delivering up all her weapons, including her fleet, to be used against her ally Britain.

It is difficult to understand what the purpose of these negotiations is. Unconditional surrender is something they could have achieved without negotiation simply by laying down their arms. As a result they would at least have saved the fleet, the airforce and the colonies for their ally, and perhaps for France's future. Why should France be behaving more shabbily than Holland and Norway? How long is it since the solemn declarations that, whatever happened, France and Britain would never ever conclude a separate peace! Hitler is not the only one to treat agreements as scraps of paper – the demoralization of the world is already well advanced.

Even the understandable desire for peace would have been served better by plain surrender. Supposedly fighting is still going on. What, in these final days which will not make one iota of difference to final subjugation, are men dying for? How demoralized the ordinary people must be becoming who are being sacrificed so senselessly. Maybe they too are having to watch those with money getting away, while the other refugees have lost their all simply to no sense or purpose. And all just to trumpet forth a few lying phrases to the world – 'Paris is being defended street by street! We shall set our names only to peace with honour!'

Even Reynaud has been toppled by such phrases. The soldiers wanted to seek a peace with honour from soldiers – Reynaud is said to have been unable to convince them that they were dealing not with chivalrous soldiers, but with Hitler. Can anyone seriously believe such rubbish? Not even generals can be so naive!

The extreme right are very likely playing a dark and evil game. Pétain is a friend of Franco; Laval, whose name turns up more and more, is a friend of Mussolini; Weygand is a reactionary Catholic, and Lebrun – a dangerous nonentity, a symbol of the failure of Democracy which has had to agree on a nonentity because real personalities have caused too much offence. The big French industrialists are probably trying belatedly to do what the German and Italian have done long since.

And so there has been no need for Hitler to bribe them with even a semi-respectable peace offer, the others are simply playing into his hands, although they are capable of knowing even this early that they themselves will be betrayed later. But people cannot be against Hitler when freedom, decency and morality no longer represent real values. In this country they still *do* – so is there hope?

Terrible too is the blow to France as *the* rallying point of anti-Fascist refugees. It is to France that the Italian anti-Fascists have come streaming, and it is there that the majority of German and Austrian refugees are – either interned or *traitors to Germany* in the French Army! There refugees from the Spanish Civil War have found a haven, a Czech and a Polish Army have already been formed, and a Belgian is in process of formation. In Hitler's eyes they are all, to a man, traitors whose lives are forfeit. They have now all been sold and betrayed in a most terrible way. The French people are affected as a whole, but the individual can hide himself amidst the mass, the refugees are specially marked individuals who cannot conceal themselves, marked out to fall victim to Hitler's vengeance, having been accepted, or even forced, to aid France who is now betraying them. Amongst them are many of my friends – it is just not possible to think out what can, or will, happen to them, or already has!

Hitler meanwhile is revelling in theatricality. The armistice has been signed at Compiègne in the very railway coach where the Germans had to sign in 1918. Hitler sat in Foch's chair. That leaves *me* cold, but maybe many Germans and the world are impressed. Hitler's understanding of mass psychology has been better than anyone's so far.

Evening

Since writing down the interpretation of the Marriage at Cana, I have been dissatisfied and uneasy.

This is, I think, because it is not good consciously and deliberately to consult the Bible too often. Otherwise it does not become a living experience and we run the danger of using the familiar vocabulary *to make something* of the Bible. We read into it what we want, filling the gaps with the conventional words, and without receiving the impetus we ought.

That was a danger I had to fight against for days, and I escaped it only when my memory of the front came flooding into the Biblical passage also. But others obviously do not escape it – even having really plausible interpretations of further particulars, but that is merely to apply the already-known from elsewhere to the still-unclear, which remains unintelligible nevertheless. The parable is transformed into an allegory used merely to show once again more of what has long been recognized, instead of to gain fresh fertilization from it.

Even Luther provides a cautionary example here. His interpretation of the Marriage at Cana as God's blessing upon matrimony is plainly pedestrian, and springs merely from a sense of duty to be complete. Jesus blessing matrimony – and yet snapping at his mother and calling her *woman?*

But why, in fact, does Jesus go to this wedding? He is preoccupied with thoughts of his final ordeal, and can feel no particular desire to go. Nor does he seem to have come simply out of reluctance to refuse a request – he certainly refuses his mother's. The sharp words seem almost to betray a regret at having come at all.

Strangely it is again precisely here that an answer lies to the question exercising me. Jesus has had years of solitude, now that he has recognized his task, he allows his inclinations and talents free play, follows, contrary to his conscious desire for ordeal, his unconscious internal desire. For his inclination is to be with people, to talk to them, to reveal and explain himself in conversation and his talent is for teaching and leading men, for awakening them, and showing them the way to, and beyond, themselves. And his inclination is a better guide than his conscious intention, and because that is what he follows, he experiences something new and decisive.

One of the most decisive distinguishing marks of inclination, talent, loving interest, is ability to immerse ourselves in ultimate, seemingly highly trivial, detail. Deliberate intention carries us with ease away and beyond seemingly uninteresting detail, and thus causes us to miss real experience: for it is only by grasping the whole context that we arrive at full consciousness, real feeling, living fulfilment of the form of our lives. To force ourselves artificially to confront our final ordeal, or to yield too often to an active desire for it, is not at all what matters, nor is it of absolute importance *what* we do. Senseless activities, certainly, are all too numerous, but even after they have been excluded, infinitely many forms of productive activity remain. The important thing above all is that what we do, we should do wholly. And it is precisely this talent – which is, of course, a mysterious gift bestowed from beyond our human limitations – which become a pointer to what we are able to do wholly. Where talent is lacking or exercise of it is impeded, inclination or allotted work

292

may take its place. But always the important thing is that we should, in this life, do something wholly, or live wholly so that we do not stray past the detail and miss it. If we artificially force ourselves to consider serious things – if we skip connections – we end in a void.

Certainly, in times of horror it may seem unworthy, wrong, frivolous, to live otherwise than in constant awareness of the supreme seriousness of death. But even that is still a relief we cannot permit ourselves absolutely; we must nevertheless live our natural lives to which we are able to give content – do what we are precisely intended to do at the given moment – must, even within the most terrible reality, so far as we are able, make a reality of the normal lives appropriate to us, only then does the death-baptism bring us to the Marriage at Cana, only then does there arise out of the horror the joy, and with it the contact with other worlds, which is in the end what matters. If Christ had persisted in concern with death instead of following his inclination, his tidings would never have been joyous; he would have been just another prophet; his death: a passing shock inflicted upon a small nation.

It is, perhaps, one of the dangers of war that we should find ourselves being all too greatly and all too often thrust away from life and on to the subject of death. But here too there are still two ways. Access to this subject is open in every man and every activity when we see deeply into it; and to do that is more terrible than to seek refuge in a ready-made religion and its established words. If we go our own way, then long familiar words from the Bible confront us anew and reveal their sense to us anew. By seeking refuge in the ready-made we run the greatest danger – that of also using up and wearing out the living supply that we bring with us. Then even the Bible can become a dead book.

25 June 1940

The German armistice conditions provide no further surprise – their simple meaning is unconditional surrender. As regards the fleet, Germany promises solemnly not to use it against Britain, from which it may be safely assumed that she is intending to. How can such promises still be given and accepted! But it may well be that the French Fascists need them simply to deceive their own people and the world.

The French also promise to hand over all German citizens as required by the Nazis. Even Czechoslovakia, occupied not partially but completely, and possessing no colonies, did not do that. The Czechs told the Germans to come and get them, and helped many to escape. The French

293

Fascists, on the other hand, are committing themselves to treachery, although no more could, in the last resort, have befallen them, had they rejected the worst conditions than will befall them anyway. Only this time, of course, it is not honourable defeat – this is hob-nobbing with the world of Fascism. Will France's famous *two hundred families* really hob-nob? It is to be feared that the French are infinitely worn and weary.

And here in Britain little rabble-rousing tales go on appearing about the ridiculously harmless misdeeds of the *foreigners*. Is the situation really so bad as to create a need for such insignificant scapegoats? Don't people trust themselves to tackle the really guilty ones?

Consideration should be given instead to what is to be done if very shortly the Germans send over two or three thousand aircraft! That provision has been made for this highly probable event ought really to be taken for granted. But unfortunately the impression is still not strong that all that is essential is seriously being done – and after the recent incredible omissions, the thing that is most improbable seems possible.

But today Russia has once again stolen the show. She denies that she is concentrating troops on the German frontier. Relations with Germany, she says, are unshakeably good, 'being based not upon transitory motives of an economic nature but upon the fundamental interests of Russia and Germany as states'. Since when have sacred economic interests been transitory? Poor Marx, poor Lenin – how they must now be turning in their graves!

26 June 1940

Italy's terms to France are surprisingly mild. Can it be that my original supposition is correct – that an attempt is being made to provide the British right wing with a basis for action?

The internment of refugees continues. When will it be our turn? I should like to think that the British had other anxieties.

But constantly still in newspapers and journals, frank, intelligent, human letters, criticisms and even leading articles appear. All the people we know fairly intimately are as frank and as positive as ever. How greatly one wishes that Britain were making a stand as a whole. About individuals I have no doubt – they have a totally different positiveness than was possible in Germany – but power even in the Democracies is a strange thing.

27 June 1940

Feelings get tugged constantly this way and that. Whereas up to now only *some* German men and women have been interned, now they are interning all male Germans. And it is becoming clearer all the time that they are being treated as enemies. They receive no papers, they are not allowed to listen to the radio. Is that not, at this time, a senseless torment? Still, it *can* be said to be necessary in order to keep the spies amongst them ignorant of the real situation.

29 June 1940

Russia, as coolly as you please, has occupied Bessarabia and Bukovina. Romania has given way. What else could she do? Now she is waiting to see whether Hungary and Bulgaria are going to collect their share. But that really is no longer of any great interest. The chances for all neutrals have been missed, and certainly for good, at least in so far as Russia is involved – for who, should this war still end well, is going to take her on? In any case, the fearful revolution presses forward.

It is making headway in the border states which are still nominally independent, but which are being obviously forced towards Sovietization from within. It is making headway in Hungary. But as she is after a piece of Romania, she is bound to accommodate herself more and more to the Nazis. And what can the other small states do now other than follow?

Of greater interest is that the Republican Party of America has now put up a candidate who is for supporting the Allies. The election was most remarkable: the Isolationist took the lead at first, but then the candidate favouring support got all the votes. The people were apparently ahead of the politicians after all – it being doubtful whether anything more can be gained through isolation. All the same I do not exactly trust the business. Now Roosevelt and his opponents have got the same foreign programme. Probably the popular mood is being made use of in order to bring about the more easily the downfall of the social appropriations which Roosevelt has after all created!

But the most disquieting thing is that Chamberlain should suddenly be popping up again and giving the Americans an interview. Obviously America is full of rumours about peace negotiations, and so the man they seem to revolve around, has been sent to deny them. And what has he had to say, the man most to blame for the fate that has befallen the world in recent weeks? He is as smug as ever! Just as after Munich. Just as after the evacuation from Norway. Everything is quite all right; not a soul thinking of peace: Hoare in Madrid is not negotiating with Franco; the Conservative Party stands united behind Churchill, its executive committee has just expressed its confidence in him, and, I'm afraid, also confirmed Chamberlain as Party Leader. And certainly since the new Government came into office much more is being done. But that is to be attributed not to the Government but to Hitler – the British have been needing the first bombs in order to wake up – it is the ordinary man to whom the increased effort is due.

30 June 1940

Gradually now many Britons are also beginning to grasp that it is a war between nations no longer, but a revolution – and that all who are prepared to stand up for the ideals of democracy ought therefore to be brought together in the same way as the Fascists mobilize their adherents in all countries. The continuing internment of refugees is gradually assuming such grotesque forms as to be working as a means of awakening. Also interned now are those pioneers of Democracy whose books the British have been warning people against for years – whose books are at this very moment being praised in all the papers – unconsciously apparently, but nevertheless plainly, people are carrying on the work of circles that have always been pro Hitler and agitating against these very valuable refugees. And from the morale point of view, people are thus being subjected to a fifth-column style of conditioning also. At the same time, valuable allies are being lost for the future. For if there is ever again to be a rational Europe, how is it to be built without the democrats of all nations? But as a result of the transition from German concentration camp to British internment camp, they are now becoming so embittered that it may be more than difficult for them ever to be fighters again.

2 July 1940

I have been talking to a German lady who has taken some part in the development of the Confessional Church in Germany. Under pressure from Hitler and as a result of his fight against the church, the ecclesiastical forms have again suddenly acquired life and meaning, and as many things have been forbidden and people have exposed themselves to danger because of them, there is a conscious sense of community in Christianity. Baptism and Holy Communion were truly sacred acts independent of the pastor himself, and as a result of the constant arrest of pastors, the value of the hard-won services was simply increased. And so this German lady thinks that the forms should be adhered to because they are the very things that oppose Christianity to Fascism.

But is that not the same as the increase of the value of freedom and democracy as a result of Fascism? That we recognize their value is after all simply an assumption – they cannot win through until they receive a new content. And the emergence of that new content will be as much impeded by the ecclesiastical forms of Christianity as by the capitalist forms of democracy.

4 July 1940

The *Arandora Star* has been sunk with fifteen hundred German prisoners of war and interned German and Austrian refugees on board. Five hundred lives appear to have been lost.

Of course, there will have been no malice in dispatching that of all vessels without a convoy, but probably carelessness and slackness. Amongst the refugees are said to have been the twenty- to thirty-year-olds interned here in Cambridge, although recognized by the tribunals as reliable. Letters from the camps take about a fortnight, and it had not been announced who was being sent to Canada. Consequently next-of-kin do not know whether their sons are still in the camp or whether they were on the ship. Nor is it possible to find out who has survived. Mothers are being passed from one Ministry to another without being given any information. Is this senseless torture really necessary?

5 July 1940

A horribly grotesque turn to the war – an Anglo-French naval battle! In spite of favourable British proposals, a section of the French Fleet attempted to return to France to fulfil the German conditions – and so the British had no alternative but to disable and sink their ships. French losses are said to be considerable. But ought the British to have trusted the Germans' word that the French Fleet would not be used against Britain? Oh, would that the British were as vigorous with Ireland!

The only alarming thing is the apparent completeness of France's moral collapse, and how considerable numbers have now been fired with that Fascism which for so long has been successfully suppressed. That section of the Fleet was free to make its own decision, and the colonies are equally free to make theirs. But they are bowing willingly to the orders of their own Fascists, and thus of the Nazis. It would have been quite unthinkable for any Czechs out of Nazi reach to have obeyed the commands of the Nazi-dependent Czech Government! And the Norwegians, Dutch and Belgians too, while not so practised in national struggle as the Czechs, have obviously and to a far greater extent, acted differently.

The French, on the other hand, are handing over four hundred German airmen – most of them shot down by the British – who will now be bombing Britain. They *were* going to hand over the Czech Army which they had forcibly recruited, and which the Nazis were threatening to hang, but the British, who have been, and still are, resisting the setting up of a Czech Army, have rescued them at great risk to themselves. The people – part in the army, part in the streets, part in the occupied zone – are completely neutralized, and so the Fascists, true to nature, are behaving like swine! The one sad thing is that a pacifist-socialist should be eagerly participating in the Government – Marxists really do seem to exist only to help the Fascists . . .

Here, however, confidence has been strengthened by this finally clear act. The more so, as it has been announced by Churchill himself in perhaps the greatest of his great speeches. His speeches have the power of giving a sense of security – it is almost like a sigh of relief – a relief reinforced by the surprising breathing space the Germans are granting us. All the same, it is to be hoped that no one will be misled into premature optimism. The decisive battle has not yet begun.

6 July 1940

Sidelights. Romania has veered off completely to the Nazis. Turkey seems slowly to be releasing herself from her obligations. Chamberlain is finding vigorous support against all attackers. Ireland is in confusion. The little news from France sounds worse and worse.

But Churchill is obviously more popular than ever, and his vigour seems to be prevailing more too. Indignation over the treatment of the refugees is gaining ground and people are being allowed to give full expression to it. Evacuation to Canada is also apparently now being better organized, and fundamentally of course may even be well intentioned. And the air attacks on Germany now seem to be being carried out more vigorously and successfully, whereas German air-raids still seem rather abortive.

But the German attack has not yet begun! And who is Mr Anderson, the Home Secretary, ill-famed for his work in India, who is so energeti-

cally anti-refugee, and so lacking in energy against the British Fascists?
And why has Churchill had to bring him into the new cabinet?

11 July 1940

I must, just for once, mention too that for ten days I have been doing
land-work, the only way we are allowed to give peaceful aid. We are
clearing scrub. Let us hope that the newly won fields will next year be to
the benefit of the Britain we love and not of the Fascists!

I have not mentioned it before because it is really without significance.
The work is unspeakably tedious. Time, which otherwise races away at
such excessive speed, creeps forward with infinite slowness. Even such
sense as can be assigned to this work from outside, does not get over the
fact that the work itself is senseless. Whoever was it invented the saying
that working in the open binds people to nature? All of us – and I have
asked – enjoy nature when walking, lying in a meadow and contemplating
the sky, or swimming or rowing. But with this work we are scarcely conscious of being in the open. Mechanical work in the open is just as deadly
as in the factory. If farm-labourers are dull-witted, it is not without good
reason. Work of this sort is merely a little healthier.

It may be different with people who have the inclination and talent for
land-work, and are doing real land-work, although the mentality of most
farmers speaks against it. It can simply be objectively established that any
work during which time crawls, i.e. is not being realized, is dangerously
deadening. Nor is it any good to keep telling ourselves that we are doing
it to beat Hitler. It is merely another bad aspect of the war that we should
not be able to help in a manner befiting our talents, when by using our
talents we could help far more effectively!

The work has just one good aspect – that most of the workers are students, conscientious objectors, obliged to do this work as war service.
That doesn't help us much, as during work it is difficult to talk properly –
still, there's an unusual atmosphere again of purity and goodness. It would
not, I believe, be possible in any other country for students thrown
together by chance to include such a large number of particularly sympa-
thetic young men – although, of course, conscientious objection represents a selection of good elements. But in what other country is
conscientious objection in this form possible?

The interesting thing is that not one of them is objecting to military
service on religious grounds, but for good, clear common-sense reasons.
A few days ago a theology student turned up – whether he is in fact sup-

posed to be missionizing, or whether he is doing it of his own accord, is not really clear, but at all events he is trying to make the young men understand Christianity. All he gets are amazed looks and smiling dismissals. Certainly, he is not very adroit and not very clever, but the complete coolness shown towards the conventional lines of thought he represents, is very characteristic. If I were in need of any further confirmation of the necessity of a fundamental renewal of Christianity for the sake of the very best of the young people, it is here!

No astonishment however over a group of Marxists – this standpoint seems more or less natural and is almost approved of. Not entirely. The Communists all too obviously say the same thing all the time for that, and are too self-satisfied and superficial. Everyone knows too precisely in advance what they are going to say, and is, in a way with which one can sympathize, too honest to join in anything they do not really believe. But in their rejection can clearly be felt regret – it would be fine to have so firm and clear a conviction!

Unfortunately the Marxists are the only ones who know what they want. How essential the aid of a firm idea – of the central idea of Christianity! All that non-Marxists are able to visualize is the imminence of Fascism in Britain too. It is something they are very much afraid of, but the fact that Fascism is the only thing that *can* be clearly visualized is of ominous assistance to it! If everyone, friend and foe, is expecting it, how is it to be prevented? Besides, no one is able to form a clear picture of what Hitler really means, and to be even half inclined towards Marxism obscures the dangers of dictatorship. What is lacking is the positive which people *have* to stand up for!

And just as much a must is social reform. A few of these randomly gathered workers have been unemployed. For them this work means a tedious and contemptible but nevertheless welcome source of help. And so already in their case the danger begins to loom which played so large a role in Germany – that of losing any feeling for the value of freedom. For freedom to them means freedom to starve, for which reason they prefer the bondage that guarantees work. After all, we shall be earning as much as we are now if Hitler comes, and work of this sort will be easier to find. For what is to become of us when the harvest's over?

Another group that does not have to fear starvation, is escaping into what in Germany we used to call 'the coffee house' – that is, into extreme intellectual and aesthetic pastimes. That too is dangerous, divesting reality of its worth and making people defenceless and indifferent. And it is not so unimportant as it may seem – even in Germany 'coffee-house' literature was an important symptom!

If only these refined aesthetics represented vital artistic feeling! But they are fed only by the intellect, not by the deeper sources of art. This nation has, on the whole, been deflected a very long way from art. It no longer plays any vital role at all. Just one small symptom – there are so many young people together here, but there is no singing. In no other European country would that be possible – only in Britain, that used before to be a particularly musical country. One of the Englishmen was telling me that Welshmen feel obliged to sing all the time, and that most Englishmen are scandalized by the fact. And all conversations confirm that small symptom to be entirely characteristic.

But how is a new, vital form to arise when feeling for the art form is dead? That is the very thing that might relax lines of thought that have become all too rigid, and is perhaps the sole remaining bridge across the abyss of today to the new that is needed.

Time and time again it is the same thing – unusually good, splendid human material, marvellous remnants of the best tradition, but nowhere anything to inspire confidence.

13 July 1940

Land-work clearly demonstrates the magic of being without responsibility, but also the dangers. It is very pleasant – at 6.45 a.m. we have to be at the corner where the lorry stops which takes us to work, and that is all we have to think about and do for ourselves. From 6.45 on, we can simply drift – all we need do beyond that is what the others do – all problems solve themselves without our contributing anything. We have no worries and no need to think, and that for the majority is undoubtedly a great relief – indeed a deliverance.

But most work only as long as they are supervised. As soon as the foreman turns his back they take a break. That is especially true of the quite young ones, but not of them only – the few who work steadily in any case, with sensible rest breaks, are clearly a minority. Lack of responsibility invites supervision – dictatorship, if anything is to be achieved!

It may be objected that clearing scrub is particularly tedious, but in this modern world the majority of jobs *are* tedious. Mechanization, in particular, means lack of responsibility, and work that is tedious and dependent on others; is dictatorship simply the necessary reverse side of this? For achievement is after all necessary and must be forced somehow.

Nevertheless I do not believe all that to be necessary. I had the task of supervising similar land-work in the last war. I told the men that as soon as they had finished that bit of field they could lie in the sun and laze. And lo and behold, the field was finished long before the time appointed. If they had been supervised and driven, they would have taken a couple of days. And even in the office I always used to try not to make each subordinate do only the preliminary work for his immediate superior, but divided the work up so that everyone had something to deal with from start to finish and be responsible for also. To begin with, most balked against it as being unusual and troublesome, and I found it very difficult at first. But gradually they took pleasure in their work and became much more efficient than before. Not all, but many, and especially the young. This principle, I am convinced, could gain wide acceptance in the field of modern technology. It might be a slow process, but after a certain period of training it would certainly emerge that the conveyor belt is, in the broadest sense of the word, the less efficient operation. It is merely more convenient, and above all for the dictators, who begin with the foreman. It is so much easier to order than to train!

Of course, there is still a second dictatorship to be disposed of – that of too small an income, of constant worries about money and making ends meet. Soldiers are relieved of the worry of earning their livelihood, and so can really enjoy lazing. Responsibility in the complex modern enterprise calls for a clear head, for a cheerful willingness to work. If the pay is too little it will not be possible to demand either greater commitment or complete concentration on the part of the worker. But if the pay is enough to stop thoughts constantly revolving around serious worries, then even luxury will lose its value. More satisfying work and a clearer head will make the little daily pleasures far more enjoyable. Only people who are overworked, care-worn and woebegone, have first to drug themselves to be able to enjoy anything at all.

I am not at all pessimistic about the possibility of socialism if approached from the individual. I am pessimistic only as to whether this path is still practicable. It is a possibility which has, I fear, already been missed.

Evening

It is no coincidence that in Germany inflation should have made so much more powerful and shocking an impression on people than the war, and that cannot be disposed of by simply saying contemptuously that people are more attached to their money than to their lives.

Danger, even in mechanized war, still has a dignity – it demands to be overcome, calls for self-sacrifice – for development on the part of a man, and allows the hope that it may be avoided. Death destroys a man, destroys many, but does not destroy life as such. Against that, the vain daily struggle for the most essential is undignified – exerting all our strength, we still do not achieve what we ought, we become worn and leached out, and with no prospect of any resting point, just reward or relief. Hope is deadened, life itself is no longer worth living. All that is left in the way of logical escape is suicide.

But do not a great many people live always in a state of inflation? The money earned is used up before they are able to buy what is most essential for themselves, their wives, their children – they use up all their time and all their strength, with never the prospect of achieving just recompense – adequate satisfaction of essential needs. Anyone deprived of rights is bound to realize in his desperation how he is using himself up without being able to do justice to life in even the most primitive sense.

But that is what eases the way to Fascism. He who is without social rights becomes dulled and unresisting, but also incapable of achievement. If the necessary achievement is to be got out of him, he has to be ordered. Thus anyone with a sense of responsibility is forced into giving orders and forcibly organizing. For society has, after all, got to work somehow – assent must be given to necessary achievement! A considerable middle section of the people abandon the struggle against Fascism, for it is only upon that path that the imperative achievement is still to be extracted from the mass. And finally, all those with a little money cling to it as a protection against sinking to the level of the masses without rights or hope. So important does money become as a protective wall that people even put up with Fascism because of it. Three different classes of society get trapped by the same basic fault – there is no longer any resistance to those who are hungry for power, who want to snatch it for themselves!

In fact, society functions the better for it too – except that man's destruction is bound to be ever more greatly intensified. Money is in fact saved for the time being, but the protective wall is destroyed nevertheless, for life as a whole becomes intolerable. The road to socialism cannot be blocked – not even by selling out to the Fascists – the only consequence of that is for Socialism, which might have been man's liberation, to become his enslavement and destruction!

Yes, but are men so blind as not to be able to see it? These consequences are, after all, now clearly enough manifest! Many *must* be blind
– with fear – yet most *can* now see what is going on before their eyes, but
are helpless – social injustice having also knocked the weapons from their
hands.

It is only a decade or two since Zola's *J'accuse!* succeeded in rousing a
whole people and shaking a state. Countless such appeals have been written against Fascism, and those of Heinrich Mann in the final years of the
German Republic have certainly not been inferior to Zola's from a literary
point of view. Why then has nothing been achieved?

Because it is not possible to summon the masses to fight for justice
when the concept of justice has been destroyed by social injustice; because
not the slightest thing can be done under the slogan *Freedom* when the
masses are held in bondage by material need; because equality before the
law becomes an empty phrase when the consequences of inequality of
wealth may be fatal; can any who are unemployed feel anything at the
deleting of the glorious words *Freedom, equality, fraternity* from the coat
of arms by the new French state?

Social disorder is not only a practical, but also a moral, preparation for
Fascism, and one that is all the more dangerous for making immediate
resistance impossible. Resistance is directed towards restoring the ultimate foundations, and that is possible only by slow and protracted labour.

14 July 1940

Meanwhile the French Republic is turning into a Fascist–National–
Socialist–Christian–Monarchist Fatherland, in so far as it is possible to
speak of Christian Fascism, and of Monarchy without a monarch. But
obviously there is nothing so grotesque but that it cannot become reality:
people are falling back on the provinces of the Bourbons; Pétain promul-
gates his dictatorial laws using the royal 'we', the 'By the Grace of God'
being all that is missing; and total submission to the Nazis is called 'a
revival in the spirit of Louis XIV' – meaning plainly neither 'submission'
nor 'revival'. More obviously than in Germany even, a criminal clique is
donning the mantle of any phrase that is going! But the enthusiastic young
people, who went along with things in Germany, are something else that
is missing, and so we may be permitted to hope that this nightmare will
not be all that long-lived.

Still, the new regime has been logical enough to forbid any celebrations today, *le quatorze juillet,* Bastille Day! Must not the memory of this be having a somewhat odd effect on the new rulers?

What memories can be stirring today, on this, France's most joyous national festival? I can see them still, those people dancing in the streets – not the great *places* with all their hustle and bustle, but the side streets – the little, ordinary people who were so happy. A gramophone blaring from a bistro – a few paper-chains and Chinese lanterns strung across the street – *madame* dancing strenuously and perspiringly with the waiter, and *monsieur* with the waitress. Of course, we had to dance too. It was so harmlessly natural and enjoyably real, everyone was really and thoroughly happy. But those good folk knew too exactly why they were rejoicing. They, as guardians of the Revolution, had a feeling of pride – *they* were still dancing around the rubble of the captured Bastille. Poor, enchanting, lovable people of France – what are their heartfelt reactions today?

Evening

Am I not again romanticizing the Revolution? Am I not overestimating the significance of external social changes? Am I not myself falling into the error against which I am constantly warning, and expecting of sudden violence what only slow, peaceful development can make reality?

Socialism is in fact facing a disastrously difficult problem. No good can result if the lower classes simply become grasping and strive for greater riches and a regrouping of property. So long as the revolutionary classes act simply out of a greed for property, they are just as much lost as the propertied classes clinging to their possessions.

The ideal would be renunciation from above – the self-sacrificial education of the lower classes to the level of that which the rulers already have. But as the propertied classes cling to property and power, and speak without noticing or considering social injustice and bondage, the change has to be striven for from below, and in the process of this the greed for property perforce intervenes. And as the inflexibility of those in power also compels the use of force, freedom and equality are again brought to nothing.

Both sides have to be seen. Justice and freedom without their needful social consequences are just as meaningless as social changes for their own sake, or for the sake of property. External and internal reality cannot be separated without both coming to naught. Justice which, in practice, proves only to the good of the rich man, is just as false as the social regrouping which means only the transfer of power and the division of property. The striving must simply be wholly for justice and freedom – the social meaning of both ought to be as obvious as their abstract principles.

Today's reality is the clearest illustration of the havoc wrought by uniform thinking. Idealists pursue their ideals without seeing reality; the realists immediately become materialistic. Genuine idealism and genuine realism, however, condition each other – a rooting in external reality is just as imperative as recognition of those fundamentals of human nature that extend beyond all that can be apprehended externally.

I speak of revolution because I see that for the sake of ideals the social order will have to be changed; but where social changes are concerned, I think of the dignity of man. But as all these concepts are made unambiguous use of today – in their superficial, obvious sense – it is probably as well to be constantly aware of their ambiguity!

The temptation today to pin our hopes on violent revolution is really of course only all too great and understandable. How is the Nazi rule of violence to be dealt with other than by employing violence?

All the same, it is essential to avoid this temptation! Violence is bound to destroy justice and freedom again and again – it cannot help replacing one form of injustice by another. The other way is infinitely difficult, and, for our patience today, bound to seem far too long and wearisome. But think of *le quatorze juillet*. That eruption of violence was a glorious bout of intoxication that seemed to portend the dawn of humanity. But it was atoned for by the rule of the guillotine, by Napoleon, by the return of the Bourbons, by Napoleon III, and that democracy was already overshadowed by that simultaneous development of Capitalism to which we owe the last war and Fascism. Experience of the other way is not yet available, but I do not believe that it will take so long. And certainly this development will not contain the seeds of its own death.

On the contrary, because even the tiniest step upon this road finds an echo in man's innermost being, it will be satisfactory in itself.

19 July 1940

Roosevelt has agreed to run for President, and that might be to some extent reassuring if the party rally which led to it had not been so grotesque. First he is adopted to loud applause, and no sooner is he adopted than people begin to attack his policy.

306

Aid for Britain, short of going to war – that obviously is the formula needed to win the election. The formulas of both parties are almost identical, which is to say that the opinion of the people is clearer and more unified than that of the politicians who do not seem at all inspired by their own claims. But foreign policy is merely the cloak under which quite different aims are pursued. At work in both parties seem to be the same capitalist forces which with the aid of foreign policy are attempting to frustrate social measures.

Churchill is very subdued in his defence of the agreement with Japan, refusing in debate to add anything to his speech – so if he, the most adept at verbal response, is sticking to the prepared text, the decision may not be his own. Even he seems to lack the power to stand up to big business.

In all countries and throughout all the old parties the conflict is between capitalism adhering with senseless rigidity to the old, and socialism seeking uncertainly after something new, and doubly uncertainly by reason of having to keep in with the Capitalists to continue the war, and of therefore being unable to stand up properly for its own convictions. The Labour Party has just expelled two M.P.s for demanding, in defiance of a Party ban, the resignation of the men of Munich!

But that is doubly to Fascism's advantage. Internal party strife is crippling the power of at least America, and very likely a good deal of power here in Britain as well. And by reason of the fact that the Socialists and many others are having, for the sake of the war, to do what they ought not to be doing at all, all those powers capable of resisting that internal Fascism perforce involved by war, are lying idle.

20 July 1940

Hitler has made his much-heralded speech, once again stressing that Britain can have peace if she is reasonable. Ostensibly he wants nothing of Britain at all.

Some regard the speech as a dangerous peace overture, others think it a sign of weakness, invasion of Britain being too difficult.

25 July 1940

British Parliamentary Democracy has again stood the test. Since the spiteful treatment of refugees there has – splendidly – been no end to letters in the press including *The Times*, demanding that this measure be reviewed, and now Sir John Anderson has had to promise a review. Still, it remains to be seen what will come of his promises – whether a number will be released again. But if not, M.P.s are bound to give him no peace. They are also persisting with questions concerning the *Arandora Star* affair about which much is still not clear.

One of the silliest measures by the Ministry of Information has been defeated in the same way. For some time there had been a big *Silent Column* campaign – people were to be stopped from talking about the war and anyone who did, was to be reported. Churchill himself had to admit that that was nonsense and would do more to weaken morale than to strengthen it.

Still, it is sad again too that this campaign, rejected by every sensible person, should, even here in Britain, have produced a whole flood of calumnies and absurd court sentences, although these too are now to be reviewed.

Scenes have been enacted as follows. Three soldiers, two British, one French, are sitting drinking each other's health with *Vive la France! Vive l'Angleterre! To hell with Hitler!* A little while later an elderly lady comes with the police claiming that the third soldier has shouted *Heil Hitler!* The soldier, understandably, tells her what she can do, gets brought before a court, and receives a sentence for using foul language.

But it has not always been so comical. People have fared similarly for discussing invasion and the inadequate counter-measures. It was clearly the beginning of that fear of informers which dominates Fascist countries – soon no one would have trusted himself to talk about anything any more when out in the street.

And yet it would be so simple to make propaganda of the good things for the sake of which Britain is really fighting. Instead of which Duff Cooper commits one blunder after another:

> What do I do if I come across German or Italian broadcasts when tuning my wireless? I say to myself: 'Now this blighter wants me to listen to him. Am I going to do what he wants?' I remember that German lies over the air are like parachute troops dropping on Britain – they are all part of the plan to get us down – *which they won't.* I remember nobody can trust a word the Haw-Haws say. So, just to make them waste their time, I switch 'em off or tune 'em-out!

Is that a timid attempt at a move towards German methods? But the Germans *do* in fact prevent foreign stations from being listened to, whereas what we have here is merely an advertisement for enemy broadcasts.

308

Everything emanating from this Ministry of Information creates an impression of unspeakable foolishness. M.P.s ought to be much harder on it. Still, since the debate in the Commons the stupider of these expensive advertisements seem to have disappeared.

M.P.s really ought to be harder on it as intelligent people are all still inclined to underestimate the effectiveness of these methods – the releasing, the justifying of stupidity, is much more dangerous than any tolerably normal person can imagine. Even in Germany we used to laugh at the stupid Nazi propaganda plugs, but the Nazis knew the masses better – and even here in Britain all too many people fall for these stupid exhortations. Pleasant music is coming from a radio in a cinema cafe – excited calls to turn it off as it's coming from Germany! – and the waiter can reckon himself lucky not to be reported to the police. In our clubroom there is a notice

> In this room we are cheerful and confident. We do not speak
> of the possibility of defeat. It does not exist.

And only a small minority of the members can be convinced that that is mobilizing stupidity against freedom of speech and of the press. Most think it right and in order. They are students, teachers, scientists, and even they are infected already.

But constantly there are some who are shocked and are entitled to be. It is however most essential that these powers for good should be actively engaged.

27 July 1940

Land-work, I'm afraid, is gradually turning into a bitter experience. Most farmers, it seems, are refusing the help of untrained and relatively expensive volunteers. It may be that, as land-workers do not have to join up, there is also no special need for volunteers. At any rate, we are not going on to harvesting work as planned, and the work we have had to do is as good as finished.

But this clear situation is being completely blurred by a couple of minor officials obviously bent on making careers. All that matters to them apparently is to be able to say – 'Look, everyone in this country can work – we're making a big effort – using our full strength for the war effort.' You cannot help wondering with some anxiety how far this eyewash extends into higher government circles.

What we are now doing is clearly senseless. To begin with the brushwood was ripped up, collected and burnt – that was boring but it obviously made sense. In spite of our slow work individually, enormous fields were daily transformed into land that could be ploughed. Then a few hedges were cleared, partly to prevent seeds being carried on to the field, and partly for ditching purposes – and that too still seemed sensible. Then the fields were gleaned again, but we were told expressly only to pick up the big bits of wood, the smaller ones didn't matter, would only be a waste of time. That was less clear, for larger bits of wood were rare and did not seem too serious an obstacle. But now we had to gather up even the smallest pieces which would have rotted away long before the autumn ploughing, and suddenly it was a waste of time no longer. And now we are clearing only one half of the hedge, as the other half is private, and so the pernicious seeds we are supposed to destroy have one yard further to go. And no question either of ditching and reclaiming land as the strip of hedge is too narrow. The idea is simply to keep us busy somehow.

The stupider the work gets, the more military the organization becomes. At first we had one foreman – now there are three deputies as well – and every minute some official turns up from the office to check or see to something or other which previously the one foreman checked or saw to with us. Always of course by car – the petrol used would, I am quite convinced, be of greater importance to the war effort than the work we are doing.

The officials' ambition is also furthered by constantly taking on new labour. But it can escape no one that for a long time now there have been too many of us – there aren't enough tools. The British conscientious objectors cannot be discharged because, of course, they have been sentenced to this work. The new people cannot be sent off again straightaway, and apparently are being paid less also. And so warnings are rained down on us aliens who were the earlier ones to arrive. The wish is to get rid of us, but in such a way that we are the guilty ones and cannot say that the organization was what was idiotic. Oh no, it is *we* who are to blame, *we* have worked badly. Clearly discernible is the rise of a Fascisto-militaristic spirit. Ordinary land-workers have been made into foremen – they are terribly timid, both towards us intellectuals as also towards their superiors – and so they are very friendly to us but then complain to their superiors that we are not working, readily and maliciously supplying the complaints which are used for the warnings, so that there is a spreading of that mistrust which I know so well from the continent, and of that method long familiar since the army – always look as if you are working –

310

whether anything actually comes of it, and whether what you do is necessary, is a matter of complete indifference.

There are scenes straight out of army life. Recently we stood around all day having finished the work assigned to us and not knowing what else to do. In the end we knocked off half an hour early. On our way we were nabbed by one of the officials who kicked up a tremendous fuss. The foreman, of course, claimed we had given him the slip, which was not true. We tried to make the official understand that we had finished our job and had not been given another, and that it was all the same whether we stood around or went home. No, he said, we could have started the next job. Yes, we said, but nobody knew what the next job was. This irrefutable argument was simply shouted down, loudly, excitedly, and uncouthly, with phrases about serving the country, cheating the government and wasting time that could never be made up.

It is sad that such things should also be possible in Britain. But here Britain does not leave one entirely without comfort. Some aliens have used devious tactics to advantage – simply chucking the work. But now some of the conscientious objectors are wanting to chuck it too. That means that they will have to reappear before the tribunal for acting in contravention of the conditions imposed on them. But it is their intention to denounce the whole ridiculous business publicly, before the tribunal and, more importantly, the journalists present. I doubt, unfortunately, whether they will achieve much, but the fact that they have the courage, and that such a thing is still possible is splendid. Even if they do not get the better of the war-machine, there are nevertheless everywhere strong forces opposed to Fascism which are bound to be effective in the intellectual decisions which sooner or later will assume sole importance.

6 August 1940

According to today's newspaper reports there are still 827,266 unemployed in Britain. How is that possible?

11 August 1940

The Italians have invaded British Somaliland, and the British are at present falling back. An Italian army is massing on the Egyptian frontier, and it seems within the realms of possibility that they are receiving support from Tunis in the shape of crucial water supplies.

The British have withdrawn troops from Northern China and Shanghai. Again and again the very greatest concessions have been made to Japan to avoid that. Up to a short while ago, this retreat could have been a powerful protest – to the effect that we were preferring to abandon an untenable position rather than buy it by means of treacherous flexibility. Today retreat is merely another sign of weakness.

New proposals to India seem to be experiencing the fate of the earlier ones – rejection and growing embitterment.

Perhaps it will be better tactics for the Nazis first to attack the Empire from all sides. Obviously there seems to be a plan to bottle up the British Fleet in the Mediterranean. If Egypt falls it will not be difficult to entice Spain into the war. And can Egypt be held against the whole Italian Army? Japan meanwhile will be loosed against French Indo-China and perhaps the Dutch Colonies also. If all that really gets going as successfully as the Nazis imagine, the consequences really cannot be foreseen. A direct attack on Britain will then perhaps no longer be necessary.

20 August 1940

The air-raids are growing more and more severe. They do not seem to be having the success the Nazis expected. Their losses are very great, and the destruction they cause may be great, but it is obviously not decisive. I really do seem to have overestimated a number of things – in at least one raid a thousand planes have been thrown in without apparently achieving anything stupendous. The field I am working in lies near an airfield. All day long planes are circling overhead with new pilots learning to fly. If the need were that great, every man would have been thrown into battle.

Nevertheless it is uncanny. These are probably crucial days. On the result of these raids will depend what happens further. But we have no idea what the decisive meaning of these events in fact is, and are not in the slightest able to judge what sort of conclusions the Nazis are drawing from them. The premature optimism of the British papers gives us just as little to go on as the intoxicated reporting of the Nazis, the unfounded nature of which is often verifiable.

Uncanny too is the lull in East Africa. Somaliland has been abandoned, and since that we have heard nothing more.

312

22 August 1940

Trotsky assassinated! In a terrible fashion, by a treacherous friend with an axe. Flight the whole way round the world to Mexico has been of no avail – he has not escaped death from the violence he himself brought into being. But with his dying words he is supposed to have saved the life of this treacherous friend . . . Whatever our attitude towards him, a great life has here come to a terrible end.

The remarkable thing is that the news should make hardly any impression on the young fellows I am working with. Is Trotsky already so far removed from the younger generation? Or is it Stalin's propaganda that has proved so effective? To us the names of Lenin and Trotsky seem linked indissolubly, but Trotsky meanwhile has been struck from the communist history books. Has he, as a result of this, really gone into obscurity? He, probably the greatest general of our time, inventor of the new tactics which led the revolution – and, unfortunately, the Fascists too – to victory; and creator – out of nothing and without resources – of an army that saved the Soviet Union which, without him, would not exist. Can such a man really be falsified into an infamous traitor?

Official Russia will go on vilifying him even after death, denying the greatness of the life now ended. They will write that he deserved the end he met. But is not the failure to concede an opponent's quality even after death, an indication that he is still feared, and is it not real proof of his greatness?

So it falls to the opponents of violence to do justice to this unfortunate apostle of violence. For it is only the opponents of the dictatorial communism which he led to victory who still recognize and feel the human and noble impulses which steered him to revolution, and who still know how to value the mind. It is they alone who are still able to gauge the enormous distance separating him from his egoistical, mindless descendents.

27 August 1940

Slowly the elderly and sick are returning from the internment camps. Some of the things they report are hair-raising. On the morning of the second day in transit they were given two pieces of bread, and then travelled all day with nothing to eat. The first camp was surrounded by an electrified barbed-wire fence guarded by machine-gun towers and floodlit at night. They had to eat without cutlery, as knives might have been used to cut the barbed wire. The huts were extremely primitive, everyone sleeping in dormitories on bedsteads which it was impossible to turn around on without waking a great number of one's neighbours. Hygienic arrangements were non-existent. Food was insufficient and had to be cooked by the internees themselves on open fires, regardless of whether they could really cook or not. Understandably, people who have been in Dachau and Buchenwald incline towards suicide, and in some camps suicides have occurred. For they are in this camp for three weeks without knowing if they will have to spend the whole of the war there – the war of whose progress they have no inkling, newspapers and wireless being forbidden, and news from outside sparse and irregular. Many go the whole three weeks without any news. They are allowed to write – on paper treated against invisible ink – only briefly and infrequently.

At Liverpool 120,000 letters are waiting at the censor's. Thirty people are supposed to be clearing them, and of course hardly any are getting through. Prepaid-answer telegrams arrive but they are not always allowed to answer them.

The British officers are friendly and concerned to help, but they are in many respects tied by senseless orders.

Still, in the end they get to the Isle of Man. There they are tolerably well accommodated in proper lodging houses – behind barbed wire, it is true, but it is a substantial part of the town that has been fenced off, and there they can move freely. They are also no longer so obviously guarded, only on longish walks. Still, there *are* now such things, and they also get taken for sea-bathing. The food is getting better, and apart from roll-call twice daily there are hardly any obstacles to a lively social and intellectual life with English lessons and lectures. A sick bay with German doctors is doing good work, newspapers are again permitted. Every week they are allowed to draw some of the money they have brought and shop in a canteen. Parcels come quickly. The letter post is slowly getting better. And the first releases are starting.

So the agitated letters, Commons debates and newspaper articles have had some success. Not enough, certainly. Obviously for the time being only the sick are being released. And the prospect of a long winter in even the best internment camp is bad enough, especially if you know that there is no justice in your being there. But for all that, the Isle of Man camps are evidently model camps. There are some much worse – worse even than the one first described, and only a few have been abandoned for having been too bad. But the British do not cease their efforts, and

314

will, I expect, gradually achieve still more – slowly, it is true – far too slowly for those affected, but all the same . . .

It is terrible that even here there should obviously be a civil service and military class fond of having its fling. Their first attack, as in Germany, has been directed against those who are most defenceless. There it has been the Jews, here it is the *dangerous enemies*. But whereas Germany kept disgracefully silent and allowed it all to go on until it was too late for anything to be said, a great number of people in Britain have put up a most energetic resistance, and with success. Here of course it is much less dangerous than in Germany – the human attitude will have first to stand the test. But I am confident that here not everyone will simply give in in silence. Here, whatever the risk, they will stand by their conviction.

31 August 1940

Romania, as could be foreseen, has had to give up a large piece – more than half of Transylvania – to Hungary. And Russia has added to the pressure from Germany and Italy.

Of interest perhaps is not only that purely Hungarian towns are still part of Romania, whereas a large Romanian minority – figures vary between 400,000 and 1,500,000 – is passing to Hungary, but above all that the German minority should have been ruthlessly divided. Of course it is well nigh impossible, in this confusion of nations, to find just frontiers as long as the right of peoples to self determination is adhered to. But there was no need for the division to be so mechanically unjust! The Peace of Versailles is supposed to be what is being fought against, but surely its mistakes are merely being made worse!

1 September 1940

Anglo-German church service – anniversary of the first at the outbreak of war. What an enormous difference between these two occasions!

What a different war we imagined then. It has been different, easier and more terrible. What we visualized then were the interminable bloody battles of the last war, and imagination added the terrible possibilities of total war in the air. Instead, bloody battles have been brief and rare, and the horror of the air war is only just beginning to develop. Instead, Hitler has gained successes which at that time were utterly inconceivable, and

315

these successes have been an icy blow to all the plans for wresting out of the war a new Europe and a new world order.

The war has descended on life like a grey veil. This month may well be crucial – on it may depend the future course of all human history. What is left but to hold our breath and wait?

Much of this is to be felt in the church service. The German pastor has been interned, and most of the men and some women of the German congregation. Occasionally they have managed to find a British preacher able to preach in German, this time they did not, which is, it is true, to be attributed not to the war but to the university vacation. But at all events the result is that the service has become a purely English one with just a mention of German participation. Today probably more courage is required for that than was for many of the earlier services in which German played a large part, and I do not doubt that this courage will hold, come what may. Nevertheless, here too one senses a feeling of 'let's hold out for a bit first, then let's see'.

This time my impression of the inadequacies of the church service is even stronger.

If the church service were, as it ought to be, vital, then no word would have to be spoken that was not of vital content – no word that was simply recited out of habit and not believed. For if, one day, the responsible members of such a congregation were to sit down together and examine the prayers, the Creed and everything that was said, word by word, they would, I believe, be bound to admit with deep horror how far the church form had deviated from life and faith!

Do they believe in the Immaculate Conception? Do they believe that it is not egoistical and unchristian to pray for individual, singled-out groups of people closely connected with themselves? Do they, clearly seeing in its unvarnished state all that is fearful and evil in this world, really believe in God? Do they believe the body and blood of Christ to be present when they receive the bread and wine at the altar?

Many, I realize, will say that they do believe. But that is not enough. To what extent is habit giving rise to a feeling that no longer has anything to do with the content of what has been said? To what extent are familiar symbols being filled with this feeling, without it being made clear whether these symbols also really represent what is being put into them? Where symbols are concerned, the content is what matters, for symbols convey knowledge. Mere form, on the other hand, appeals to feeling. Are we not, with symbols, adhering to form without noticing that its content can

316

no longer be believed in at all? And do we not cut countless people off from Christianity when, seduced by form, we cling to old symbols which aware people can no longer accept?

It has seldom been so shockingly manifest as it is today how very greatly content is concealed by form, and Christianity by custom. The lesson contained the words 'I came not to send peace, but a sword.' Are not those words that ought time and time again to create uproar – in the middle of a war especially? There are, of course, countless ways of interpreting them, or explaining them away, but ought they not always to break through any sense of comfort? Today they simply got read with the rest and I doubt whether anyone considered their significance. The service, rolling steadily onward, killed them dead.

But why then do I still attend? Is it not better to hold to those ethical laws which convey a purely developed system of ethics in less adulterated fashion than Christianity does? What does Christ mean to me? What does the church?

Ethical laws are, I believe, what matter first and foremost: they alone lead man to make human quality a reality. Yet for that very reason I also believe Christ to be of wholly decisive significance.

Ethics must not be imposed on man from without. They must spring from, and correspond to, his inner reality. They must be the language and expression of the Absolute within him. But how uncertain our knowledge of that Absolute is, and how great the danger of ethics remaining a loose collection of rules which is too little binding on us, which fails to do justice to our feeling; or of their becoming wholly abstract and therefore stating too little about real life; or of their becoming a self-sufficient science that deflects us from the Absolute! How easy it is for ethics to restrict themselves to the visibly human and the tangibly social!

But that is the very thing that must not happen. Ethics must not become abstract. They must be fed unceasingly from the mysterious sources which flow from within man, and must be the means by whose aid we experience and express the divine in man. We cannot know the Absolute, but we can experience and apprehend it within us and elevate it into reality. But that is precisely what the task of ethics is – ethics are the connecting link between the existing and the realized Absolute. Only when, with the aid of ethics, we experience each new situation anew from deep down, and, as a result, use that situation further to illuminate that which is profoundly mysterious – only then do ethics have human meaning, and only then can they remain genuine and pure.

It is in Christ that this Absolute, this divine quality in man, has wondrously been made reality, and to him alone was granted the gift of a pure and perfect life – the Absolute, in us concealed, uncertain and often apparently powerless, is here bestowed upon us in blessed perfection. It is *bestowed* upon us, for it has become an inexhaustibly vital example that can be re-experienced by everyone – faced with Christ, the Absolute within us becomes vital and conscious, the mystery is clear, the deep sources begin to flow freely.

If Christ is set at the centre of ethics, the dispersed rules of ethics receive their firm core. The abstract becomes concrete, all rigidity is resolved in the constant flow – in the countless real situations of our real life. Now there is no longer any uncertain groping, for the Absolute stands before us in overwhelming clarity and vitality, but at the same time too there is no rigidity – for at every step we take, the example has to be experienced, felt and interpreted anew. It conveys not the abstract rule but the exact living form. Thinking and feeling, wish and will, knowledge and experience – here they can, and must, be constantly examined – constantly taken to their human and ethical content, and thus become an expression of the Absolute. Ethics become what ethics must be; our every step is, through Christ, always a step taken anew in the face of the Absolute; ethics make real, as life, what knowledge and metaphysics have striven for upon an abstract way and not achieved.

But what then do I look for in the church? Does not the church conceal and destroy the example of Christ, instead of leading us to him? Combining ethics with Christ also reacts upon Christianity, destroying abstract theology, forcing us to refer every word and every act of Christ's directly to our human life. Is not the church at that point merely an obstacle?

Yes and no. The reproaches are correct, but at the same time too the reflected glory of the Christian tradition creates in many people an attitude very close to *the essential*. One of the greatest impediments of our time is the difficulty of achieving understanding – for most people the same words mean different things. But even church Christianity, if only it is honest, creates a foundation upon which definite essential principles can clearly be built up. Decisive principles without some previous understanding, are simply natural assumptions. But here in Britain – and in present-day Germany too – there are within the church and thanks to the church, people who can be trusted without reservation. Are these possibilities for creating understanding which have been preserved within the church, to be renounced too?

Revolutionary opposition to the church is part of the youthful experience of my generation. We had, we thought, only to smash all the false things that had sprung up around man – antiquated tradition, dead form, bad practice – then simple man who is at the same time pure and perfect man, would appear again entirely of his own accord. Simplicity seemed to us a beginning to which the way back could be found, not an end to which to find a way upon new paths. The new paths which we too tried, were therefore first and foremost destruction of the accustomed – revolt against the existing – not the careful building up of a new world. Meanwhile the process of destruction had its success, but what made its appearance was animal, blind-instinct-enslaved, hopelessly-lost-in-the-herd man, and National Socialism and Fascism. We learnt that the highest civilization is represented by simplicity, purity, humanity, and just as any artist only really achieves simplicity, having achieved highest perfection, so in human life too purity and simplicity can only be achieved when all the obscure and confused urges, all the complicated fears, ecstatic outbursts and mystical ideas of primitive man are overcome.

Today it is a question of rescuing what still can be rescued of European civilization so that a foundation for reconstruction shall remain. Christianity is one, perhaps the most important, of these foundations; the church too can help preserve Christianity if, within the church, people remain aware – and make as many others as possible aware – of what Christianity, as opposed to church, really means. The revolution against the church can safely be left to the Nazis: coming from that quarter it will bring about a consciousness of Christianity; coming from us it would lead to a hardening of that which is false – would therefore be regrettably destructive. The important thing is to be in contact with people with whom we can still achieve understanding concerning what is essential – concerning the foundations of our civilization – whether within the church or outside it does not matter.

For the sake of this consciousness, we must also not complain at the Anglo-German church services having changed – quite the reverse. It is only to the good for external sensation – for the externally simple fulfilment of a Christian commandment to be scrapped – what matters is to be mindful of the essential. Nor does the church stand alone in this – the war has let all the rashly superficial plans for a new Europe die off in the same way – it is not enough for us to correct details, there must be a radically new beginning. Maybe it will be not just a month of waiting – very likely we shall have to hold our breath for considerably longer – the two possibilities which seem open today: victory by Hitler or a long war, today mean a terribly long wait. But it is just such a period as this that must be used to advantage – only not externally, for externally our hands are tied: what matters *now*, and only now matters, is that internal work should be done.

INDEX

Absolute, the, 245–9,254,256–7,258,269–70,317–18
Abyssinia, 4,262
achievement, 45–7,51–2,55
act, an *or* the, 41,51–3,55,73,78–82
activity, 51–2; external, 80–4
Albania, 262
ambiguity, 45,171,180,306
America, 56–7,138,269,295
Anderson, Sir John, 298,307
Anglo-German church services, 20,26,61,140,315–17,319; sermons at, 17–18,66–7,266
architecture, 187–9; *see also* Cambridge
art, 31–2,135–7,167,170,189–90: *see also* Giotto, Holbein, Masaccio, Rembrandt, Tintoretto
Asia, 69,70
astronomy, 109–10,116
Austria, 4,68,262

Balkans, the, 56–7,68,69,115
Baltic states, 57,68,69,86,115,193
beauty, 123–4,176
Belgium, 179,274,275; invasion of, 264,265,266,273
Beneš, 126,127,215
Bergson, xi
Berlin, in 1920s, vii–viii,150–2
Bessarabia, 295
Bismarck, 259
Bolshevism, Bolshevization, 38,39,57,70,179,186
Briand, 178
Britain, 54,55,72,129,160–1,301; and Czechoslovakia, 125–6; and Russia, 86,185,186,193; and Turkey, 114–15; 'the other', 99; unemployed in, 257,311
British attitude to political refugees, 6,17,20–1,122,138–9,140–2,187,211,260, 265,275,281
British character and attitudes, 63,64,205,222–3,259–60,263,277
British Government statement, 133–5
British optimism, 68–71,124–5,259
British policy, 35,57,86,296,100–1
British press, 16,56,57,161,174,186,201,202,214,216, 260–1,265–6,294,312

British war aims, 33
Brüning, 216
Bukovina, 295
Bulgaria, 53,295

Cambridge, vii,xiii,154–5,187,283,297; architecture of, 29–30,54,143,159–60,176; gardens of, 30,123
Canada, 297,298
Capitalism, capitalist attitudes, 6,223,267; and communism, 179,194,204; and democracy, 5,306; and Marxism, 36,272
causality, 163–6,242–4,245
Chamberlain, 177,257,264,268; and Munich Agreement, 262,295; support for, 100,274,298
China, 57,262
Christ, 41,113,135,160,163,248; and death, 27–8,50,75,108–9; and Last Supper, 190–2,199; and Marriage at Cana of Galilee, xi,51,286–9,291–3; and peace, 115,21; and sin, 218–21; and the Absolute, 317–18; crucified, 11,16,58,250; example of, x,10–11,12,15,20,24,27–8,32,48–51,67,68,103,104,105,133,172, 253,270,271,276; *Life* of, 148–9; literal belief in, 163,316; teachings of, x,xi,8, 40,66,208
Christianity, x–xi,42,210,217,256,276; and conscientious objection, 7,132–3; and Judaism, 40–1; and knowledge, 116–17; and Marxism, 36,300; and suffering, 192; and the Absolute, 269; and war, 10–16; in Britain, 205,266; 'of the churches', 160,316–19; revitalization of, necessary, 17–26,66–7,121–2,204; Tolstoy and, 59–61,135
Christmas, 210–12,214
Church, churches, 36,40,115–16,160,164,205; Confessional, 17–21,296–7,316–19
Churchill, 264,282,296,298,299; speeches of, 268,283,307
circumstances, external, 47,48,75
civilization, 38,52,76,187,189,271; and the Church, 205,319–20; defence of, 18,56; destruction of, 6,65; Western, 62,278
civilizations, past, 184–5
Claudius, Matthias, ix,xiii,3,94–6,197–9

321